Critical Essays on
Kurt Vonnegut

Critical Essays on Kurt Vonnegut

Robert Merrill

G. K. Hall & Co. ● Boston, Massachusetts

printing number

10 9 8 7 6 5 4 3

Library of Congress Cataloging-in-Publication Data

Merrill, Robert, 1944–
　　Critical essays on Kurt Vonnegut / Robert Merrill.
　　　　p.　cm.—(Critical essays on American literature)
　　Includes index.
　　ISBN 0-8161-8893-9 (alk. paper)
　　1. Vonnegut, Kurt—Criticism and interpretation.　I. Title.
II. Series.
PS3572.05Z78　1989
813'.54—dc20
　　　　　　　　　　　　　　　　　　　　　　　　　89-11130
　　　　　　　　　　　　　　　　　　　　　　　　　CIP

This publication is printed on permanent/durable acid-free paper
MANUFACTURED IN THE UNITED STATES OF AMERICA

CRITICAL ESSAYS ON AMERICAN LITERATURE

This series seeks to anthologize the most important criticism on a wide variety of topics and writers in American literature. Our readers will find in various volumes not only a generous selection of reprinted articles and reviews but original essays, bibliographies, manuscript sections, and other materials brought to public attention for the first time. *Critical Essays on Kurt Vonnegut* contains the most comprehensive collection of criticism on this author yet assembled. The book presents both a sizable gathering of reviews of the major works and a broad selection of more modern scholarship, including essays on Vonnegut's early fiction, *Slaughterhouse-Five,* and later works. Among the reprinted essays are those by Tony Tanner, Terry Southern, Robert Scholes, Loree Rackstraw, John Updike, Charles B. Harris, and Kathryn Hume. In addition to Robert Merrill's important introduction, which surveys Vonnegut's career and the history of scholarship on his fiction, there are original essays commissioned specifically for publication in this volume by John L. Simons, David Cowart, and Charles Berryman. We are confident that this book will make a permanent and significant contribution to American literary study.

JAMES NAGEL, GENERAL EDITOR

Northeastern University

For Dotson

CONTENTS

INTRODUCTION

In 1973 Jerome Klinkowitz could confidently refer to Kurt Vonnegut as "the most talked-about American novelist since Ernest Hemingway." In 1980 he could reprint this opinion without qualification.[1] One must wonder what Klinkowitz would say about Vonnegut's reputation today. The recent reception of Vonnegut's *Bluebeard* (1987) and Jane Vonnegut Yarmolinsky's *Angels without Wings* (1987) is somewhat discouraging for anyone who takes Vonnegut to be one of the major American novelists of the past forty years. *Bluebeard* received many good reviews, but one could make a long list of the major journals and magazines that chose not to review the book—among others, *Newsweek*, the *Times Literary Supplement*, the *New York Review of Books*, and the *New Yorker*. The review in the *New York Times Book Review* was almost embarrassingly brief.[2] Like the novel that preceded it, *Galápagos* (1985), *Bluebeard* sold enough copies to make the various best-seller lists but did not reach the top of these lists. And though there is little literary merit in Jane Yarmolinsky's account of how she and Kurt came to raise the three eldest children of Kurt's sister Alice, it is still surprising that a work of such obvious relevance to Vonnegut's biography inspired almost no critical interest.[3] In sum, recent evidence suggests that people are neither talking about nor reading Kurt Vonnegut as much as they did in the years immediately following his first great popular and critical success with *Slaughterhouse-Five* (1969).

Of course, major American writers have rarely achieved great popular success within their lifetimes, so the oddity is perhaps that Vonnegut was talked about so much for so many years, not that his works no longer provoke Hemingwayesque discussion. Certainly it should not surprise us that Vonnegut's critical reputation is now unstable, for its earlier fluctuations are among the most pronounced in American literary history. Almost totally ignored for the first twenty years of his career, Vonnegut suddenly became, in the late 1960s, the sort of writer whose portrait graces the cover of *Harper's* and whose books are reviewed everywhere. In the 1970s and early 1980s Vonnegut's popularity translated into a vast critical industry that produced 265 critical studies, including eight books and two journal issues almost entirely

1

devoted to his works.[4] If such massive evidence of critical interest has begun to abate, this may only mean that a lot of people have had their say about Vonnegut. In any case, the following account of Vonnegut's critical reputation will chart the curves of his fascinating career in order to characterize what has already been said and what perhaps still needs to be said about one postmodern American novelist who really matters.

The story of Vonnegut's critical reputation prior to 1969 is a very short story indeed. Vonnegut first began to write fiction in 1949 and published his first story in *Collier's* in 1950; subsequently he published forty-five stories through 1963, plus one additional story in 1968 and one in 1972.[5] Yet there was no criticism on his short fiction until the early 1970s. And Vonnegut's first novel, *Player Piano* (1952), was his only book to be reviewed until *God Bless You, Mr. Rosewater* (1965). Vonnegut's strange publishing history is involved here, of course, for seven years elapsed between Vonnegut's first novel and his second, *The Sirens of Titan* (1959), and both *The Sirens of Titan* and *Mother Night* (1962) first appeared as paperback originals (as did Vonnegut's first collection of stories, *Canary in a Cat House* [1961]). Original paperback publication is a good way to reach a large audience, but the only critical reputation it secures is that of a hack (in Vonnegut's case, a science-fiction hack). Though the reviews of *Player Piano* were friendlier than is often suggested,[6] there is no denying that Vonnegut's serious reputation was almost nonexistent prior to the republication of his early novels in hardcover in 1966 and the redistribution of all his novels in new paperback editions in 1967. In 1961 Mark Hillegas discussed *Player Piano* as one of several recent examples of dystopian science fiction, and in 1963 the *New York Times Book Review* and the *Spectator* published the only reviews of *Cat's Cradle* (1963).[7] The rest was silence.

Republication of Vonnegut's earlier works in 1966 generated the first serious reviews of his career. Historically speaking, the most important review was C. D. B. Bryan's "Kurt Vonnegut on Target" in the *New Republic*. Bryan's command of the facts was seriously flawed, as he claimed that *Mother Night* was published a few months ago, characterized *Canary in a Cat House* as a novel, and said that *Player Piano* preceded *Cat's Cradle* by nine years. But his very favorable review alluded to four of Vonnegut's novels, *Player Piano, Mother Night, Cat's Cradle* and *God Bless You, Mr. Rosewater*, each of which was praised as the work of a serious new writer. Never before had Vonnegut's early achievement received such conspicuous publicity. Moreover, Bryan's most severe reservation inspired the first serious academic study of Vonnegut's art the following year. Bryan characterized Vonnegut as a satirist who seems always to fall short of the great satiric models: "all the anger, the shame, the shock, the compassion, the irony, the control to produce great satire are *there*. . . . Why, then, does Vonnegut settle for such lovely, literate, amusing attacks upon such simple targets as scientists, engineers, computer technicians, religion, the American legion, artists, company picnics?"[8]

In 1967 Robert Scholes answered this question in his chapter "Fabulation and Satire" in *The Fabulators*. Here Scholes argues that the black humorists—Vonnegut among them—are in fact fabulators and not satirists. Black humor lacks "the rhetoric of moral certainty" that we expect from satire and seeks to make us "thoughtful" rather than to reform us. Its primary instrument is not invective but laughter. For Scholes, then, Vonnegut does not write great satire because his ends are not satiric. Instead, he writes a distinguished form of intellectual comedy. Scholes illustrates these generalizations by discussing *Cat's Cradle* and *Mother Night*, works that "exhibit an affection for the world and a desire to improve it—but not much hope for improvement." Scholes's essay is one of the most cogent ever published on Vonnegut. Scholes was the first scholar to point out the excellence of Vonnegut's craft, and the questions Scholes addressed remain crucial to all formal considerations of Vonnegut's art—is Vonnegut a satirist, and if not, what kind of fiction does he write?[9]

Klinkowitz once remarked that except for Scholes's work no scholarly articles on Vonnegut appeared in American journals until 1971.[10] This is true, but Tony Tanner's well-known chapter on Vonnegut in *City of Words* (1971) first appeared in *Critical Quarterly* in 1969, so Tanner should be recognized as the first critic to publish a comprehensive study of Vonnegut's novels from *Player Piano* to *Slaughterhouse-Five*. Tanner is the first of many critics to see *Slaughterhouse-Five* as the artistic climax to Vonnegut's early career, for Tanner's essay is essentially a thematic discussion of Vonnegut's first six novels as they build toward the "masterly" *Slaughterhouse-Five*. Tanner argues that man's peculiar status as "agent-victim" is Vonnegut's recurring subject, as Vonnegut sees man's dreams or illusions as not only resisting but also contributing to his own victimage. Tanner is especially good on Howard W. Campbell's embodiment of this schizophrenic condition in *Mother Night*. With *Cat's Cradle* and *Slaughterhouse-Five*, Tanner formulates the philosophical issues posed by these two books, especially their Bokononistic and Tralfamadorian responses to life. Though writing only a few months after the publication of *Slaughterhouse-Five*, Tanner deftly defines what is at issue in this novel and, somewhat less obviously, Vonnegut's earlier works. Tanner is perhaps a bit evasive about answering his own question as to whether Vonnegut, like his protagonist Billy Pilgrim, is a moral quietist; but no one has surpassed Tanner in demonstrating the urgency of this question. Inevitably dated and marked by a few minor errors of fact, this first extended discussion of Vonnegut's career remains one of the best.[11]

The Scholes and Tanner pieces were excellent first efforts to define Vonnegut's early achievement, but of course it was the publication of *Slaughterhouse-Five* that prompted widespread revaluation of his art. Among the many enthusiastic reviews of *Slaughterhouse-Five*, Scholes's assessment for the *New York Times Book Review* was probably the most important.[12] Scholes's front-page review anticipated overviews of Vonnegut's career in a number of major magazines and journals. In 1970, for example, Jack Richardson attacked Vonnegut in the *New York Review of Books* as "a soft, sentimental satirist . . . a compiler of easy-to-read truisms about society," while Leslie Fiedler praised Vonnegut in *Esquire* for being precisely such a sentimentalist. A year later, in the *Saturday Review*, Benjamin DeMott straddled these two positions by "praising" Vonnegut for an inartistic sentimentality that the young found immensely appealing.[13] These relatively early critiques initiated the popular view of Vonnegut as a sentimental champion of the young or what Fiedler called the new romanticism, a view that Vonnegut and his academic supporters have been challenging ever since; but these studies also pointed up Vonnegut's emergence as a major figure, one who deserves full-scale attack in the *New York Review of Books*. Another sign of Vonnegut's emerging reputation was the appearance of the first book chapter entirely devoted to his works, recognizing that Vonnegut seemed to stand out among his contemporaries as a representative figure.[14]

By 1971 this view of Vonnegut as a serious artist was widely shared throughout the academy. In this year *Summary* published an entire issue on Vonnegut's life and works, *Critique* published four essays and the first substantial bibliography on Vonnegut, Charles Harris treated Vonnegut as one of four major American novelists of the absurd, and Mary Sue Schriber and L. J. Clancy published excellent scholarly articles on Vonnegut.[15] The essays in *Summary* are often brief and impressionistic, but the volume does include Scholes's "Chasing a Lone Eagle," a pioneering study of Vonnegut's journalism at Cornell; Seymour Lawrence's reflections on how Vonnegut became one of his writers in the late 1960s; and John Rauch's biography of the Vonneguts of Indianapolis, Indiana. (Rauch, an uncle of Vonnegut's, is not named as the author here, but Vonnegut identifies him in *Palm Sunday* [1981].) The essays in *Critique* are far more substantial as literary criticism. Max Schulz's "The Unconfirmed Thesis: Kurt Vonnegut, Black Humor, and Contemporary Art" extends Scholes's suggestion that Vonnegut is a black humorist who lacks the classical satirist's ethical certainty; indeed, Schulz ends up arguing that Vonnegut's major point is the absolute unverifiability of *any* moral or ethical position. Stanley Schatt complements Schulz's argument in "The World of Kurt Vonnegut, Jr.," a general essay that emphasizes Vonnegut's pragmatic, pluralistic response to a radically relativistic universe. Jerome Klinkowitz's "Kurt Vonnegut, Jr., and the Crimes of Our Time" is the first of Klinkowitz's many studies of Vonnegut. Klinkowitz disputes the tendency to identify Vonnegut with such black humorists as Terry Southern and offers as evidence an extended discussion of the themes and techniques of *Mother Night* and *Cat's Cradle*. Subsequently revised in 1973 for Klinkowitz's *The Vonnegut Statement*, this essay is still one of the shrewdest assessments of these early novels, especially *Cat's Cradle*, a book Klinkowitz understands as well as anyone who has written on Vonnegut. Finally, Leonard Leff provides the first essay-length reading of *God Bless You, Mr. Rosewater*. Leff highlights Vonnegut's somewhat didactic treatment of money as power and defends Eliot Rosewater as an exemplary figure who must struggle against an inhumane, capitalistic status quo. The *Critique* essays and the formidable checklist provided by Schatt and Klinkowitz effectively introduced continuous rather than sporadic scholarly attention to Vonnegut.

Charles Harris's book chapter helped to focus this attention, for Harris offered the first decisive evaluation of Vonnegut's philosophical "progress" from *Player Piano* to *Slaughterhouse-Five*. Harris argues that Vonnegut tends to distinguish between two kinds of human illusions. Bad illusions are those that make life more miserable than it should be: nationalism, materialistic notions about success, racial prejudice. Vonnegut's early novels attack such illusions. Good illusions are those that help prevent despair: Bokononism, Tralfamadorianism. A later novel such as *Slaughterhouse-Five* offers "almost total resignation" as the proper response to a universe that is absurd in Camus's sense of the term. Harris's very clear presentation initiates the ongoing debate as to where Vonnegut stands vis-à-vis the deterministic philosophies presented in all his novels, but especially in *Slaughterhouse-Five*. Together with the essays in *Critique* and the fine essays by Schriber and Clancy, Harris's chapter helped make 1971 the true beginning of serious Vonnegut criticism.

The surge of interest in Vonnegut following the publication of *Slaughterhouse-Five* reached its first climax in 1972, the year in which the first book-length critical studies appeared. The signs of critical interest were many and various, including the reminiscences of colleagues, critical notes and articles, and Raymond Olderman's important chapter on Vonnegut in *Beyond the Waste Land*, a book that rivals Tanner's *City of Words* as the best treatment of American fiction of the 1960s.[16] But the major publications were the books by David Goldsmith and Peter Reed.[17] To be fair, Goldsmith's work is in fact a forty-four-page pamphlet in which he traces Vonnegut's thematic development from the "nihilism" of *The Sirens of Titan* to the "tentative affirmation" embodied in *Slaughterhouse-Five*. But if the brevity of Goldsmith's essay is a handicap, its major problem is an excessive reliance on quotation and plot summary. Goldsmith is especially dubious as a critical guide, for he argues that *God Bless You, Mr. Rosewater* is "unquestionably" Vonnegut's best novel and that *Slaughterhouse-Five* is "his most poorly written novel." Peter Reed's book is superior in every respect. Reed offers what is still the most detailed analysis of the first six novels. Common techniques and themes are explored throughout and summarized in an excellent concluding chapter. Reed's patient handling of textual details is sometimes laborious and his stress on Vonnegut's ambiguities sometimes permits him to avoid critical judgments that seem called for. But Reed is very good on Vonnegut as a fabulator (though the term is never used), especially when he demonstrates the aesthetic coherence of Vonnegut's "fantastic" tales. This balanced but sympathetic study only covers Vonnegut's early career, but it can be supplemented by Reed's publications on the later novels.[18]

Reed's book was followed a year later by a collection of essays written by Vonnegut's most enthusiastic academic readers. Edited by Klinkowitz and John Somer, *The Vonnegut Statement* is a diverse work supposedly devoted to showing "that *Slaughterhouse-Five* constituted a resolution of sorts to themes and techniques developing throughout [Vonnegut's] previous work." A few essays do address this topic, but most develop their own subjects. Parts 1 and 2 deal with Vonnegut as a public and literary figure, part 3 with his novels. The first two parts include Klinkowitz's superb study of the short fiction, Scholes's essay on the Cornell journalism (reprinted from *Summary*), Dan Wakefield's reminiscences, and an extremely interesting Vonnegut interview with Scholes at Iowa. Part 3 is a mixed affair: the notes of a fan (Tim Hildebrand); a protracted and vague generic discussion (Karen and Charles Wood); an interesting study of Vonnegut's formal innovations in his first two novels (James Mellard); a revised version of Klinkowitz's *Critique* essay on *Mother Night* and *Cat's Cradle*; two very sympathetic but misleading studies of Vonnegut's thought and art, especially in *Slaughterhouse-Five* (Glenn Meeter, John Somer); and an excellent bibliography by Klinkowitz, Asa Pieratt, Jr., and Stanley Schatt. Mellard's essay is one of the most important discussions of Vonnegut's early fiction. Mellard traces Vonnegut's first efforts to get "beyond" the realistic or Jamesian mode of fiction to one that has its origin in popular oral tradition. Mellard shows how the conventions of the mimetic novel are revised in *Player Piano*, then overthrown in *The Sirens of Titan*, as Vonnegut achieves a modern form of "naive" literature that allows him "to reinstate popular sentimental values as commands—to love, to be courageous, to be kind." Meeter also emphasizes Vonnegut's "rejection" of the traditional novel, but he sees this aesthetic decision as linked to Vonnegut's rejection of conventional religion and even "a sense of history." Indeed, Meeter argues that "for the most part [Vonnegut's] work accepts the loss of tradition rather gladly as a fact, and even demands that it become a fact." Readers of the later Vonnegut, especially *Slapstick* (1976), will be surprised to learn that Vonnegut is so grateful for the loss of tradition; they may even think that Vonnegut regrets this loss very much. Meeter also argues that Bokononism and Tralfamadorianism are equally desirable versions of the same "faith," one of the crucial points of view in the debate as to what Vonnegut thinks of his invented religions. Meeter agrees with Somer, who argues that Vonnegut's continuing search is for "a hero who [can] survive with dignity in an insane world." Like Meeter, Somer thinks that Vonnegut ends this search with Billy Pilgrim, who achieves what is said to be a sublime serenity. Somer is rather more explicit than Meeter, but both critics see Vonnegut as espousing the benefits of what Harris calls "resigned acceptance." As this is consistent with what Klinkowitz also argues, the real "thesis" of *The Vonnegut Statement* seems to be that *Slaughterhouse-Five* is the most powerful expression of Vonnegut's stoical, even quietistic views on life. Whether one agrees or not, the long essays by Meeter and Somer are required reading for anyone interested in the thematic implications of Vonnegut's novels.

The emergence of a true Vonnegut "industry" can be traced from 1973 to 1976 (when the next book on Vonnegut appeared). In 1973 the Vonnegut phenomenon was remarked by a number of prominent critics and writers. Pearl Bell deplored Vonnegut as one of several recent "celebrants of unreason, chaos, and inexorable decay," Ihab Hassan labeled Vonnegut a fatalist but included him among "prominent" contemporary novelists, Charles Nicol and Michael Wood wrote admiringly of Vonnegut's work while questioning the uncritical enthusiasm expressed in *The Vonnegut Statement,* and Alfred Kazin and Doris Lessing offered extremely interesting evaluations of individual novels.[19] Kazin's comments illustrate the misunderstanding that mars the work of even the best critics when they deal with writers they know only superficially. Among other misstatements, Kazin refers to chapter one of *Slaughterhouse-Five* as an "introduction" (a view he subsequently reaffirmed by reprinting chapter one in a collection of essays) and suggests that Vonnegut "has no politics." Kazin strongly endorses the fatalistic reading of *Slaughterhouse-Five,* arguing that "Vonnegut deprecates any attempt to see tragedy that day in Dresden. . . . He likes to say with arch fatalism, citing one horror after another, 'So it goes.' " By contrast, Doris Lessing's belated review of *Mother Night* both praises Vonnegut ("one of the writers who map our landscape for us") and offers a major insight into *Mother Night* and Vonnegut's work in general. Lessing argues that "what Vonnegut deals with, always, is responsibility," and that Vonnegut refuses to succumb to "the new and general feeling of helplessness." In effect responding to the views of Meeter, Somer, and Kazin, Lessing anticipates many later defenses of Vonnegut's moral position in *Slaughterhouse-Five.*

The more scholarly essays published on Vonnegut in 1973 were all very good. The 1972 film version of *Slaugherhouse-Five* gave rise to several interesting studies of the relationship between George Roy Hill's film and Vonnegut's novel.[20] In addition, Arlen Hansen treated Vonnegut briefly but perceptively as an example of what Hansen calls "The Celebration of Solipsism: A New Trend in American Fiction." Hansen's most useful insight is that "in creating Bokononism, Vonnegut rejects the premise that mankind has no alternative but to adapt himself passively to the dictates of his environment." In "Vonnegut's Cradle: The Erosion of Comedy," Stanley Trachtenberg discussed Vonnegut's use of comic form in *Cat's Cradle.* Trachtenberg distinguishes Vonnegut's brand of comedy from that of the black humorists, but also from more traditional comedy as defined by Susanne Langer and Northrop Frye. Donald Greiner, in "Vonnegut's *Slaughterhouse-Five* and the Fiction of Atrocity," highlighted Vonnegut's unique treatment of war by relating his war novel to Robert Jay Lifton's concept of "the guilt of survival" and to several historical accounts of the firebombing of Dresden. Finally, Jerome Klinkowitz reviewed "The Literary Career of Kurt Vonnegut, Jr." in one of the best pieces on Vonnegut to this date. In this essay Klinkowitz argues that Vonnegut is "our great public writer." Klinkowitz's account of Vonnegut's career is filled with telling information, but it also develops a definite thesis concerning Vonnegut's themes. Klinkowitz quite accurately summarizes Vonnegut's social theme as his desire to "change the social ethic and treasure people for something other than what they can produce." Klinkowitz then identifies Vonnegut's metaphysical theme as his belief that mankind should reject responsibility for an absurd universe, as "the consummate horrors of the twentieth century have made it an unbearable trial for man to identify himself with the center of the Universe." In his otherwise excellent essay Klinkowitz does not explain how these apparently contradictory themes can be reconciled.[21]

The major essays of 1974 varied a great deal, though even the weaker efforts provided good evidence of an emerging critical debate about the nature of Vonnegut's themes. David Vanderwerken's "Pilgrim's Dilemma: *Slaugherhouse-Five*" presented a brief but compelling argument that in this novel Vonnegut rejects both Tralfamadorianism and divinely oriented Christianity. These philosophies or religions share the deterministic belief that we cannot avoid wars and other social disasters; the inevitable result if we adopt such beliefs is moral apathy. Vanderwerken was the first critic to argue that *Slaughterhouse-Five* espouses "a humanistic Christianity, which may also be an illusion, but yet a saving one." At the other extreme, philosophically speaking, David Ketterer pointed out that the Tralfamadorian philosophy is "handy" as a way of dealing with life's horrors, for individual responsibility "shrinks" from view in this perspective. Ketterer's chapter, "Vonnegut's Spiral Siren Call: From Dresden's Lunar Visits to Tralfamadore," deals with *The Sirens of Titan* and *Slaugherhouse-Five* as examples of Vonnegut's science fiction. Unfortunately, Ketterer's grasp of textual details is either faulty or excessively ingenious, as when he remarks that Billy Pilgrim comes "unstuck in time" due to the example of his captives on Tralfamadore, or when he suggests that in *The Sirens of Titan* Mercury and Venus should be equated because Beatrice Rumfoord, in her cookbook, recommends young Harmoniums (from Mercury) filled with Venusian cottage cheese. Billy Pilgrim comes unstuck in time many years before he travels to Tralfamadore, the Tralfamadorians are hardly Billy's captives, and most readers would no doubt expect a stronger "tie" between Mercury and Venus. Arnold Edelstein's "*Slaughterhouse-Five:* Time Out of Joint" was a far more useful discussion of Vonnegut's sixth novel. Edelstein provides an extensive chronology of events to show that "all the significant details of Billy's life on Tralfamadore have sources in Billy's life here on Earth"—thus proving that Tralfamadore is Billy's own creation. As Edelstein points out, this only becomes clear at the end of the novel, a late revelation that powerfully reorders our entire sense of the book. This fine point about the novel's structure leads Edelstein to conclude that Billy's space-travel is made up of "escapist, regressive fantasies." Yet Edelstein ends his essay by insisting that Vonnegut shares Billy's

Tralfamadorianism. As there is no evidence offered for this view, nor any discussion of its implications, Edelstein's final remarks seem oddly out of place. The same might be said of everything in Sanford Pinsker's "Fire and Ice: The Radical Cuteness of Kurt Vonnegut, Jr." Pinsker is one of the better critics of contemporary American writing, but his essay on Vonnegut seems either hastily or carelessly done. Pinsker refers to Robert "Heinlan" and speaks repeatedly of Vonnegut's "Harry" Campbell and Dr. Felix "Hoeniker."[22] The quality of Pinsker's response to Vonnegut is suggested by the following comment: "But while the baggage that is history may have been a heavy burden for Joyce or Eliot, it is a lightweight affair for Vonnegut." In a relatively short essay Pinsker discusses the first six novels in a brisk, breezy fashion—all too brisk and breezy.[23] This sort of casual, unsympathetic treatment of Vonnegut was still possible as of 1974, but it was to become almost extinct within the next year or so. Hereafter critics might dislike Vonnegut, but they would take his works far more seriously.

This kind of critical but scrupulous attention marks two other essays of the 1974–75 period, Peter Messent's "*Breakfast of Champions:* The Direction of Vonnegut's Fiction" and Clinton Burhans's "Hemingway and Vonnegut: Diminishing Vision in a Dying Age." Messent's 1974 article was the first serious discussion of *Breakfast of Champions* (1973). Messent is finally quite critical of Vonnegut's new novel, but he does Vonnegut the honor of analyzing his book at great length. In 1975 Burhans paid Vonnegut an even greater compliment by suggesting that Vonnegut represents his age as distinctly as Hemingway represents his. One must wonder, however, whether Burhans's contrast is really valid. Hemingway is said to offer "an essentially tragic vision of man" in which we achieve meaning by imposing aesthetic form on life's harsh realities, whereas Vonnegut presents man as "a silly and pitiful creature" who must turn away from truth to embrace comforting illusions. Burhans's Vonnegut is a despairing pessimist, an absurdist who should be linked with Beckett and Ionesco. Burhans makes many fine points in passing about such topics as Vonnegut's ambivalence toward love, especially sexual love, but he projects a Vonnegut who is all too neatly Hemingway's foil, someone who is blind to everything but humanity's silliness. Moreover, Burhans consistently quotes such Vonnegut characters as Winston Niles Rumfoord, Malachi Constant, and Billy Pilgrim as if they were mouthpieces for their creator. This extremely dubious practice leads Burhans to reverse what may be the appropriate conclusion, for many readers would argue that Hemingway is in fact the more pessimistic writer.[24]

Whatever one may think of Burhans's conclusions, the appearance of his article in *Modern Fiction Studies* marked a new stage in Vonnegut's assimilation into the American canon. Additional evidence was provided by Robert Uphaus's "Expected Meaning in Vonnegut's Dead-End Fiction," a review of Vonnegut's work in general and *Breakfast of Champions* in particular. Uphaus's very sympathetic essay asks a fundamental question, "what is the apparent meaning of Vonnegut's novels?," and proceeds to offer one of the most interesting answers yet proposed. For Uphaus, Vonnegut's novels demonstrate that "self-actualization" can only be "imaginatively achieved" and so can never influence human history. Vonnegut therefore celebrates the human imagination while acknowledging its extreme limitations. This very tempting theory prepares the way for Uphaus's reading of *Breakfast of Champions* as a "moving, tortured, and honest" book, one that dramatizes its author's extreme ambivalence about human powers. The publication of Uphaus's review in *Novel* was yet another signal of Vonnegut's emerging status; other signs in 1975 were the prominent role assigned to Vonnegut in Thomas LeClair's and Jean Kennard's lengthy treatments of contemporary American writing and Lynn Buck's essay on Vonnegut in yet another major journal, *Studies in American Fiction*.[25]

In 1976 a number of important essays were published, including Maurice O'Sullivan's "*Slaughterhouse-Five:* Kurt Vonnegut's Anti-Memoirs," Thomas Wymer's "The Swiftian Satire of Kurt Vonnegut, Jr.," and Charles Harris's "Time, Uncertainty, and Kurt Vonnegut, Jr.: A Reading of *Slaughterhouse-Five*." O'Sullivan and Wymer reinforce Vanderwerken's reading of *Slaughterhouse-Five*, and Harris's essay complements his earlier work by treating Vonnegut's narrative techniques in *Slaughterhouse-Five* as thoroughly as Harris analyzed the novel's themes in his book chapter. Harris's essay is especially recommended to anyone interested in the chronological errors—deliberate or unintended—in *Slaughterhouse-Five*.[26] It is rather harder to recommend the major publication of 1976, Stanley Schatt's Twayne book.[27] Schatt consistently fails to evaluate or even characterize Vonnegut's formal achievement (or failure) as he reviews all of Vonnegut's works through *Slapstick*. Whether discussing Vonnegut's formal innovations in *Player Piano*, the role of the artist in *Mother Night*, the supposed "third" narrator of *Slaughterhouse-Five*, or the themes of *Slapstick*, Schatt comes to no real conclusions about the large topics he introduces. (Schatt's treatment of *God Bless You, Mr. Rosewater* provides a significant exception. The chapter on this book—Vonnegut's "richest and most complex novel"—is easily his best.) Formal questions are almost never addressed, belying Schatt's prefactory promise to engage just such questions. In addition, one could hardly count the typographical and factual errors that plague this book. A few random examples: *Between Time and Timbuktu* (1972) is cited as *From Time to Timbuktu;* Kilgore Trout's *The Big Board* is renamed *The Big Barrel;* Theodore Roethke's "I learn by going where I have to go," quoted in the first chapter of *Slaughterhouse-Five,* is rendered "dream by going where I have to go"; Vonnegut is said to have quit General Electric in 1951, at least a year later than he actually did so; *The Sirens of Titan* is omitted from the chronology of Vonnegut's life and works; Amanita Buntline, a minor character in *God Bless You, Mr. Rosewater,* is rechristened Amanda. Moreover, a number of the notes do not correspond to the numbers in the text and the index is virtually worthless, as it refers to none of the critics cited in the book. Schatt's critical judgments are also suspect, as when he says that in *Player Piano* "Finnerty and his followers also believe that they cannot possibly fail," or when Billy Pilgrim is said to "realize" that he cannot comfort others with the Tralfamadorian philosophy. Finnerty and his followers are very much aware that they cannot *succeed* (see their conversation at the end of the book), and what is Billy doing at the very end of his life if not trying to comfort others with the good news from Tralfamadore? Schatt's typos and factual errors are minor but tend to undermine the reader's confidence; his critical misjudgments are rather more serious and severely limit the value of his book.

Three more books on Vonnegut appeared in 1977, another major year in the history of his critical reputation. The best of these was James Lundquist's contribution to the Ungar series. Lundquist begins with a long chapter that summarizes Vonnegut's recurring themes. Marred by excessive reliance on plot summaries, this discussion nonetheless offers a good paraphrase of Vonnegut's works. The next chapter responds to charges of artistic incompetence directed against *Slaugherhouse-Five*. Lundquist has many good things to say about the novel's structure, though he hints that Vonnegut agrees with Billy Pilgrim's "philosophy" without really arguing the matter. Lundquist's final two chapters are more successful. The first deals authoritatively with Vonnegut's relationship to science fiction, a subject Lundquist knows much better than most of Vonnegut's critics. The second offers a brief but effective summary of Vonnegut's basic methods. What is missing here, as elsewhere in the book, is a more detailed elaboration of Lundquist's main points. Nonetheless, Lundquist's book is far more reliable than Richard Giannone's *Vonnegut: A Preface to His Novels*. Like Schatt, Giannone first claims that he will study the form of Vonnegut's novels, then proceeds to say almost nothing on the subject. At most, Giannone offers a one- or two-sentence aesthetic judgment that has little connection to the chapter in which it appears. Following Giannone's argument is difficult enough in most chapters, but especially those on *Player Piano* and *Cat's Cradle*. In all fairness, one should add that others have liked Giannone's book a great deal; in his review for *American Literary Scholarship*, for example, James Justus calls it "the best of the new work on Vonnegut."[28] The third book on Vonnegut to appear this year was another collection of essays edited by Klinkowitz (with Donald L. Lawler), *Vonnegut in America*. Most of the essays here are revised versions of talks delivered at a 1975 MLA session on Vonnegut, and the book as a whole does not measure up to *The Vonnegut Statement*. Still, there are many good things included. Klinkowitz's "Vonnegut in America" is the single best biographical account yet published. William Veeder's "Technique as Recovery: *Lolita* and *Mother Night*" is a fascinating comparison in which more is revealed about Nabokov's novel than Vonnegut's. Veeder's essay illustrates the problems that result when a writer's formal or generic intentions are misconstrued, for Veeder treats *Lolita* and *Mother Night* as if they were realistic actions in which Humbert Humbert and Howard W. Campbell function as the respective protagonists of contemporary bildungsromane. This approach is appropriate to *Lolita*, but it ignores the fabulistic nature of Vonnegut's "novel." Conrad Festa's "Vonnegut's Satire" presents a good argument that, pace Scholes and others, Vonnegut does indeed write satire. And Peter Reed's long essay on "The Later Vonnegut" offers a very good reading of *Breakfast of Champions* and the first extended treatment of *Slapstick*. Other essays discuss Vonnegut's status abroad, another sign of his developing reputation, and Klinkowitz again provides a remarkably comprehensive bibliography.[29]

If the three books on Vonnegut in 1977 were of mixed quality, several essays advanced the study of his work considerably. Dolores K. Gros-Louis's "*Slaughterhouse-Five*: Pacifism vs. Passiveness" and John Tilton's "*Slaughterhouse-Five*: Life against Death-in-Life" continued reaction against the quietistic reading of *Slaughterhouse-Five*. Gros-Louis presents a strong argument that Vonnegut and Billy Pilgrim should not be identified, for Vonnegut represents pacifism and Billy a form of Tralfamadorian passivity. One limitation to her essay is that Gros-Louis never quite explains why Billy's experiences parallel Vonnegut's if the two men are finally so different. Tilton's long book chapter is a major study for anyone who takes Vonnegut or *Slaughterhouse-Five* seriously. Tilton points out that the parallels between Vonnegut and Billy Pilgrim are ultimately ironic, that Billy invented Tralfamadore in 1968 (not 1967, the year he claims to have been kidnapped by the Tralfamadorians), that Somer's distinction between hallucinations and time-travel ignores the fact that both are forms of human invention, and that the Kilgore Trout of this novel is much more cynical than the Trout of *God Bless You, Mr. Rosewater*. Tilton is less convincing when he discovers no fewer than four narrators in the novel, two of whom are supposed to be third-person narrators. These proliferating narrators permit Tilton to identify in the text a Kurt Vonnegut who neither recognizes nor embraces his "Billy Pilgrim-self," that is, the side of himself that "would welcome release from the world of familial, professional, and moral responsibility." But the Kurt Vonnegut who drinks too much, who notes anxiously the presence of clocks, and who reflects on the fate of Lot's wife is someone who would very much welcome "release." Tilton is also a bit reductive in presenting Billy Pilgrim as Vonnegut's satirical target, pure and simple. Most readers will feel that Vonnegut sympathizes with Billy even if he does not share his character's point of view. In sum, Tilton's extremely detailed argument goes too far in rejecting misleading theories advanced in *The Vonnegut Statement*. My own "Vonnegut's *Breakfast of Champions*: The Conversion of Heliogabalus" complemented Tilton's essay by arguing that in *Breakfast of Champions* Vonnegut exorcises the seductive appeal of Tralfamadorian fatalism. This argument may reflect Vonnegut's intentions rather than his achievement, for in this novel Vonnegut renders his fear of a totally mechanized universe far more persuasively than his "conversion" to a more humane optimism. Finally, in "Bringing Chaos to Order: The Novel Tradition and Kurt Vonnegut, Jr.," Mary Sue Schriber presented the interesting idea that four of Vonnegut's novels—*Mother*

Night, Cat's Cradle, Slaughterhouse-Five, and *Breakfast of Champions*—
all explore "the novel's relationship to reality and truth and, consequently,
its contemporary value." Schriber is able to show that Vonnegut comments
on the novelistic tradition within his own novels, but she is not very convincing when she suggests that *Cat's Cradle* is "cast in traditional novel
form," or when she uses the phrase "the novel tradition" to refer exclusively to the more naive forms of realism. It may be that Vonnegut shares
this very limited conception of the novelistic tradition, but one would want
better evidence than is presented here. On the other hand, Schriber's
Vonnegut is a sophisticated man of letters who self-consciously manipulates
the conventions of traditional and more recent narrative—a Vonnegut many
readers will recognize from their own experience with the novels.[30]

The next year, 1978, marked something of a turning point in Vonnegut's
critical fortunes. From that year to the present the volume of criticism has
been consistent but smaller than in the early 1970s, and aside from
Klinkowitz's short book for Methuen in 1982 there have been no book-length
studies. The quality of this work is not in question, however, for Klinkowitz's
book is perhaps the best single study of Vonnegut, and many of the best essays
appeared in the 1980s. Unfortunately, two of the better-known discussions of
1978 do not measure up to this standard. In *On Moral Fiction* John Gardner
suggests that it is natural for Vonnegut's "cynical disciples" to see him as a
nihilist, for "Vonnegut's moral energy is forever flagging, his fight forever
turning slapstick." Gardner's rather moralistic point is that Vonnegut's writing
suffers from a "lack of commitment." This strange reading was matched by
Josephine Hendin's in her *Vulnerable People*. Hendin says many astute things
about Vonnegut's treatment of fathers and sons, but she also believes that
"spacing out is Vonnegut's answer to death, war, and human glaciers" and that
"dumbness is precisely his solution" in *Slaughterhouse-Five*. This extreme
version of the quietistic reading betrays its shallowness, or so Peter Scholl and
I argued this same year in "Vonnegut's *Slaughterhouse-Five:* The Requirements of Chaos." This essay was written as the pieces by Vanderwerken,
O'Sullivan, Wymer, Gros-Louis, and Tilton were appearing, and is perhaps
best seen as summarizing the case that Vonnegut does *not* recommend "resigned acceptance" of life's injustices. Scholl and I differ from others who
deplore the quietistic reading by acknowledging such complicating factors as
Vonnegut's sympathetic treatment of Billy Pilgrim. Finally, however, we
agree that Vonnegut's primary purpose is to challenge the Tralfamadorian
point of view when it is adopted by human beings in a position to know better
and to act upon what they know.[31]

The debate about *Slaughterhouse-Five* continued in 1979 even when
the critic showed no awareness of other points of view. Thus, in Thomas
Hartshorne's "From *Catch-22* to *Slaugherhouse-V* [*sic*]: The Decline of the
Political Mode," *Slaughterhouse-Five* was seen as a political fable that
preaches quietism: "One cannot control one's fate, so one should simply
allow things to happen." For Hartshorne, Vonnegut's novel illustrates "the

decay of reformist hopes," a dour mood that characterized the late 1960s. This emphasis on Vonnegut's "resignation" anticipates the argument that Vonnegut's vision is "relentlessly pessimistic." So David Bosworth argued in "The Literature of Awe," an essay in which Vonnegut is said to recommend "pessimism, cynicism, resignation, despair." But resignation need not be equated with despair, as Philip Rubens insisted in one of the year's more important essays, " 'Nothing's Ever Final': Vonnegut's Concept of Time." According to Rubens, *Slaughterhouse-Five* embodies a Bergsonian concept of time that frees us from "a linear, deterministic universe" by validating Billy Pilgrim's discovery, that is, "a multiple and ever-present now composed of good moments." Tralfamadorianism therefore offers comfort instead of freedom, an extremely desirable exchange because free will is nothing but an illusion in any case. Rubens refers to Vonnegut's "personal belief that the destruction of Dresden was not a final act, and, by extension, that death does not represent a final act for all men," a position attributed to Vonnegut almost entirely on the basis of a 1970 interview in which Vonnegut remarks that "nothing in this world is ever final—no one ever ends—we keep on bouncing back and forth in time, we go on and on ad infinitum."[32] A single Vonnegut quote can serve almost any purpose, but why not embrace Vonnegut's comment in his 1966 introduction to *Mother Night*, "When you're dead you're dead"? If Vonnegut really wants to reconcile us to what happened at Dresden, how does he go about it in *Slaughterhouse-Five*? Rubens raises the most tantalizing of issues, but his treatment of *Slaughterhouse-Five* itself is sketchy at best. Far more persuasive were Loree Rackstraw's excellent review of *Jailbird* (1979), the second of four essay-reviews she has published on Vonnegut since 1976,[33] and Ellen Cronan Rose's "It's All a Joke: Science Fiction in Kurt Vonnegut's *The Sirens of Titan*," a suggestive attempt to show how Vonnegut's use of science-fiction conventions differs from that of Isaac Asimov, Arthur Clarke, and Frank Herbert. Among other reviews of *Jailbird*, John Irving's "Kurt Vonnegut and His Critics" deserves mention. A student of Vonnegut's, Irving offers a moving tribute to the influence and integrity of Vonnegut's fiction.[34]

In 1980 Jerome Klinkowitz either published or republished a number of his essays on Vonnegut. A slightly earlier piece, "Kurt Vonnegut Jr.'s SuperFiction," included interesting information concerning the manuscript of *Breakfast of Champions*. Contrary to rumor, *Breakfast of Champions* was unfinished as of 1971, at which time the book was about the narrator of Kilgore Trout's *Now It Can Be Told*. Also, the novel originally ended with "Kurt Vonnegut" and Dwayne Hoover in the same loony bin, an ending Vonnegut changed just before the book was published.[35] In 1980 Klinkowitz republished "The Dramatization of Kurt Vonnegut, Jr." in his book *The Practice of Fiction in America*. This 1975 essay on *Happy Birthday, Wanda June* (1970) offers an interesting perspective on the post-*Slaughterhouse* Vonnegut. Klinkowitz also included a long chapter on Vonnegut in the second edition of his *Literary Disruptions* (a book first published in 1975). This chapter is an expanded version of Klinkowitz's excellent *Modern Fiction Studies* essay of 1973, but curiously it does not have the same impact. The longer piece is a bit rambling, punctuated by suggestive facts that do not quite come together to make a thesis. Klinkowitz stresses Vonnegut's emphasis on the imaginative re-creation of an all too dismal reality, but he does not address the charge of escapism and never engages, here or elsewhere, the question of how we should respond to Billy Pilgrim. In "Kurt Vonnegut and Donald Barthelme: The American Image," a chapter in his *The American 1960s*, Klinkowitz deals with the same topic but to better effect. Here he argues that the novels of the 1960s are "demonstrations of the Bokononist fiction-making principle," an appropriate response to the period's more demoralizing "realities." Though he still fails to discuss Billy Pilgrim, Klinkowitz offers a far more definite reading of *Slaughterhouse-Five*. Nonetheless, this version of Klinkowitz's argument still betrays a fundamental contradiction. In Klinkowitz's reading of the early novels, man is free to create imaginatively but does not have free will—a Bokononist paradox, perhaps, but one that is insufficiently explained.[36]

Three other essays of note appeared in 1980. Richard Ziegfeld's "Kurt Vonnegut on Censorship and Moral Values" published Vonnegut's letter to the head of the Drake, North Dakota, school board that burned thirty-two copies of *Slaughterhouse-Five*. Ziegfeld also comments on the case, rightly concluding that Vonnegut wrote his letter "to promote a better world in which people are kinder to each other than they are presently." Russell Blackford's "The Definition of Love: Kurt Vonnegut's 'Slapstick' " presented a thorough but possibly misleading interpretation of Vonnegut's thematic intentions in *Slapstick*. Blackford's reading is open to the same charge as my essay on *Breakfast of Champions*, for what Vonnegut intended does not square with most readers' disappointment at what he in fact did. Finally, Robert Nadeau published the first extensive study of Vonnegut's use of science. Nadeau suggests that unlike other science-fiction writers Vonnegut uses scientific concepts for "metaphysical" rather than "spectacular" effects. Nadeau explains and relates quantum and relativity theories to *The Sirens of Titan, Cat's Cradle*, and *Slaughterhouse-Five*. He argues, for example, that Bokononism is based on our new belief in "the approximate or relative nature of truth," and that the theory of relativity "justifies" time-travel and Billy Pilgrim's Tralfamadorian beliefs. Nadeau may be right about all this, but his discussion is unpersuasive. The parallels cited are analyzed very briefly, Vonnegut's texts and even titles are miscited all too frequently (Vonnegut's most famous novel is referred to throughout as *Slaughter House-Five*), and Nadeau asserts that Vonnegut and the Tralfamadorians share a common philosophy without saying a word about the issue of determinism.[37]

The essays of 1981 continued to treat Vonnegut as an established, perhaps even major writer. In his *Alternative Pleasures* Philip Stevick praised Vonnegut's ability to combine irony with sentimentality and explored the naive narrative mode of the later novels. Writing on "Elements of Dostoevsky in the Novels of Kurt Vonnegut," Donald Fiene established that the allusions to Dostoyevski in *Breakfast of Champions* and *Slapstick* do not reflect anything Vonnegut remembered from Dostoyevski's texts. Fiene also quotes from correspondence that confirms Vonnegut's respect for the major Russian writers. Peter Reed's entry on Vonnegut in *American Writers: A Collection of Biographies* was of even greater biographical interest. This thirty-page essay complements Klinkowitz's earlier studies while proposing several crucial connections between Vonnegut's life and works. Richard Giannone and Barry Chabot provided the more substantial critical studies of 1981. Giannone's "Violence in the Fiction of Kurt Vonnegut" is an important article that repeats points from his earlier book but advances a far more striking (and unifying) thesis. Unfortunately, this thesis is an extreme one. Giannone traces a "pervasive" violence in Vonnegut's works, then argues that Vonnegut's response is one of "wacky despair." In Giannone's view, Vonnegut sees no hope in curbing life's violence. Indeed, Vonnegut's fatalism is so great that his books are parables of "the unalterable law of natural disorder." Giannone acknowledges that Vonnegut's public statements are much more hopeful, but he does not account for the discrepancy between these public utterances and the novels. Giannone fails to distinguish between the *kinds* of violence depicted in Vonnegut's fiction. More important, Giannone sees no difference between natural and man-made forms of violence. Perhaps Vonnegut himself makes no distinction, but Giannone offers no evidence to confirm this. Barry Chabot's "*Slaughterhouse-Five* and the Comforts of Indifference" presents a fascinating theory about Vonnegut's stance toward Tralfamadorianism. Chabot sees that the Tralfamadorian point of view is "cruelly inadequate," but he argues that Vonnegut still wants to achieve this perspective and its "comforts of indifference." The novel dramatizes Vonnegut's inability to maintain this stoical stance, a "problem" that many readers would see as altogether to Vonnegut's credit but which Chabot seems to take as a genuine failure. Chabot argues that "[Vonnegut's] allusion to Lot's wife is instructive, for *Slaughterhouse-Five* is a novel written by a man who would be stone," and he interprets Vonnegut's praise of Mary O'Hare as "a comment I can only read as gratuitous irony." These remarks expose the eccentricity of Chabot's case, for Vonnegut admires Lot's wife because she felt compelled to look back, not because she was turned to stone, and no other critic has read what Vonnegut says about Mary O'Hare as ironic. In each case Vonnegut praises someone who will not settle for the comforts of indifference.[38]

If the body of criticism on Vonnegut has diminished since 1977, 1982 was the major exception to this trend. Not only did a goodly number of essays and one book appear, the work published in 1982 represents perhaps the high point in Vonnegut criticism so far as quality is concerned. Lucien Agosta presented an acute psychological reading of *Cat's Cradle*, John Cooley emphasized Bokonon's complexity while presenting him as "one of the rare examples of a basically successful black portrait by a white writer,"

Thomas Wymer added to his earlier argument by tracing Vonnegut's complex attack on technology, Michael McGrath made a strong if exaggerated case for Vonnegut as an almost complete pessimist concerning the liberal tradition in a postindustrial society, and Jerome Klinkowitz discussed "The Hyannis Port Story" as an example of postmodernist anti-illusionism or what Klinkowitz calls "self-apparency."[39] But the year's major publications were Klinkowitz's *Kurt Vonnegut* in the Methuen contemporary authors series and Kathryn Hume's three substantial essays on different features of Vonnegut's career. These pieces are, arguably, the best book and the best individual essays yet published on Vonnegut.

Klinkowitz's book is only ninety-six pages long, but it provides an extremely well-written and informative overview of Vonnegut's career prior to *Deadeye Dick* (1982). Klinkowitz describes Vonnegut's shift from a genre writer to a modern experimentalist to perhaps the major postmodernist. He assimilates material from his earlier studies, especially his work on the short fiction, and adds incisive discussions of *Slaughterhouse-Five* as a book about Vonnegut's problems in writing it, the thematic thrust of *Slapstick*, and Vonnegut's most recent achievement in *Jailbird*. No one knows more about Vonnegut, of course, and Klinkowitz's critical judgments are usually as reliable as his information. The latter is truly impressive here, for in this short book one learns a remarkable number of new things about Vonnegut, for example, that he used one of his proposed master's theses in *Player Piano*, that the stories published in science-fiction magazines were first rejected by mainstream magazines, that Vonnegut intended to call the narrator of *Cat's Cradle* "Vonnegut" but was overruled by his publisher, that *Between Time and Timbuktu* was put together by a committee rather than by Vonnegut, that changes were made in *Happy Birthday, Wanda June* even as the play was in production. Though not exactly a biographical critic, Klinkowitz brings his information to bear in such a way as to illuminate whatever he discusses. One might wish that his critical judgments were as frequent as they are reliable, for Klinkowitz tends to avoid distinguishing between Vonnegut's greater and lesser efforts. Thus he manages to discuss *Slapstick* for several pages without a hint of the novel's relative inferiority. More important, perhaps, Klinkowitz has little to say about the structure of Vonnegut's novels. But Klinkowitz has so much to say about so many other things, one can only regret that his one book-length treatment of Vonnegut is so short.[40]

Kathryn Hume's three essays overlap a bit, but each advances a major argument. "Kurt Vonnegut and the Myths and Symbols of Meaning" derives from Hume's vast knowledge of myth as well as Vonnegut (she has written extensively about myth, especially as it relates to fantasy).[41] She describes in detail Vonnegut's almost step-by-step rejection of traditional mythic patterns, especially "the hero mónomyth" as described by Joseph Campbell and others. Vonnegut rejects mythic plots because they "clash" with his personal experiences. Thus, in Vonnegut's fiction, "evil" women are not conquered and good women are extremely rare; dragonlike embodiments of evil are hard to find, let alone defeat; atonement with the father never occurs; and "questing" heroes bring back no "boon" or special knowledge from their trials. Homecoming, the traditional end of the monomyth, is a particularly dismal experience (see especially *Mother Night, Happy Birthday, Wanda June,* and *Jailbird*). Vonnegut's most direct use of mythic "exostructures" occurs in *Breakfast of Champions* and *Happy Birthday, Wanda June,* where parallels to the *Odyssey* are frequent and invariably ironic. Yet Hume does not see Vonnegut as nihilistic. "He is no Pollyanna, but neither is he totally pessimistic or cynical," she concludes, citing his efforts in the 1970s to find sustaining modes of behavior to replace mythic clichés. Hume's "The Heraclitean Cosmos of Kurt Vonnegut" also argues that Vonnegut is more hopeful than many have thought. Vonnegut's world may be chaotic, but he continues to believe that in the flux and flow of things it is still possible to honor what is distinctively human. Hume offers a wonderfully detailed portrait of Vonnegut's "cosmos," his constantly shifting fictional world that can only be understood by looking at all his works rather than any one book. She is especially good on Vonnegut's "recycled" characters, such as Kilgore Trout, who always seem to change when introduced into a new work. She offers the best published account of how Vonnegut treats traditional society, romantic love, and religion as momentary stays against confusion. Finally, she defines Vonnegut's position on his shifting cosmos by comparing it with similar worldviews in Ovid, Shakespeare (*Hamlet*), Heraclitus, and Gerard Manley Hopkins. This is a splendid essay tht paraphrase only beings to characterize. Finally, in "Vonnegut's Self-Projections: Symbolic Characters and Symbolic Fiction," Hume treats Vonnegut's main characters as "straightforward projections of some part of his psyche." This sort of analysis may seem suspect, but Hume's critical practice is exemplary. A good example is her claim that in *Slaughterhouse-Five* "the various responses of Billy, of the Vonnegut persona, and of Trout together provide a kind of symphonic score for rendering human reaction to such a disaster." She goes on to offer extremely perceptive readings of Kilgore Trout and the later novels, *Breakfast of Champions, Slapstick,* and *Jailbird*. Without exaggerating the value of these novels, Hume clarifies their relatively positive themes as well as anyone has yet done.[42]

As noted earlier, the flow of Vonnegut criticism since 1982 has been steady but diminished. In 1983 John Aldridge revived the opinions of more traditional critics such as Alfred Kazin and Charles Samuels. Aldridge berates Vonnegut for his "adolescent stoicism" and his retreat into "cuteness." Frederick Karl offered a far more extensive but no less critical commentary in his *American Fictions 1940 / 1980.* "His provenance," Karl suggests, "belongs not with serious practitioners of fiction but with the Beatles, McLuhan, and those who have probed into popular culture as ways of directly interpreting us." But Karl does not find Vonnegut's "probe" to be very profound, for he characterizes the novels as "drenched by sentimental whimsy," attacks such works as *God Bless You, Mr. Rosewater* for their "obviousness," and

laments Vonnegut's artlessness in *Slaughterhouse-Five* as well as *Breakfast of Champions* and *Slapstick*. Karl's grasp of Vonnegut is suggested by his definition of *foma* as "evil." Moreover, the organization of Karl's book is particularly frustrating, for the discussions of Vonnegut's individual novels occur in five separate chapters. Fragmentation and repetition are the almost inevitable results. Kermit Vanderbilt's "Kurt Vonnegut's American Nightmares and Utopias" was a much more successful review of Vonnegut's utopian instincts, especially as they inform *Slapstick* and *Jailbird*. But the year's two most valuable studies were by Joseph Schöpp and Lawrence Broer. Schöpp's "*Slaughterhouse-Five*: The Struggle with a Form that Fails" is a well-written essay that notes Vonnegut's determined effort to avoid the conventions of traditional narrative because they imply a coherence and rationality that do not apply to Dresden. Schöpp argues that Vonnegut "fails" in this effort, for his readers doggedly piece together the novel's chronology, assign praise and blame, and even end up providing a moral. Thus, Schöpp argues, Vonnegut's structural ploy forces us to confront the grim realities of Dresden. Curiously, Schöpp's otherwise skillful analysis says nothing about Vonnegut's use of the Tralfamadorians. Broer's "Pilgrim's Progress: Is Kurt Vonnegut, Jr., Winning His War with Machines?" identifies the technological horrors of the twentieth century as Vonnegut's prevailing theme. Broer is especially good at showing how Vonnegut's attack on Tralfamadorian complacency begins with his first novel, *Player Piano*, a book Broer reads as well as anyone. Broer's Vonnegut does seem terribly optimistic, however. According to Broer, Vonnegut "knows too that with a little imagination and heart we can, like Salo in *Sirens of Titan*, dismantle our own self-imprisoning machinery and become whatever we choose to become." Vonnegut knows all too well that this will require more than a "little" imagination and heart.[43]

The essays of 1984 ranged from very modest to excellent. Robert Hipkiss's chapter on Vonnegut in his *The American Absurd: Pynchon, Vonnegut, and Barth* is marred by numerous editorial or factual errors and excessive plot summaries for all works discussed. Hipkiss is very good on *Jailbird* and other specific topics, but he is committed to the undemonstrated idea that Vonnegut is a determinist and offers what almost seem to be random notes without a controlling thesis. It also seems odd that in a chapter relating Vonnegut to "the American absurd" Hipkiss makes no reference to Charles Harris. T. J. Matheson's " 'This Lousy Little Book': The Genesis and Development of *Slaughterhouse-Five* as Revealed in Chapter One" is a more successful essay even if one does not agree with it. Matheson argues that Vonnegut's persona undergoes a crucial conversion while writing *Slaughterhouse-Five*. At first "Vonnegut" is callous and cynical in his attitude toward Dresden, and his artistic aims are "those of a mechanic or laborer" rather than "a truly creative artist." This "Vonnegut" is shocked into a more responsible stance by Mary O'Hare, who recommends confronting the horrors of Dresden rather than "romanticizing or flatly ignoring events that are intrinsically sordid, unpleasant, or ugly." This evasive, irresponsible Vonnegut is largely Matheson's creation. Why did Vonnegut have so much trouble writing about the firebombing of Dresden if he simply wanted to romanticize the event? Matheson is right to emphasize the Mary O'Hare episode, but the role he assigns it in Vonnegut's "development" is greatly exaggerated. An even more successful discussion was R. B. Gill's "Bargaining in Good Faith: The Laughter of Vonnegut, Grass, and Kundera." This first-rate essay links the three artists cited in its title as modern comedians who must be read against the expectations of traditional comedy: "Open-eyed and without illusion, they do not suggest that their comic imaginations can transform reality; nevertheless, they attempt to salvage what they can from their worlds, to accommodate themselves to what must be in any case. Their novels, then, record a comic impulse compromised by an unillusioned realism." Gill's views recall those of Robert Scholes, but Gill's Vonnegut is slightly more optimistic. For Gill, Vonnegut's laughter bespeaks a "healthy adjustment to a sad world," and the rituals proposed in a work such as *Slapstick* offer "respite from pain even if they do not offer meaningfulness." Gill is especially good on *Jailbird*, but his essay is recommended for everything he has to say about Vonnegut.[44]

In 1985 Vonnegut was the subject of five brief but highly suggestive discussions, several of them in essays or books on broader topics. Arthur Saltzman cited Vonnegut as a prime example of what he called "The Aesthetic of Doubt in Recent Fiction," arguing that Vonnegut struggles mightily with his lack of faith but ends up expressing "bewilderment and resignation, not affirmation." Saltzman suggests that Vonnegut's genius is to make this spiritual drama his most moving subject. In his *Literary Subversions* Jerome Klinkowitz returned to *Slaughterhouse-Five* to point out that this novel is "an anthropological reinvention," a work that confirms the fact our world is a cultural creation.[45] Despite his far-reaching title, "Physics and Fantasy: Scientific Mysticism, Kurt Vonnegut, and *Gravity's Rainbow*," Russell Blackford argued the rather narrow point that John Somer is wrong to insist Vonnegut authenticates Billy Pilgrim's space-travel in *Slaughterhouse-Five*. And in his book chapter "Kurt Vonnegut: The Cheerfully Demented" David Punter presented an astute if dour assessment of Vonnegut's social views. But the year's major piece was Charles Berryman's "After the Fall: Kurt Vonnegut." Berryman notes that each of Vonnegut's protagonists from *Slaughterhouse-Five* through *Deadeye Dick* is "haunted by images of death and destruction." These characters try to exorcise their terrible vision but fail. Indeed, their efforts to achieve a childish innocence lead to a remarkable string of deaths involving their women. As Berryman remarks, it is as if the later Vonnegut wanted to verify Poe's famous claim that the most poetical topic is the death of a beautiful woman. Berryman points out that Vonnegut has acknowledged a recurring bad dream in which he murders an old woman—a strong hint that Vonnegut's later novels are very personal indeed. Berryman's review of the later fiction presents a Vonnegut far less free from alienation than the writer Klinkowitz describes in "The Dramatization of Kurt Vonnegut, Jr.," but perhaps both Vonneguts are real. At times the later novels depict a Vonnegut who seems liberated from the paralyzing matter of Dresden, at times they present a Vonnegut who continues to fight internal demons we cannot trace to a single calamity such as Dresden. In any case, as Klinkowitz himself has noted, Berryman's essay is one of the best recent discussions of Vonnegut.[46]

Only three essays were published on Vonnegut in 1986 but two were important contributions. Leonard Mustazza's "Vonnegut's Tralfamadore and Milton's Eden" is the best essay on *Slaughterhouse-Five* in many years. Mustazza shows that "Billy continually tries to construct for himself an Edenic experience out of materials he garners over the course of some twenty years." Billy's effort reflects "his own yearnings for peace, love, immutability, stability, and an ordered existence"—everything he has *not* known in reality. Billy creates a "myth" that shares much with Milton's Eden: "a prepared habitat, instruction by a higher power, a mate who is different from yet perfect for him." These parallels are ironic, however, for "contrary to Adam and Eve, Billy Pilgrim begins from the fallen state and expresses an overpowering desire to move backwards to a prior state, to go from horrid experience into a dimension where will and action are unnecessary or inconsequential." Unlike Adam, then, Billy seeks to reject his knowledge, to avoid what Mustazza calls "ethical action." Mustazza insists that Billy Pilgrim is not Kurt Vonnegut, that Vonnegut presents his character as a sympathetic but pitiable example of our own fate if we cannot resolve the problems that drove Billy to Tralfamadore. Joseph Sigman's "Science and Parody in Kurt Vonnegut's *The Sirens of Titan*" provides an excellent review of modern physics—Einstein, Planck, Heisenberg, Bohr—in order to demonstrate Vonnegut's use of the new concepts in *The Sirens of Titan*. Sigman is at his best in discussing Winston Niles Rumfoord's status as a false deity and Vonnegut's creation of "a totally relativistic cosmos." He is less convincing in claiming a correspondence between quantum jumps and the book's many scene changes, for the narrative shifts are almost always explained within the novel. Nor does Sigman ever quite formulate what he calls "the philosophical implications of modern physics." Nonetheless, his discussion is much more persuasive than Nadeau's earlier treatment of the same subject.[47]

Since 1986 very little has appeared on Vonnegut. By far the most important publication of 1987 was *Kurt Vonnegut: A Comprehensive Bibliography* by Asa Pieratt, Jr., Julie Huffman-klinkowitz, and Jerome Klinkowitz. Updating their 1974 bibliography, the authors identify "all the published material both by and about Vonnegut from 1950 through 1985." Anyone who uses this book will quickly realize how remarkably complete it is. Its sheer size implies a kind of canonization, as the reviewer for *American Literature* remarked,[48] which seems quite at odds with the dwindling criticism devoted to Vonnegut's works. In 1987 only one short article was published, Robert A. Martin's "*Slaughterhouse-Five:* Vonnegut's Domed Universe," while Brian McHale referred to Vonnegut throughout his book *Postmodernist Fiction*.[49] The one essay published early in 1988, William H. E. Meyer, Jr.'s "Kurt

Vonnegut: The Man with Nothing to Say," is an eccentric effort to link Vonnegut with virtually every major figure in the American tradition, though Meyer's purpose in doing this is extremely fuzzy.[50] This sparse critical material, coupled with the lukewarm response to *Bluebeard*, seems to point to Vonnegut's declining reputation. But this may be a premature conclusion, for at least two major essays are forthcoming, Leonard Mustazza's "The Machine Within: Mechanization, Human Discontent, and the Genre of Vonnegut's *Player Piano*" and Lawrence Broer's "Kurt Vonnegut vs. Deadeye Dick: The Resolution of Vonnegut's Creative Schizophrenia." Mustazza's study of *Player Piano* illustrates that there is still much to be said about even the earliest of Vonnegut's novels, and Broer's essay is easily the best study to date of *Deadeye Dick*. These essays suggest that serious criticism of Vonnegut will continue, less voluminous perhaps but more discriminating.[51]

I suspect that Vonnegut criticism is about to undergo a marked resurgence. Mustazza, Broer, and Loree Rackstraw are all close to completing new books on Vonnegut, sophisticated studies that answer one of our obvious needs by taking into account the recent novels. (Indeed, Broer's *Sanity Plea: Schizophrenia in the Novels of Kurt Vonnegut* [Ann Arbor, Mich.: UMI Research Press, 1988] is the best thematic study of Vonnegut's works yet written. Though I have only read this book in galleys, I especially recommend its treatment of the later Vonnegut.) I would also suggest that we still need a formal study in which Vonnegut's generic experiments are assessed as well as described. We also need a book-length biography, though Klinkowitz's many fine studies will no doubt suffice for some time to come. And we need serious critical evaluations of many individual novels other than *Slaughterhouse-Five*. Notice, for example, how often I have praised what individual critics say about *Jailbird*, yet so far no one has devoted an entire essay to this book. Also, no essay has appeared on *Galápagos*, which I would rank as Vonnegut's second best novel. Finally, Vonnegut needs to be more firmly related to the American and postmodern literary traditions, though Meyer's recent essay illustrates the kind of Americanist criticism we do *not* need, and Klinkowitz has already done much to relate Vonnegut to his postmodern peers. Perhaps I should simply say that Vonnegut needs to be taken even more seriously by even more critics, who will presumably undertake these and other tasks commonly associated with the reassessment of a major writer. Indeed, behind additional studies of Vonnegut's life, his individual works, and his literary relationships stands the fundamental question of whether Vonnegut is in fact a major writer. The large body of work already done suggests that the answer may well be yes. Future work of the sort described above will allow us to answer this question— at least for our own time—with greater confidence than most of us feel at present.

The four essays I commissioned for this collection do not provide a definitive answer to the question of Vonnegut's stature, but they move us closer to such an answer. John L. Simons's "Tangled Up in You: A Playful Reading of *Cat's Cradle*" is a serious revaluation of an early Vonnegut novel.

No one has presented a better case for the book's own seriousness. Charles Berryman's essay on *Breakfast of Champions* offers a chastening reminder of Vonnegut's comic, even self-parodic intentions, while his lively discussion of *Galápagos* is the first essay-length interpretation of one of Vonnegut's finest novels. David Cowart's "Culture and Anarchy: Vonnegut's Later Career" is an excellent thematic overview of the novels since *Slaughterhouse-Five,* a general study that has the advantage of encompassing all the novels except *Bluebeard.* These four essays treat Vonnegut with a respect each piece amply justifies. I believe they constitute a significant response to the dearth of recent criticism.

I would like to thank John L. Simons, Charles Berryman, and David Cowart for agreeing to write essays for this collection. They have been more prompt than I in fulfilling their tasks. My thanks to Judy Sokol, Lynn Herman, and Sandy Lucash for their assistance in gathering and preparing the relevant materials. My thanks, too, to Asa Pieratt, Jr., Julie Huffman-klinkowitz, and Jerome Klinkowitz, whose bibliography was indispensable to my work. Jerome Klinkowitz also read my introduction to help save me from factual if not critical sin. Finally, I am grateful to James Nagel for permitting me to undertake this task, one I have very much enjoyed doing.[52]

ROBERT MERRILL

University of Nevada, Reno

Notes

1. Jerome Klinkowitz, "The Literary Career of Kurt Vonnegut, Jr.," *Modern Fiction Studies* 19 (1973):57, and *Literary Disruptions,* 2nd ed. (Urbana: University of Illinois Press, 1980), 33.

2. See Julian Moynahan, "A Prisoner at War in the Hamptons," *New York Times Book Review,* 18 October 1987, 12.

3. Vonnegut and Yarmolinsky separated in 1971 after twenty-six years of marriage. Published by Houghton Mifflin, Yarmolinsky's memoir uses fictional names to protect the innocent and the guilty, but Vonnegut's role as "Carl" is unmistakable.

4. I take these numbers from Asa B. Pieratt, Jr., Julie Huffman-klinkowitz, and Jerome Klinkowitz, *Kurt Vonnegut: A Comprehensive Bibliography* (Hamden, Conn.: Archon Books, 1987), 223–68. A few of the items included are reviews, but the overall figure would not change much if all reviews were excluded.

5. See the section on Vonnegut's short fiction in Pieratt, Huffman-klinkowitz, and Klinkowitz, *Vonnegut: Bibliography,* 177–82. Technically only forty-four stories were published through 1963, as "The Hyannis Port Story" was sold to the *Saturday Evening Post* in 1963 but did not appear because of the assassination of President Kennedy. The story was first published in *Welcome to the Monkey House* (1968).

6. Favorable 1952 reviews included Charles Lee, "New Terms and Goons," *Saturday Review,* 30 August 1952, 11; Don Fabun, "Anti-Utopian Novel," *San Francisco Chronicle,* 29 August 1952, 15; Granville Hicks, "The Engineers Take Over," *New York Times Book Review,*

17 August 1952, 5, 16; James Hilton, "Glum, Satiric Look Ahead," *New York Herald Tribune Book Review*, 17 August 1952, 5.

7. See Mark Hillegas, "Dystopian Science Fiction: New Index to the Human Situation," *New Mexico Quarterly* 31 (1961):238–49; Terry Southern, "After the Bomb, Dad Came Up with Ice," *New York Times Book Review*, 2 June 1963, 20; *Spectator*, 2 August 1963, 158–59.

8. C. D. B. Bryan, "Kurt Vonnegut on Target," *New Republic*, 8 October 1966, 21–22, 24–26.

9. Robert Scholes, *The Fabulators* (New York: Oxford University Press, 1967), 35–55. This chapter is expanded and revised from " 'Mithridates, He Died Old': Black Humor and Kurt Vonnegut, Jr.," *Hollins Critic* 3 (1966): 1–12, and is incorporated into Scholes's *Fabulation and Metafiction* (Urbana: University of Illinois Press, 1979), 144–62.

10. See Jerome Klinkowitz, "Kurt Vonnegut, Jr.: The Canary in a Cathouse," in *The Vonnegut Statement*, ed. Jerome Klinkowitz and John Somer (New York: Delacorte Press / Seymour Lawrence, 1973), 12.

11. Tony Tanner, "The Uncertain Messenger: A Study of the Novels of Kurt Vonnegut, Jr.," *Critical Quarterly* 11 (1969):297–315. This essay is reprinted in *City of Words* (New York: Harper and Row, 1971), 181–201.

12. See Robert Scholes, review of *Slaughterhouse-Five*, *New York Times Book Review*, 6 April 1969, 1, 23.

13. Jack Richardson, "Easy Writer," *New York Review of Books*, 2 July 1970, 7–8; Leslie A. Fiedler, "The Divine Stupidity of Kurt Vonnegut," *Esquire* 74 (September 1970): 195–97, 199–200, 202–4; Benjamin DeMott, "Vonnegut's Otherwordly Laughter," *Saturday Review*, 1 May 1971, 29–32, 38. See also Charles Thomas Samuels, "Age of Vonnegut," *New Republic*, 12 June 1971, 30–32.

14. See Jerry H. Bryant, *The Open Decision* (New York: Free Press, 1970), 303–25.

15. *Summary* 1, no. 2 (1971); *Critique* 12, no. 3 (1971); Charles B. Harris, *Contemporary American Novelists of the Absurd* (New Haven, Conn.: College and University Press, 1971), 51–75; Mary Sue Schriber, "You've Come a Long Way, Babbitt! From Zenith to Ilium," *Twentieth Century Literature* 17 (1971):101–6; L. J. Clancy, " 'If the Accident Will': The Novels of Kurt Vonnegut," *Meanjin Quarterly* 30 (1971):37–45.

16. See especially Vance Bourjaily, "What Vonnegut Is and Isn't," *New York Times Book Review*, 13 August 1972, 3, 10; John R. May, "Vonnegut's Humor and the Limits of Hope," *Twentieth Century Literature* 18 (1972):25–36 (expanded in May's *Toward a New Earth: Apocalypse in the American Novel* [Notre Dame, Ind.: University of Notre Dame Press, 1972], 172–200); Peter A. Scholl, "Vonnegut's Attack upon Christendom," *Newsletter of the Conference on Christianity and Literature* 22 (1972):5–11; Raymond M. Olderman, *Beyond the Waste Land: The American Novel in the 1960s* (New Haven, Conn.: Yale University Press, 1972), 189–219.

17. David H. Goldsmith, *Kurt Vonnegut: Fantasist of Fire and Ice*, Popular Writers Series Pamphlet No. 2 (Bowling Green, Ohio: Bowling Green University Popular Press, 1972); Peter J. Reed, *Kurt Vonnegut, Jr.* (New York: Warner, 1972).

18. See especially Reed's "The Later Vonnegut," in *Vonnegut in America*, ed. Jerome Klinkowitz and Donald L. Lawler (New York: Delacorte Press / Seymour Lawrence, 1977), 150–86, and the Vonnegut entry in *American Writers: A Collection of Biographies* (New York: Scribner's, 1981), 753–84.

19. Pearl K. Bell, "American Fiction: Forgetting Ordinary Truths," *Dissent*, Winter 1973, 26–34; Ihab Hassan, *Contemporary American Literature, 1945–1972* (New York: Ungar, 1973), 45–47, 65, 86; Charles Nicol, "The Ideas of an Anti-Intellectual," *National Review*, 28 September 1973, 1064–65; Michael Wood, "Dancing in the Dark," *New York Review of Books*, 31 May 1973, 23–25; Alfred Kazin, *Bright Book of Life* (Boston: Little, Brown, 1973), 82–83, 86–90;

Doris Lessing, "Vonnegut's Responsibility," *New York Times Book Review*, 4 February 1973, 35.

20. See especially Joyce Nelson, "*Slaughterhouse-Five:* Novel and Film," *Literature / Film Quarterly* 1 (1973):149–53, and Neil D. Isaacs, "Unstuck in Time: *Clockwork Orange* and *Slaughterhouse-Five*," *Literature / Film Quarterly* 1 (1973):122–31. Other, later treatments of this subject include Stephen Dimeo, "Novel into Film: So It Goes," in *The Modern American Novel and the Movies*, ed. Gerald Peary and Roger Shatzkin (New York: Ungar, 1978), 282–92, and Joanna E. Rapf, " 'In the Beginning Was the Work': Steve Geller on *Slaughterhouse-Five*,' *Post-Script* 4 (1985):19–31.

21. Arlen J. Hansen, "The Celebration of Solipsism: A New Trend in American Fiction," *Modern Fiction Studies* 19 (1973): 5–15; Stanley Trachtenberg, "Vonnegut's Cradle: The Erosion of Comedy," *Michigan Quarterly Review* 12 (1973):66–71; Donald J. Greiner, "Vonnegut's *Slaughterhouse-Five* and the Fiction of Atrocity," *Critique* 14 (1973):38–51; Klinkowitz, "The Literary Career of Kurt Vonnegut, Jr.," 57–67.

22. Curiously, these errors were not corrected six years later when Pinsker republished his essay in *Between Two Worlds: The American Novel in the 1960's* (Troy, N.Y.: Whitston, 1980), 87–101.

23. David L. Vanderwerken, "Pilgrim's Progress: *Slaughterhouse-Five*," *Research Studies* 42 (1974): 147–52; David Ketterer, *New Worlds for Old: The Apocalyptic Imagination, Science Fiction, and American Literature* (Bloomington: Indiana University Press, 1974), 296–333; Arnold Edelstein, "*Slaughterhouse-Five:* Time Out of Joint," *College Literature* 1 (1974): 128–39; Sanford Pinsker, "Fire and Ice: The Radical Cuteness of Kurt Vonnegut, Jr.," *Studies in the Twentieth Century* 13 (1974): 1–19.

24. Peter B. Messent, "*Breakfast of Champions:* The Direction of Vonnegut's Fiction," *Journal of American Studies* 8 (1974): 101–14, and Clinton S. Burhans, Jr., "Hemingway and Vonnegut: Diminishing Vision in a Dying Age," *Modern Fiction Studies* 21 (1975): 173–91.

25. Robert W. Uphaus, "Expected Meaning in Vonnegut's Dead-End Fiction," *Novel* 8 (1975): 164–75; Thomas LeClair, "Death and Black Humor," *Critique* 17 (1975): 5–40; Jean E. Kennard, *Number and Nightmare: Forms of Fantasy in Contemporary Literature* (Hamden, Conn.: Archon Books, 1975), 101–28, 131–33, 203–4; Lynn Buck, "Vonnegut's World of Comic Futility," *Studies in American Fiction* 3 (1975): 181–98.

26. Maurice J. O'Sullivan, Jr., "*Slaughterhoue-Five:* Kurt Vonnegut's Anti-Memoirs," *Essays in Literature* 3 (1976): 44–50; Thomas L. Wymer, "The Swiftian Satire of Kurt Vonnegut, Jr.," in *Voices for the Future*, ed. Thomas D. Clareson (Bowling Green, Ohio: Bowling Green University Popular Press, 1976), 238–62; Charles B. Harris, "Time, Uncertainty, and Kurt Vonnegut, Jr.: A Reading of *Slaughterhouse-Five*," *Centennial Review* 26 (1976):228–43.

27. Stanley Schatt, *Kurt Vonnegut, Jr.* (Boston: Twayne Publishers, 1976).

28. James H. Justus, "Fiction: The 1950s to the Present," in *American Literary Scholarship 1977*, ed. James Woodress (Durham, N.C.: Duke University Press, 1979), 311.

29. James Lundquist, *Kurt Vonnegut* (New York: Ungar, 1977); Richard Giannone, *Vonnegut: A Preface to His Novels* (Port Washington, N.Y.: Kennikat Press, 1977); Klinkowitz and Lawler, *Vonnegut in America*.

30. Dolores K. Gros-Louis, "*Slaughterhouse-Five:* Pacifism vs. Passiveness," *Ball State University Forum* 18 (1977):3–8; John W. Tilton, *Cosmic Satire in the Contemporary Novel* (Lewisburg, Pa.: Bucknell University Press, 1977), 69–103; Robert Merrill, "Vonnegut's *Breakfast of Champions:* The Conversion of Heliogabalus," *Critique* 18 (1977): 99–109; Mary Sue Schriber, "Bringing Chaos to Order: The Novel Tradition and Kurt Vonnegut, Jr.," *Genre* 10 (1977):283–97.

31. John Gardner, *On Moral Fiction* (New York: Basic Books, 1978), 87; Josephine Hendin, *Vulnerable People: A View of American Fiction Since 1945* (New York: Oxford University

Press, 1978), 30–40; Robert Merrill and Peter A. Scholl, "Vonnegut's *Slaughterhouse-Five:* The Requirements of Chaos," *Studies in American Fiction* 6 (1978): 65–76.

32. Patricia Bosworth, "To Vonnegut, the Hero is the Man Who Refuses to Kill," *New York Times*, 25 October 1970, sec. D, 5.

33. For Rackstraw's reviews of *Slapstick, Jailbird, Deadeye Dick*, and *Galápagos*, respectively, see "Paradise Re-Lost," *North American Review* 261 (1976): 63–64; "Vonnegut the Diviner, and Other Auguries," *North American Review* 264 (1979):74–76; "The Vonnegut Cosmos," *North American Review* 267 (1982):63–67; "Blue Tunnels to Survival," *North American Review* 270 (1985): 78–80. Her review of *Bluebeard* is forthcoming in the *North American Review*.

34. Thomas L. Hartshorne, "From *Catch-22* to *Slaughterhouse-V* [*sic*]: The Decline of the Political Mode," *South Atlantic Quarterly* 78 (1979):17–33; David Bosworth, "The Literature of Awe," *Antioch Review* 37 (1979): 4–26; Philip M. Rubens, " 'Nothing's Ever Final': Vonnegut's Concept of Time," *College Literature* 6 (1979): 64–72; Ellen Rose Cronan, "It's All a Joke: Science Fiction in Kurt Vonnegut's *The Sirens of Titan*," *Literature and Psychology* 29 (1979):160–68; John Irving, "Kurt Vonnegut and His Critics," *New Republic*, 22 September 1979, 41–49.

35. Jerome Klinkowitz, "Kurt Vonnegut, Jr.'s SuperFiction," *Revue Française d'Études Américaines* (Sorbonne), no. 1 (1976): 115–24. This essay was revised for Klinkowitz's *The Life of Fiction* (Urbana: University of Illinois Press, 1977), 84–93.

36. Jerome Klinkowitz, *The Practice of Fiction in America* (Ames: Iowa State University Press, 1980), 98–105; Klinkowitz, *Literary Disruptions*, 33–61, 196–205; Klinkowitz, *The American 1960s* (Ames: Iowa State University Press, 1980), 47–58.

37. Richard E. Ziegfeld, "Kurt Vonnegut on Censorship and Moral Values," *Modern Fiction Studies* 26 (1980–1981): 631–35; Russell Blackford, "The Definition of Love: Kurt Vonnegut's 'Slapstick,' " *Science Fiction* 2 (1980): 208–28; Robert L. Nadeau, "Physics and Metaphysics in the Novels of Kurt Vonnegut, Jr.," *Mosaic* 13 (1980): 37–47. Nadeau's essay was reprinted in his *Readings from the New Book of Nature* (Amherst: University of Massachusetts Press, 1981), 121–33.

38. Philip Stevick, *Alternative Pleasures: Postrealist Fiction and the Tradition* (Urbana: University of Illinois Press, 1981), 77–93 (reprinted from Stevick's "Naive Narration: Classic to Post-Modern," *Modern Fiction Studies* 23 [1977–1978]: 531–42); Donald M. Fiene, "Elements of Dostoevsky in the Novels of Kurt Vonnegut," *Dostoevsky Studies* 2 (1981): 129–42; Reed, "Kurt Vonnegut, 1922–.," 753–84; Richard Giannone, "Violence in the Fiction of Kurt Vonnegut," *Thought* 56 (1981): 58–76; C. Barry Chabot, "*Slaughterhouse-Five* and the Comforts of Indifference," *Essays in Literature* 8 (1981): 45–51.

39. Lucien L. Agosta, "Ah-Whoom! Egotism and Apocalypse in Kurt Vonnegut's *Cat's Cradle*," *Kansas Quarterly* 14 (1982): 257–72; John Cooley, *Savages and Naturals: Black Portraits by White Writers in Modern American Literature* (Newark: University of Delaware Press, 1982), 161–73; Thomas L. Wymer, "Machines and the Meaning of the Human in the Novels of Kurt Vonnegut, Jr.," in *The Mechanical God: Machines in Science Fiction*, ed. Thomas P. Dunn and Richard D. Erlich (Westport, Conn.: Greenwood Press, 1982), 41–52; Michael J. Gargas McGrath, "Kesey and Vonnegut: The Critique of Liberal Democracy in Contemporary Literature," in *The Artist and Political Vision*, ed. Benjamin R. Barber and Michael J. Gargas McGrath (New Brunswick, N.J.: Transaction Books, 1982), 363–83; Jerome Klinkowitz, *The Self-Apparent Word* (Carbondale: Southern Illinois University Press, 1982), 23–29.

40. Jerome Klinkowitz, *Kurt Vonnegut* (London: Methuen, 1982).

41. See especially Hume's *Fantasy and Mimesis: Responses to Reality in Western Literature* (New York: Methuen, 1984).

42. Kathryn Hume, "Kurt Vonnegut and the Myths and Symbols of Meaning," *Texas Studies in Literature and Language* 24 (1982):429–47; "The Heraclitean Cosmos of Kurt Vonne-

gut," *Papers on Language and Literature* 18 (1982): 208–24; "Vonnegut's Self-Projections: Symbolic Characters and Symbolic Fiction," *Journal of Narrative Technique* 12 (1982): 177–90.

43. John W. Aldridge, *The American Novel and the Way We Live Now* (New York: Oxford University Press, 1983), 7, 74, 106, 138; Frederick R. Karl, *American Fictions 1940 / 1980* (New York: Harper and Row, 1983), 168–69, 174, 245–47, 344–47, 499–502, 521, 529–31; Kermit Vanderbilt, "Kurt Vonnegut's American Nightmares and Utopias," in *The Utopian Vision: Seven Essays on the Quincentennial of Sir Thomas More* (San Diego: San Diego State University Press, 1983), 137–73; Joseph C. Schöpp, *"Slaughterhouse-Five:* The Struggle with a Form that Fails," *Amerikastudien* 28 (1983): 335–45; Lawrence Broer, "Pilgrim's Progress: Is Kurt Vonnegut, Jr., Winning His War with Machines?" in *Clockwork Worlds: Mechanized Environments in Science Fiction,* ed. Richard D. Erlich and Thomas P. Dunn (Westport, Conn.: Greenwood Press, 1983), 137–61. The Erlich and Dunn collection also includes Thomas P. Hoffman, "The Theme of Mechanization in *Player Piano,"* 125–35.

44. Robert A. Hipkiss, *The American Absurd: Pynchon, Vonnegut, and Barth* (Port Washington, N.Y.: Associated Faculty Press, 1984), 43–73; T. J. Matheson, " 'This Lousy Little Book': The Genesis and Development of *Slaughterhouse-Five* as Revealed in Chapter One," *Studies in the Novel* 16 (1984): 228–40; R. B. Gill, "Bargaining in Good Faith: The Laughter of Vonnegut, Grass, and Kundera," *Critique* 25 (1984): 77–91.

45. I take this particular paraphrase from the relevant annotation in Pieratt, Huffman-klinkowitz, and Klinkowitz, *Vonnegut: A Bibliography,* 244.

46. Arthur M. Saltzman, "The Aesthetic of Doubt in Recent Fiction," *Denver Quarterly* 20 (1985):89–106; Jerome Klinkowitz, *Literary Subversions* (Carbondale: Southern Illinois University Press, 1985), xviii–xxiii, xxviii, xxx, 51, 54, 98–99, 104, 149–53, 171–79, 183, 185–90, 193; Russell Blackford, "Physics and Fantasy: Scientific Mysticism, Kurt Vonnegut, and *Gravity's Rainbow," Journal of Popular Culture* 19 (1985): 35–44; David Punter, *The Hidden Script* (London: Routledge & Kegan Paul, 1985), 78–93; Charles Berryman, "After the Fall: Kurt Vonnegut," *Critique* 26 (1985): 96–102. Klinkowitz praises Berryman's essay in his "Fiction: The 1960s to the Present," in *American Literary Scholarship 1985,* ed. J. Albert Robbins (Durham, N.C.: Duke University Press, 1987), 290–91.

47. Leonard Mustazza, "Vonnegut's Tralfamadore and Milton's Eden," *Essays in Literature* 13 (1986): 299–312, and Joseph Sigman, "Science and Parody in Kurt Vonnegut's *The Sirens of Titan," Mosaic* 19 (1986): 15–32.

48. "Brief Mention," *American Literature* 59 (1987): 717. I should add that the earlier bibliography, *Kurt Vonnegut, Jr.: A Descriptive Bibliography and Annotated Secondary Checklist* (Hamden, Conn.: Shoe String Press, 1974), was itself an important stage in Vonnegut studies. Here Asa Pieratt and Jerome Klinkowitz established the canon, including foreign editions, stories, essays, and interviews, at a crucial time in Vonnegut's career.

49. Robert A. Martin, *"Slaughterhouse-Five:* Vonnegut's Domed Universe," *Notes on Contemporary Literature* 17 (1987):5–8, and Brian McHale, *Postmodernist Fiction* (London: Methuen, 1987), 72, 110, 153, 210, 214, 223.

50. William H. E. Meyer, Jr., "Kurt Vonnegut: The Man with Nothing to Say," *Critique* 29 (1988): 95–109.

51. Mustazza's essay will appear in *Papers on Language and Literature* (1988). Broer's essay will appear in *Spectrum of the Fantastic,* an anthology edited by Donald Palumbo for the Greenwood Press (1988).

52. I would like to thank the University of Nevada, Reno, for a sabbatical leave that allowed me to complete this project.

Reviews

New Terms and Goons
[Review of *Player Piano*]

Charles Lee*

To the long list of worries coming off the assembly line of the Age of Anxiety—atomic energy, Anzus, iron curtains, inflation, and flying saucers—Mr. Vonnegut has a new one to add: automation. His mordantly amusing first novel deals with an America that has become one vast interlocked corporate machine so expertly mechanized that almost nobody has to work. The Third World War has been won, permanent peace has been declared, the machines have moved off the battlefield into the factories, and about the only thing people can die of is boredom.

The scene of Mr. Vonnegut's streamlined nightmare is Ilium, New York, whose topless towers house one of the massive sets of push-button workshops that distribute materialism to the American public in a complete security package. Its personnel consists of a few technocrats and one woman, all of whom are under the direction of a governing body of managers and engineers in Washington. This elite lives apart from the "people," whose diversions seem to be television, dope, alcohol, divorce, suicide, and assorted other delinquencies when they are not in the Army or the Reconstruction and Reclamation Corps.

The manager of Ilium is one Dr. Paul Proteus, whose occasional visits among the people at length begin to convince him (his own wheels turn slowly) that the computing machines have somehow left out character, that the tinkering talents of America have finally gadgeted it into a humming terror of uniformity and frustration, that efficiency can neither provide for nor understand the needs of the spirit. Proteus becomes sicklied o'er with the pale cast of thought, and if it is paler than you might like you must remember that he has been trafficking in vacuum tubes for most of his thirty-five years.

His first notion is to retire from Ilium with his wife, Anita, a "sexual genius" whose concept of the richer life includes a fanatical devotion to TV commercials. Anita resists Paul's emancipation proclamation, complete with

*Reprinted by permission from *Saturday Review*, 30 August 1952, 11.

farm, kerosene illumination, and ordinary wash-tubs, and turns her genius in more rewarding directions.

The results are protean, indeed, for Paul, and he is soon involved in more switches of loyalties than even his tabulator mind is prepared for. He is given a sudden assignment to act as a secret agent for the Government, his chief duty being to inform on a disaffected bureaucrat who has joined a revolutionary group of the people and who just happens to be his own best friend. Turning to the revolutionaries himself, and being trusted by neither side, Paul finally discovers himself to be the head of the rebellion, with consequences that no one (excepting perhaps the infallible machines against which he marches) could predict.

Mr. Vonnegut's glimpse of the future may strike some as being over-drawn to the point of grotesqueness, and wanting in Orwellian depth, but it has macabrely playful pertinence at a time when the workerless factory is all but upon us. He would ask us, out of his own electronic literacy (he is himself a graduate engineer), whether this new phase of the Industrial Revolution will be geared to the spiritual and intellectual growth of the American people or whether it will grind their dream into a kind of abundant discontent of the sort satirized in his ingenious book. "Player Piano" has its bright side as entertainment, and its witty moments. But it's not funny.

After the Bomb, Dad Came Up with Ice [Review of *Cat's Cradle*]   Terry Southern*

The narrator of "Cat's Cradle" purports to be engaged in compiling a responsibly factual account of what certain interested Americans were doing at the precise moment the atomic bomb was dropped on Hiroshima. Through correspondence with the three children of the late Felix Hoenik-ker, Nobel Prize winner and so-called "father of the atomic bomb," he evolves a portrait of the man in relation to his family and the community.

We learn that at the eventful moment in question Dr. Hoenikker was, in fact, "playing with a bit of string," having made of it a "cat's cradle"—and that his youngest son, to whom he had never previously spoken, was fright-ened when Dad came up to him, jerking the string back and forth, saying: "See the cat! See the cradle!"

We further learn that on the night of his death, years later, he was again "playing around"—in the kitchen this time, with some water and bits of ice. With his characteristically pure-science approach ("Why doesn't someone do something about *mud*?" the Marine Corps general had asked him) he has isolated crystals of ice in such a way that water can now be caused to freeze at

*Reprinted by permission from the *New York Times Book Review*, 2 June 1963, 20. Copyright © 1963 by the New York Times Company.

a relatively high temperature. "Ice-9" it is called. The family dog laps at a bowl of water which has been touched with a piece of Ice-9 and is promptly frozen stiff. The Hoenikker children carefully divide this last gift to mankind from Dr. Hoenikker.

Following the doctor's death, the story devotes itself to what happens to the three children and to Ice-9. Frank, the eldest, has become the right-hand man of Monzano, the President of a Carribean island. The daughter and the younger brother visit the island to celebrate the forthcoming marriage of Frank to the regional sex-goddess; we soon learn that he has bought his position of power with a piece of Ice-9—which President Monzano then uses to commit suicide, thereupon naming Frank his successor.

Frank declines the responsibility and offers the post to the narrator. As the two of them try discreetly to dispose of the President's frozen corpse, the narrator realizes how extensive the spread and acquisition of Ice-9 has become. The younger brother, Newt, a midget, has exchanged his share for a few mad nights with a Russian circus performer, also a midget. The unmarriageable daughter, a six-foot bean-poler, has used hers to buy a handsome physicist. Finally events reach their inevitable conclusion—the freezing of all the earth's waters, and life itself.

"Cat's Cradle" is an irreverent and often highly entertaining fantasy concerning the playful irresponsibility of nuclear scientists. Like the best of contemporary satire, it is work of a far more engaging and meaningful order than the melodramatic tripe which most critics seem to consider "serious."

Kurt Vonnegut on Target C. D. B. Bryan*

Kurt Vonnegut, Jr., is 44 years old and lives with his wife and six children in West Barnstable on Cape Cod. During the 1955–56 term he taught at the Writers' Workshop of the University of Idaho, and now teaches English in a private school on the Cape.[1] He once worked for General Electric, his biography tells us, but Vonnegut "is a scientist only in as much as he is interested in the science of living reasonably and kindly." He was also volunteer fireman in Alplaus, New York—Badge 155. He has written six books and over a hundred short stories, articles, and reviews. Among his fans are Conrad Aiken, Nelson Algren, Marc Connelly, Jules Feiffer, Graham Greene, Granville Hicks, Terry Southern. Still Vonnegut has not received the acceptance due him from the reading public. Four of his books are available: *Mother Night*, published a few months ago; *God Bless You, Mr. Rosewater, or, Pearls Before Swine*, 1965; *Cat's Cradle*, 1963; and *Player Piano*, 1952 reissued this year. Out of print are his two other novels, *Canary*

*Reprinted by permission from the *New Republic*, 8 October 1966, 21–22, 24–26. © 1966 the New Republic, Inc. Review of *Player Piano, Mother Night, God Bless You, Mr. Rosewater*, and *Cat's Cradle*.

in a Cathouse and the science fiction paperback, *Sirens of Titan*. What prevents Vonnegut from being a major satirist on the order, say, of John Barth is that Vonnegut takes very little seriously, and although he excels at that more gentle barb Irony, he lacks the anger and impatience which great satire demands. Nevertheless, he is the most readable and amusing of the new humorists.

Mother Night is narrated by Howard W. Campbell, Jr., an American citizen who broadcasts anti-Semitic propaganda for the Nazis during the Second World War. Campbell had been recruited by a US counterintelligence agent in 1938, and Campbell's broadcasts carried coded information out of Germany. Campbell never knew what the information was. (Once the information was that Campbell's wife was captured and presumed dead.) Towards the end of the war Campbell is captured by Lt. Bernard B. O'Hare of the American Third Army, and taken to a nearby German concentration camp so that the American "traitor" would see the lime pits, the stacks of emaciated dead and the gallows capable of hanging six at a time. From the end of each rope hangs a camp guard. Campbell expects also to be hanged:

> I took an interest in the peace of the six guards at the ends of their ropes.
> They had died fast.
> My photograph was taken while I looked up at the gallows. Lieutenant O'Hare was standing behind me, lean as a young wolf, as full of hatred as a rattlesnake.
> The picture was on the cover of *Life*, and came close to winning a Pulitzer Prize.

So that the Americans will not have to admit that he had been a counterspy, Campbell is freed on nonexistent technicalities. He returns to New York, moves into an attic in Greenwich Village and tries to start a new life. One of his neighbors is an alcoholic with the alias George Kraft, actually Colonel Iona Potapov, resident Soviet agent in the United States since 1935. Another character is the Reverend Doctor Lionel Jason David Jones, DDS, DD, who believes the teeth of Jews, Negroes, Catholics and quite possibly Unitarians prove beyond question that these groups are degenerate, a theory he advances in his publication, *The White Christian Minuteman*. Jones is also founder of the Western Hemisphere of the Bible, a university which "held no classes, taught nothing, did all its business by mail. It awarded doctorates in the field of divinity, framed and under glass, for eighty dollars a throw." Campbell's wartime activities had made him a hero to Jones and his followers, one of whom is Jones's chauffeur, a 73-year-old Negro, Robert Sterling Wilson, the "Black Fuehrer of Harlem," who had been imprisoned as a Japanese agent during the war. The first time Campbell meets him, Wilson says:

> "The colored people are gonna rise up in righteous wrath, and they're gonna take over the world; White folks gonna finally lose!"
> "All right, Robert," Jones said patiently.

"The colored people gonna have hydrogen bombs all their own," he said. "They working on it right now. Pretty soon gonna be Japan's turn to drop one. The rest of the colored folks gonna give them the honor of dropping the first one."

"Where are they going to drop it?" I said.

"China, most likely," he said.

"On other colored people?" I said.

He looked at me pityingly. "Whoever told you a Chinaman was a colored man?" he said.

Because of the publicity given Campbell by Jones's White Christian Minute-men, Campbell again comes to the attention of ex-lieutenant O'Hare, now the Americanism Chairman of the Francis X Donovan Post of the American Legion, who writes, "I was very surprised and disappointed to hear you weren't dead yet." Both O'Hare and the reverend dentist Jones had been informed of Campbell's whereabouts by the Soviet spy, George Kraft. Kraft wants to pressure Campbell into going to Mexico where he would then be kidnapped and flown to Moscow to be put on display "as a prime example of the sort of Fascist war criminal this country shelters."

What lifts *Mother Night* out of the realm of easy entertainment is Campbell's awareness of his guilt. His desire for punishment compels him to give himself up; and another neighbor, a Jewish doctor who had survived Auschwitz, reluctantly arranges Campbell's capture by "Israeli agents"—a tailor, watchmaker and a pediatrician who, with Campbell's consent, turn him in the next morning to Israeli officials. While in Israel Campbell meets Eichmann who asks, "Do you think a literary agent is absolutely necessary?" Campbell replies, "For book clubs and movie sales in the United States of America, absolutely." Campbell knows that if the Israeli government will not punish him, he must. In the end he executes himself.

In his introduction to *Mother Night*, Vonnegut offers the following: "This is the only story of mine whose moral I know. I don't think it's a marvelous moral; I simply happen to know what it is: We are what we pretend to be, so we must be careful what we pretend to be." Howard W. Campbell, Jr., pretended to be a vicious, anti-Semitic Nazi. His guilt lay in his knowledge that he had been far more successful at it than he needed to be.

Cat's Cradle is the account of a writer who wanted to record what important Americans had done on the day the first atomic bomb was dropped on Hiroshima. The book, to be called *The Day The World Ended*, "was to be a Christian book. I was a Christian then," explains the author-narrator. "I am a Bokonist now." Bokonism is a religion invented by Vonnegut. The first sentence in the Books of Bokonon is: "All of the true things I am about to tell you are shameless lies." Another is, "Pay no attention to Caesar. Caesar has no idea what's *really* going on." Most of Bokonon's teachings are found in calypso "psalms" but the gist of it is captured in its "Genesis":

In the beginning, God created the earth, and he looked upon it in His cosmic loneliness.

And God said, "Let Us make living creatures out of mud, so the mud can see what We have done." And God created every living creature that now moveth, and one was man. Mud as man alone could speak. God leaned close as mud as man sat up, looked around, and spoke. Man blinked, "What is the *purpose* of all this?" he asked politely.

"Everything must have a purpose?" asked God.

"Certainly," said man.

"Then I leave it to you to think of one for all this," said God. And He went away.

Vonnegut's theology is also voiced in his science fiction novel, *Sirens of Titan,* in which religion is celebrated in the Church of God the Utterly Indifferent. Vonnegut is a proponent of the God is Dead theory and is convinced that all the evil in this world is perpetrated by man upon man. He is appalled by scientists and engineers. In *Cat's Cradle,* the author-narrator interviews Dr. Breed, head of the Research Laboratory of the General Forge and Foundry Company—the laboratory in which Dr. Felix Hoenikker developed the atomic bomb. Dr. Breed is dismayed because "every question I asked implied that the creators of the atomic bomb had been criminal accessories to a murder most foul."

Dr. Breed was astonished and then he got very sore. He drew back from me and grumbled, "I gather you don't like scientists very much."

"I wouldn't say that, sir."

"All your questions seem aimed at getting me to admit that scientists are heartless, conscienceless, narrow boobies, indifferent to the fate of the human race, or maybe not really members of the human race at all."

"That's putting it pretty strong."

Vonnegut's hero in *Player Piano,* the novel which preceded *Cat's Cradle* by nine years, is again a man against science. But this time he is an insider, Dr. Paul Proteus, manager of the Ilium Works, a fully automated factory which produces just about everything. The time is the Electronics Age, perhaps 100 years in the future. But whereas in *Cat's Cradle* the rebellion is against that segment of science which produces better methods by which man can annihilate himself, in *Player Piano* Vonnegut attacks the science of automation through which man produces machines which replace man's pride, his usefulness, his meaning.

Vonnegut's best-known book is *God Bless You, Mr. Rosewater, or, Pearls Before Swine.* Eliot Rosewater, whom Marc Connelly describes as "the most truthful picture of a saint since El Greco's Sebastian," is heir to the Rosewater fortune which provides an income of $3.5 million a year. The antagonists are everywhere, but the best articulated is Norman Mushari, a Lebanese hired by the Washington, D.C. law firm of McAllister, Robjent, Reed and McGee, designers of the Rosewater Foundation and Rosewater Corporation. The author points out that Mushari "would never have been hired if the other partners hadn't felt that McAllister's operations could do with just a touch more viciousness." Mushari's guiding principle in law had been stated by one of his former law school professors:

> In every big transaction there is a magic moment during which a man has surrendered a treasure, and during which the man who is due to receive it has not yet done so. An alert lawyer will make that moment his own, possessing the treasure for a little microsecond, taking a little of it, passing it on. If the man who is to receive the treasure is unused to wealth, has an inferiority complex and shapeless feelings of guilt, as most people do, the lawyer can often take as much as half the bundle, and still receive the recipient's blubbering thanks.

God Bless You, Mr. Rosewater hinges upon Mushari's knowledge that all he need do is prove Eliot Rosewater insane, and the fortune is transferred to the lesser branch of Rosewaters living in Rhode Island. Mushari has a good case. In every telephone booth in Rosewater, Indiana, where Eliot lives, there is a sticker: "Don't kill yourself. Call the Rosewater Foundation." The stickers had been placed there by Eliot. If a person called, he was usually given some money, often with the suggestion that the caller take two aspirin with a glass of wine. Eliot had been under psychoanalysis; but the night after the psychiatrist resigned from the case, Eliot Rosewater and his wife, Sylvia, attend a new staging of *Aida* at the Met, for which the Rosewater Foundation had provided the costumes. "Everything was fine until the last scene of the opera, during which the hero and the heroine were placed in an airtight chamber to suffocate. As the doomed pair filled their lungs, Eliot called out to them, 'You will last a lot longer if you don't try to sing.' Eliot stood, leaned far out of his box, told the singers, 'Maybe you don't know anything about oxygen, but I do. Believe me, you must not sing'." Eliot's wife led him away "like a toy balloon."

The only people with whom Eliot Rosewater feels complete identification are volunteer firemen. "We few, we happy few, we band of brothers," he tells them, "joined in the serious business of keeping our food, shelter, clothing, and loved ones from combining with oxygen." The one other group he admires are science fiction writers. On one of his alcoholic binges, Eliot crashes a science fiction writers convention held in a motel in Milford, Pennsylvania. He interrupts their meeting to say, "I love you sons of bitches. You're all I read any more. You're the only ones who'll talk about the *really* terrific changes going on, the only ones crazy enough to know that life is a space voyage, and not a short one either, but one that will last for billions of years. You're the only ones with guts enough to *really* care about the future, who *really* know what machines do to us, what cities do to us, what big, simple ideas do to us, what tremendous mistakes, accidents, and catastrophes do to us. You're the only ones zany enough to agonize over time and distances without limit, over mysteries that will never die, over the fact that we are right now determining whether the space voyage for the next billion years or so is going to be Heaven or Hell."

Vonnegut was born in Indianapolis in 1922. During the Second World War he was a battalion scout in the US Army and was captured by the Germans. He became part of a prisoner work group employed by a Dresden factory which made a vitamin-enriched malt syrup for pregnant women. Dresden contained no troop concentrations or war industries. It was an "open city"—not to be attacked—and yet on the night of February 13, 1945, British and American bombers attempted to obliterate Dresden through the meticulous and scientific creation of a fire storm. They were about 75 percent successful. In his introduction to *Mother Night,* Vonnegut writes:

> There were no particular targets for the bombs. The hope was that they would create a lot of kindling and drive the firemen underground.
>
> And then hundreds of thousands of tiny incendiaries were scattered over the kindling, like seeds on freshly turned loam. More bombs were dropped to keep the firemen in their holes, and all the little fires grew, joined one another, became one apocalyptic flame. Hey presto: fire storm. It was the largest massacre in European history, by the way. . . .
>
> We didn't get to see the fire storm. We were in a cool meat-locker under a slaughterhouse with our six guards and ranks and ranks of dressed cadavers of cattle, pigs, horses and sheep. We heard the bombs walking around up there. Now and then there would be a gentle shower of calcimine. If we had gone above to take a look we would have been turned into artifacts characteristic of fire storms: seeming pieces of charred firewood two or three feet long—ridiculously small human beings, or jumbo fried grasshoppers, if you will.
>
> The malt syrup factory was gone. Everything was gone but the cellars where 135,000 Hansels and Gretels had been baked like gingerbread men. So we were put to work as corpse miners, breaking into shelters, bringing bodies out. And I got to see many German types of all ages as death had found them, usually with valuables in their laps. Sometimes relatives would come to watch us dig. They were interesting, too.
>
> So much for Nazis and me.
>
> If I'd been born in Germany, I suppose I would have *been* a Nazi, bopping Jews and gypsies and Poles around, leaving boots sticking out of snowbanks, warming myself with my secretly virtuous insides. So it goes."

And so goes Vonnegut's most powerful writing. All the anger, the shame, the shock, the guilt, the compassion, the irony, the control to produce great satire are *there.* For sheer barbarity the fire storms of Dresden and Hamburg surpass the atomic bombing of Hiroshima and Nagasaki. Why, then, does Vonnegut settle for such lovely, literate amusing attacks upon such simple targets as scientists, engineers, computer technicians, religion, the American Legion, artists, company picnics?

Note

[1. Editor's note: Vonnegut taught at Iowa, not Idaho, and the year was 1965–66, not 1955–56. Other factual errors here include the following: *Mother Night* was first published in

1962, not 1966; *Canary in a Cat House* is a collection of stories, not a novel; Vonnegut's invented religion in *Cat's Cradle* is Bokononism, not Bokonism; *Cat's Cradle* was published eleven years after *Player Piano*, not nine; Vonnegut's introduction to *Mother Night* was added to the 1966 edition.]

[History as Fabulation:]
Slaughterhouse-Five   Robert Scholes*

Kurt Vonnegut speaks with the voice of the "silent generation," and his quiet words explain the quiescence of his contemporaries. This is especially true of his sixth novel, "Slaughterhouse-Five," in which he looks back—or tries to look back—at his wartime experience. In the first chapter he tells us how for over 20 years he has been trying to re-create a single event, the bombing of Dresden by American and British pilots. Vonnegut had an unusual perspective on that event. Safe, as a prisoner of war in a deep cellar under the stockyards, he emerged to find 135,000 German civilians smoldering around him. Dresden had been an open city. We closed it. We. We Anglo-Saxons, as the present ruler of France likes to term us.

For 20 years Vonnegut has been trying to do fictional justice to that historical event. Now he has finished, and he calls his book a failure. Speaking of the Biblical destruction of Sodom and Gomorrah (like Dresden, subjected to a fire-storm), Vonnegut writes:

"Those were vile people in both those cities, as is well known. The world is better off without them.

"And Lot's wife, of course, was told not to look back where all those people and their homes had been. But she looked back, and I love her for that, because it was so human.

"So she was turned to a pillar of salt. So it goes.

"People aren't supposed to look back. I'm certainly not going to do it any more.

"I've finished my war book now. The next one I write is going to be fun.

"This one is a failure, and had to be, since it was written by a pillar of salt."

The connection between that Biblical act of God and the destruction of Dresden is not accidental. Vonnegut's book is subtitled "The Children's Crusade." The point is a simple one, but it should serve to illustrate just where the gap opens between the "silent generation" and the present group of childish crusaders who are so vocal in preparing for a Holy Revolution. The cruelest deeds are done in the best causes. It is as simple as that. The best writers of our time have been telling us with all their imaginative power that our problems are not in our institutions but in ourselves.

*Reprinted by permission from the *New York Times Book Review*, 6 April 1969, 1, 23. Copyright © 1969 by the New York Times Company.

Violence is not only (as Stokely Carmichael put it) "as American as apple pie." It is as human as man. We like to hurt folks, and we especially like to hurt them in a good cause. We judge our pleasure by their pain. The thing that offends me equally in our recent Secretary of State and his most vicious critics is their unshakable certainty that they are right. A man *that* certain of his cause will readily send a bunch of kids off to rescue his Holy Land. His rectitude will justify any crimes. Revolution, war, crusades—these are all ways of justifying human cruelty.

It may seem as if I have drifted away from considering Vonnegut's book. But I haven't. This is what his book keeps whispering in its quietest voice: Be kind. Don't hurt. Death is coming for all of us anyway, and it is better to be Lot's wife looking back through salty eyes than the Deity that destroyed those cities of the plain in order to save them.

Far from being a "failure," "Slaughterhouse-Five" is an extraordinary success. It is a book we need to read, and to reread. It has the same virtues as Vonnegut's best previous work. It is funny, compassionate, and wise. The humor in Vonnegut's fiction is what enables us to contemplate the horror that he finds in contemporary existence. It does not disguise the awful things perceived; it merely strengthens and comforts us to the point where such perception is bearable. Comedy can look into depths which tragedy dares not acknowledge. The comic is the only mode which can allow itself to contemplate absurdity. That is why so many of our best writers are, like Vonnegut, what Hugh Kenner would call "Stoic Comedians."

Vonnegut's comic prose reduces large areas of experience to the dimensions of a laboratory slide. Consider how much of human nature and the nature of war he has managed to encompass in this brief paragraph:

"Billy . . . saw in his memory . . . poor old Edgar Derby in front of a firing squad in the ruins of Dresden. There were only four men in that squad. Billy had heard that one man in each squad was customarily given a rifle loaded with blank cartridge. Billy didn't think there would be a blank cartridge issued in a squad that small, in a war that old." The simple-minded thought processes of Billy Pilgrim are reflected in those ultra-simple sentences. But the wisdom and verbal skill of the author shaped the final, telling phrases: "in a squad that small, in a war that old."

That deceptively simple prose is equally effective when focused on peacetime American life. In speaking of Billy's mother (who acquired an "extremely gruesome crucifix" in a Santa Fe gift shop) Vonnegut says, "Like so many Americans, she was trying to construct a life that made sense from things she found in gift shops." The pathos of human beings enmeshed in the relentless triviality of contemporary American culture has never been more adequately expressed.

Serious critics have shown some reluctance to acknowledge that Vonnegut is among the best writers of his generation. He is, I suspect, both too funny and too intelligent for many, who confuse muddled earnestness with profundity. Vonnegut is not confused. He sees all too clearly. That also is the problem of the central character of "Slaughterhouse-Five," Billy Pilgrim, an optometrist from Ilium, N.Y. Billy sees into the fourth dimension and travels, or says he does, to the planet Tralfamadore, in a distant galaxy. Only Billy's time-warped perspective could do justice to the cosmic absurdity of his life, which is Vonnegut's life and our lives. Billy's wartime capture and imprisonment, his ordinary middle-class life in America, and his visionary space-time traveling are reference points by which we can begin to recognize where we are.

The truth of Vonnegut's vision requires its fiction. That is what justifies his activity as a novelist and all imaginative writing, ancient and modern. Art, as Picasso has said, is a lie that makes us realize the truth. Kurt Vonnegut, Jr. is a true artist.

Nothing Sacred [Review of *Breakfast of Champions*]

Peter S. Prescott*

Here's further evidence that as a thinker and literary stylist Kurt Vonnegut is fully the equal of Kahlil Gibran, Rod McKuen, even Richard Bach. These writers, gurus and soothsayers apparently fill a need for some of us, adolescents of all ages who clutch at any sentimental positivism: Gibran's perfumed religiosity; McKuen's mawkish romanticism; Bach's can-do optimism dipped in mystical shellac; and Vonnegut's smug pessimism with its coy implication that the reader is one of the author's initiates, one of the happy few. The comfortable banalities advanced by these writers in place of ideas are totally incompatible, but that doesn't bother the groupies. *Anything* will do for them—as long as it's self-assured, as long as it's presented in a lobotomized English that these writers feel is appropriate for their audience.

Listen (as Vonnegut likes to say). Here is the plot of "Breakfast of Champions" reduced so small you could stuff it in an earthworm's ear. Kilgore Trout, the prolifically unsuccessful science-fiction writer, is beaten and robbed as he sets off for an arts festival in Midland City, where, when he arrives, his knuckle will be bitten off by Dwayne Hoover, who runs a Pontiac agency and is going insane. Dwayne blows his mind when he reads one of Kilgore's novels, which seems to Dwayne to tell him that only he has free will in a world populated by machines. He runs amok, is carted off. Vonnegut himself comes onstage to bleed for a while and fend off suicide, and then (Oh, massa! Let my people go!) he frees his characters. What that means I'm not sure, but Vonnegut, who has provided childlike drawings to match his Dick-and-Jane prose, concludes with a self-portrait that, like any peasant's Madonna, shows a tear leaking from his eye.

Kiddy: Enough of plot; it serves only as an armature for Vonnegut's

*From *Newsweek*, 14 May 1973, 114, 118. All rights reserved. Reprinted by permission.

specialty: gratuitous digressions. Here we find Vonnegut in his customary pose of satirizing attitudes that only Archie Bunker could love. Vonnegut is against racism and pollution and poverty, oh my. "A Nigger was a human being who was black." Note the past tense: Vonnegut knows all is lost. Taking care to please his audience, he snipes at teachers: they tell kids that human beings came to America in 1492, and they flunk kids who "failed to speak like English aristocrats before the First World War." By any standard, this is sucking up to kiddy grievances. It fits well with the eighth-grade obscenities—the anal imagery and the fascination with measuring penises—and the village blasphemy: for whores to surrender to pimps, he says, is like surrendering to Jesus; they can live "unselfishly and trustingly."

Well. There is just something a little *arrested* about all this. The simple-minded summations: Communists "had a theory that what was left of the planet should be shared more or less equally," but Americans were opposed to Communism. The cretinous philosophizing: "There was nothing sacred about myself or any human being," except, of course, our awareness, "an unwavering band of light." Otherwise, "human beings are robots, are machines." In a particularly charmless phrase, Vonnegut calls a girl "a machine made of meat." *That* kind of wisdom. People shoot each other because life imitates fiction, he says, and so Vonnegut, who thinks literature should be therapy, chooses to write aimlessly: "I would bring chaos to order."

Manure, of course. Pretentious, hypocritical manure. From time to time, it's nice to have a book you can hate—it clears the pipes—and I hate this book for its preciousness, its condescension to its characters, its self-indulgence and its facile fatalism: all the lonely people, their fates sealed in epoxy. Mostly, I hate it for its reductiveness, its labored denial of man's complexity and resilience. Life cannot, as Vonnegut insists, be summed up with "And so on" and "ETC."—or at least not without more wit and insight than Vonnegut can muster. Samuel Beckett is not noticeably more optimistic about the human condition than is Vonnegut, but he does not condescend to Vladimir and Estragon. He does not think they are machines. "We are what we pretend to be," Vonnegut wrote in "Mother Night," and if we pretend that we are only machines we cannot pretend to be interesting enough for a novel.

All's Well in Skyscraper National Park [Review of *Slapstick*]   John Updike*

Kurt Vonnegut abjures the appellation "Junior" in signing his new novel, "Slapstick, or Lonesome No More!" (Delacorte), and, indeed, the author, after his furious performance in the preceding work, "Breakfast of

*From *Hugging the Shore* by John Updike. Copyright © 1983 by John Updike. Reprinted by permission of Alfred A. Knopf, Inc. Originally appeared in the *New Yorker*.

Champions," does seem relatively at peace with himself, his times, and the fact of his writing a novel at all. He introduces this one with the customary noises of exasperation over his "disagreeable profession" ("He asked me politely how my work was going. . . . I said that I was sick of it, but that I had always been sick of it"), but, once launched, the tale floats along without interruption, and is something of an idyll. A hundred-year-old man, Dr. Wilbur Daffodil-11 Swain, who has been President of the United States ("the final President, the tallest President, and the only one ever to have been divorced while occupying the White House"), lives with his granddaughter, Melody Oriole-2 von Peterswald, and her lover, Isadore Raspberry-19 Cohen, in the otherwise empty Empire State Building, on the almost deserted island of Manhattan, which has been decimated by plague and is variously known as "The Island of Death" and "Skyscraper National Park." The awkward middle names of the inhabitants, we might as well explain now, have been assigned them in the last and only reform of the Swain Presidency, a measure to combat "American loneliness" (the root of all our evil: "all the damaging excesses of Americans in the past were motivated by loneliness rather than a fondness for sin") through the division of the population into huge (ten thousand siblings, one hundred and ninety thousand cousins) artificial families by means of computer-bestowed middle names, "the name of a flower or fruit or nut or vegetable or legume, or a bird or a reptile or a fish, or a mollusk, or a gem or a mineral or a chemical element." This scheme, the basis of President Swain's successful campaign (slogan: "Lonesome No More!") for the highest office in the land, was concocted years before, when Wilbur and his twin sister, Eliza, like himself a monstrous "neanderthaloid" two metres high, enjoyed in a secluded Vermont mansion an emotional and intellectual symbiosis that amounted to sheer genius, though separately the two were dullards named Bobby and Betty Brown.

Lost already? "Slapstick," whose main present action consists of the narrator's hundred-and-first birthday party, which kills him, is a reminiscence about the future, a future braided of a half-dozen or so scientific and sociological fancies. The lonesome-no-more-thanks-to-new-middle-names notion is about the silliest of them, the least charming and provocative, however dear to the author's heart. The others, roughly in descending order of charm and provocation, are:

1. That gravity on earth has become variable, like the weather. "Well—the gravity . . . is light again today," Wilbur writes in his memoir. On days of light gravity, all males have erections, and lovers build a pyramid of large rubble at the intersection of Broadway and Forty-second Street. When the gravity is heavy, men crawl about on all fours, and the insides of horses fall out. Heavy gravity first struck when Wilbur Swain was fifty, and had just learned that his sister had died in an avalanche on Mars:

> An extraordinary feeling came over me, which I first thought to be psychological in origin, the first rush of grief. I seemed to have taken root

on the porch. I could not pick up my feet. My features, moreover, were being dragged downward like melting wax.

The truth was that the force of gravity had increased tremendously.

There was a great crash in the church. The steeple had dropped its bell.

Then I went right through the porch, and was slammed to the earth beneath it. . . .

In other parts of the world, of course, elevator cables were snapping, airplanes were crashing, ships were sinking, motor vehicles were breaking their axles, bridges were collapsing, and on and on.

It was terrible.

In this superbly simple fancy (and why not? what do we know about gravity, except that it is always there, and has not yet broken its own "law"?) Vonnegut gives enormous body to his own moodiness, and springs a giddy sense of menace upon the city he inhabits.

2. That the Chinese, on the other side of the world from the lonely, destructive Americans, have succeeded in miniaturizing themselves, to the size first of dwarfs, then of dolls and elves, and finally of germs; the plague, called the Green Death, it turns out "was caused by microscopic Chinese, who were peace-loving and meant no one any harm. They were nonetheless invariably fatal to normal-sized human beings when inhaled or ingested." This last *reductio* is a bit much, but a radical divergence of the Chinese from our own brand of *Homo sapiens* sounds right; we laugh in recognition when the Chinese ambassador, sixty centimetres tall, severs diplomatic relations "simply because there was no longer anything going on in the United States which was of any interest to the Chinese at all." China is another planet, Vonnegut has discovered.

3. That a brother and sister might "give birth to a single genius, which died as quickly as we were parted, which was reborn the moment we got together again." In childhood, Wilbur, who does the reading and writing, and Eliza, who makes the intuitive leaps and juxtapositions, concoct theories and manuscripts that a half century later are of interest even to the Chinese. In adulthood, after a long separation, the siblings reunite in a kind of psychosexual explosion that produces, besides a houseful of wreckage, a manual on child-rearing which becomes the third most popular book of all time.

Vonnegut in his prologue claims this novel to be "the closest I will ever come to writing an autobiography" and movingly writes of the Indianapolis Vonneguts and of his sister Alice—her importance to him as "an audience of one," her death at the age of forty-one of cancer, her final days in the hospital, her hunched posture, her description of her own death as "slapstick." In "Slapstick" these memories become:

She was so bent over that her face was on level with Mushari's—and Mushari was about the size of Napoleon Bonaparte. She was chain smoking. She was coughing her head off. . . .

"Oh, Wilbur, Wilbur, Wilbur—" said my mother as we watched, "is that really your sister?"

I made a bitter joke—without smiling, "Either your only daughter, Mother, or the sort of anteater known as an *aardvark*," I said.

The image shocks us, offends us, twists us inside, and successfully asks to be recognized as sombre and tender. It is a moment peculiarly Vonnegutian, tapping the undercurrents of pure melancholy which nurture the aggressively casual surface growths of his style. These moments arise unexpectedly, and seem to take the author unawares as well—the pathetic valedictory conversation, for instance, between Salo and Rumfoord near the end of "The Sirens of Titan" (1959), or the odd interlude, amid the "impolite" "junk" of "Breakfast of Champions" (1973), wherein the homeless, jobless black ex-convict Wayne Hoobler, hanging out in a used-car lot, in his extreme of lonesomeness begins to talk to the highway traffic:

> He established a sort of relationship with the traffic on the Interstate, too, appreciating its changing moods. "Everybody goin' home," he said during the rush hour jam. "Everybody home now," he said later on, when the traffic thinned out. Now the sun was going down.
> "Sun goin' down," said Wayne Hoobler.

It will vary, where Vonnegut's abashed and constant sorrow breaks through to touch the reader; here, though, in this fantasy, as it pays tribute not to the extended family he hopes for but to the nuclear family he has known, he places his rather mistrustful art in frank proximity to the incubator of his passion for—to quote his prologue—"common decency."

4. That the United States, as the world's energy sources dried up, has pleasantly settled back into a rural society, powered by slaves and horses as before; that the old Inca capital of Machu Picchu, in Peru, has become "a haven for rich people and their parasites, people fleeing social reforms and economic declines"; and that when the White House, containing President Wilbur Swain, who is stoned on tribenzo-Deportamil, quite ceases to rule, the nation falls into a feudal anarchy dominated by such guerrilla chieftains as the King of Michigan and the Duke of Oklahoma.

5. That a religion has arisen called the Church of Jesus Christ the Kidnapped, which holds that Jesus has come again but has been kidnapped by the Forces of Evil and is being held captive somewhere. The members of this cult, the most popular ever in America, distinguish themselves by an incessant jerking of the head, as if to discover the Kidnapped Jesus peering out "from behind a potted palm tree or an easy chair."

6. That a scientist named Dr. Felix Bauxite-13 von Peterswald has discovered a way to talk to the dead, who irritably and disconsolately inhabit a dreary hereafter known as the Turkey Farm. The late Eliza reports to her living brother, "We are being bored stiff."

This saucy spaghetti of ideas, strange to report, seems in the consumption as clear as consommé, and goes down like ice cream. "Slapstick" has more science fiction in it than any other novel by Vonnegut since "The Sirens of Titan" and lays to rest, in an atmosphere of comic exhaustion and serene self-parody, the obsessive Prospero figure who first came to life there. The Prospero in "Sirens" is Winston Niles Rumfoord, a Rhode Island aristocrat who acquires superhuman powers by steering his spaceship straight into a "chrono-synclastic infundibulum" and who thenceforth arranges an interplanetary war so that its guilt-engendering slaughters may form the basis for a new religion, the worship of God the Utterly Indifferent. With a demonic elaborateness that argues a certain demon of overplotting in the author, Rumfoord furthermore manipulates Malachi Constant (one of Vonnegut's long line of boob heroes) and his little family through a ramshackle series of space flights and changes of identity toward an ultimate goal that turns out to be the delivery, in Constant's son's pocket, of a replacement part for a spaceship from the planet Tralfamadore. The unseen Tralfamadorians are manipulating not only Rumfoord but much of the planet Earth; Stonehenge, the Great Wall of China, and other terrestrial wonders of human enterprise are in truth messages ("Replacement part being rushed with all possible speed"; "Be patient. We haven't forgotten about you") in the Tralfamadorian language to the messenger Salo, who in the course of delivering from "One Rim of the Universe to the Other" a message consisting of a single dot ("Greetings" in Tralfamadorian) has become stranded on Saturn's biggest moon, Titan, for hundreds of thousands of years. Well, it's some book, full of laughs yet operatically flaunting Vonnegut's concern with the fundamental issues of pain, purpose, and Providence. Though raised in a family of atheists, Vonnegut quarrels with God like a parochial-school dropout. In "Mother Night" (1961), Prospero has shrunk to the dimensions of a Second World War master-spy; Colonel Frank Wirtanen, the Blue Fairy Godmother, controls the hero's life by appearing to him only three times, and his final act of magical intervention is rejected. In "Cat's Cradle" (1963), the idea of a religion devoted to an indifferent God is codified as Bokononism, and Prospero retreats to still lower visibility; Bokonon, the black founder of the cult, emerges from the underbrush of the Caribbean island of San Lorenzo only at the novel's end, to direct the hero (called John, and rather less of a boob) to commit suicide, while thumbing his nose skyward, at You Know Who. But Bokonon, who like Rumfoord has the gifts of foresight and cynicism, oversees the events on this island of survivors—a most "Tempest"-like setting. There is even a Miranda, called Mona.

   In "God Bless You, Mr. Rosewater" (1965), Prospero and the boob have merged; the very prosperous Eliot Rosewater, after exercising the powers of the rich rather inchoately in the isolation of Rosewater County, Indiana, stands to full stature when threatened by a usurper, whom he smites down with a surprising disposition, both regal and cunning, of his fortune. In "Slaughterhouse-Five" (1969), Billy Pilgrim, like Winston Rumfoord, communicates with the Tralfamadorians and sees future and past as parts of a single panorama—"All moments, past, present, and future, always have existed, always will exist." But his prescience is impotent to change the sad course of Earthly events; planes crash, bombs fall, though he knows they will. His access to Tralfamadore merely gives him the wonderful accessory bubble of the second life he lives there, more Ferdinand than Prospero, mated with the gorgeous Montana Wildhack in a transparent dome in a Tralfamadorian zoo. "Breakfast of Champions" reveals the author himself as Prospero, "on a par with the Creator of the Universe," sitting in the cocktail lounge of a Holiday Inn wearing mirroring sunglasses, surrounded by characters of his own creation, whom he frees in the end: "I am going to set at liberty all the literary characters who have served me so loyally during my writing career." (Nevertheless, "Slapstick" revives the obnoxious lawyer Norman Mushari from "God Bless You, Mr. Rosewater"; Vonnegut's ongoing puppet show is irrepressibly self-cherishing.)

> Now my charms are all o'erthrown,
> And what strength I have's mine own,
> Which is most faint . . .

"Slapstick" gives us the Prospero of Shakespeare's epilogue, his powers surrendered, his island Manhattan, his Miranda his granddaughter Melody. Vonnegut dreamed the book, he tells us, while flying to a funeral. "It is about desolated cities and spiritual cannibalism and incest and loneliness and lovelessness and death, and so on. It depicts myself and my beautiful sister as monsters, and so on." It is about what happens after the end of the world. The end of the world is not an idea to Vonnegut, it is a reality he experienced, in Dresden, as a prisoner of war, during the holocaustal air raid of February 13, 1945. He has described this repeatedly, most directly in the introduction to "Mother Night" added in 1966:

> We didn't get to see the fire storm. We were in a cool meat-locker under a slaughterhouse with our six guards and ranks and ranks of dressed cadavers of cattle, pigs, horses, and sheep. We heard the bombs walking around up there. Now and then there would be a gentle shower of calcimine. If we had gone above to take a look, we would have been turned into artifacts characteristic of fire storms: seeming pieces of charred firewood two or three feet long—ridiculously small human beings, or jumbo fried grasshoppers, if you will.

Vonnegut's come-as-you-are prose always dons a terrible beauty when he pictures vast destruction.

> Eliot, rising from his seat in the bus, beheld the fire storm of Indianapolis. He was awed by the majesty of the column of fire, which was at least eight miles in diameter and fifty miles high. The boundaries of the column seemed absolutely sharp and unwavering, as though made of glass.

> Within the boundaries, helixes of dull red embers turned in stately harmony about an inner core of white. The white seemed holy.

The end of the world can come by fire, as in the quotation above, from "God Bless You, Mr. Rosewater," or by ice, as in "Cat's Cradle":

> There was a sound like that of the gentle closing of a portal as big as the sky, the great door of heaven being closed softly. It was a grand AH-WHOOM.
> I opened my eyes—and all the sea was *ice-nine*.
> The moist green earth was a blue-white pearl.

The New York of "Slapstick" has been destroyed several times over. Gravity has pulled down its elevators and its bridges, plague has devoured its population. An ailanthus forest has grown up, and a rooster crowing in Turtle Bay can be heard on West Thirty-fourth Street. Amid collapse, the fabulous is reborn. Wilbur Swain's nearest neighbor, Vera Chipmunk-5 Zappa, arrives at his hundred-and-first birthday party encrusted with diamonds, in a sedan chair. "She had a collection of precious stones which would have been worth millions of dollars in olden times. People gave her all the jewels they found, just as they gave me all the candlesticks." Swain has become the King of Candlesticks, the possessor of a thousand. For a birthday present Vera Zappa gives him a thousand candles she and her slaves have made from a Colonial mold. They set them about on the floor of the Empire State Building lobby and light them. Swain's last written words are "Standing among all those tiny, wavering lights, I felt as though I were God, up to my knees in the Milky Way." He dies, happy, but the narrative carries on, relating how Melody arrived in New York, fleeing the seraglio of the King of Michigan, helped along the way by her fellow-Orioles.

> One would give her a raincoat. . . .
> Another would give her a needle and thread, and a gold thimble, too.
> Another would row her across the Harlem River to the Island of Death, at the risk of his own life.

The novel ends "*Das Ende*," reminding us of German fairy tales and of Vonnegut's pride in his German ancestry; in "Mother Night" he even dared to be a poet in the German language. In "Slapstick" he transmutes science fiction into something like medieval myth, and suggests the halo of process, of metamorphosis and recycling, that to an extent redeems the destructiveness in human history to which he is so sensitive. The end of the world is just a Dark Age. Through a succession of diminishingly potent Prosperos, the malevolent complexities of "The Sirens of Titan" have yielded to a more amiable confusion.

"Slapstick" enjoys a first printing of a cool one hundred thousand copies, and Vonnegut's popularity, which has grown even as his literary manner becomes more truculent and whimsical, has attracted comment from many reviewers, who usually find it discreditable to author and audience alike. But there need be no scandal in Vonnegut's wide appeal, based, as I believe it is, on the generosity of his imagination and the honesty of his pain. Who of his writing contemporaries strikes us as an imaginer, as distinguished from a reporter or a self-dramatizer? There is a fine disdain in Vonnegut of the merely personal. His prologue to "Slapstick" says, "I find it natural to discuss life without ever mentioning love," and his fiction, stoic in an epicurean time, does have a pre-sexual, pre-social freshness; he worries about the sort of things—the future, injustice, science, destiny—that twelve-year-old boys worry about, and if most boys move on, it is not necessarily into more significant worries. Vonnegut began as a published writer with the so-called slick magazines—the credits for the stories in "Welcome to the Monkey House" feature *Collier's, The Saturday Evening Post,* and the *Ladies' Home Journal.* Rereading such exercises as "D.P.," "Deer in the Works," and "The Kid Nobody Could Handle" is a lesson in what slickness, fifties vintage, was: it was a verbal mechanism that raised the spectre of pain and then too easily delivered us from it. Yet the pain in Vonnegut was always real. Through the transpositions of science fiction, he found a way, instead of turning pain aside, to vaporize it, to scatter it on the plane of the cosmic and the comic. His terse flat sentences, jumpy chapters, interleaved placards, collages of stray texts and messages, and nervous grim refrains like "So it goes" and (in "Slapstick") "Hi ho" are a new way of stacking pain, as his fictional *ice-nine* is a new way of stacking the molecules of water. Such an invention looks easy only in retrospect.

Vonnegut the Diviner and Other Auguries [Review of *Jailbird*]   Loree Rackstraw*

It is one of those "accidents" Vonnegut is so fond of telling us about that the release of his new novel, *Jailbird,* and the professional theatre opening of *God Bless You, Mr. Rosewater* in Manhattan occurred nearly simultaneously this fall. Both, in their kooky and kind ways, are stories about our economy, probably very much like the science fiction novel Kilgore Trout is writing from prison at the end of *Jailbird.*

The *Rosewater* production is an adaptation of the 1965 novel, in which Eliot Rosewater boozily runs a volunteer fire department and administers the estate of his wealthy family by giving away money to the "useless people" of Rosewater County in Indiana. Kilgore Trout is in that novel, too, as Eliot's favorite science fiction writer, an avowed socialist who is a free-enterpriser "through no choice of [his] own." At the novel's end, Eliot is seemingly

*Reprinted by permission from the *North American Review* 264 (Winter 1979): 75–76). © 1979 by the University of Northern Iowa.

inspired by Trout—and by the question of a bird ("Poo-tee-weet?") in the garden of a mental institution—to prove his sanity and save the Rosewater millions from the selfish grasp of the Rhode Island wing of the family. His solution: declare himself the father of all the useless children in Rosewater County so they will inherit his fortune.

There are birds in a garden in *Jailbird*, too. Only this time, the garden is the penthouse of the Chrysler Building in New York, the paradise showroom of the American Harp Company, owned by the RAMJAC Corporation, "a place of unearthly beauty and peace within the building's stainless-steel crown." Inhabiting the seventy feet of space beneath the crown are "Myriads of bright yellow little birds . . . perched on the girders, or flitting through the prisms of light admitted by the bizarre windows, by the great triangles of glass that pierced the crown." Beneath the crown is a vast floor carpeted in grassy green and furnished with a fountain, garden benches, statues, "and here and there a harp." The birds are prothonotary warblers who have multiplied from the two set free in 1931 to preside over this paradise prison. It is significant that a meaning of prothonotary is "a priest of the chief college of the papal curia who keeps records of consistories and canonizations." It is also significant that this setting is a haven for Mary Kathleen O'Looney, a Manhattan shopping bag lady who is the chief female protagonist in the novel.

Because—you guessed it—this setting is the Paradise of the divine capitalistic comedy Vonnegut creates in *Jailbird*. His Dante is Walter Starbuck, whose story is the autobiography of a son of immigrants adopted by their millionaire employer—a pathological stutterer, made so after witnessing the massacre of protesting iron workers at his father's iron works in 1894. The accidental shaping of Walter's life by this event is one in a series that sends him to Harvard, where he becomes a temporary idealistic Communist and runs a radical newspaper; to Washington, where he works for the government and inadvertently betrays his best friend in a pre-McCarthy investigation, and eventually to prison, where he goes as an accidental victim of Watergate. And we remember that Dante, too, held a government position in Florence and was convicted of an improbable charge of graft. Like Walter, his best friend was arrested and banished by the government Dante served.

Walter's Beatrice is Mary Kathleen, his first lover, a volunteer writer for his radical paper when he was a student at Harvard. He has forgotten her until he accidentally meets her as the shopping bag lady at the intersection of Forty-Second Street and Fifth Avenue in Manhattan on the day he is released from prison at age 64. Unbeknownst to Walter, she is disguised so no one will know she is the owner of the RAMJAC Corporation. The melodrama of this meeting swells with the simultaneous encounter he has with the friend he betrayed, Leland Clewes. This bizarre trio takes on an additional zany edge from our knowledge that Leland has married another former sweetheart of Walter, Sarah Wyatt, whose father owned the clock company in whose employ Mary's mother was accidentally poisoned by the radium used to paint the faces of the clocks.

And there's more, smooth as syrup in pure Vonnegut vintage, crafted to near perfection: Walter's Virgil, the voice of reason, is not Virgil Greathouse, the corrupt Secretary of State who enters prison the day of Walter's release. Rather, it is probably Bob Fender, the ex-veterinarian mistakenly sentenced to life for treason, who is chief clerk—another prothonotary warbler—and listens to old Edith Piaf records in the prison where Walter is incarcerated as the novel begins. Fender, under the pseudonym of Kilgore Trout, writes the science fiction stories that elucidate Walter's autobiography—that is, the novel.

The Inferno of this not-so-divine comedy is the empty catacombs beneath Grand Central Station, the graveyard garage for defunct steam locomotives, the elegant machines that made free enterprise work. And it's also another secret haven for Mary Kathleen, because she fears for her life. Her fear is legitimate, since she is really the widow of Jack Graham, a union leader who left her a fortune. This is the fortune she is using to fulfill the socialist dream inspired by Kenneth Whistler, the union organizer who spoke in Cambridge when she and Walter were young idealists. It is a dream she never forgot and is determined to fulfill as owner of the RAMJAC Corporation. Her mission? To buy up the American economy and give it back to the people.

And what is the Gospel that makes it all work? "The Sermon on the Mount, sir." Every kind person Mary finds is immediately made a vice president of a firm owned by RAMJAC. The titular head of the Corporation is Arpad Leen, whose service to Mary Kathleen is a "religious experience," and who buys up whatever she tells him by phone.

And does it *really* work? No, of course not. It turns out to be another Great Ponzi Scheme. Walter learns about Ponzi schemes from Dr. Carlo di Sanza, a Doctorate in Law from the University of Naples who is a naturalized American citizen serving his second term at Walter's prison for using the mails to defraud. Dr. di Sanza is ferociously patriotic and has made many people happy and rich. He offers fools enormous rates of interest for the use of their money, uses it to buy luxuries for himself, returns part of the money as the high interest he promised, gets more money from grateful investors to write more interest checks—"and on and on."

Walter is moved to suppose "that every successful government is of necessity a Ponzi scheme." And indeed, two years following Mary's accidental death (after she is hit by a taxi probably owned by RAMJAC) the great corporation crumbles. Her beneficiary, the American people via the government, takes over RAMJAC and hires twenty thousand bureaucrats, half of them lawyers, to oversee the job of selling off the corporation to the highest bidders. The highest bidders are foreign investment firms. "There are plenty of dollars, it turns out, to buy all the goodies the federal government has to sell . . . There was a photograph on an inside page of the *Daily News* yesterday of a dock in Brooklyn. There was about an acre of bales that looked like cotton on the dock. These were actually bales of American currency from Saudi Arabia, cash on the barrelhead, so to speak, for the McDonald's Hamburgers Division of RAMJAC. The headline said this: 'HOME AT LAST!' " And these dollars will serve Americans at home with new roads, military equipment, and partial payment of the national debt.

And Walter, after successfully running his Down Home Records division of RAMJAC for the two years following Mary Kathleen's death, will be sent to prison again for committing a class E felony: unlawfully concealing Mary's will.

The Purgatorio of Vonnegut's comedy is the limbo of life, the literal and figurative prison where the air is "unacceptable" and where all the folks of the novel live or have lived their mythical or actual lives. And there are a lot of folks: there are no fewer than 215 entries in the Index of *Jailbird*, from "Adam" to "Zola, Emil." They all help contribute to the development of the existential theme of absurdity—of the indifference of nature and of humans to fellow humans. A limbo where "The economy is a thoughtless weather system—and nothing more. Some joke on the people, to give them such a thing." It is a theme Vonnegut has played before, but which he plays now with a new variation: the role of women.

This is the first of his novels with so strong a female protagonist. She is a parody of Beatrice to be sure, the bizarre Mary Kathleen who wears immense purple and black basketball shoes containing love letters, stock certificates, and her will, among other valuables. One of her most treasured secrets is the row of toilets in her private catacomb beneath Grand Central: "You know there are millions of poor souls out on the street," she tells Walter, "looking for a toilet somebody will let them use?" Nonetheless, she represents faith, hope and love. She never forgot the impassioned speech of Kenneth Whistler back in Walter's Harvard days when she was only 18: ". . . Whistler promised us that the time was at hand for workers to take over their factories and to run them for the benefit of mankind. Profits that now went to drones and corrupt politicians would go to those who worked, and to the old and the sick and the orphaned . . ." Mary had told Walter, back in their youth, that he would be just like Whistler, but Walter, now in his sixties, confesses that the most distressing thing about his autobiography "is its unbroken chain of proofs that I was never a serious man. I have been in a lot of trouble over the years, but that was all accidental. Never have I risked my life, or even my comfort, in the service of mankind. Shame on me."

Mary, however, *was* serious. After Walter left Harvard and forgot her, she hitchhiked to Kentucky to help Whistler in the coal mines. There she met her husband, Jack Graham, whose legacy she used to begin her corporation. She is growing old and tired, but her chance meeting with Walter after all those years has renewed her. "I'll rescue you, Walter . . . Then we'll rescue the world together." And rescue him she does, at least temporarily, from another accidental arrest in the American Harp paradise where she has taken him. Then she makes new vice presidents of RAMJAC out of him and all the people who had been kind to him on the day he left prison.

There are those who see Dante's *Comedy* as a reflection of 14th century Florentine and European life fraught with the evils of Church, State, and individuals in need of the redeeming powers of reason and divine love. If Vonnegut's *Jailbird* is a parodied allegory of that allegory, it, too, is a reflection of 20th century life in Washington, New York, and a United States where old drunks are burned alive by teenagers on Skid Row, where the child of an impoverished mother is ravaged by the watch dog left to protect it, where Sacco and Vanzetti are wrongfully executed and forgotten, and where corrupt and uncaring educational, religious, and political institutions have failed in their responsibilities to the people.

If "Kilgore Trout" is Virgil, his science fiction warns us about the planet Vicuna where people ran out of time after having "found ways to extract time from topsoil and the oceans and the atmosphere—to heat their homes and power their speedboats and fertilize their crops . . . and a million years of future were put to the torch in honor of the birthday of the queen." He questions quasi-religious interpretations of life in his "sacrilegious story," "Asleep at the Switch," in which people trying to get into heaven must submit to a full review of how they mis-handled the business opportunities God offered them on earth. The hero is the ghost of Albert Einstein, chastised by a heavenly public accountant because he failed to invest money in uranium before telling the world that $E = Mc^2$. The point the public accountant is trying to make is that Einstein's life had been fair, that he shouldn't blame God because he had been "asleep at the switch." Such a voice of "reason" is perhaps the only one that makes sense in the absurdity of 20th century America, where time and money and the power of fossil fuels are the values which seem to blind humans to faith, hope, and love.

A person not so blinded in *Jailbird* is Mary Kathleen. Walter, as Dante, says that he believes women are "more spiritual, more sacred than men." All four women he has loved, he says, "seemed more virtuous, braver about life, and closer to the secrets of the universe than I could ever be." Two of those women were his sweethearts, Mary and Sarah; a third was Ruth, his wife. The Biblical versions of all three, we remember, have their place of honor at the highest circle of heaven in the 32nd Canto of Dante's "Paradiso." And the fourth woman Walter loved was Anna Kairys Stankiewicz, his mother. In Dante's poem, Anna, the mother of the Virgin Mary, sits at the feet of the Lord.

As Dante was inspired by his love for Beatrice in his youth, and redeemed by her in his poem, so Walter receives atonement from Mary, his first lover, not in Paradise but in the underground cavern of Grand Central where she is dying: "You couldn't help it that you were born without a heart," she tells him. "At least you tried to believe what the people with hearts believed—so you were a good man just the same."

Walter gives Mary a decent burial under her maiden name, so it will not be known that Mrs. Jack Graham, the owner of RAMJAC, has died. And for two years he serves, with considerable comfort, as vice president of the Down Home Records division of RAMJAC that Mary has given him. Down Home Records owns Gulf & Wester, *The New York Times,* Universal Pictures, Ringling Bros. and Barnum & Bailey, Dell Publishing (Vonnegut's own paperback publisher), the Marlborough Gallery, and Associated American artists, among other enterprises. During his vice presidency, his division and its subsidiaries win "eleven platinum records, forty-two gold records, twenty-two Oscars, eleven National Book Awards, two American League pennants, two National League pennants, two World Series, and fifty-three Grammies—and we never failed to show a return on capital of less than 23 percent." But then, by a bizarre coincidence, Mary's death is discovered and Walter's fortune is eaten up by lawyer's fees.

At a party in his honor, the night before he is to be sent to prison for the third time, Walter is surrounded by his new friends, all recent vice presidents of RAMJAC because of their kindness to him. He becomes depressed by their levity, especially in the face of how the corporation is being devoured by "foreigners and criminals and endlessly greedy conglomerates," to say nothing of the new government bureaucracy administering Mary's legacy to the people.

So Walter attempts to behave as though he were the good man Mary said he was: "You know what is finally going to kill this planet?" he asks his friends. "A total lack of seriousness . . . Nobody gives a damn anymore about what's really going on, what's going to happen next, or how we ever got into such a mess in the first place." And indeed, not one of his friends will either be serious or take him that way, so he gives up on saying anything serious and tells a joke.

Which, of course, is Vonnegut's own ploy: to try to say something serious by telling a joke. And, of course, it works. Like his protagonist, Walter, Vonnegut knows the cynicism and carelessness of the American public.

John Ciardi, hardly a fan of Vonnegut, once wrote a two-part essay for *Saturday Review* (May 15, 1965) entitled "700 Years After: The Relevance of Dante." In it Ciardi, who has done a fine translation of *The Divine Comedy,* said that "Dante will remain relevant to mankind for exactly as long as those values we call the humanities are relevant to it.

"If in some future time the nations of this world turn to systematic indoctrination of their people, making them over into the automatons of a self-justifying technology, then, of course, these meditative and intuitive perceptions for which we honor Dante will have been dismissed as an antiquarian idiocy, and he can have, at best, only a bootleg existence among the outcasts of society or among the secretly subversive."

In his essay Ciardi recognized that the future he dreaded had a likelihood of fulfillment, and certainly Vonnegut writes critically of such self-justifying technology in *Jailbird*—and in other novels as well. Mr. Ciardi undoubtedly knows by now that the humanities are not faring well in American universities, and, alas, that Dante is not at the top of many reading lists today. Vonnegut is. .At this writing, *Jailbird* has joined other Vonnegut novels of the past as number one on the best seller list. This probably gives Mr. Ciardi fits; in a scathing article in the September 30, 1967 *Saturday Review*, he attacked Vonnegut's *New York Times Book Review* piece on summer writing conferences, and implied that Vonnegut was a hack writer who "writes like a slob and thinks like a blob."

So it is ironic to imagine that Vonnegut may be one of those outcasts or secret subversives who still honors Dante, and who recognizes his relevance enough to transpose Dante's perceptions into an idiom that maybe, just *maybe*, even a corporate capitalist of the 20th century would read and be moved by. Certainly if there is a literary moralist writing today, it's Vonnegut. Although he has gone to considerable length to explain that he did not receive formal training in literature, he is hardly illiterate in the humanities. (Indeed, if my students know something about all the people listed in the Index to *Jailbird*, I would guess they would come close to having what we call a liberal arts education.)

Vonnegut writes for and of a culture in which the Sermon on the Mount is seen as naïve sentimentality. It is a culture in which the President wrongly thinks he has control of a real steering wheel. It is a culture which insists upon burning time with no thought for the future, a culture in which the air is unacceptable, and in which impoverished old women live out of shopping bags on the streets of our cities.

Despite élitist critics who are either embarrassingly unable or unwilling to understand, Vonnegut continues to insist that we give a damn about what's really going on. And he does so in a delightfully imaginative and coherent form. *Jailbird* is his best novel since *Slaughterhouse-Five*.

The Vonnegut Cosmos
[Review of *Deadeye Dick*]
Loree Rackstraw*

Kurt Vonnegut once wrote that Joseph Heller's first two novels are full of excellent jokes, but neither is funny; ". . . they tell a tale of pain and disappointment experienced by mediocre men [and women] of good will." This same judgment might be made about Vonnegut's work, including his new novel, *Deadeye Dick*.

Like the Rolls-Royce in the book, *Deadeye Dick* has "scraped up against

*Reprinted by permission from the *North American Review* 267 (December 1982):63–67. © 1982 by the University of Northern Iowa.

something blue." That blue is the quiet penance of the protagonist, Rudy Waltz, whose father was a maniacal failed artist famed only for befriending Adolph Hitler before the war, and whose mother was a mindless ornament unable to care for herself or family until her death from brain tumors that "bloomed" from a radioactive fireplace.

Rudy Waltz is "Deadeye Dick," a nickname he earned on Mother's Day at age 12 when he was initiated into manhood by being given the care of his father's gun collection. Rudy is caressing a Springfield rifle in the cupola atop his house when he squeezes the trigger and sends a bullet across Midland City into an unseen target, directly between the eyes of a pregnant woman vacuuming in her second floor guest room.

Deadeye Dick will likely stand as Vonnegut's most tightly crafted and complex work to date. It is an artful dance of fictional skill that interweaves ideas he has expressed before with new and old characters who are spin-offs from previous novels and from figures out of his own life he has discussed in print. The novel's form unfolds as though it were a kaleidoscopic deck of cards magically transformed from a linear order of successive suits into a new pattern of intricate and vaguely familiar design. This is not a book to be read quickly. Rather, it is to be savored, slowly and repetitively, for the benefit of its rich density.

It's not likely that *Deadeye Dick* will receive immediate critical acclaim. That the perceptions of Vonnegut's novels are largely misunderstood is exactly the point he writes to. As a former student of his, I can remember a boozey literary argument in Iowa City, where he taught back in 1965, when one of my fellow students in the Writers Workshop said: "If what Vonnegut is saying in his novels is true, then there's no reason to even stay alive." That, of course, is Vonnegut's very point: Life is often a cruel accident; the dilemma of humanity is how to stay alive with decency in the face of that reality.

If one had the talent of a Vonnegut, one could make a whimsical novel from any morning paper: disasters interlaced with a few jokes, some recipes, and some music. But probably it would be ill-received. Someone would say that the paper should print the *good* news. Alas, there's not a lot of it around. Vonnegut's novels are saying that if we can perceive the realities of the chaos around us, it might be possible for us to cut through the glaze of false hope that blinds us to the truth of our own self-destructive history, a history that got stuck, as he says in *Deadeye Dick*, in the Dark Ages. Perhaps, if we could do that, we might be able to think and act more responsibly about the future of our planet.

What are the false hopes his novels suggest distort our vision, and thus sustain our repetitive self-destruction? They come from our misuse of just about everything held sacred in Western civilization: organized religion, love, money, war, firearms, righteousness, parenthood, marriage, medicine, technology, art, and even language itself.

What might prevent us from destroying ourselves? The practice of common decency might help, along with the ability to laugh at ourselves. Recipes don't seem to do much harm, nor do music or restroom graffiti. Birdsong imitations and scat-singing can help "shoo the blues away. . . ."

So Vonnegut is a scandal. He refuses to honor traditional institutions, and his uncritically loving fans of the sixties have largely joined those institutions they, too, once decried. His inventive narrative structures are distressing to the literary establishment, and his language is unseemly.

Should we then take *Deadeye Dick*, his tenth novel, seriously as a work of literary art even if he, presumably, does not? Yes, indeed. In so doing, we will see a master shaman at work again in one of the most finely tuned and complex of all his books, even if one of the more painful.

As a prelude to reading this book, I would suggest the reader take another look at his 1973 novel, *Breakfast of Champions*. There, Vonnegut, the inventor of this fiction, enters the story as himself and expresses his credo as a writer, one central to the shaping of *Deadeye Dick:*

> As I approached my fiftieth birthday, I had become more and more enraged and mystified by the idiot decisions made by my countrymen. And then I had come suddenly to pity them, for I understood how innocent and natural it was for them to behave so abominably, and with such abominable results: They were doing their best to live like people invented in story books. This was the reason Americans shot each other so often: It was a convenient literary device for ending short stories and books. . . .
>
> Once I understood what was making America such a dangerous unhappy nation of people who had nothing to do with real life, I resolved to shun storytelling. I would write about life. Every person would be exactly as important as any other. All facts would also be given equal weightiness. Nothing would be left out. Let others bring order to chaos. I would bring chaos to order, instead, which I think I have done.
>
> If all writers would do that, then perhaps citizens not in the literary trades would understand that there is no order in the world around us, that we must adapt ourselves to the requirements of chaos instead.
>
> It is hard to adapt to chaos, but it can be done. I am living proof of that. It can be done.

Certainly *Deadeye Dick* is a story about adaptation to chaos, but the Preface to the novel hints of another connection to *Breakfast* when Vonnegut says he is writing this book as his sixtieth birthday "winks" at him, and identifies the symbolism of "an unappreciated, empty arts center in the shape of a sphere," which is to be seen as his own head. In *Breakfast*, the same Center, named for Mildred T. Barry, is located in the same Midland City of *Deadeye Dick*. Furthermore, the Preface to *Breakfast* tells us that Vonnegut is throwing out the characters from his previous books, and is trying to empty his head of things that other people have put into it. In that book, he says goodbye to Kilgore Trout, the perennial science fiction writer of past Vonnegut novels. (Trout is probably reincarnated in *Deadeye Dick* as the Haitian voodoo artist, Hippolyte Paul DeMille, who can raise ghosts from the dead, even as Vonnegut does when he resurrects characters from his previous books.) In *Deadeye Dick*, many of the newly invented characters of *Breakfast* are reinvented and given further development. Dwayne Hoover, the Pontiac dealer, and his wife Celia appear again, and we learn why the Celia of *Breakfast* killed herself by drinking Drāno.

The connection between the two novels is inescapable, and it tempts us to look more deeply for other ties to Vonnegut's literary past, a move that could very well result in a bibliophilic orgy. For not only will one find a re-crystallization of old characters, but one will find further development of old refrains and images that take us back at least as far as *God Bless You, Mr. Rosewater* for an earlier incarnation of Rudy Waltz. It includes *Happy Birthday Wanda June* and *Palm Sunday*, where Vonnegut tells us his father was a "gun nut," rather like Rudy's father, Otto Waltz. It takes us to *Slapstick* where we are told that "Life ideally . . . should be like the Minuet or the Virginia Reel or the Turkey Trot, something easily mastered in dancing school." Rudy's waltz in *Deadeye Dick* is not easily mastered, but he does survive the chaotic accidents of his life by adapting, and by quietly and decently becoming a house servant to his helpless and now financially ruined parents. As an adult he becomes a night-shift pharmacist at Schramm's Drug-store where he dispenses aspirin and hemorrhoid remedies, temporary re-liefs for life's pains and congestions, along with perfumes and cheap wristwatches—little gifts for buyers who have forgotten the birthday of a friend. Rudy's ministrations, like Rosewater's, are the harmless but useful prescriptions Vonnegut offers readers with his stories.

Which is to say, the anachronistic immediacy of *Deadeye Dick* is a highly crafted example of the Vonnegut art he has always insisted he is trying to invent: time, action, characters, setting, all have equal balance in the kaleidoscopic picture that real life is. Vonnegut doesn't bother with slicing it up. We get the whole thing at once, in a form which can free us from our addiction to the linearity of time and causality—an addition which often cripples us with simplistic, pompous and myopic perceptions.

Not that Rudy Waltz is to be seen as a great visionary. He tells us as the novel opens that he "was a wisp of undifferentiated nothingness, and then a little peephole opened quite suddenly. Light and sound poured in. Voices began to describe me and my surroundings. Nothing they said could be appealed." The peephole image, introduced in *Breakfast* and central to Vonne-gut's 1980 *Sun Moon Star* (a story he made up to fit illustrations by Ivan Chermayeff), is used throughout the novel to insist that the perceptions and behaviors of all his characters are accidental to their cultural surroundings.

Vonnegut's novels have long argued against the philosophical concept of free will. In the Preface to *Deadeye Dick*, he tells us that Rudy's nickname was originally for a sailor. "A deadeye," he explains, "is a rounded wooden block usually bound with rope or iron, and pierced with holes. The holes receive a multiplicity of lines, usually shrouds or stays, on an old-fashioned sailing ship. But in the American Middle West of my youth, a 'Deadeye Dick' was a honorific often accorded a person who was a virtuoso with firearms. So it is a sort of lungfish of a nickname. It was born in the ocean, but it adapted to life ashore." And of course, this is what the protagonist of the novel and his fellow characters try to do. Adapt to the chaos of life ashore, with their bodies bound by genetic structures and their perpetual holes open to the lines of the culture which shapes them.

Not all the characters are successful in their adaptation. One of the least successful is Celia Hildreth Hoover, a woman who we are given to understand is launched on her painful course to drug addiciton and suicide by the accident of her remarkable beauty. It was a beauty which made her "ready to die at any time, she said, because what men and boys thought about her and tried to do to her made her so ashamed." Her shame is heightened on the night she has her first and only date with Rudy's brother, Felix, to attend the high school prom. Felix has promised his father to bring her to his parents' home before going to the party. Unbeknownst to him, however, father Otto Waltz has extracted that promise in order to enact one of the legend-based fantasies through which he enlivens his otherwise drab life. He greets Felix and beautiful Celia as the "King of the Early Evening," attired in the scarlet-and-silver uniform of a major in the Hungarian Life Guard, complete with sable busby and panther skin. Otto garbles up the legend of Helen with the myth of Aphrodite, and addresses a stunned Celia with "Let Helen of Troy come forward—to claim this apple if she dare!" Whereupon Celia, in humiliation and fear, sheds her golden dancing shoes and corsage and takes off running, in one of those hilariously painful scenes Vonnegut is famed for.

What we see in this scene is the careful thematic and character development the author is unfolding. Rudy and Felix are used to their father's antics, and are relatively unmuffled by them. Their mother's only life is as a participant in her husband's fantasies. But when the myth is imposed on a newcomer like Celia, "a goddess who could not dance, would not dance" (cannot live adaptively), it can be misinterpreted and result in painful destructiveness, even as Vonnegut has shown, in *Breakfast of Champions,* that Celia's husband Dwayne turns homicidal when he believes he is truly the character with free will in one of Kilgore Trout's novels. It is what Vonnegut has been warning us about all along: if we take romantically violent myths or legends (or novels) like the Trojan War seriously as truth, we may find ourselves unconsciously shaped into destructiveness by them. This is not a new idea for Vonnegut. His first novel in 1952, *Player Piano,* is set in Ilium (Troy).

Celia's dilemma figures strongly in two other developments in the book. It is suggested that the one joyful experience of her life occurred when she portrayed a character in a play written by Rudy. The play, which failed miserably in a one-night performance in New York, was produced later in Midland City by the local Mask and Wig Club. Celia played the role of the ghost of the hero's wife in a Shangri-la type play about John Fortune, Rudy's boyhood hero, who sought paradise in Katmandu after his wife's death. The closing lines of the play, spoken by Fortune as he dies, are: "Come on over. There's room for everybody in Shangri-la." Which is to say, everybody can enjoy the temporary illusion of the arts, but don't take them too seriously. For, as Rudy discovered in his research for the play, the real story of John Fortune is that he never experienced Katmandu. He was carried, dying, on a stretcher to the paradise.

The beautiful fantasy of that play, however, had been taken seriously by Celia. We see her later in her life in a vivid scene with Rudy at night in the drugstore—a store, it's useful to remember, once a part of the Waltz family fortune derived from the production of "a quack medicine known as 'Saint Elmo's Remedy.' It was grain alcohol dyed purple, flavored with cloves and sarsaparilla root, and laced with opium and cocaine. As the joke goes: It was absolutely harmless unless discontinued."

Celia's despair is no joke when we see her in this scene, although it is developed in a kind of slapstick drama in the actual form of a play, a device Rudy uses throughout the novel to stylize and cope with embarrassing memories. Rudy sees a small, wretched customer inspecting dark glasses on a carousel, a customer who turns to face him with "the addled, raddled, snaggle-toothed ruins of the face of Celia Hoover, once the most beautiful girl in town." Celia is by now a hopeless drug addict on the eve of her suicide. She has come to Rudy ostensibly to ask for another play, for more beautiful words to say to an appreciative audience. She wants Rudy to "Write a crazy old lady play" with words that should come out of her new face, which is now—much to her relief—ugly. She wants Rudy to be her doctor with the medicine of his magic words.

With tired cynicism Rudy speculates that this adoring woman really wants amphetamines without a prescription—and he refuses. When Celia responds by saying "What makes you so afraid of love?" the telephone rings, and Rudy returns from a brief conversation to report that "Someone wanted to know if I was Deadeye Dick." He then tells Celia that he knows she will soon become abusive because of her longterm use of amphetamines. "I can take that if I have to," Rudy says, "but I'd rather get you home some way." Celia tells him her husband is gone, her son hates her, and that her doctor has been beaten up by her husband for prescribing the pills that destroyed her. She throws gold coins worth thousands of dollars at his feet against the damage she may do, and begs him to hug her. When he instead telephones the police, she begins to destroy the drugstore, starting with the carousel of dark glasses.

This five-page drugstore scene is representative of the novel's density, and it's worth unraveling. First of all it functions to develop the character of the woman who has been crippled for living by the cultural response to her beauty. As a result, she substitutes the chemical energy of drugs and the artistic energy of literary fantasy for the adaptive dance of life. This addiction drives her to destroy herself and others, a destruction she is now able to justify because she has money to pay for the damages. This characterization reflects again Vonnegut's view of the destructiveness that can come from living by illusions, a destructiveness that somehow seems acceptable if one has money. The development of Celia's character also suggests that stories traditionally stereotype the female, and that the myth of feminine pulchritude can be devastating to that sex. And certainly Vonnegut's longtime concern with drug abuse and physicians who prescribe destructive drugs reaches us through the vehicle of Celia.

Rudy's response to her develops several more Vonnegut themes: first, that Rudy cannot protect Celia from the harsh realities of life. He and, one presumes, Vonnegut refuse to write prescriptive stories that can blind the reader to reality: they can take hostile criticism if they have to, but they would rather speak a truth that can take readers home to reality, a place actually safer than illusion. Second, Rudy develops an old theme about the misinterpretation and abuse of love, a theme found in many Vonnegut novels, most especially in *Jailbird*. Rudy mistrusts love: when Celia asks why he is afraid of it, a telephone call reminds him of his accidental murder of the pregnant woman on Mother's Day (the day Vonnegut's own mother died from an overdose of drugs). Rudy lives with his painful reality and knows that love will not make it go away. His best response to Celia is common decency, honesty, kindness.

Finally, there are the sunglasses on the carousel that Celia first observes and later destroys. That image is elucidated in a later scene at Celia's funeral when Rudy is daydreaming about the purpose of life. He imagines Celia and all humans to be cells of a larger animal that are naturally sloughed off, as though "by a pancreas the size of the Milky Way," and he smiles when he thinks: "How comical that I, a single cell, should take my life so seriously!" Then, aware that he has been smiling at a funeral, he looks around to see if anyone has noticed. One person, at the other end of the pew, has. He is gazing at Rudy, and he does not look away. He is wearing large sunglasses with mirrored lenses. "He could have been anyone." Since the stranger has not been seen before, and is given no further development, he attracts the reader's attention. His enigma is clarified by a return to *Breakfast of Champions*. There, when Vonnegut enters the novel as himself, the inventor of the fantasy, he goes in a disguise of mirrored sunglasses to the arts festival in Midland City. And one of the honored guests there is Kilgore Trout, a science fiction writer who sees mirrors to be "leaks" or openings (peepholes?) into another universe. The sunglasses on the carousel in *Deadeye Dick* represent Vonnegut's vision into another fictional universe, a vision of life and history as "circles within circles," as a series of accidents ironically interrelated.

To attempt a full explication of this novel would no doubt result in an essay longer than the work itself. Such an attempt is neither possible nor nearly so much fun as reading the book, and re-reading it, for its complex nuances and the integrity of its interweaving with other Vonnegut works. A few further observations are too tempting to resist, however.

A pair of relatively minor characters in the novel (who also appeared in *Breakfast of Champions*) offer an interesting foil to Rudy's parents. Fred T. Barry, the millionaire bachelor philanthropist who builds the arts center in Midland City, and his aging mother, Mildred, for whom the center is named, live a vital mythic fantasy life that somewhat parallels that of Rudy's parents, except that the Barrys do not take themselves or their fantasies seriously. They fly about the world taking joy from all cultural events, piloted in their Lear jet by Tiger Adams—the name, incidentally, of one of Vonnegut's adopted sons, also a pilot. The Barrys are the only ones in an audience of twenty people who are enthusiastic about Rudy's failed play in New York, whereas Rudy's parents wouldn't even read the play. The fortune which made the Mildred Barry Arts Center possible came ironically from Barrytron, Ltd., a manufacturer of sophisticated weapons systems. Mr. Barry, a self-educated inventor, "had entered the armaments business more or less by accident. The timer on an automatic washing machine which he had been manufacturing . . . turned out to have military application." By contrast, Rudy's parents had lost their inherited fortune for which they never worked, because of the accident of Rudy's "crime." His responsibility for the murder would have gone undetected had not his father hysterically assumed the blame for letting Rudy use the gun. The result was that Otto Waltz was sent to prison for two years and was ruined financially in a lawsuit brought by the dead woman's husband. (Never mind that Rudy and his brother retire on funds from a lawsuit brought—by the same lawyer— against those responsible for the radioactive fireplace that accidentally killed their mother.)

In contrast to Emma Waltz's passive dependency, Mildred Barry finds delight in amusing herself and her servants by imitating birds, like "the bulbul of Malaysia and the morepork owl of New Zealand." Rudy observes "a basic mistake my parents had made about life: They thought that it would be very wrong if anybody ever laughed at them."

Ironically, it is Rudy's useless mother who, energized by the tumors growing in her brain, prevents the Arts Center from operating by her campaign against the two pieces of abstract art Barry purchased to begin the Center's collection. One is a statue by Henry Moore which Emma Waltz thinks looks like a "figure eight on its side," the other is a painting by Rabo Karabekian—a huge green painting with one vertical orange stripe called "The Temptation of Saint Anthony." We might see the Henry Moore sculpture as the symbol of eternity without much difficulty. But what of "The Temptation of Saint Anthony?" The answer is found in *Breakfast of Champions* again, where the same painting and artist provide Vonnegut, the intruding author, with his "born again" experience in the Mildred Barry Center, at what he calls "the spiritual climax of this book. . . ."

When Karabekian is hatefully criticized in *Breakfast* for his painting, he rises to his own defense by saying that his picture:

shows everything about life which truly matters, with nothing left out. It is a picture of the awareness of every animal. It is the immaterial core of every animal—the 'I am' to which all messages are sent. It is all that is alive in any of us . . . unwavering and pure, no matter what preposterous adventure may befall us. A sacred picture of Saint Anthony alone is one vertical, unwavering band of light. Our awareness is all that is alive and maybe sacred in any of us. . . ."

When we are also told in *Breakfast* that Saint Anthony was an Egyptian who founded the "first monastery, which was a place where men could live simple lives and pray often to the Creator of the Universe, without the distractions of ambition and sex. . . ." we realize that this painting in *Deadeye Dick* functions as a foil to other representational religious paintings in the book, paintings which express the violence of Christian history. The irony, of course, is that it is Rudy's mother who makes empty the Mildred Barry Center, the Center which Vonnegut has told us is symbolic of his own head, a head he presumably wishes to free from cultural fantasies so his vision will be as pure as Karabekian's. And the further irony is that Emma Waltz has brain tumors because she stood so often in front of the radioactive fireplace to look at her dead husband's one good painting, a work he never finished, an illusion on which she depended, having no dance of her own.

The clusters of multiple ironies in this book whirl toward ever greater density, as if each were a vortex connected with all others—and with the whole constellation of *Deadeye Dick* dynamically intertwined with others from Vonnegut's literary and life experience. One feels that the author's entire history and perception come together in this novel, a fictional cosmos with everything held in animated balance by a playful, magic energy. Its quiet spectacularity seems to require the participation of the reader in its whole. The result is voodoo, as practiced in the novel by Hippolyte Paul DeMille. The shaman is Vonnegut—with the deterministic philosophy of a Hippolyte Taine, the commitment of a Paul to spread the Beatitudinal word, and the savvy to put it into a literary DeMille production. *Deadeye Dick* is truly a novel that could never work in any other genre. In fact, it is *not* any other genre—it is Vonnegut's own.

And now, lest readers take this review too seriously, let me remind them that my response is written mostly in present tense—the tense Vonnegut tells us is the easiest for beginners learning to speak the Creole language of *Deadeye Dick*'s Haitian voodoo shaman.

God Bless You, Mr. Darwin, for Kurt Vonnegut's Latest [Review of *Galápagos*]

Peter J. Reed*

"Galapagos" is Kurt Vonnegut's 11th novel. It comes 30 years after his first, "Player Piano." That's a long career, and a productive one, especially if one adds his essays, plays and many short stories that enrich it. It is hard to think of this writer, who is so often iconoclastic, fresh, and youth-oriented, as an established major figure of American letters, but he unquestionably is. And "Galapagos" proclaims it. Three years in the making, it shows the labor in a polish and density that bespeak an experienced craftsman.

But this sounds solemn, and the book isn't. Though "Galapagos" has a smooth fluidity (as contrasted with, say, the fragmentation of the earlier "Breakfast of Champions"), it contains much of the wacky wit and irreverent imagination one expects of Vonnegut. And it employs the full range of technical innovations that have made him America's preeminent experimental novelist.

For this novel Vonnegut takes as his *mantra,* if you will, Darwin and the theory of evolution. The plot recounts the intricate coincidences whereby 10 people end up on Santa Rosalia, one of the Galapagos Islands. They evade the insidious virus that ends the human race, not in the usual apocalyptic bang but in the whimper of infertility.

A million years later humans have evolved to have fur, flippers and streamlined heads like seals. This is the result of adapting to existence on a barren rock with fish as principal food source. They're much happier, of course, because without hands they can't use tools or weapons. And they've shed the huge, overactive brains that invented lies and caused trouble, and that were as burdensome (and probably as lethal) to humans as the vast antlers of the long-extinct Irish elk.

Evolution permeates the book. It certainly governs the form. Vonnegut has described his books as mosaics in which each tile is a joke. That fits here, too, as chapter after chapter ends with the punch line of a joke. But each joke evolves from the last, and the larger joke of the whole situation—be it the first step of selecting the final 10 survivors and getting them to the island, or the evolution one million years on—evolve out of a sea of coincidence and happenstance, as if everything conspires to thwart an inevitable destiny.

The longer, first part of the book, "The Thing Was," seems at first confusing because of this. There are so many names and complications. One must relax and enjoy it: story and character evolve. Eventually our ship of fools-cum-human Noah's Ark sets forth.

The second segment, "And the Thing Became," gets us to the island,

*Reprinted by permission from the *Minneapolis Star and Tribunal,* 20 October 1985, 10G.

shows us what happens there, with forward glimpses to how humans evolve a million years later.

Evolution may seem like a curious topic to invent a novel around, but Darwin has always fascinated Vonnegut. He's obviously never liked "survival of the fittest" (a precept he casts some doubt upon), where every death is a triumph of progress. He's always had a warm heart for animals (in his high-school writing he borrowed the *nom de plume* "Ferdy" from that wonderful children's book, "Ferdinand the Bull") and has frequently drawn on the deep impressions made by a visit to the Galapagos. He's also interested in the way evolution theory has often been adopted by what Jerry Falwell calls "secular humanists" as a kind of religious dogma.

As a locus, though, evolution offers Vonnegut a long-term viewpoint from which to look at human endeavors with his characteristic mixture of detached amusement and compassion, despite seeing cause for despair. After all, he takes as his epigraph Anne Frank's stubborn assertion: "In spite of everything, I still believe people are really good at heart." That reflects the tone of this novel, although as usual Vonnegut shows us a fair amount in our collective behavior to give us pause.

Another evolution in "Galapagos" comes in narration. Vonnegut does not enter this novel to speak directly, as he often has in the past. Instead, his narrator is the son of his fictional alter ego, the science fiction writer Kilgore Trout. A warming trail of clues will lead most Vonnegut regulars to guess this identity before its satisfying confirmation.

There are other old touches, too: a few favorite places (the top of the Chrysler Building), characters (Dwayne Hoover), the dog's name Kazakh (the "h" is new), and a pet word (susurruing—you look it up!). But the sort of familiar repetitions ("hi ho," "and so on") which in the past have incensed cantankerous reviewers, are gone. There's nothing here that even looks lazy or easy or warmed-over.

"Galapagos" is an entertaining book, with an element of surprise, some sharp social comment, Twain-like satire of human foible and plenty of joking. Much of the joke is in the plot itself, and in its convoluted, coincidence-riddle unfolding. There are lots of embedded jokes, too, in context, but which I'd flatten dead if I picked out to illustrate. Many are provided by Mandarax (the computer evolved from Gokubi), who has a familiar quotation for every situation. They are often apt, but in an outrageously ironic sense.

At the same time, the book is thoughtful. Vonnegut says he agonized over "Galapagos" because he had to get it right scientifically as well as artistically. He's always been one of our most astute writers, outspoken but not merely opinionated, informed by a diverse and continuing education. This book is often thought-provoking and morally challenging but without being strident. It amuses as it educates, while its whimsy never devalues its substance.

Poking Holes in the Social Fabric
[Review of *Bluebeard*]

Paul Skenazy*

What is it about Kurt Vonnegut that makes his work so special to so many people? He's been pumping out words for more than three decades. His books continue to sell well, and some of them, like "Cat's Cradle" and "Slaughterhouse-Five," have an almost cult status.

But all Vonnegut's tales have their dull, flat sections, and that mild and undemonstrative voice of his can become droning at times. His satiric if embattled love for America and its mad version of civilization is heartening to the disenchanted but hardly original or exclusive. And if he's often brilliant at pointing to the emperor's nakedness, he barely suggests how we might clothe the monarch more decently.

To be cynical, you could say his fame rests on the easy wisdom he offers with his winsome, playful one-liners and his resistance to taking himself, or Art, or Writing, too seriously. And there is that dependable Vonnegut tone, too, that incorporates inanities and inhumanities, and keeps trying to storytell its way to sanity. However unsuspenseful a narrative device that voice sometimes seems, it's a voice you can trust to keep poking holes in the social fabric. Vonnegut is not going to let God have the last laugh at the bad joke called life; like so many of his heroes, he may be imagined benignly, if resignedly, thumbing his nose at the heavens.

"Bluebeard" is Vonnegut's 12th novel, and a classic example of its kind—endearing enough to disarm criticism, bland enough to warrant some, and finally so effective that the whole issue of judgment more or less fades into pleasure and admiration.

It purports to be the autobiography of Rabo Karabekian, whom we met a few Vonnegut books ago (in "Breakfast of Champions") as a snotty minimalist painter who created huge canvas fields of color, crossed by strips of reflecting tape, which sold for outrageously high prices. Now, years later and something of a comic footnote to art history (all of his paintings self-destructed because of the way the paint he used reacted with the canvases and tape, glue and air), Rabo takes a few months to record what he realizes is both his life's story and "a *diary* of this past troubled summer."

We ramble back through time from his cushy mansion in East Hampton to the Turkish extermination of the Armenians that turned his parents into exiles in Egypt. Snookered out of their fortune (and future) by promises of milk and honey in San Ignacio, California, where Rabo's scholarly father becomes a poor cobbler, Rabo grows up with a masterful facility for illustration and a failed immigrant's despair as his legacy.

And from there, fitful jumps take him and us to New York City, where a woman's loneliness and her lover / painter's cruelty provide Rabo with a

*Reprinted by permission from the *San Francisco Chronicle Review*, 4 October 1987, 1, 10.

fortuitous if fractious apprenticeship to Dan Gregory, the greatest illustrator of his time; to a camouflage unit in World War II consisting entirely of artists; and to the loss of an eye in combat, which leaves Rabo a cyclopean painter. After the war, Rabo bankrolls a bunch of improvident Abstract Expressionist artists (and gets repaid in canvases they can't sell elsewhere), loses his wife and two sons, has his own brief moment of glory and watches as the geniuses of the movement burn themselves out in success.

Then there's the story of the troubled summer, while Rabo lives in the mansion he inherited from his second wife, where he feels like something of a "museum guard" to the collection of Abstract Expressionist masterpieces that cover the walls. A novelist, Paul Slazinger, occasionally shares his digs, and the two men are taken up by a beautiful younger woman named Circe Berman, who is spending the summer writing her late husband's biography. It is Circe who adds new threat and meaning to Rabo's world with her insistent questions and very different artistic tastes. The conflict of her insufferably energetic if haunted will with his indifference provides the admittedly artificial tension that keeps Rabo's reminiscences readable.

As a psychological document, or pseudodocument, "Bluebeard" is a rambling, gangly piece of work, meandering from vignette to vignette and afraid of its own emotional material. To Vonnegut's credit, he can write more or less humorously about just about anything; on the other hand, he can't seem to, or won't, look misery in the face for more than an instant. Here as elsewhere in his work, the flippancy shoves the pain aside, and charming brief scenes substitute for the record of people's attachments and experiences.

But plot is more the excuse than the purpose of this novel, something like a spider web to catch the stray, random whims and whimsies of Vonnegut's flighty imagination. As a writer, Vonnegut is something akin to the Fool in Shakespeare's plays, his characters mere masks and fronts for a comic soothsayer's meditations. He's a master of the anecdote, giving inordinate weight and significance to gossip about a tailor, a cobbler's mumbled asides, the war experiences of the women servants at an Italian villa, or the thumbnail biographies of Rabo's neighbors.

Vonnegut sets up his political salvos—whether about Nancy Reagan and drugs, or our tastes in art, or what men do to women—with the skill of a Woody Allen who's finally managed to forget about himself for a while. And he fills his books with so many suggestive metaphors, like Rabo's one-eyed condition and self-erasing paint, that you finally believe he's not so much graceless as a narrator as someone who's just abandoned old-time plots and stories as too confining, like a sport coat he's outgrown.

The title of the novel comes from the legend of Bluebeard, who kept one room that he forbade a new bride to enter (and where all the former brides who couldn't resist temptation were hung for their intrusion). Rabo has a secret, too: A potato barn that used to be his studio, which he keeps locked away from Circe's prying and Paul's inquisitiveness and the reader's desire to peek without having to pay the emotional and moral price of admission.

When we finally do "see" what's in there, we discover more meaning in illusion than we know what to do with. It's in silly little games like this that Vonnegut really shines.

Vonnegut's way is to do a little jig around ideas, a sort of verbal two-step that is something between a guerrilla action and a hummingbird's erratic attacks on a flower. That unstable combination is what keeps his readers absorbed and his art buoyant, however gloomy his takes on our world often are. Hidden inside his shenanigans in "Bluebeard" is a study of history, memory and art. Rabo's personal story is meant to remind us of how Americans pretend to a convenient historical amnesia that allows us to ignore our part in what Rabo calls "the genocide century."

Rattling the backward-looking brain cells into animation, Vonnegut is also exploring the ways artists have, and might, serve our culture's need to know what we have done to ourselves and others. There are painters and writers of every kind littering the pages: Rabo's mentor Dan Gregory with his sentimental illustrative precision and hatred of modernism; Rabo's own abortive career as illustrator, abstract painter and now writer; Circe Berman's multiple lives as a biographer and (under a pseudonym) the author of teenage "problem" novels; Paul Slazinger's arty fictions.

And most importantly, there are the Abstract Expressionists, who created the first art movement to originate in America. As Rabo and Vonnegut muse on the artistic desires and deaths of painters real (Arshile Gorky, Pollack, Rothko) and imagined (Terry Kitchen, Rabo's closest friend in the novel, and another suicide), they make us think about abstract canvases ("about absolutely nothing but themselves"), representational work, and what we agree as writers and painters and readers and lookers to allow to be represented to us about us.

By the time we're done, we realize that Vonnegut has managed to make us laugh our way through a study of men at war—in and with themselves, with the women who serve and are abused by them, with other times and cultures they seek to dominate, with the ways they've learned to recreate and relish their world in art. Like the patch he wears over his wounded eye, Rabo's goodwill conceals an incapacity we're a bit ashamed to acknowledge to others: our self-generated blindness.

The Early Works

Why They Read Vonnegut
Jerome Klinkowitz*

In Spring of 1970 Kurt Vonnegut, Jr., studied the campus popularity of *Steppenwolf* and *Siddhartha* in an essay, "Why They Read Hesse." His answer: "America teemed with people who were homesick in bittersweet ways, and . . . *Steppenwolf* was the most profound book about homesickness ever written." Of the basic sort as "I miss my Mommy and Daddy,"[1] this homesickness ascribed to Hesse may be the clue to Vonnegut's own popularity with the young. I will not offer a lengthy analysis of his individual novels; that, more incisively than for J. D. Salinger a decade ago, has already been done, and the third section of this book [*The Vonnegut Statement*] presents a careful synthesis of Vonnegut's literary achievement. But there are many answers to be found in Vonnegut's career as a writer, a career now in its twenty-first year. During it Vonnegut did much "to finance the writing of the novels," as he tells us in the preface to *Welcome to the Monkey House* (p. xiv), and just what he did, within and without fiction, gives sounder basis to an understanding of his appeal.

For one thing, he became a paperback writer. "And I need a job, so I want to be a paperback writer," the Beatles sang a few years ago; in 1949 Vonnegut quit as a General Electric p.r. man to be a writer, the very Sherwood Anderson-like act which, like Anderson, he continued to celebrate in much of his fiction thereafter. American publishers must have thought that this material wouldn't sell in hard covers, because they marketed Vonnegut in unreviewed pulp editions. Yet Vonnegut reached a large if uncritical public: the greater majority of Americans buy less than one hardbound book a year, but drugstores remain crowded with racks of paperbacks—among them, the works of Kurt Vonnegut, Jr.

Popular magazines accepted Vonnegut's work, and he favored middle-class America with dozens of stories appearing in both sides of the competition, including *Redbook* and *Cosmopolitan*, *Esquire* and *Playboy*, *The Ladies' Home Journal* and *McCall's*, and at one time in the same weekly issues of *Collier's* and *The Saturday Evening Post*. His appeal was broad: several

*Reprinted by permission from *The Vonnegut Statement*, ed. Jerome Klinkowitz and John Somer (New York: Delacorte Press / Seymour Lawrence, 1973), 18–30.

stories pleaded for pacifism and deplored military uses of science, while one, "Harrison Bergeron," was reprinted in the hawkish *National Review*.[2] Because the subject of his first novel, *Player Piano*, was in part technology, Vonnegut earned the reputation of a science-fiction writer. But *Player Piano* and the science-oriented stories he published in *Collier's* and the *Post* in fact considered the effect of innovation on contemporary culture, and even the four stories Vonnegut did write for science-fiction journals emphasized the workings of science and technology among very conventional middle-class American lives. "I supposed," he has said, "that I was writing a novel about life, about things I could not avoid seeing and hearing in Schenectady, a very real town, awkwardly set in the gruesome now."[3] Some magazine stories, such as "Report on the Barnhouse Effect,"[4] consider questions—military misuse of science, peacetime harnessing of atomic energy—that were debated on other pages of the same issue. Most are focused, despite their futurism, on present habits of existence. Narcoticlike radio waves from outer space are marketed on earth like color TVs or frozen pizzas;[5] cranky oldsters, treated to a preservative fountain of youth, simply persevere in their crankiness;[6] and future citizens, who are blessed with the ability to live ideal lives apart from their imperfect bodies, nevertheless retain all their human foibles.[7] For better or for worse, Vonnegut's science-fiction stories read at times like television situation comedies. The hallmark of these stories is that although technology changes, sociology remains the same. Familiar people encountering a new life have nevertheless familiar problems. Vonnegut's most radical departure from the *status quo* comes when Eliot Rosewater forecasts the eventual obsolescence of all workers, when the problem will become "How to love people who have no use" (p. 210). His solution is to relocate the Rosewater Foundation in a shabby walk-up office over a lunchroom and liquor store, serving the public like any small businessman.

By far the greater majority of Vonnegut's stories feature no science or technology at all, and are simple, sometimes sentimental tales of middle-class America. Again, some have the flavor of contemporary magazines, especially "All the King's Horses,"[8] which suggests Korean War topicality with its brave American P.O.W.s facing a sinister Oriental guerrilla and a dispassionate Russian officer. "Long Walk to Forever," presented as "a sickeningly slick love story from *The Ladies' Home Journal*," was drawn from Vonnegut's own life. "Shame, shame," he reflects, "to have lived scenes from a woman's magazine."[9] Conventional life, as depicted by such magazines, is at the center of such stories (which may, as Leslie Fiedler suggests, "fit formulas which are often genuine myths").[10] Some deal with small, frivolous incidents and ironies (interior-decorating schemes, summer vacations), while others are telling critiques of morals and manners. Most are written from a very stable point of view, that of an average citizen, often "a salesman of storm windows and doors, and here and there a bathtub enclosure."[11] Vonnegut's salesman leads a generally mundane life, but on one occasion sells a tub enclosure to a movie star, and on another, a full set of his top-line windows to a neighbor of the Kennedys at

Hyannis Port. His experience conforms to that of other Vonnegut narrators in similar positions—real-estate salesmen, contact men for investment-counseling firms—who learn that people rich and famous sorely lack the blessings of simple, middle-class life. One story, "The Foster Portfolio,"[12] treats this theme with a touch of irony. Herbert Foster, who has inherited a large fortune, insists on remaining in his "jerry-built postwar colonial with expansion attic," with his discount-store furniture, and even with his worries about payments on his second-hand car—all so that he has the excuse to moonlight weekends as a honky-tonk pianist. But most of Vonnegut's stories are more honestly homely. "Custom-Made Bride"[13] features a designer who has crafted for himself a showpiece wife, but who misses the girl's former simple qualities. In many stories wealth is compared with middle-class frugality; the latter always wins. In "Bagombo Snuff Box"[14] a showoff tries to embarrass his ex-wife in her "small, ordinary home," but ends up profoundly humiliated himself. "The Package"[15] shows a retired businessman trying to impress an old friend with his luxury house; he is, of course, shamed by the other's life of poverty and self-sacrifice. "Hal Irwin's Magic Lamp"[16] tells of a poor man who makes half a million on the stock market, cleverly revealing the bounty to his wife by means of a "magic lamp." The wife, however, wishes for their simple life; her wish is answered by the Great Depression, and they are happy again. In "Poor Little Rich Town"[17] Vonnegut sets several forces at work: a quiet upstate town is chosen as the site for a new electronics complex; high-salaried technocrats will be moving in, real-estate values will soar; and the plant's efficiency expert himself has already arrived, habitually setting about improving all aspects of town life. For a time the townspeople carry on a flirtation with the new life, but in the end they soundly reject it, to the detriment of their pocketbooks but not of their souls.

Whether Vonnegut's magazine pieces of the 1950's are great fictional art, and whether they conform to myths indicative of our deepest cultural feelings, need not be debated here. What I have hoped to establish is that Vonnegut wrote these stories, dozens of them, from a consistently middle-class point of view. This point of view is often their best asset, offering Vonnegut some of his strongest plots, clearest themes, and funniest lines. The middle-class slant is not simply a requirement of the form; if we look at Vonnegut's nonfictional work, we will see that it is an integral part of his expression. His review of *The Random House Dictionary*,[18] for instance, is written as a middle-class appreciation: "Prescriptive, as nearly as I could tell, was like an honest cop, and descriptive was like a boozed-up war buddy from Mobile, Ala." He often uses the same standards when called to appear on television talk shows and documentaries. For the WBBM-TV (Chicago) report on the generation gap, "Nothing Like Us Ever Was" (Jaunary 27, 1971), Vonnegut made a simple comparison. "This is an alcoholic nation," he said. "Much big business is done by people four sheets to the wind." When we learn to deal so well with the other part of the population high on pot, he concluded, the generation gap will be bridged. The American middle class is a constant point of reference in Vonnegut's commentary on life. His review of Len Deighton's *Bomber* leads him to generalize on "War as a Series of Collisions."[19] "During the Great Depression in Indianapolis," he remembers, "collisions between steam locomotives were arranged at the Indiana State Fairgrounds—to cheer up the folks. The folks enjoyed the suspense and then the crunch and the steam. They marveled at the wreckage, picked up pieces of steel which had been bent like taffy, saying reverently, 'My God—looky there.' " "Looky there," like "So it goes" in *Slaughterhouse-Five*, is his refrain to a series of grisly quotes from Deighton's book, suggesting the ultimately prosaic nature of modern, mechanized warfare. In another essay, after he is surprised to learn so many of his high-school classmates died in the war, "I read those casualty lists again . . . made old friends and enemies stop mowing lawns and barbecuing steaks in my imagination, made them climb back into their graves." But he was also amazed to find that among his living classmates was Mrs. Melvin Laird, wife of the Secretary of Defense. "When you get to be our age, you all of a sudden realize that you are being ruled by people you went to high school with. You all of a sudden catch on that life is nothing *but* high school."[20] Daily life as a measure of judgment pervades Vonnegut's work. High school, big and small business, are frequent standards: so is family life. His playlet, "The Very First Christmas Morning,"[21] characterizes children at the inn as selfish, middle-class kids—who are blessed in becoming selfless. Even heaven, as depicted in *Happy Birthday, Wanda June,* is a middle-class vision: " 'In heaven, shuffleboard is everything. It was almost worth the trip to find out that Jesus Christ in heaven is just another guy who plays shuffleboard. He wears a blue and gold warmup jacket.' "

When Vonnegut criticizes middle-class American life, he does not do it from a position of superiority. In *God Bless You, Mr. Rosewater* Eliot's sophisticated wife is herself criticized because "She had never seen Rosewater County, had no idea what a night-crawler was, did not know that land anywhere could be so deathly flat, that people anywhere could be so deathly dull." Vonnegut knows it well, and, like Asa Leventhal in Bellow's *The Victim,* is frequently mindful of that part of humanity which "did not get away with it," in this case those who have not escaped the Middle West. Returning for a writers' conference at Western Illinois University, he describes the institution's reputation as "such a jerkwater school," the town's as "such a hell-hole." He admits that things weren't that bad, but feels sorry for everyone as they sit at a party at the TraveLodge Motel, listening to "the Muzak and the sounds of drag races out on Route 136."[22] Like Thoreau, Vonnegut sees people living lives of "quiet desperation."[23] But instead of retreating to a Cape Cod Walden, Vonnegut keeps near these sources in his fiction; like Eliot Rosewater, he confides that " 'I'm going to love these discarded Americans, even though they're useless and unattractive. *That* is going to be my work of art.' "

The most conclusive proofs for Vonnegut as a spokesman of the middle class are that he does not view himself as an intellectual writer, and that in fact much of his material is grossly anti-intellectual. In *Player Piano* he expressed the same aversion to rule by "experts" that Richard Hofstadter says anchors anti-intellectualism in middle-class American life. Vonnegut complains that he was for years dismissed as a science fictionist because "The feeling persists that no one can simultaneously be a respectable writer and understand how a refrigerator works."[24] And although he attends writers' conferences, he regards them as finally irrelevant: "You can't teach people to write well. Writing well is something God lets you do or declines to let you do."[25] That comment drew a bitter attack from John Ciardi, who pilloried Vonnegut's argument and even the prose it was written in, preferring instead the writer who is "a member of a group." "That group," said Ciardi, "might have met in a Greek agora, in a Roman bath, in a Parisian café, or at an English university, but it met, argued, agreed, conspired, hated, and loved."[26] Vonnegut is no such writer. "I am self-taught," he says. "I have no theories about writing that might help others."[27] When he did teach at the University of Iowa Writers Workshop, his major goal was to instill, not critical axioms, but a simple "sense of wonder."[28] He sees himself as neither intellectual nor prophet, but rather as "an old fart with his memories and his Pall Malls."[29] Of his writing career: "It seems like a perfectly straightforward business story."[30]

"You can safely ignore the arts and sciences," advised Eliot Rosewater. "They never helped anybody. Be a sincere, attentive friend of the poor." Art fails several Vonnegut heroes—Rosewater, Howard Campbell, and Billy Pilgrim— and in "Physicist, Purge Thyself," an address delivered before the American Association of Physics Teachers, Vonnegut criticized both art and science. "I sometimes wondered what the use of any of the arts was with the possible exception of interior decoration," he admitted.[31] On the other hand, "a virtuous physicist is a humanistic physicist. . . . He wouldn't knowingly hurt people. He wouldn't knowingly let politicians or soldiers hurt people. If he comes across a technique that would obviously hurt people, he keeps it to himself."[32] When Vonnegut traveled to Biafra during its last days, he found the occasion to again consider the role of the intellectual. He was amazed to find out that the dot on the map that was Biafra contained "700 lawyers, 500 physicians, 300 engineers, eight million poets, two novelists of the first rank, and God only knows what else—about one third of all the black intellectuals in Africa. Some dot." He recounts how "Biafrans got the best jobs in industry and the civil service and the hospitals and the schools, because they were so well educated," and that "They were hated for that—perfectly naturally."[33] But he wonders "if there was a chance that one thing that had killed so many Biafrans was the arrogance of Biafra's intellectuals."[34] Vonnegut forever speaks from the point of view of that middle-class citizen who, according to Hofstadter, suspects "experts working in any area outside his control."[35] Such thinking is easily categorized as McCarthyism of the 1950's, and Vonnegut's work written at the center of the 1950's experience at times responds with an eerie echo. But Vonnegut was unknown in the 1950's, and is famous only in the 1970's. The appeal of his statements may be a new style of anti-intellectualism, a protest against what a *Time* reviewer described as "a persistent attempt to adjust, smoothly and rationally, to the unthinkable, to the unbearable."[36] In the cold-war years Americans were taught to live under the bomb, in an eroding ecology, in deteriorating cities; against all of this, as an increasingly public personality, Vonnegut protests.

Yet there is a continuity to Vonnegut's works, stretching, he himself claims, back to the 1930's. His "youth-minded notions" which have made him so popular derive, he claimed in a *Life* interview, "from my parents. I thought about it and decided they were right."[37] In "Times Change" he wrote, "I've wanted to record somewhere, for a long time, something easily forgotten: my generation was raised to be pacifistic, but it fought well in a war it felt was just. This is surely true of the pacifists in the present high-school generation: they aren't cowards, either."[38] Vonnegut's appeal has been compared to the popularity of Senator Eugene McCarthy in 1968; each, as Wilfrid Sheed has indicated, "operated out of a venerable Midwestern culture that came as complete news to most Americans."[39] Maybe it is surprising that a youth hero should be able to say to himself, "Look at me . . . I have kids, a car, and I pay my bills on time."[40] Yet Vonnegut's views are after all not revolutionary; he represents in fact a counterrevolution to the real direction of "progress," ever the path of advancing technology and of science for its own sake.

I shall conclude with references to one of Vonnegut's most obscure stories, and then to his most famous speech. In "Runaways,"[41] published in *The Saturday Evening Post* in 1961, he pictured a teen-age couple who at length find themselves "not too young to be in love," but in fact "Just too young for about everything else that goes with love." The story gently mocks youthful rebellion, counseling that there are some responsibilites that kids, for a while, should simply not have to bear. In his commencement address at Bennington College in May 1970, only a few weeks after the killings at Kent State, Vonnegut gave the same advice. In the intervening years a youth culture had been born, and all generations had been willing to accede young people the responsibility for changing, and indeed saving, the world. That is "a great swindle," Vonnegut complained. In all seriousness he advised the graduates that for at least part of the time after they received their diplomas "they should go swimming and sailing and walking, and just fool around."[42] Young people, Vonnegut insisted, cannot themselves change the world: they don't have the money or the power. Moreover, it is an impossible responsibility to bear. I will argue in Chapter Eleven that Vonnegut's major novels speak against man's position as romantic center of the universe, a posture which makes him responsible for all evil and hence hopelessly alienated from himself. When Vonnegut applies the same distinctions to youth he is clearly repeating statements characteristic of his writing for middle-class magazines. He is a pacifist; he distrusts the unbridled intellect; he argues for simple, humane values. All are elements of a fundamental American decency, dating to his childhood in the 1930's and sustained in his writings of the 1950's, which perhaps in the last decade has been submerged under new forces and ideas against which youth rightly protests. When Vonnegut so accurately reflects that protest, it should be no surprise that he is forty-eight years old, has kids, a car, and pays his bills on time. He is simply speaking for its ultimate origins.

Notes

1. Kurt Vonnegut, Jr., "Why They Read Hesse," *Horizon*, 12 (Spring, 1970), 30.

2. 17 (November 16, 1965), 1020–1021.

3. "Science Fiction," *Page 2*, ed. Francis Brown (New York: Holt, Rinehart and Winston, 1969), p. 117.

4. *Collier's*, 125 (February 11, 1950), 18–19 ff.

5. "The Euphio Question," *Collier's*, 127 (May 12, 1951), 22–23 ff.

6. "Tomorrow and Tomorrow and Tomorrow" [orig.: "The Big Trip Up Yonder"], *Galaxy Science Fiction*, 7 (January, 1954), 100–110.

7. "Unready to Wear," *Galaxy Science Fiction*, 6 (April, 1953), 98–111.

8. *Collier's*, 127 (Febraury 10, 1951), 14–15 ff.

9. *Welcome to the Monkey House*, p. xv.

10. "The Divine Stupidity of Kurt Vonnegut," *Esquire*, 74 (September, 1970), 196.

11. "Who Am I This Time" [orig.: "My Name is Everyone"], *Saturday Evening Post*, 234 (December 16, 1961), 20.

12. *Collier's*, 128 (September 8, 1951), 18–19 ff.

13. *Saturday Evening Post*, 226 (March 27, 1954), 30 ff.

14. *Cosmopolitan*, 137 (October, 1954), 34–39.

15. *Collier's*, 130 (July 26, 1952), 48–53.

16. *Cosmopolitan*, 142 (June, 1957), 92–95.

17. *Collier's*, 130 (October 25, 1952), 90–95.

18. "The Latest Word," *New York Times Book Review*, October 30, 1966, p. 56.

19. *Life*, 69 (October 2, 1970), 10

20. "Times Change," *Esquire*, 74 (February, 1970), 60.

21. *Better Homes and Gardens*, 40 (December, 1962), 44 ff.

22. "Teaching the Unteachable," *New York Times Book Review*, August 6, 1967, pp. 1, 20.

23. *Welcome to the Monkey House*, p. 55.

24. "Science Fiction," pp. 117–118.

25. "Teaching the Unteachable," p. 1.

26. "Manner of Speaking," *Saturday Review*, 50 (September 30, 1967), 18.

27. *Welcome to the Monkey House*, p. ix.

28. Franklin Dunlap, "God and Kurt Vonnegut, Jr., at Iowa City," *Chicago Tribune Magazine*, May 7, 1967, p. 84.

29. Kurt Vonnegut, Jr., *Slaughterhouse-Five*, p. 2.

30. "The High Cost of Fame," *Playboy*, 18 (January, 1971), 124.

31. *Chicago Tribune Magazine,* June 22, 1969, p. 44.

32. *Ibid.,* p. 48.

33. "Biafra," *McCall's,* 97 (April, 1970), 135.

34. *Ibid.,* p. 138.

35. *Anti-Intellectualism in American Life* (New York: Vintage, 1963), p. 12.

36. "The Price of Survival," *Time* (April 11, 1969), p. 108.

37. Wilfrid Sheed, "The Now Generation Knew Him When," *Life,* 67 (September 12, 1969), 66.

38. "Times Change," p. 60.

39. Sheed, p. 66.

40. Rollene W. Saal, "Pick of the Paperbacks," *Saturday Review,* 53 (March 28, 1970), 34.

41. *Saturday Evening Post,* 234 (April 15, 1961), 27–28.

42. "Up Is Better Than Down," *Vogue* (August 1, 1970), pp. 54, 144–145.

[Kurt Vonnegut and Black Humor]   Robert Scholes*

. . . The satirical kind of Black Humor is qualified by the modern fabulator's tendency to be more playful and more artful in construction than his predecessors: his tendency to fabulate. Fabulative satire is less certain ethically but more certain esthetically than traditional satire. This causes the special tone that the phrase Black Humor so inadequately attempts to capture. The spirit of playfulness and the care for form characteristic of the modern fabulators operate so as to turn the materials of satire and protest into comedy. And this is not a mere modern trick, a wayward eccentricity. These writers reflect quite properly their heritage from the esthetic movement of the nineteenth century and the ethical relativism of the twentieth. They have some faith in art but they reject all ethical absolutes. Especially, they reject the traditional satirist's faith in the efficacy of satire as a reforming instrument. They have a more subtle faith in the humanizing value of laughter. Whatever changes they hope to work in their readers are the admittedly evanescent changes inspired by art, which need to be continually renewed, rather than the dramatic renunciations of vice and folly postulated by traditional satire.

The special tone of Black Humor, often derived from presenting the materials of satire in a comic perspective, is perfectly illustrated in a passage from Vonnegut's *Cat's Cradle.* The narrator in this passage is interviewing the son of a Schweitzer-type jungle doctor on a small Caribbean island:

"Well, aren't you at all tempted to do with your life what your father's done with his?"

*Reprinted by permission from *The Fabulators* (New York: Oxford University Press, 1967), pp. 41–55.

Young Castle smiled wanly, avoiding a direct answer. "He's a funny person, Father is," he said, "I think you'll like him."

"I expect to. There aren't many people who've been as unselfish as he has."

"One time," said Castle, "when I was about fifteen, there was a mutiny near here on a Greek ship bound from Hong Kong to Havana with a load of wicker furniture. The mutineers got control of the ship, didn't know how to run her, and smashed her up on the rocks near 'Papa' Monzano's castle. Everybody drowned but the rats. The rats and the wicker furniture came ashore."

That seemed to be the end of the story, but I couldn't be sure. "So?"

"So some people got free furniture and some people got bubonic plague. At Father's hospital, we had fourteen hundred deaths inside of ten days. Have you ever seen anyone die of bubonic plague?"

"That unhappiness has not been mine."

"The lymph glands in the groin and the armpits swell to the size of grapefruit."

"I can well believe it."

"After death, the body turns black—coals to Newcastle in the case of San Lorenzo. When the plague was having everything its own way, the House of Hope and Mercy in the Jungle looked like Auschwitz or Buchenwald. We had stacks of dead so deep and wide that a bulldozer actually stalled trying to shove them toward a common grave. Father worked without sleep for days, worked not only without sleep but without saving many lives, either."

[After an interruption]

"Well, finish your story anyway."

"Where was I?"

"The bubonic plague. The bulldozer was stalled by corpses."

"Oh, yes. Anyway, one sleepless night I stayed up with Father while he worked. It was all we could do to find a live patient to treat. In bed after bed after bed we found dead people.

"And Father started giggling," Castle continued.

"He couldn't stop. He walked out into the night with his flashlight. He was still giggling. He was making the flashlight beam dance over all the dead people stacked outside. He put his hand on my head, and do you know what that marvelous man said to me?" asked Castle.

"Nope."

" 'Son,' my father said to me, 'someday this will all be yours.' "

In the passage an excess of the horrible is faced and defeated by the only friend reason can rely on in such cases: laughter. The whole episode is a comic parable of our times. Progress, that favorite prey of satirists from Swift and Voltaire onward, means that some people get free furniture and some get the plague. Some get Biarritz and some get Auschwitz. Some get cured of cancer by radiation; others get radiation sickness. But the spuriousness of progress is not seen here with the *saeva indignatio* of the satirist. Progress is seen not as a conspiracy but as a joke. The Black Humorist is not concerned with what to do about life but with how to take it. In this respect Black Humor has certain affinities with some existentialist attitudes, roughly distinguishable in terms of the difference between seeing the universe as absurd and seeing it as ridiculous—a joke. The absurd universe is a pretty dismal affair. The best, in fact, that Camus found to offer humanity as a response to the human condition was "scorn." In "The Myth of Sisyphus" he told us that "there is no fate that cannot be surmounted by scorn." The Black Humorists offer us something better than scorn. They offer us laughter. The scorn of Sisyphus leads finally to resignation—"He, too, concludes that all is well." Beneath the hide of this scornful hero beats the heart of Dr. Pangloss after all. Vonnegut's fictional prophet Bokonon suggests a better posture for man on the mountain top than that of Camus's Sisyphus, who simply starts down again to pick up his burden. At the end of *Cat's Cradle,* with the world nearly all frozen, Bokonon gives one of his last disciples a bit of advice:

> If I were a younger man, I would write a history of human stupidity; and I would climb to the top of Mount McCabe and lie down on my back with my history for a pillow; and I would take from the ground some of the blue-white poison that makes statues of men; and I would make a statue of myself, lying on my back, grinning horribly, and thumbing my nose at You Know Who.

What man must learn is neither scorn nor resignation, say the Black Humorists, but how to take a joke. How should one take a joke? The best response is neither acquiescence nor bitterness. It is first of all a matter of perception. One must "get" the joke. Then one must demonstrate this awareness by playing one's role in the joke in such a way as to turn the humor back on the joker or cause it to diffuse itself harmlessly on the whole group which has participated in the process of the joke. Even at the punch line of apocalypse, feeble man can respond with the gesture prescribed by Bokonon, suggesting an amused, tolerant defiance. Of course, a joke implies a Joker, as Gloucester observed amid the cosmic tomfoolery of *King Lear:* "They kill us for their sport." But I do not think the Black Humorists mean to present us with a new diety, crowned with a cap and bells in place of thorns. No more than Paul Tillich do they wish to "bring in God as a *deus ex machina*" to fill the great hole in the modern cosmos. To see the human situation as a cosmic joke, one need not assume a Joker.

Some accidents are so like jokes that the two are indistinguishable. Moreover, it is possible to conceive of all human history as part of a master plan without thinking of the Planner in quite the traditional way. In an early science fiction novel, now re-released in paperback, Kurt Vonnegut developed such a view. In *Sirens of Titan* he presented a cosmos in which the whole of human history has been arranged by intervention from outer space in order to provide a traveler from a distant galaxy with a small spare part necessary for his craft to continue its voyage to the other side of the universe. Such purposefulness to entirely extra-human ends is indeed a cosmic joke, but is not intended as such by those superior beings who have manipulated earthly life for their own ends. This novel suggests that the joke is on us every time we attribute purpose or meaning that suits us to things which are either accidental, or possessed of purpose and meaning quite different from those we would supply. And it doesn't matter which of these mistakes we make.

Samuel Johnson, whose *Rasselas* is a rather solemn ancestor of *Cat's Cradle,* picked on just this aspect of the vanity of human wishes in one of his finest works—an *Idler* paper so black and humorous that Johnson later suppressed it. In this essay Johnson presented a dialogue between a mother vulture and her children, in which the wise old bird, looking down at a scene of human carnage from a recent European battle, tells her young that men do this at regular intervals as part of a divine plan which has shaped the best of all possible worlds—for vultures. In presenting this view of life as a joke on all those who think this is the best of all possible worlds for men, Johnson is very close to his modern descendants. For the joke is one key to the fabulative impulse, especially to the impulse behind Black Humor. To present life as a joke is a way of both acknowledging its absurdity and showing how that very absurdity can be encompassed by the human desire for form. A joke like Dr. Johnson's acknowledges and counteracts the pain of human existence. In the best of all possible worlds there could be no jokes.

Of all the things that men must endure, war is one of the worst. Certainly war brings the contrast between human ideals and human actions to the highest possible degree of visibility. In time of war the drums, the rituals, the rhetoric all collaborate to suppress reason and its ally laughter, to prevent any rational scrutiny of such an irrational process. But satirists and picaresque novelists have subjected these phenomena to their fierce scrutiny nonetheless. Grimmelshausen's *Simplicissimus* is an honored ancestor of Céline's *Journey to the End of Night,* and the king of Brobdingnag's pronouncement on European history still reverberates in our ears with an eerie relevance to modern contitions. The Black Humorists of today, of course, have found the fields of Mars as fertile as ever. *Catch-22* and *Dr. Strangelove* are among the triumphs of modern comic fiction. Thus it should not surprise us to find that two of Kurt Vonnegut's strongest performances deal with modern war: one with World War II, and one with the scientific discovery of an ultimate weapon.

CAT'S CRADLE AND *MOTHER NIGHT*

These two works will serve well to indicate the range and quality of Vonnegut's achievement to date and also will help to reinforce the distinction I have been trying to make between the modern fabulator's comedy of extremity and the method of traditional satire. The need to insist on this distinction is demonstrated continually, but I can illustrate it by citing a retrospective review of Vonnegut's work which appeared in the *New Republic* between the time when I wrote most of this chapter and the moment I am writing these words:

> And so goes Vonnegut's most powerful writing. All the anger, the shame, the shock, the guilt, the compassion, the irony, the control to produce great satire are *there*. . . . Why, then, does Vonnegut settle for such lovely, literate amusing attacks upon such simple targets as scientists, engineers, computer technicians, religion, the American Legion, artists, company picnics?

These words are a comment on a passage from the introduction to *Mother Night*, which will be quoted below, but they are meant as a reaction to all of Vonnegut's work, and could serve as a typical reaction to much of Black Humor. The review from which I have taken this criticism is long and favorable, but the reviewer is finally baffled by Vonnegut's refusal to turn his material into satire. Such a reaction, it seems to me, is clearly better than assuming either that Vonnegut has produced works of satire or that he is trying to and failing. But it is still an unfortunate reaction and, in a word, wrong. It is based, I should judge, on the assumption that satire is "better" than comedy. Why anyone should assume this, I do not know, though I suspect such an assumption goes along with a belief that the world is sick and the satirist can cure it by rubbing its nose in the filth it produces. This assumption is one that I want to reject. The world, in any fair historical perspective, is about as sick or healthy as it has been. These times are perhaps more dangerous than some moments in the past, because man's weapons are stronger, but that goes for his weapons against disease as well as for his weapons against life. But whether the world is especially sick, now, or not, there is no evidence that satire ever cured any human ailment, or any social disease either. In fact the whole notion of "great satire" seems rather suspect from this point of view. What *are* the great satires? And what are the hard targets they attack? Is Dr. Pangloss a hard target? Or Stalinist Communism? Even Jonathan Swift's finest achievement, the fourth book of *Gulliver's Travels*, is hard to call a great satire, precisely because its greatness is problematic and not satiric at all.

If I tried to pin down the nature of Vonnegut's fabulation—to find a phrase more descriptive than Black Humor and more precise—I would, borrowing a phrase Hugh Kenner used in another connection, call Vonnegut's work stoical comedy. Or perhaps I would go one step further and call it Epicurean comedy—if I could take my definition of Epicureanism from Walter Pater's elaborate fabulation on that subject. Like Pater's *Marius*, Vonnegut's works exhibit an affection for this world and a desire to improve it—but not much hope for improvement. (In making this suggestion toward a name for Vonnegut's fabulation, I do not mean to suggest that it resembles Pater's work in any respect. The slow, dreamy movement of *Marius* is a far cry from Vonnegut's crisp deftness. If we can call Vonnegut's work Epicurean comedy, let us be sure to put the emphasis on the noun—he is a comic artist first and last.)

In *Cat's Cradle* Vonnegut brings his comic perspective to bear on contemporary aspects of the old collision between science and religion. The book is dominated by two characters who are offstage for the most part: a brilliant scientist and the founder of a new religion. The scientist, "Nobel prize physicist Felix Hoenikker," is presented as a child-like innocent who is finally as amoral as only an innocent child can be. He is a "father" of the atomic bomb (rather more of a father to it than to his three children) and he finally develops a much more potent device—*ice-nine*—which can (and does) freeze all the liquid on this watery globe. One of his children tells the narrator this anecdote about him:

> For instance, do you know the story about Father on the day they first tested a bomb out at Alamagordo? After the thing went off, after it was a sure thing that America could wipe out a city with just one bomb, a scientist turned to Father and said, "Science has now known sin." And do you know what Father said? He said, "What is sin?"

This anecdote parallels that told of the jungle doctor by *his* son, which I quoted earlier. The contrast between the aware humanity of the one and the terrible innocence of the other is pointed up by the parallel structure of the anecdotes. The doctor, however, is a minor figure, almost eclipsed by the major opposition between the sinless scientist and the distinctly fallen religious prophet, Bokonon. As the scientist finds the truth that kills, the prophet looks for a saving lie. On the title page of the first of the *Books of Bokonon,* the bible of this new religion, is the abrupt warning: "Don't be a fool! Close this book at once! It is nothing but *foma!*" *Foma* are lies. Bokonon, a Negro from Tobago in the Caribbean, has invented a religion for the island of San Lorenzo (where he arrived, a castaway, after considerable experience of the world). His "Bible" includes some parable-like anecdotes, some epigrams, and many psalm-like calypsos, such as this one:

> I wanted all things
> To seem to make some sense,
> So we all could be happy, yes,
> Instead of tense.
> And I made up lies
> So that they all fit nice,
> And I made this sad world
> A par-a-dise.

The epigraph to Vonnegut's book reads this way:

> Nothing in this book is true.
> "Live by the *foma** that make you brave and
> kind and healthy and happy."
>
> *The Books of Bokonon. 1:5*
> *harmless untruths

The author's disclaimer is partly a parody of the usual "any resemblance to actual persons . . ." hedge against libel suits. But it is also a way of encircling Bokononism and making *Cat's Cradle* a repository of religious untruth itself. The very confrontation in the book between science and religion is aimed at developing the "cruel paradox" that lies at the center of Bokononist thought as it lies at the center of our world: "the heartbreaking necessity of lying about reality, and the heartbreaking impossibility of lying about it."

The ideas I have been trying to sketch out briefly here are only the string for Vonnegut's cat's cradle. The life of the book is in its movement, the turns of plot, of character, and of phrase which give it vitality. Vonnegut's prose has the same virtues as his characterization and plotting. It is deceptively simple, suggestive of the ordinary, but capable of startling and illuminating twists and turns. He uses the rhetorical potential of the short sentence and short paragraph better than anyone now writing, often getting a rich comic or dramatic effect by isolating a single sentence in a separate paragraph or excerpting a phrase from context for a bizarre chapter-heading. The apparent simplicity and ordinariness of his writing mask its efficient power, so that we are often startled when Vonnegut pounces on a tired platitude or cliché like a benevolent mongoose and shakes new life into it: "Son . . . someday this will all be yours."

Despite his mastery of the prose medium, and a sense of the ridiculous which is always on duty, Vonnegut never abandons himself to relentless verbal cleverness of the Peter De Vries sort. Sometimes we may wrongly suspect him of this kind of self-indulgence, as in the opening sentence of *Cat's Cradle*—"Call me Jonah"—which seems like a gratuitous though delightful parody of the opening of *Moby Dick*, until we realize that by invoking Jonah and *his* whale, along with the biblical Leviathan, Vonnegut is preparing us for a story on the Job theme, with the anti-Joblike conclusion provided by Bokonon's advice to the narrator on the proper posture for death in response to the plague of *ice-nine*.

Vonnegut's prose always serves his vision and helps to make narrative structures of that vision. This process is illustrated nicely by a longish passage from the introduction he wrote in 1966 for the new edition of *Mother Night*. In it he speaks of his actual experience as a prisoner of war in Dresden, in prose which has the lucidity of the best journalism enriched with the poetic resources of a born storyteller. (One falls naturally into the word "speaks" in discussing this prose, which gives a strong sense of a voice behind the words.)

> There were about a hundred of us in our particular work group, and we were put out as contract labor to a factory that was making a vitamin-enriched malt syrup for pregnant women. It tasted like thin honey laced with hickory smoke. It was good. I wish I had some right now. And the city was lovely, highly ornamented, like Paris, and untouched by war. It was supposedly an "open" city, not to be attacked since there were no troop concentrations or war industries there.

But high explosives were dropped on Dresden by American and British planes on the night of February 13, 1945, just about twenty-one years ago, as I now write. There were no particular targets for the bombs. The hope was that they would create a lot of kindling and drive firemen underground.

And then hundreds of thousands of tiny incendiaries were scattered over the kindling, like seeds on freshly turned loam. More bombs were dropped to keep firemen in their holes, and all the little fires grew, joining one another, became one apocalyptic flame. Hey presto: fire storm. It was the largest massacre in European history, by the way. And so what?

We didn't get to see the fire storm. We were in a cool meatlocker under a slaughterhouse with our six guards and ranks and ranks of dressed cadavers of cattle, pigs, horses, and sheep. We heard the bombs walking around up there. Now and then there would be a gentle shower of calcimine. If we had gone above to take a look, we would have been turned into artifacts characteristic of fire storms: seeming pieces of charred firewood two or three feet long—ridiculously small human beings, or jumbo fried grasshoppers, if you will.

The malt syrup factory was gone. Everything was gone but the cellars where 135,000 Hansels and Gretels had been baked like gingerbread men. So we were put to work as corpse miners, breaking into shelters, bringing bodies out. And I got to see many German types of all ages as death had found them, usually with valuables in their laps. Sometimes relatives would come to watch us dig. They were interesting, too.

So much for Nazis and me.

If I'd been born in Germany, I suppose I would have *been* a Nazi, bopping Jews and gypsies and Poles around, leaving boots sticking out of snowbanks, warming myself with my secretly virtuous insides. So it goes.

The admission at the end of this passage suggests one reason why Vonnegut and other Black Humorists write the way they do. And in this respect they are close to the traditional satirists. They would like to prevent us from "warming ourselves with our secretly virtuous insides" while we condone the freezing of others. And as long as we persist in fire-bombing other human beings they would like to blow our cool for us. Comically but relentlessly they seek to make us thoughtful—in all the senses of that most sensible word.

Mother Night is the autobiography of a fictional hero / criminal of World War II, Howard W. Campbell, Jr. This Campbell is a hero or criminal depending on how one looks at him. He is an American who stayed in Germany during the war to broadcast for the Nazis a special line of virulent anti-semitism and other hateful stuff: a Nazi hero, an American traitor. But in his broadcasts he was secretly sending back coded messages for American intelligence: an American hero, a Nazi traitor. The novel begins with Campbell in prison—"a nice new jail in old Jerusalem"—awaiting trial along with Adolph Eichmann. As Campbell unravels his life story we begin to find out how he got there and to worry about what will happen to him. These affairs are managed very skillfully. With perfect aplomb, Vonnegut juggles three distinct time schemes: the present, the past of the war period, and the past of the post-war period; and three distinct settings: Israel, Germany, and New York. The effect of this juggling is superbly controlled. It operates not so as to call attention to the juggler himself but so as to combine the narrative suspense involved in resolving these actions with a moral and intellectual suspense generated by them. From *what* and *how* we progress to *why* and *why not*—but without ceasing to care about *what* and *how*. I am not going to give away the lines of narrative development here. The reader deserves the pleasure of experiencing them firsthand, without warning. But I will give away one of the morals because Vonnegut himself mentions it in the first paragraphs of his new introduction:

> This is the only story of mine whose moral I know. I don't think it is a marvelous moral; I simply happen to know what it is: We are what we pretend to be, so we must be careful about what we pretend to be.

In Vonnegut, as in his contemporaries, we do not find the rhetoric of moral certainty, which has generally been a distinguishing characteristic of the satirical tradition. The writers of modern dark comedy do not seek the superior position of the traditional moralists. Nor do they point to other times and customs as repositories of moral values, or to any traditional system as The Law. Even in essaying to abstract a moral from his own book, Vonnegut makes no special claim for its virtues, or his. The book itself must be the test. Our experience of it must be satisfying and healthy. If this is so, then it may nourish our consciences without requiring reduction to a formula. My feeling is that, far from manifesting sickness (as some critics seem to feel it does), Black Humor is a sign of life and health.

Vonnegut, in his fiction, is doing what the most serious writers always do. He is helping, in Joyce's phrase, "to create the conscience of the race." What race? Human certainly, not American or German or any other abstraction from humanity. Just as pure romance provides us with necessary psychic exercise, intellectual comedy like Vonnegut's offers us moral stimulation— not fixed ethical positions which we can complacently assume, but such thoughts as exercise our consciences and help us keep our humanity in shape, ready to respond to the humanity of others.

Mother Night, Cat's Cradle, and the Crimes of Our Time
Jerome Klinkowitz*

Kurt Vonnegut, Jr., through six novels and more than forty stories, has crafted for his readers an exceedingly mad world. He holds his own with the

*Reprinted by permission from *The Vonnegut Statement*, ed. Jerome Klinkowitz and John Somer (New York: Delacorte Press / Seymore Lawrence, 1973), 158–77.

black humorists, matching Yossarians with Howard Campbells, Guy Grands with Eliot Rosewaters, and Sebastian Dangerfields with Malachi Constants. But unlike Joseph Heller, Vonnegut is prolific, tracing his vision through many different human contexts. He surpasses Terry Southern by striking all limits from human absurdity: destruction by nuclear fission is for Vonnegut the most passé of apocalypses. Moreover, he teases us with a Mod Yoknapatawpha County; "Frank Wirtanen" and "Bernard B. O'Hare" (originally characters in his third novel, *Mother Night*) and others appear again and again, always (as befits the modern county) in a maddening metamorphosis of roles. Favorite cities such as "Rosewater, Indiana" and "Ilium, New York" are storehouses for the paraphernalia of middle-class life which so delight Vonnegut, whose religion is one of cultural value rather than geographical place. But unlike Southern and Bruce Jay Friedman, who mock such culture in the sociosatiric mode of Evelyn Waugh (Southern scripted *The Loved One* for the movies), Vonnegut uses his roots more like John Barth uses Maryland: interest lies beneath the surface, and the surface itself is constantly changing. Vonnegut, in short, demands independent investigation. One finds at the end of Vonnegut's vision a "fine madness" indeed, but a madness at the same time more clinical and more cosmic than found in conventional black humor—or, indeed, nearly anywhere else.

Perhaps a reason for the long critical neglect of Kurt Vonnegut is that his vision is superficially akin to that of Orwell, Huxley, and others who have written dolefully of the mechanical millennium to come. His first novel, *Player Piano*, warns of the familiar *Brave New World* future, while the much-praised title story of *Welcome to the Monkey House*, with its Ethical Suicide Parlors and waning sentimental romanticism, recalls Evelyn Waugh's alternatives of "Love Among the Ruins" and *Scott-King's Modern Europe*. Karen and Charles Wood have shown how Vonnegut's material moves beyond the bounds of science fiction, the label used so long to restrain his recognition. But to justify a reputation for Vonnegut, one must also recognize the essential elements in his technique which surpass the efforts of a black humorist like Terry Southern, and understand the complexity of his vision.

Both technique and theme are well represented by two novels published well into his career: *Mother Night* and *Cat's Cradle*. In *Mother Night*, Vonnegut's panorama of the Nazi world is a black humorist's dream: all the stuff of middle-class life is present, but the people in the picture are not G. E. flaks or Indiana brewers but rather honest-to-goodness "criminals against humanity." Rudolph Hoess, Heinrich Himmler, and Adolf Eichmann himself (the book was published in 1962 when Eichmann was in the news) are presented to the reader, who gasps and giggles like a tourist on a Beverly Hills sightseeing bus. And Vonnegut exploits our fascination by giving us these men in their utter banality. This, of course, is orthodox black-humor technique, and signals Vonnegut's departure from the standard humanistic approach to the subject of the rise and fall of the Third Reich: in all of William L. Shirer's heavily documented book there is not a single Ping-Pong tournament, which is one of the things Vonnegut gives us.[1] But the absurdity of this world yields more than an affectatious glimpse behind the scenes, as Terry Southern offers in *Dr. Strangelove*. Life in Vonnegut's Nazi realm is more properly absurd: the hero, Howard W. Campbell, Jr., acts out an Ionesco drama as he broadcasts vital secrets to the Allies in coded gestures he cannot understand. Vonnegut toys with ironic *déjà-vu* as the documents of 1960's "White Christian Minutemen" are recognized as crafted a generation earlier by Howard Campbell when in the service of the Nazis. The morbid dance of life reaches its black-humor climax when no less than the neo-Nazi journalist Rev. Doctor Lionel Jason David Jones, D.D.S., D.D., the unfrocked Paulist Father Patrick Keeley, Robert Sterling Wilson (the "Black Fuehrer of Harlem"), Russian agent Iona Potapov, Legion Post Americanism Chairman, Lt. Bernard B. O'Hare, O.S.S. spy-maker Col. Frank Wirtanen, and various FBI agents and sundry nineteen-year-old Minutemen from New Jersey battle over the body and soul of Vonnegut's hero.

Neither does Vonnegut's absurd humor stop here. Terry Southern's *The Magic Christian* is equal in single absurdities; Vonnegut surpasses him by working in triplets. Campbell's wartime buddy Heinz Schildknecht is not merely comically robbed of his dearer-than-life motorcycle; on the second turn Heinz shows up as a gardener for a rich expatriate Nazi in Ireland, courting fame as an authority on the death of Hilter ("Hello out there, Heinz. . . . What were you doing in Hitler's bunker—looking for your motorcycle and your best friend?" [p. 89]), and on the third is revealed to have been a secret Israeli agent all the time, gathering evidence for Campbell's prosecution. Vonnegut's is a spiraling, madly rebounding absurdity. A hangman's noose suggestively placed in Campbell's apartment by the American Legion is not merely laughed at and discarded. Instead, "Resi put the noose in the ash can, where it was found the next morning by a garbageman named Lazlo Szombathy. Szombathy actually hanged himself with it—but that is another story" (p. 112). Double turn: Szombathy is despondent because as a refugee he is barred from practicing his profession of veterinary science. Triple turn: Szombathy is particularly despondent because he has a cure for cancer, and is ignored. Absurdity to the third power rules the entire world: not only is Campbell's dramatic work pirated and plagiarized by a looting Soviet soldier, but the best of the loot turns out to be Campbell's secret and sensitive love memoirs, which at once become the *Fanny Hill* of postwar Russia. Third turn: the soldier is caught and punished, but not for plagiarism: " 'Bodovskov had begun to replenish the trunk with magic of his own,' said Wirtanen. 'The police found a two-thousand-page satire on the Red Army, written in a style distinctly un-Bodovskovian. For that un-Bodovskovian behavior, Bodovskov was shot' " (p. 157). Other examples abound: Arndt Klopfer, official Reich chancellery portrait photographer, turns up in Mexico City as the country's greatest brewer. But not for long; he's really a Russian spy. We are teased with the knowledge that one of the world's greatest admirers of Lincoln's *Gettysburg Address* is Paul Joseph Goebbels. But *the* greatest admirer, literally brought to tears by the document, is Adolf Hitler. Triple turn: the most gleeful fan of Campbell's anti-Semitic broadcasts is Franklin Delano Roosevelt.

The triplet madness, besides being an ingenious technique, serves to introduce Vonnegut's more serious theme. George Kraft, alias Iona Potapov, becomes at one and the same time Howard Campbell's most sincere friend plus the agent who is working most seriously to engineer his exploitation, torture, and death in Moscow. Moreover (triplets again), Kraft is widely acknowledged as the best of modern artists ("surely the first man to under- stand the whole of modern art," according to a *Herald Tribune* review sup- plied by the Haifa Institute). Others besides Kraft-Potapov lead double lives. One of Campbell's Israeli prison guards is Arpad Kovacs, who spent the war as a Jewish spy among the S.S. in Germany. He boasts to Campbell:

> "I was such a pure and terrifying Aryan that they even put me in a special detachment. Its mission was to find out how the Jews always knew what the S.S. was going to do next. There was a leak somewhere, and we were out to stop it." He looked bitter and affronted, remembering it, even though he had been that leak (p. 10).

Campbell himself, of course, had lived a double life for the years of World War II. He was, at the same time, *the best* Nazi radio propagandist and *the best* spy in the service of the Allies. He understands this apparently contra- dictory situation, even finding the clinical name for it: " 'I've always known what I did. I've always been able to live with what I did. How? Through that simple and widespread boon to modern mankind—schizophrenia' " (p. 136). Schizophrenia indeed seems the proper name for the madness devouring Vonnegut's world. When federal agents raid the basement quarters of the White Christian Minutemen, an incredulous G-man wonders how the pro- fessedly anti-Catholic and anti-Negro Reverend Jones can have as his two most loyal cohorts Father Patrick Keeley and Robert Sterling Wilson, the black Fuehrer of Harlem, the latter who announces plans for killing all whites. Campbell's explanation is worth seeing at length:

> I have never seen a more sublime demonstration of the totalitarian mind, a mind which might be likened unto a system of gears whose teeth have been filed off at random. Such a snaggle-toothed thought machine, driven by a standard or even a substandard libido, whirls with the jerky, noisy, gaudy pointlessness of a cuckoo clock in Hell.
>
> The boss G-man concluded wrongly that there were no teeth on the gears in the mind of Jones. "You're completely crazy," he said.
>
> Jones wasn't completely crazy. The dismaying thing about the classic totalitarian mind is that any given gear, though mutilated, will have at its circumference unbroken sequences of teeth that are immaculately main- tained, that are exquisitely machined.
>
> Hence the cuckoo clock in Hell—keeping perfect time for eight min-

utes and thirty-three seconds, jumping ahead fourteen minutes, keeping
perfect time for six seconds, jumping ahead two seconds, keeping perfect
time for two hours and one second, then jumping ahead a year.

The missing teeth, of course, are simple, obvious truths, truths available and comprehensible even to ten-year-olds, in most cases.

The willful filing off of gear teeth, the willful doing without certain
obvious pieces of information—

That was how a household as contradictory as one composed of Jones,
Father Keeley, Vice-Bundesfuehrer Krapptauer, and the Black Fuehrer
could exist in relative harmony—

That was how my father-in-law could contain in one mind an indifference toward slave women and love for a blue vase—

That was how Rudolf Hoess, Commandant of Auschwitz, could alter-
nate over the loudspeakers of Auschwitz great music and calls for corpse-
carriers—

That was how Nazi Germany could sense no important differences
between civilization and hydrophobia—

That is the closest I can come to explaining the legions, the nations of
lunatics I've seen in my time. And for me to attempt such a mechanical
explanation is perhaps a reflection of the father whose son I was. Am.
When I pause to think about it, which is rarely, I am, after all, the son of an
engineer (pp. 168–70).

The key to Vonnegut's vision, however, is not merely this clinical diagnosis of the illness of an age. The traditional desire to maintain the integrity of
self in the face of a too chaotic world has always been a schizophrenia of sorts.
Faced with the pressures of Nazi Germany, Campbell takes a solace not
unusual in Western culture: he retreats first to art, and then to love. Crucial
to this solace is that man have a self to flee to, a self which cannot be reached
and abused by others. Like any fictive artist of the ages, Campbell offers "lies
told for the sake of artistic effect." His self knows that on their deepest level
his fictions are "the most beguiling forms of truth" (p. ix), but the surface is
all art. Hence in the thirties, when Hilter's war machine is building, Campbell is the apparent escapist, scripting "medieval romances about as political
as chocolate *éclairs*" (p. 26). When forced as a spy into the service of the
Nazis, he finds refuge in parody and satire. "I had hoped, as a broadcaster, to
be merely ludicrous" (p. 122). Campbell's second traditional refuge is that of
love, where the escapist and even schizoid tendencies are more marked.
From the terrors of daily social existence Vonnegut's hero flees to *Das Reich
der Zwei*. "It was going to show how a pair of lovers in a world gone mad
could survive by being loyal only to a nation composed of themselves—a
nation of two" (p. 27). Its geography, he admits, "didn't go much beyond the
bounds of our great double bed" (p. 33). In both artistic and emotional form,
Campbell's theme becomes "Reflections on Not Participating in Current
Events" (p. 92), and he honestly states that "My narcotic was what had got
me through the war; it was an ability to let my emotions be stirred by only
one thing—my love for Helga" (p. 36). Art and love are two traditional ways

of coping with the chaos of the outside world. Come what may, the self should be inviolate, and it is here that Campbell places his hope.

Vonnegut's point, however, is that in this modern world the self can indeed be violated, and is so at every turn. Campbell's love is the first casualty. Helga is captured on the Russian front, but this alone is no more than a challenge to Campbell's romantic imagination. He will nurture his grief and celebrate his melancholy. Modern espionage, however, not only mocks his grief, but uses him to do the mocking.

> This news, that I had broadcast the coded announcement of my Helga's disappearance, broadcast it without even knowing what I was doing, somehow upset me more than anything in the whole adventure. It upsets me even now. Why, I don't know.
>
> It represented, I suppose, a wider separation of my several selves than even I can bear to think about.
>
> At that climactic moment in my life, when I had to suppose that my Helga was dead, I would have liked to mourn as an agonized soul, indivisible. But no. One part of me told the world of the tragedy in code. The rest of me did not even know that the announcement was being made (p. 140).

Neither will history let his love rest. The intimate diary of his life with Helga is plagiarized and made into pornography, complete with fourteen plates in lifelike color. "That's how I feel right now," Campbell admits, "like a pig that's been taken apart, who's had experts find a use for every part. By God—I think they even found a use for my squeal" (pp. 155–56).

Art is no safer a refuge. Campbell had hoped, as a propagandist, to be satirically ludicrous—on the one hand, it would cover his self-respect, while on the other it might indeed, by *reductio ad absurdum*, bring down the Nazi regime in gales of laughter. "But this is a hard world to be ludicrous in," Campbell learns, "with so many human beings so reluctant to laugh, so incapable of thought, so eager to believe and snarl and hate. So many people wanted to believe me!" (p. 122).[2] At the end of the war Campbell is confronted with the awful possibility that his intended satire may have in fact prolonged the war. His high-ranking father-in-law confides, " 'I realized that almost all the ideas that I hold now, that make me unashamed of anything I may have felt or done as a Nazi, came not from Hilter, not from Goebbels, not from Himmler—but from you.' He took my hand. 'You alone kept me from concluding that Germany had gone insane' " (p. 75). Campbell reflects on the fate of his several selves: "The part of me that wanted to tell the truth got turned into an expert liar! The lover in me got turned into a pornographer! The artist in me got turned into an ugliness such as the world has rarely seen before" (p. 156). Throughout the book Campbell has been priding himself on his integrity. He has devoted a full chapter to the lunatic Reverend Doctor Jones "in order to contrast with myself a race-baiter who is ignorant and insane. I am neither ignorant nor insane" (p. 52). Unlike the trite and banal Eichmann, Campbell knew right from wrong, "the only advantage" being "that I can sometimes laugh when the Eichmanns can see nothing funny" (pp. 126–27). But the self, Campbell finally learns, offers no refuge. Art and love are impossibilities, themselves easily manipulated into cruel absurdities. The self is not inviolate; there is no place to hide.

To this point Vonnegut is on firm if traditional ground. Howard Campbell has in these terms learned no more than Winston Smith did in *1984*, and Vonnegut's vision seems one with Wylie Sypher's: the loss of the self in modern art and literature (and love) is exactly what has happened to our hero.[3] Vonnegut, however, has more to say. His vision extends backward as well as to the fore. How has the modern world come to be such a chamber of horrors? Where lies the cause for the loss of the self? Vonnegut answers that the very cause may be found in the traditional notion of the inviolate self. Because men have abandoned all else and have selfishly fled to their selves as the romantic center of the universe, when the self collapses, everything, quite literally, is lost. This is what Vonnegut's character finally recognizes. Campbell, after all, does not follow through on his offer to surrender to the Israelis and accept punishment for his crimes against humanity. At the last moment, on the eve of his trial, when in fact conclusive evidence for his innocence has come with the day's mail, he makes his decision: "I think that tonight is the night *I* will hang Howard W. Campbell, Jr., for crimes against *himself*" (p. 202, italics added). In spite of all humanistic arguments to the contrary, Campbell sees the absurd use that he has made of his self, and the evil which has come of it. Vonnegut's indictment, in his own signed headnote to the story, is no less severe: "This book is rededicated to Howard W. Campbell, Jr., a man who served evil too openly and good too secretly, the crime of his times" (p. xii).

Mother Night remains, to date, Vonnegut's only book with an explicitly stated moral: "We are what we pretend to be, so we must be careful about what we pretend to be" (p. v). The author has been clear in his condemnations: art and love are selfish, false escapes. But if one is "careful," can there be a valid pretense? *Cat's Cradle*, Vonnegut's next novel, presents a tempting program. Its opening disclaimer is also an imperative: "Nothing in this book is true. / Live by the *foma* that make you brave and kind and healthy and happy" (p.[v]). "Foma" are the magic elements, correcting the rampant cowardices, cruelties, sicknesses, and sadnesses of *Mother Night*. A comparison to the "soma" of *Brave New World* is alarming but intentionally immediate: sounding similar, working similar, Vonnegut dares to confront us with something too good to believe: a pain pill for the ills of the world.

Mother Night presents the destructive pretenses that make modern life a nightmare; *Cat's Cradle*, however, offers *foma* as "*harmless* untruths" [italics added]. They are the key elements in the book's religion, Bokononism. Why is religion a valid pretense, whereas love and art are not? The answer lies with the peculiar state of modern man, and with his need for a unique religion. Other modern novelists, particularly Saul Bellow, have written of the "romantic over-valuation of the Self"[4] which most terrifyingly makes "each of us . . . responsible for his own salvation."[5] But Vonnegut's Bokononism is a religion after alienation, for it seeks a way for man to be comfortable in a world he no longer wishes to admit is his own. The "lies" of this particular religion are purgative, restoring man's happiness, balance, and comfort. Bokononism reorders our notion of the finite world so that we may accept it, rather than simply rebel against it in fruitless anger. It is the first step toward accommodating oneself to the schizophrenic reality given full treatment in *Slaughterhouse-Five*.

The danger that Vonnegut actively courts in *Cat's Cradle* is religion's becoming an opiate. His writer-narrator is told that "When a man becomes a writer . . . he takes on a sacred obligation to produce beauty and enlightenment and comfort at top speed" (p. 189). The writer accepts the methodology of religion by seeking the ultimate meaning of things. Bokononism cooperates by teaching that "humanity is organized into teams, teams that do God's Will without ever discovering what they are doing. Such a team is called a *karass*" (p. 14). Therefore the writer tries to include in his book "as many members of my *karass* as possible," and "to examine strong hints as to what on Earth we, collectively, have been up to" (p. 16). If one sought the reason for the madly twisted life of Howard W. Campbell, Jr., the answer might be found in *Cat's Cradle*: " 'If you find your life tangled with somebody else's life for no very logical reason,' writes Bokonon, 'that person may be a member of your *karass*' " (p. 14). Hence the writer studies the affairs of Dr. Felix Hoenikker, for, as his memorial states, "THE IMPORTANCE OF THIS ONE MAN IN THE HISTORY OF MANKIND IS INCALCULABLE" (p. 53).

Bokononism follows tradition in its eschatological imperative; it departs, however, when at the same time it calls any such search absurd:

> "In the beginning, God created the earth, and he looked upon it in His cosmic loneliness.
>
> "And God said, 'Let Us make living creatures out of mud, so the mud can see what We have done.' And God created every living creature that now moveth, and one was man. Mud as man alone could speak. God leaned close as man sat up, looked around, and spoke. Man blinked. 'What is the *purpose* of all this?' he asked politely.
>
> " 'Everything must have a purpose?' asked God.
>
> " 'Certainly,' said man.
>
> " 'Then I leave it to you to think of one for all this,' said God. And He went away" (pp. 214–15).

The first axiom of this religion, then, is that if there is to be an ultimate meaning for things, it is up to man's art to find it. But as we know from *Mother Night*, his art can be selfish and escapist. Vonnegut's writer is at one point mistaken for a drug salesman, and is then encouraged to write a book for "people who are dying or in terrible pain." The writer suggests an impro-

visation on the Twenty-Third Psalm, and is told "Bokonon tried to overhaul
it" but "found out that he couldn't change a word" (pp. 128–29).

Whether religion is an opiate, and whether the "consolations of literature" are little more than the wares of drug salesmen, must be decided by
comparison with men's other eschatological artifices. For consolation Felix
Hoenikker played games: one resulted in the chance invention of the atom
bomb, another in the creation of *ice-nine*. His daughter Angela's "one escape" is playing weirdly authentic blues clarinet, but "such music from such a
woman could only be a case of schizophrenia or demonic possession" (p. 150),
and from the lessons of *Mother Night* must be dismissed. Little Newt paints,
but his works appear "sticky nets of human futility hung up on a moonless
night to dry." Art lies, we are told again. Recalling the game of cat's cradle
his father played with him, Newt comments:

> "No wonder kids grow up crazy. A cat's cradle is nothing but a bunch
> of X's between somebody's hands, and little kids look and look at all those
> X's . . ."
> "And?"
> *"No damn cat, and no damn cradle"* (p. 137).

Newt is objecting that the cat's cradle has excluded the real, or the
finite. The necessary artifice is one which will handle the finite on its own
terms, without recourse to "lies." Finite existence in San Lorenzo is depressingly futile, and so "the religion became the one instrument of hope" (p.
143). McCabe and Bokonon, founders of the Republic, "did not succeed in
raising what is generally thought of as the standard of living," the writer is
told. "The truth was that life was as short and brutish and mean as ever." But
Vonnegut's world cannot remain Hobbesian; Bokononism provides a system
whereby "people didn't have to pay as much attention to the awful truth. As
the living legend of the cruel tyrant in the city and the gentle holy man in the
jungle grew, so, too, did the happiness of the people grow. They were all
employed full time as actors in a play they understood, that any human being
anywhere could understand and applaud" (p. 144). The writer learns that "for
the joy of the people, Bokonon was always to be chased, was never to be
caught" (p. 178). Vonnegut speaks elsewhere in *Cat's Cradle* of "the brain-
less ecstasy of a volunteer fireman" (p. 157), anticipating the role Eliot
Rosewater will find most comfortable in *God Bless You, Mr. Rosewater*.
Here the idealized, sustained game is part of a "dynamic tension" which
argues that "good societies could be built only by pitting good against evil,
and by keeping the tension between the two high at all times" (p. 90). Not
surprisingly, we learn that as a student in Episcopal schools Bokonon was
"more interested in ritual than most" (p. 91).

Vonnegut's religion is a type unto itself: heretical, in fact, but to a
particular purpose. Within the situation of San Lorenzo one finds both tragic
and comic possibilities; it is the daily life which is tragic, however, while its
religion is comic. Nathan Scott, in relating the comic to the religious, has

remarked that only comedy can tell us "the whole truth."[6] When the whole truth is not told, when a salient element of reality is denied concrete existence, we have the heresy of Gnosticism, which posits "a God unknowable by nature . . . and utterly incommensurable with the created order."[7] Vonnegut's impetus is in the opposite direction. The finite is granted a real existence, rather than being an imperfect shadow of some higher ideal. Pushed far enough, such doctrine would constitute the heresy of Manicheanism. The value of Bokononism, however, is that it makes possible what Scott terms the "cosmic *katharsis*," which involves "such a restoration of our confidence in the realm of finitude as enables us to see the daily occasions of our earth-bound career as being not irrelevant inconveniences but as possible roads into what is ultimately significant in life."[8] A Gnostic approach to the evils of San Lorenzo would indeed encourage a flight from "meaningless" finitude. But such flight would be hopeless, as Vonnegut demonstrated in *Mother Night*. Modern man, romantically placed at the center of the universe and responsible for his own salvation, cannot flee from evil, even into himself; for in himself he will find only evil's deepest source. Vonnegut's alternative in Bokononism is a recognition of the finite for what it is: an external repository of certain elements, some of which may be evil but none of which are egocentrically identified with Man. Wylie Sypher, whose discussion of the loss of the self coincides with the theme of *Mother Night*, makes a plea for a new fiction which is answered in *Cat's Cradle*. Sypher speaks of "our need for unheroic heroism" or "anonymous humanism"[9] which will relieve man of his untenable position as center of the universe, a position which the terrible amounts of evil wrought in the twentieth century have caused man to become alienated from his very self. Bokononism is a religion after alienation because it carefully removes evil from the self and deposits it in a finitude granted real existence, not a finitude vaguely (and Platonically) reflective of Ideal Man.

Bokononism is not an opiate, nor is it irresponsible. It is not a turning away at all, but rather an acceptance of the finite for what it is, as part of the whole truth. The single identified saint in *Cat's Cradle* is Julian Castle, who "forestalled all references to his possible saintliness by talking. out of the corner of his mouth like a movie gangster" (p. 138). Castle heroically saves countless lives, but can also appreciate the grotesqueness of his situation; as Robert Scholes agrees, "an excess of the horrible is faced and defeated by the only friend reason can rely on in such cases: laughter."[10] If evil is securely located in a coexisting finitude, there is no compulsive need "to concentrate on [Castle's] saintly deeds and ignore entirely the satanic things he thought and said" (p. 140). Bokononism is one religion which accommodates the finite. In a whimsical manner, a psalmlike "Calypso" reminds us that "We do, doodley do . . . What we must, muddily must . . . Until we bust, bodily bust" (p. 216). And the last rites of this curious Church simply affirm, "I loved everything I saw" (p. 181).

The theme of *Cat's Cradle* is repeated in Vonnegut's later work, where, perhaps because of his growing prominence,[11] he writes more directly and even personally. To a new edition of *Mother Night* in 1966 Vonnegut added an introduction, speaking not as "editor" of the "American edition of the confessions of Howard W. Campbell, Jr." (p. ix), but as an individual who has had "personal experience with Nazi monkey business" (p. v). In *Slaughterhouse-Five* Vonnegut includes a great deal of autobiography and comment as the first chapter of his otherwise fictional work. Here he contrasts his anthropology courses at the University of Chicago, where he was taught that man is a benign creature, with his after-school work as a police reporter. The deliberately retrospective preface to *Welcome to the Monkey House* features the same duality; recalling his brother's adventures with a newborn son and his sister's dignified death from cancer, Vonnegut states: "And I realize now that the two main themes of my novels were stated by my siblings: 'Here I am cleaning the shit off of practically everything' and 'No pain' (p. xiv). When in *Slaughterhouse-Five* Vonnegut's father accuses him that "you never wrote a story with a villain in it" (p. 7), we need not fear that Vonnegut has been an irresponsible jokester or even a blithe optimist. Indeed, Vonnegut's public pronouncement has been that he is "a total pessimist," and has been since the experiences of Dresden, Hiroshima, and Dachau.[12] Writing on the fall of Biafra, he admits that "joking was my response to misery that I can't do anything about,"[13] but he has also reminded us that "to weep is to make less the depth of grief."[14] The joking in Bokononism is not a palliative: instead it is a fundamental reordering of man's values, solving the problem which has made man uncomfortable as the center of the universe. Wylie Sypher decries egocentric romanticism, and charges that it has alienated man from himself; Vonnegut begs that we still trust "the most ridiculous superstition of all: that humanity is at the center of the universe,"[15] proving that to sustain such a position "all that is required is that we become less selfish than we are."[16] That selfishness, however, is strong enough to have spawned a heresy and determined man's expression in art. Shaping a new religion is no small achievement.

Despite their rogues' galleries of unpleasant incidents, both *Mother Night* and *Cat's Cradle* are finally optimistic works. Howard W. Campbell, Jr., commits not so many "crimes against humanity" as "crimes against himself," the latter which, once recognized, can be successfully and personally purged. *Cat's Cradle* goes a step farther by relieving man of his unbearable egocentric responsibility for the conditions of existence. Granted that the world can become absurd, and that any good life may be unliveable: at this point Vonnegut's man can responsibly bow out, having "the good manners to die" (p. 220), and with great composure and respectability "turn the humor back on the joker."[17] Modern life, for all its errors, has a great clarifying power in helping man find his proper place in the universe. Rightly positioned, the Vonnegut hero can honestly say of his life, "Everything was beautiful, and nothing hurt."[18]

Notes

1. The respected German historian Klaus Epstein harshly criticized Shirer's *The Rise and Fall of the Third Reich* ("Shirer's History of Nazi Germany," *Review of Politics*, 23 [1961], 230–45) because of its "curious inability to understand the nature of a modern totalitarian regime" (p. 230); Epstein singles out Shirer's failure to study "the entire domestic history of wartime Germany" (p. 236) as a key to understanding the "defiance of self-interest and sanity" (p. 239).

2. *The Goebbels Diaries*, ed. Louis P. Lochner (New York: Doubleday, 1948), contain a fascinating comment on Campbell's closest real-life counterpart: "The English speaker, Lord Haw Haw, is especially great at biting criticism, but in my opinion the time for spicy debate is past . . . During the first year of war the people still listen to the delivery; they admire the art and the spiritual qualities of the presentation. Today they want nothing but facts" (p. 227).

3. Wylie Sypher, *Loss of the Self in Modern Art and Literature* (New York: Random House, 1962).

4. Saul Bellow, "Recent American Fiction," lecture delivered under the auspices of the Gertrude Clarke Whittal Poetry and Literature Fund (Washington: Library of Congress, 1963). Reprinted in *Encounter*, 21 (November, 1963), 23.

5. Saul Bellow, *Dangling Man* (New York: New American Library, 1965 [first published in 1944]), p. 59.

6. Nathan Scott, "The Bias of Comedy and the Narrow Escape into Faith," *The Christian Scholar*, 44 (Spring, 1961), 20–21. Scott refers to Aldous Huxley's essay, "Tragedy and the Whole Truth."

7. Scott, p. 13.

8. Scott, p. 32.

9. See Sypher's last chapter, "The Anonymous Self: A Defensive Humanism," pp. 147–65.

10. Robert Scholes, *The Fabulators* (New York: Oxford, 1967), p. 43.

11. In the fall of 1965 Vonnegut began a two-year lectureship at the University of Iowa Writers Workshop, followed by a Guggenheim fellowship (1967–68) and a creative-writing post at Harvard University (1970–71).

12. Kurt Vonnegut, Jr., "Up Is Better Than Down" (commencement address at Bennington College, 1970), *Vogue* (August, 1, 1970), pp. 54, 144.

13. Kurt Vonnegut, Jr., "Biafra," *McCall's* (April, 1970), p. 135.

14. Vogue, P. 144. He quotes *Henry VI, Part Three*, II, i. l. 85.

15. *Vogue*, p. 144.

16. *Vogue*, p. 145.

17. Scholes, p. 44.

18. *Slaughterhouse-Five*, p. 106.

Tangled Up in You: A Playful
Reading of *Cat's Cradle*   John L. Simons*

> . . . the two most potent
> spiritual forces in contention
> today have nothing to do with
> nations, political parties or
> economic philosophies.
>
> The opposing forces are these:
> those who enjoy childlike play-
> fulness when they become adults
> and those who don't.
> —Kurt Vonnegut[1]

Cat's Cradle (1963) remains one of Kurt Vonnegut's least understood achievements. Sometimes the novel's complexity is underrated, as when Peter J. Reed writes, "Compared with the two preceding novels, it seems thinner in plot, more superficial and fragmentary in characterization, weaker in its ability to evoke emotions or concern, and consequently less substantial."[2] Sometimes the novel's implications are misconstrued, as when Richard Giannone speaks of "the inquisitional cruelty of Bokononism."[3] These problems are related, for it is necessary to grasp Vonnegut's stance toward his Bokononist materials if one is to appreciate the complexity of his fictional argument.

The crucial question is whether Vonnegut embraces the virtually nihilistic views on life expressed by a number of his characters. Vonnegut's narrator, John, originally intends to write a book about what the rest of civilization was doing on the day the first atomic bomb was dropped on Hiroshima. This book was to be entitled *The Day the World Ended*. Eventually, however, John, who is clearly his author's alter ego,[4] chooses a different title, one that is emphatically antiapocalyptic: *Cat's Cradle*. He does so because everything in Vonnegut's fictional universe resists the impulse toward fixity, finality, or "ends" in general. As Kathryn Hume has remarked, Vonnegut sees the world as flux, involving metamorphoses, instabilities, exaggerations, and distortions. The essential "elasticity of Vonnegut's universe," Hume notes, "is just one more way of focusing attention on underlying ideas. His cosmos, consisting of endless transformations, provides him with many of his literary techniques for guiding the reader's attention."[5] What the reader is guided to see here is a fragmented world poised at the edge of chaos but potentially responsive to the far from nihilistic view of life embodied in John's and Vonnegut's title.

It is surprising how little attention has been paid to the cat's cradle as a crucial symbol in a novel of the same name. In fact Peter Reed, whose

---

*This essay was written specifically for this volume and is published here for the first time by permission of the author.

reading of *Cat's Cradle* remains the best single treatment of the book, seems to view the cat's cradle pejoratively, seeing it through the disillusioned eyes of Felix Hoenikker's midget son, Newt, as a kind of betrayal of any symbolic or meaning-making possibilities. "All incomprehensible X's. No cat. No cradle. That sums up man's dilemma as the novel shows it," writes Reed,[6] echoing Newt's cynical observation about the string figure his father makes for him: "*No damn cat, no damn cradle.*"[7] But both critic and character have missed the point about the importance of cat's cradles in the novel. It is not the string figures themselves that Vonnegut vilifies, but rather Felix's willfully thrusting a cat's cradle at his terrified son instead of allowing the boy to play with it, in his own way, by himself.

Cat's cradles are children's playthings, but in primitive cultures they are also very popular among adults. In her book *String Figures and How to Make Them: A Study of Cat's Cradle in Many Lands*,[8] Caroline Furness Jayne makes a number of striking observations that would seem to address the interests of a writer who received his master's degree in cultural anthropology from the University of Chicago. (Indeed, Vonnegut's thesis was *Cat's Cradle* itself.) A cat's cradle is an "endless string," that is, a cord tied together at the ends, usually about six feet long and circular. Often depicted as a symbol of infinity, it has no beginning and no end, and can be constructed into innumerable designs. Primitive cultures use cat's cradles to give shape to their own mythologies, in particular their creation tales. For example, a cat's cradle is called "Maui" in New Zealand, and as one ethnoanthropologist writes of the many string figures the natives construct, "these are said to be different scenes in their mythology, such as Hine-nui-te-po, Mother Night bringing forth her progeny, Maru and the gods, and Maui fishing up the land."[9] *Mother Night* is, of course, the title of Vonnegut's third novel (directly preceding *Cat's Cradle*), and "Maru" recalls the foot-touching rite of "boku-maru," which is considered one of the most sacred and sensual acts of the Bokononist religion that Vonnegut invents in *Cat's Cradle*.

Foot-touching may be seen as analogous to tribesmen playing cat's cradle with each other, using two pairs of hands and often reenacting "a whole drama . . . by means of changing shapes."[10] Groups such as the Eskimos, mentioned in *Cat's Cradle*, attach "magical" properties to their cat's cradle games, while others seem to regard them far more lightly. Vonnegut, who laments the death of magic in the modern scientific world, understands both the serious and the playful sides of cat's cradle construction. He would be charmed by the notion that ethnologists, who are after all "scientists" of culture, do not agree about the ultimate significance of string figures.

For Jayne the real interest of cat's cradles lies in "the methods employed by different races in making the figures and a comparison of those methods," not in "the study of the relations between the finished patterns."[11] She is more concerned with the ways in which particular string figures are conceived in the minds of their makers than with the final product. How close she comes to Jerome Klinkowitz's description of the way in which Bokononism "structures" the lives of the pitiful inhabitants of Vonnegut's Caribbean island, San Lorenzo: "Here is *Cat's Cradle's* aesthetics of belief: meaning lies not in the content of a novel or the materials of a religion, but rather in the business of dealing with them. Once that process, that act of play, is complete, content should be forgotten. If not, it becomes the stuff of great mischief."[12] Klinkowitz follows Jayne in valuing form over content, method over pattern, process over product.

This does not mean that patterns are utterly unimportant, only that they are subject to perpetual alternation and can never be hypostasized into fixed absolutes. Nevertheless, Jayne does attempt to define three different kinds of string games that offer uncanny insights into Vonnegut's fictional creations:

1. "those figures whereof the purpose is to form final *patterns*, supposed to represent definite objects;"

2. "those which are *tricks*, wherein, after much complex manipulation of the strings, the entire loop is suddenly drawn from the hand by some simple movement; and"

3. "those which are *catches*, wherein, when certain strings are pulled, the hand or some of the figures may be unexpectedly caught in a running noose."

Jayne concludes, "Of course, there is no hard and fast rule of classification; several very pretty patterns may be converted into catches."[13] As she implies, it is possible to combine "patterns," "tricks," and "catches" within a single cat's cradle, thus offering a sense of stability while at the same time undermining the stability, or trapping it in the web (cradle) of one's own creation. All of these allotropic elements are playfully at work in Vonnegut's own literary cat's cradle, as we see most clearly in the chapter called, appropriately, "Cat's Cradle." But before we look at that chapter we should first consider the crucial scene when little Newt Hoenikker is frightened by his father's sudden appearance bearing a string figure.

In chapter five Newt Hoenikker describes the day Dr. Felix Hoenikker plays (or so it seems) with his six-year-old son for the first and last time. By chance Dr. Hoenikker has just received the manuscript of a novel tied with mailing string. This novel was written in prison by a convicted fratricide named Marvin Sharpe Holderness. Holderness's novel concerns how "mad scientists made a terrific bomb that wiped out the whole world" (16); he writes to Felix Hoenikker, the inventor of the atomic bomb, because he wants to know just what to put into the bomb to make it sound authentic. Unfortunately for Marvin Holderness, Felix Hoenikker, who has never, according to his son, "read a novel or even a short story in his whole life, or at least not since he was a little boy" (16–17), sets aside the manuscript and, momentarily fascinated by the loop of string he holds in his hands, "started playing with it. His fingers made the string figure called a 'cat's cradle' " (17). The scene is poignant because Newt, the essentially orphaned son of a living father, realizes that it was probably through a human tie, perhaps with his tailor father, that Felix learned to build cat's cradles. But Felix has long since abandoned imaginary "made-up games" for what he calls "real games," with all too real consequences for his family and for humanity. "He must have surprised himself when he made a cat's cradle out of that string," Newt continues, "and maybe it reminded him of *his own childhood*. He all of a sudden came out of his study and did something he had never done before. He tried *to play with me*. Not only had he never played with me before; he had hardly ever spoken to me" (17; my emphases). This towering figure, impersonal and abstract as a god, then went down on his knees, showed Newt his teeth, and waved that tangle of string in his face. " 'See? See? See?' he asked. 'Cat's cradle. See the cat's cradle? See where the nice pussycat sleeps? Meow. Meow' " (17).

The scene appears to be harmless, even charming. But within the larger structure of the novel, and in direct relation to a particular day when nuclear Hell was unleashed on Hiroshima, it looms as darkly sinister in a book in which another kind of Hell is let loose upon the nuclear family typified by the Hoenikker children, but also the book's other physically and spiritually maimed families—the Breeds, the Mintons, the Castles, even the twice-divorced, booze-and-cigarette surfeited narrator himself.

As Felix draws nearer, Newt recoils, terrified. At a distance the father may seem a remote deity, but up close he resembles some satanic monster out of a science-fiction film. "His pores looked as big as craters on the moon," writes Newt. "His ears and nostrils were stuffed with hair. Cigar smoke made him smell like the mouth of Hell. So close up, my father was the ugliest thing I had ever seen. I dream about it all the time" (18–19). Here we have what may be a gruesome parody of Joyce's description of little Stephen Dedalus, "Baby Tuckoo," gazing up at his father at the beginning of *A Portait of the Artist as a Young Man*. Joyce's scene represents, as Hugh Kenner has written apropos of the "father with the hairy face," "a traditional infantile analogue of God the Father."[14] But here in Vonnegut we witness the devil's almost Moloch-like appearance, his smoky rictus akin to the malodorous "mouth of Hell." The reference may be more deeply Dantean than we initially suspect. Considering that Felix Hoenikker is a form of anti-Christ, inflicting on man both nuclear war and perpetual winter, his actions as a scientist echo the words of Dante's Charon, ferryman to the underworld, who tells Dante and Virgil that he comes to lead them "into eternal dark, into fire and ice."[15] The journey through the Inferno parallels Felix Hoenikker's inventions of the atomic bomb and *ice-nine*. In the initial stages of Dante's descent Hell's circles are generally hot, but when Dante arrives in the last circle, the ninth, he finds instead a "huge frozen lake," filled with those sinners whose sins involved "denials of love and of all human warmth,"[16] which is another way of defining Felix Hoenikker's relationship to his late wife, his children, and people in general.

At the very center of Dante's final circle of Hell, immobilized and up to his neck in ice, is Satan, perpetrator of the most destructive of all impulses, nihilism. In this vein he resembles the more comic but no less nihilistic Felix Hoenikker. Seemingly childlike and often referred to as "innocent," Felix nevertheless wreaks the same kind of doomsday havoc as Satan. In fact Vonnegut makes one of his strongest anti-nihilistic statements by pairing a would-be artist named Krebbs, who destroys John's apartment, with Hoenikker himself. As his final act of devastation Krebbs kills a cat by hanging it on the refrigerator door handle and placing under it a sign written in excrement that reads "Meow" (59). This, of course, is no cradle but a cat's gallows, and Krebbs, like Hoenikker, is a man who really believes in nothing. Krebbs destroys a cat, Felix Hoenikker a cat's cradle (symbol of imagination). Felix's insistent "Meow, Meow" is really no less nihilistic than Krebbs's sign. Neither science nor art can function without some respect for humanity, as both Felix (whose first name ironically evokes a famous cartoon cat) and Krebbs illustrate.

Felix Hoenikker's nihilistic egotism is fully in evidence in the scene with the cat's cradle. The father puts a tangled mass of string before his cowering child, who sees through it into Felix's horrific face. The father then proceeds to hold up *his* version of a cat's cradle and to sing *his* version of the nursery rhyme lullaby "Rockaby Baby," where a baby's cradle or human arms as a cradle figure so importantly. In the conceit of the cat's cradle metamorphosing into the baby cradle, Newt becomes the cat (or baby) falling when the wind blows, but with no one there to catch him. No wonder the boy "burst into tears" and "jumped up and ran out of the house as fast as I could go" (18). For Newt, no cat's cradle means no "catch" and no catcher for the falling boy. The image is Salingeresque, the experience a nightmare; when he "grows up," Newt continues to paint that traumatic nightmare in the form of black "blasted landscapes," post-nuclear in their evocation of a ruined world. Newt's cynical *"No damn cat! No damn cradle"* underscores his sense, screened and deflected of course, of his own personal damnation before his father's indifference.

Any knowledgeable student of child psychology or of play therapy knows that Felix Hoenikker is not really *playing* with his son because it is he and not Newt who is manipulating the string figure. Devoid of a proper "mother," whom Alice Miller defines as "the person closest to the child during the first years of life,"[17] someone who can properly "mirror" the child's emerging identity and allow that child to grow *as a self,* Newt can only blame the cat's cradle for holding no cat and being no cradle. In essence he negates his own imagination, though the real cause of this crippling loss is not the string figure but his father, the absent "mother," the missing cradle rocker. What Newt fails to understand is that cat's cradles are not meant to be "real" in a scientific or factual sense. Rather they are games for us to play with and to act upon. They are useful fictions. Without them we cannot "invent" our own lives, are doomed to repeat endlessly (as Newt does with his paintings) our moment of loss.

What does "play" accomplish for a child, and why is its absence felt so profoundly? As defined by Bruno Bettelheim, play "refers to the young child's activities characterized by freedom from all but personally imposed rules (which are changed at will), by free-wheeling fantasy involvement, and by absence of any goals outside the activity itself."[18] Remove play and games from a child and he or she loses the "chance to work through unresolved problems of the past, to deal with pressures of the moment, and to experiment with various roles and forms of social interaction in order to determine their suitability for himself."[19] Bettelheim emphasizes that *real play* (a delicious Bokononist paradox) is "a child's true reality; this takes it far beyond the boundaries of its meaning for adults."[20] Without play a child is shaped, formed, carved—like a statue—by the adult world. With play the child develops an "inner life," a fluid self that nevertheless begins to explore, to experiment "with moral identities." Games like "cops and robbers" are salutary, even if they deal in mimed violence, because "such conflicts between good and evil represent the battle between tendencies of the asocial id and those of the diametrically opposed superego," and they permit as well "some discharge of aggression either actually or symbolically, through conflict."[21] Once again "play" sounds acutely Bokononist in its acting out of both sides of a moral struggle. And while Bettelheim seems to identify the formation of an ego with the forces of the superego gaining "ascendancy to control or overbalance those of the id,"[22] both Bettelheim and Vonnegut are conscious of the need to play in order to become a self. Nor would Bettelheim dispute Bokonon's exhortation to his followers to become "actors in a play they understood, that any human being anywhere could understand" (120). Little wonder then that Bokonon describes growing up as "a bitter disappointment for which no remedy exists, unless laughter can be said to remedy anything" (134). It is a tragedy for an adult to lose the ability to play, but unlike a child, and unlike the infantile, narcissistic Felix Hoenikker as well, the adult who plays can only be a good Bokononist if he realizes that he *is* playing, that his actions may have negative consequences (the A-bomb, *ice-nine*), and that if this is so they should be abandoned. That is what Vonnegut means by the epigraph to *Cat's Cradle*, where he instructs his audience to "Live by the foma ("Harmless untruths") that make you brave and kind and healthy and happy." The key word here is "Harmless."

A discussion of play is important to art because creativity is an aspect of play and functions only when the artist-self exists in what D. W. Winnicott calls an "unintegrated state of personality," a condition in which the artist is able to act upon the "formless experience" of his or her life and to play with it, make something mysterious, flexible, and free out of it. Like Bettelheim and Vonnegut, Winnicott believes that without play the child's growth process is stunted and self-making cannot take place. As Winnicott writes, "To get to the idea of playing it is helpful to think of the *preoccupations* that characterize the playing of a young child. *The content does not matter*. What matters is the near-withdrawal state. . . ."[23] (first emphasis Winnicott's, second emphasis mine). Play is one of the "transitional phenomena" that Winnicott has explored so extensively in his work. It inhabits a mediating middle ground between the empirical and the invented worlds: "This area of playing is not inner psychic reality. It is outside the individual, but it is not the external world."[24] Once again play is very Bokononist because, while Bokononism refuses to blink at the hard truth of a reality it cannot alter, it nevertheless fictionalizes that reality. Bokonon's principle of "Dynamic Tension," which derives from Charles Atlas and has appeared in children's comic books for years, closely follows the double vision (internal and external) of play. "Dynamic Tension" also resembles the making of string figures: "It is the same principle whereby if you hold your hands apart, pulling in opposite directions, you can string a cat's cradle on them; with no tension, of course, you would just have a muddle of string."[25] Just as Bokononism is tough work for its followers, a point that few critics seem to note, play is tough work for its earnest youthful adherents. This is so because in play a child attempts to give constructive form to the world's fundamental disorder. That is what makes it, in Winnicott's words, "inherently exciting and precarious."[26]

It is no happenstance that Winnicott himself employed string therapy games, analogous offshoots of cat's cradles, in treating disturbed children. And it is no chance occurrence that in one of those string games a boy named Edmund took a mound of tangled string, placed it "at the bottom of [a] bucket like bedding, and began to put [his] toys in, so that they had a nice soft place to lie in, like a cradle or a cot."[27] Or a cat's cradle. What Edmund learns, and what both Bettelheim and Winnicott have taught us, is the vital necessity of play in the development of a child's psychic life. Without it we have the blighted freakish children of Felix Hoenikker, father of the atomic bomb, father of *ice-nine*, but failed father to his own children. This leads us, finally, to the most important section of *Cat's Cradle*.

In the chapter called "Cat's Cradle" Newt describes one of his scratchy morbid paintings as the depiction of a cat's cradle. John asks if the scratches are string. Newt responds, "One of the oldest games there is, cat's cradle. Even the Eskimos know it! . . . For maybe a hundred thousand years or more, grownups have been waving tangles of string in their children's faces." John's only response is "Um," but Newt proceeds, obviously anxious to make his point. He holds out his black painty hands (a gesture John himself unconsciously imitates throughout the novel) as though a cat's cradle were strung between them: "No wonder kids grow up crazy. A cat's cradle is nothing but a bunch of X's between somebody's hands, and the little kids look and look and look at all those X's." "And?" John asks. Newt replies, "*No damn cat, and no damn cradle*" (114). For Newt, then, cat's cradles represent lies, betrayals, perfidy, the end of imagination rather than the beginning. "X" equals nothing, and all possibility for creation is denied.[28] It is a nihilistic image and functions in direct relation to other forms of closure or death in the novel, specifically the dropping of the atomic bomb and the end of the world through *ice-nine*.

Everything about Vonnegut's fictional world rebukes closure and confutes endings, apocalyptic or otherwise. Thus Vonnegut begins to deconstruct Newt's pointed observations at the same moment Newt makes them. Vonnegut does so initially through a description of the fantastic house built by Mona Aamons Monzano's father, Nestor, one of the few good fathers in any of Vonnegut's novels. Understanding this house is vital to understanding how the cat's cradle figure (itself architectural) dominates this chapter. The house resembles in part Coleridge's stately pleasure dome, for it is clearly a Bokononist home, grounded in physical reality but transcending that reality at the same time. Built on the side of the putatively mythic Mount McCabe, highest point on the island of San Lorenzo, and rising through ethereal mists, the house is formed out of "a cunning lattice of very light steel posts and beams," with interstices "variously open, chinked with native stone, glazed or curtained by sheets of canvas" (113). Such terms as "cunning lattice," "variously open," "curtained," and "canvas" seem deliberately to evoke the structure's clever design, its freedom (openness), its artfulness (curtain and canvas allude to both drama and painting), as well as to cat's cradles themselves (the criss-crossed lattice), and are all used to undercut Newt's debunking of string figures. Of Nester Aamons John writes, "The effect of the house was not so much to enclose as to announce that a man had been whimsically busy there" (113). Like the house, Vonnegut's fiction defies definition, shows a man "Busy, busy, busy," or what "we Bokononists say when we feel that a lot of mysterious things are going on" (121). The real mystery, sourceless, inexplicable, and "measureless to man," as Coleridge would put it, is the mystery of creation or play, the magic of cat's cradles themselves, fragile and fantastic forms, stretched delicately over an abyss (here the mountainside), yet infinitely free.

Asleep in a butterfly chair on that improbably poised "giddy terrace," itself "framed in a misty view of sky, sea, and valley," making it a part of nature and yet different from it, Newt dreams his grim dreams, then wakes to describe for John his spooky, grotesque paintings. And they *are* repellent, "small and black and warty," consisting of "scratches made in a black, gummy impasto." "The scratches formed a sort of spider's web," continues John, "and I wondered if they might not be the sticky nets of human futility hung upon a moonless night to dry" (113). Here is the opposite image of a cat's cradle, which liberates the mind, for this cradle is a sticky "spider's web," image of human futility, that which entraps us in our own natures and finally kills us. There can be little doubt that Vonnegut himself identifies in part with this vision. But only in part. This is a vision halved, unfinished, all darkness without light, evil without good, despair without hope. It is, in short, an anti-Bokononist perception of the world, the specter of a fallen cradle, a blighted childhood (like Newt's), lacking the "Dynamic Tension" that precariously balances its paradoxical oppositions so that human life is possible despite our pathetic condition.

Appropriately Newt, whose dreams are violent, wakes to the sound of gunfire, an explosion not unlike a bomb blast, that propels him into the previously cited "reading" of his own painting. But there is little difference between Newt and what he paints. Here is Newt putting "his black, painty hands to his mouth and chin, leaving black smears there. He rubbed his eyes and made black smears around them too" (113). His painting may be "something different" to others who see it, as a work of art should be, but to Newt it is one thing only, the objectification of his father's betrayal of Newt's childhood, symbolized by the destruction of a cat's cradle. In an important sense Newt has not yet been born because he has not been allowed to experience his childhood. We see the little man "curled" prenatally (perhaps even like a cat!) in that big butterfly chair, still waiting to metamorphose, to fly himself.

Everything that surrounds Newt and John on that wondrous terrace seems to symbolize the fertile life-affirming impulse. The mountain, whale-shaped and hump-like at the top, may also have connotations relating it to Mona Aamons Monzano, the would-be earth goddess with whom John is in love and whom he marries. Surely Vonnegut intends the pun on "a mons," as in "mons veneris." But if the mountain represents in part female fertility, then the stream and waterfall that flow down its side imply the opposite or male potential for life. These two forces, male and female, unite in Nestor Aamons's house, which, in a sexually charged image, "straddled a waterfall" (112). In addition the mountain and the waterfall share the Bokononist oppositions of fixity and flow, what might be called the novel's flexible form, its ceaseless mediation between chaos and order.

Having suffered at birth the loss of his natural mother, little Newt cannot comprehend the abundant powers that nature itself figures forth around him. Nor can he see how Nestor Aamons's own design unites the natural with the human-made, the artful creation out of what is already there. Vonnegut makes this apparent in an outrageous pun that underscores the union between art and life in *Cat's Cradle*. The pun turns on a parody of Stanley's search for the lost explorer Livingstone through the "heart" of darkest Africa. In the novel a plump servant—rare in poverty-ridden San Lorenzo—guides John to his room, a journey "around the heart of the house, down a staircase of *living stone*, a staircase sheltered or exposed by steel-framed rectangles at random. My bed was a foam-rubber slab on a stone shelf, a shelf of *living stone*. The walls of my chamber were canvas. Stanley demonstrated how I might roll them up or down, as I pleased" (113; my emphases). Led by the servant Stanley, John journeys into the "heart" of Nestor Aamons's house to a bedroom hard by the "living stone" of the mountainside, stone that contains an even more female image of a cave beneath the waterfall, festooned with what resemble ancient prehistoric drawings but which, in contradistinction to Newt's morbid modernistic paintings, are primitive drawings that "treated endlessly the aspects of Mona Aamons Monzano as a little girl" (131). These apparently ancient but actually quite recent playful paintings refute Newt's limited vision and make an indirect comment on his never having been born out of the womb of creation, while the sensual earth mother, Mona, revels in her own fertility / creativity.

Vonnegut offers one final negative verdict on little Newt's vision of art and life through the saintly yet sinister figure of Julian Castle, famous Schweitzer-like doctor at the House of Hope and Mercy. It is Castle whom John originally intended to visit on his journey to San Lorenzo, and it is Castle who gives the final verdict on Newt's jaundiced artistic vision. Castle, who has witnessed and attempted to give comfort to the worst kinds of human misery, including bubonic plague, gazes upon Newt's canvas and says, "It's *black*. What is it—hell?" (115). Receiving no help from Newt, Castle snarls, in his best Edward G. Robinson voice, "Then it's hell." From someone who has seen the hell of human suffering on his god-forsaken island, this seems to ring true. But Castle is a true Bokononist and really means the opposite of what he says. Therefore when he learns from John that the painting is of a cat's cradle, he replies that it is in fact "a picture of the meaninglessness of it all! I couldn't agree more" (116). Castle is really mocking Newt's cynical attitudinizing, pushing Newt into either agreeing with him or abandoning his pose. "You may quote me," Castle continues. "Man is vile, and man makes nothing worth making, knows nothing worth knowing!" (116). At this point, after winning Newt's uneasy assent (Newt seems "to suspect momentarily that the case had been a little overstated"), Castle picks up the "blasted landscape" of a painting and hurls it off the cantilevered terrace, from which it boomerangs and slices into the waterfall.

The painting flows into the maelstrom of the waterfall and down the mountainside, where it "ends" (or seems to) in a "big stone bowl," across which the poor natives have woven out of chicken wire a net (a cat's cradle?) that they use to catch and hold whatever flows down from above. Here is what they find: "Four square feet of gummy canvas, the four milled and mitred sticks of the stretcher, some tacks, too, and a cigar. All in all, a pretty nice *catch* for some poor, poor man" (121; my emphasis). The proper "use" to which Newt's limited and limiting "artwork" has been put belies its maker's original intention. As we have seen, a "catch" is also a kind of cat's cradle. This time it is used not only to catch Newt's painting, but figuratively to "catch" Newt himself in an unbokononist lie.

Although "Cat's Cradle" concludes with another of Newt's cynical refrains, this time in criticism of his sister Angela's loveless marriage, Newt once again sees only part of the picture. His gloss on Angela's deluded love for her ruthless husband, "See the cat? See the cradle?" (122), can hardly be gainsaid. But the way in which, out of *her* art, Angela translates her suffering into the cadenzaed grief and grandeur of her music leads to transcendence of that miserable marriage. This cannot be said of Newt.

At the end of the book, when John searches for a "magnificent symbol" (190) to carry with him to the top of Mount McCabe to give a central meaning to his life (he still is a Christian, and to a Christian such "centers" are important), John can find nothing, least of all a cat's cradle, to take with him. By this time *ice-nine* has nearly destroyed the world, leaving only a small enclave of survivors, among them John and Newt, still alive on San Lorenzo. What could one possibly bring to the top of a supposedly holy mountain, and what use would it be? We already know what Bokonon thinks of such gestures. As Frank Hoenikker tells John, Mount McCabe may have once been "sacred or something," but no more. John then asks, "What *is* sacred to Bokononists?" and receives the terse reply, "Man. That's all. Just man!" (144). Nevertheless, John continues to seek the proper symbol to carry to the top of the mountain and, one might argue, to "end" the novel on which he has been working for the past six months. He does not find that symbol by undergoing a conventional quest. Instead, unwittingly, he enacts a Bokononist "solution"—open-ended, inconclusive, ambiguous, and decentered—to his search. He discovers, whether he knows it or not, a cat's cradle.

Driving across San Lorenzo, John proffers his scheme to Newt, who by this time has become somewhat of a Bokononist. "I took my hands from the wheel for an instant to show him how empty of symbols they were. 'But what in hell would the right symbol *be*, Newt? What in hell would it *be?*' I grabbed the wheel again." Then a little later: " 'But what, for the love of God, is supposed to be in my hands?' " (190). Holding up his empty hands, as if to pantomime the making of a cat's cradle, John, a writer for whom that cat's cradle functions as a metaphor for writing, can only put them down in defeat. Still, he is beginning to speak the paradoxical language of a Bokononist. His parallel but thematically contrasting phrases, "What in hell" and "what, for the love of God," seem to fit perfectly with the Bokononist counterpointing of those two "separate" forces of good and evil, heaven and hell, which are a part of the Bokononist mythology. In addition, that same phrase, "for the love of God," echoes an earlier exhortation on the part of Julian Castle to his son and John, both writers, not to abandon their craft just because it all seems so hopeless: "for the love of God, both of you, please keep writing!" (156). We remember as well that it is Julian Castle who offers a capsule definition of the very writing style, cat's cradlelike, that Vonnegut invents for his novel. That something "sacred" John hopes to carry to the top of the mountain affiliates writing with responsibility as Julian Castle imagines it, for to write is to create books that entail "a *sacred* obligation to produce beauty and enlightenment and comfort at top speed" (156; my emphasis).

John also believes that one of his chief purposes in climbing Mount McCabe is to discover the identity of his *karass*. "If you find your life *tangled* up with somebody else's life for no very logical reasons," writes Bokonon, "that person may be a member of your *karass*" (12). John learns that the "tendrils" of his life "began to *tangle* with those of [the Hoenikker] children" (14; my emphases). Vital to understanding how a *karass* works is to view it as a creation of God, not man. Thus we can never know for certain who is part of our *karass*, and it is difficult to exclude anyone from it. One thing we do know is that "a 'karass' ignores national, institutional, occupational, familial, and class boundaries" (12). A *karass* is, finally, "as free-form as an amoeba" (12)— or a cat's cradle. It is those words "tangled" and "tangle," associated throughout the novel with cat's cradles (beginning with Felix Hoenikker's waving a "tangled mass of string" before his cowering son, and culminating with

Newt's own tangled splotchy paintings of cat's cradles), that imply a connection with the flexible, playful strutures called cat's cradles, which we make and unmake, tangle and untangle, never arriving at any final synthesis of their polymorphous possibilities, never knowing what the Platonic essence of a cat's cradle could possibly be. The same is true of our *karass,* for if it is a successful *karass* we never learn who belongs to it and who does not. It is analogous to the Christian notion of grace, of being chosen for eternal salvation out of God's mysterious and ineffable love. It should make us more loving, more "human," for Bokonon worships the human above all other values.

The final chapter of *Cat's Cradle,* entitled "The End," may represent the end of *The Books of Bokonon,* of John's book, and of Vonnegut's book as well (not to mention the end of the world), but it is not a true ending. It can be no more than a cat's cradle, circular, supple, full of possibilities. If each of the many chapters in *Cat's Cradle* is a mini-cat's cradle itself, open to innumerable interpretations, then what is its ending but a beginning? By allowing Bokonon, wise but perdurably mendacious (as in the sense of "foma"), to utter the novel's final words, Vonnegut suggest that those words are suspect. Bokonon in fact duplicates John's own desperate gesture and in so doing gives it the lie. Here is the last "book" in *The Books of Bokonon:*

> If I were a younger man, I would write a history of human stupidity; and I would climb to the top of Mount McCabe and lie down on my back with my history for a pillow; and I would take from the ground some of the blue-white poison that makes statues of men; and I would make a statue of myself, lying on my back, grinning horribly, and thumbing my nose at You Know Who. (191)

Those words are not really addressed so much to the plight of the crazy old Bokonon as to the "young man," John, to whom Bokonon speaks. In the fabulist hyper-fictional world of *Cat's Cradle,* Bokonon, the first half of whose name is an obvious respelling of the word "book," is really the author's creation. We recall that Bokonon's "real" name is Johnson, that Johnson, alias Bokonon, is really "John's son," his author's imagined progeny, and that each of them is Von's son since Johnson became the maker of *The Books of Bokonon* the year he landed on the fictional (but all too real) island of San Lorenzo, which was 1922, the year Kurt Vonnegut was born. Wheels within wheels, and cat's cradles generating newer and more elaborately concatenated cat's cradles in the perpetual process of creation, without beginning and without end.

That is the true meaning of Vonnegut's book, and that is why, despite the imminent demise of the world and of Bokonon himself (now that his creator has become a Bokononist, as he tells us in the novel's first pages, Bokonon's existence is no longer necessary; he has been assimilated into John), suicide is the least Bokononist solution to the desperate situation we witness at the end of *Cat's Cradle.* This, plus the realization that Bokonon is always lying, should prevent us from assuming that John intends to follow

Bokonon's advice (an anti-Bokononist response). Indeed, John assumes Bokonon's conditional phrase, "If I were a younger man," into his own writing, takes the last page of *The Books of Bokonon*, and, by changing that conditional "If" to an emphatic "When," incorporates them into the beginning of his own book. John is really satirizing his own pre-Bokononist youth, its failures and its futility, when he writes, "When I was a younger man—two wives ago, 250,000 cigarettes ago, 3,000 quarts of booze ago . . . When I was a much younger man, I began to collect material for a book to be called *The Day the World Ended*" (11). But the world does not quite end in *Cat's Cradle*, and its author, holding in his hands the only cat's cradle he knows, that is his fictional world, can hardly take the advice of Bokonon and thumb his nose at "You Know Who," since he does not in fact know who "You Know Who" is, or whether "He" even exists. Bokononism is referred to as a religion in *Cat's Cradle*, but if it is it is a very different, undogmatic religion, built out of the creative, playful, childlike aspects of human nature, out of our enduring ability to invent meanings in an essentially meaningless world (or a world whose meanings are hidden permanently from us). By *not* following Bokonon's advice, John enacts his own conversion to Bokononism.

Bokononism is a philosophy of flow, resisting entropy and harrowing the fixities that reduce societies to monomaniacal obsessions, to one-sided "truths." Everything it stands for opposes the destructive science of Felix Hoenikker, and for that reason it is fiercely if amusingly unquietistic, refusing to accept that all human action is ultimately futile. Thus it is stridently unlike another Vonnegutian "philosophy" with which it is often paired, the deterministic Tralfamadorianism of *Slaughterhouse-Five*.[29] Because they hold that we are powerless to alter history (in fact "history" has already happened, and the universe has already been destroyed), Vonnegut's Tralfamadorians believe that our only solution is to time-travel, to live in selected "happy moments," to ignore the burden of human misery that drives Bokonon mad but which also forces him to invent a religion of compassion and compensation against our grim human lot. Contrastingly, the Tralfamadorians see humankind in the lowliest terms, as "bugs trapped in amber" for whom they have little sympathy.[30]

Although their reductivist philosophy appeals to such a pathetic and limited person as Billy Pilgrim, the protagonist of *Slaughterhouse-Five*, it is difficult to believe that Vonnegut wants us all to become Tralfamadorians. Bokononism, on the other hand, is Dostoevskian in its riddling contradictions. A true Tralfamadorian would never accept Bokononism's life-lie, its "cruel paradox," which acknowledges "the heartbreaking necessity of lying about reality, and the heartbreaking impossibility of lying about it" (189). For "heartbreaking" read "tragic," a word utterly alien to Tralfamadorian hedonism. So much deeper and more complicated than Tralfamadorianism, Bokononism is at bottom a comic response to a tragic world, yet a response that simultaneously *contains*, in its artful dualism (really a delicate balancing), both the tragic and the comic aspects of human nature.

There is no better gloss on Bokononism than the celebrated description of the artistic imagination offered by F. Scott Fitzgerald in *The Crack-Up*. "[L]et me," writes Fitzgerald, "make a general observation—the test of a first-rate intelligence is the ability to hold two opposed ideas in the mind at the same time, and still retain the ability to function." What follows is critical if we are to comprehend Vonnegut's tragicomic Bokononist vision. "One should, for example," Fitzgerald continues, "be able to see that things are hopeless and yet be determined to make them otherwise."[31] Kurt Vonnegut could easily have penned these words. What's more, Vonnegut's own rhetoric follows Fitzgerald's in the latter's summation of his hope-against-hope philosophy: "I must hold in balance the sense of the futility of effort and the sense of the necessity to struggle: the conviction of the inevitability of failure and still the determination to succeed."[32] This is, of course, the language of Vonnegut's "cruel paradox." It is the voice of tragedy, which for Vonnegut, confirmed Bokononist that he is, can only be expressed by its opposite, the author's courageous comedy.

Notes

1. Kurt Vonnegut, "Prague's Fun-Haters Are Out to Silence Toe-Tappers," *Rocky Mountain News*, 17 December 1986, 62.

2. Peter J. Reed, *Kurt Vonnegut, Jr.* (New York: Warner, 1972), 119.

3. Richard Giannone, *Vonnegut: A Preface to His Novels* (Port Washington, N.Y.: Kennikat, 1977), 59.

4. See Jerome Klinkowitz, *Kurt Vonnegut* (London: Methuen, 1982), 55. Klinkowitz says that "except for an editorial veto," Vonnegut's narrator would have been named "Vonnegut."

5. Kathryn Hume, "The Heraclitean Cosmos of Kurt Vonnegut," *Papers on Language and Literature* 17 (Spring 1982): 210, 215.

6. Reed, *Vonnegut*, 139. Although he acknowledges that *Cat's Cradle* is fundamentally a comic novel, Reed still believes the book's title is ironic: "In using that image of the cat's cradle—or of no cat, no cradle—for the title and the central symbol of the book, Vonnegut implies an endorsement of Newt's assessment" (141).

7. Kurt Vonnegut, Jr., *Cat's Cradle* (New York: Dell, 1970), 114. All subsequent references will appear within the text.

8. Caroline Furness Jayne, *String Figures and How to Make Them: A Study of Cat's Cradle in Many Lands* (New York: Dover, 1963). This book first appeared in 1906.

9. Alfred C. Haddon, introduction to *String Figures and How to Make Them*, xviii–xix.

10. Ibid., xix.

11. Jayne, *String Figures*, 3–4.

12. Klinkowitz, *Kurt Vonnegut*, 54–55.

13. Jayne, *String Figures*, 4.

14. Hugh Kenner, "The *Portrait* in Perspective," in *Joyce's Portrait: Criticism and Critiques*, ed. Thomas E. Connolly (New York: Appleton-Century-Crofts, 1962), 30.

15. Dante, *The Inferno*, trans. John Ciardi (New York: New American Library, 1954), 44.

16. Ibid., 266.

17. Alice Miller, *Prisoners of Childhood* (New York: Basic Books, 1981), 8.

18. Bruno Bettelheim, "The Importance of Play," *Atlantic Monthly*, 259 (March 1987): 37.

19. Ibid., 38.

20. Ibid., 39.

21. Ibid., 46.

22. Ibid.

23. D. W. Winnicott, *Playing and Reality* (London: Tavistock, 1971), 51.

24. Ibid., 51.

25. Tony Tanner, *City of Words: American Fiction 1950–1970* (New York: Harper & Row, 1971), 191.

26. Winnicott, *Playing and Reality*, 52.

27. Ibid., 43.

28. In the mathematical world of Felix Hoenikker an "X" stands for an unsolved problem, an imminent solution, an algebraic "truth." This runs completely counter to Bokononism's "foma" thesis and is underscored by the nickname of Frank Hoenikker, who most resembles his father in his indifference to other humans. As a young man Frank is called "Secret Agent X-9" by his classmates. Thus in a neat stroke Vonnegut allies the search for truth, for the meaning of "X," with the death of the world, through *ice-nine*. X equals *ice-nine*.

29. Cf. the pairing of Bokononism and Tralfamadorianism in Glenn Meeter, "Vonnegut's Formal and Moral Otherworldliness: *Cat's Cradle* and *Slaughterhouse-Five*," in *The Vonnegut Statement*, ed. Jerome Klinkowitz and John Somer (New York: Delta, 1973), 204–19, and Michael Wood, "Dancing in the Dark," *New York Review of Books*, 31 May 1973, 23–25. That both Meeter and Wood see Bokononism and Tralfamadorianism as nearly synonymous would seem to indicate they understand neither philosophy. For a convincing refutation of the notion that Vonnegut presents Tralfamadorianism as a valued form of "foma," see Robert Merrill and Peter A. Scholl, "Vonnegut's *Slaughterhouse-Five*: The Requirements of Chaos," *Studies in American Fiction* 6 (1978): 65–76.

30. Kurt Vonnegut, Jr., *Slaughterhouse-Five* (New York: Dell, 1971), 77. Could there be a less Bokononist notion than the idea that humans (revered above everything else) are nothing but "bugs," insects helplessly "trapped in amber," with no vestiges of freedom whatsoever?

31. F. Scott Fitzgerald, *The Crack-Up*, ed. Edmund Wilson (New York: New Directions, 1945), 69.

32. Ibid., 70.

[Economic Neurosis: Kurt Vonnegut's *God Bless You, Mr. Rosewater*]

Peter J. Reed*

In his 1973 *Playboy* interview (reprinted in *Wampeters, Foma and Granfalloons*),[1] Kurt Vonnegut plays down what is often thought of as the most influential episode among his experiences. "The importance of Dresden in my life has been considerably exaggerated because my book about it

*Reprinted by permission of the author from *Kurt Vonnegut, Jr.* (New York: Warner, 1972), 146–71. The chapter has been slightly revised.

became a best seller. If the book hadn't been a best seller, it would seem like a very minor experience in my life. And I don't think people's lives are changed by short-term events like that" (*WFG* 263). What Vonnegut points to, in that interview and elsewhere, as a more significant long-term influence on him is the Great Depression. In fact, he says, "everything I believe I was taught in junior civics during the Great Depression" (*WFG* 274). Nowhere are those lessons more apparent than in *God Bless You, Mr. Rosewater* (1965), the novel which begins by declaring, "A sum of money is a leading character in this tale about people. . . ." In the interview Vonnegut asserts, "That Depression has more to do with the American character than any war" (*WFG* 282). *God Bless You, Mr. Rosewater* takes as its subject the impact of money, of economic policy and personal greed, upon the individual and upon the character of American society. In so doing, it may indeed be closer to the mainstream of Vonnegut's work than the great Dresden novel it precedes, for the social injustice of economic systems has been a persistent theme throughout his fiction.

No doubt *God Bless You, Mr. Rosewater* has been somewhat overshadowed by the two books it stands between chronologically—the ever-popular *Cat's Cradle* (1963) and the best-selling *Slaughterhouse-Five* (1969). Compared with them, *Rosewater* appears to be a reconventionalized novel, shorn of the experimentation with language, fragmentation, narration-within-narration, and self-reflexive fictionality that are their hallmarks. Yet while it returns to the novel's traditional preoccupations with money and social morality, it does so in a manner appropriate to its own era, and it is not without elements of the innovation that so characterizes the other two books. *Rosewater* has its metafictional aspects, such as its sustained intertextuality with Shakespeare's *Hamlet,* some of which is overt and some implied. Eliot's version of history in the letter to his descendants becomes the text on which the rest of the novel builds as *surfiction*. That the senator and Eliot encapsulate their conflicting ideas in two rival quotations from William Blake emphasizes the fact that *Rosewater* embodies a dialogue between two competing fictions to describe the American experience. And by the end, Kilgore Trout has invented his own fiction to explain Eliot's actions, while Eliot himself imposes another fiction by proclaiming pretenders heirs. Most obviously, *Rosewater* retains the fragmentation (the short paragraphs separated by "R"s) of multiple plot lines characteristic of much of the post–*Cat's Cradle* fiction.

Vonnegut's treatment of his central theme was bold for its day even though one might argue it was in keeping with the progressive social programs of the time. *God Bless You, Mr. Rosewater* was written, after all, at a time when Kennedy-Johnson social programs were still building toward the Great Society and the "War on Poverty." The counter voice of conservatism, raised most vociferously by Senator Barry Goldwater, expressed a growing opposition to liberal social legislation, but was not yet strong enough to stop it, as the 1964 election demonstrated. At the time, then, Vonnegut's message, while tempered by some skepticism of expensive social programs, was read primarily as applauding compassion ("Goddamn it, you've got to be kind!") and ridiculing the rising right. In the more conservative climate of the 1980s, its position might be seen as almost reversed, now expressing the outsider's criticism of the decade of Reaganomics. In that sense, Eliot Rosewater is the forerunner of Walter Starbuck and Mary Kathleen O'Looney of *Jailbird* (1979), who try to redistribute wealth in the conglomerate age.

There is a characteristic toughness in Vonnegut's treatment of the issues of poverty, social justice, and economic morality in *God Bless You, Mr. Rosewater*. In the first place, of course, the novel is not simply concerned with the effects of poverty and economic deprivation; it is equally concerned to show that wealth can be damning, and that the great financial inequality in America takes its toll on everyone. Vonnegut is a compassionate man with a lively social conscience, but he is neither sentimental nor doctrinaire on this subject. Behind this novel's skepticism of grand-scale philanthropy and money hand-outs, one senses the writer from the mid-American middle class who has spoken of managing his own literary career like a small business: "I started out with a pushcart, and now I've got several supermarkets at important intersections. My career grew just the way a well-managed business is supposed to grow" (*WFG* 278). Thus the author's perspective remains distinct from his protagonist's; Eliot is often undercut and his father is given enough respect to impart a toughening balance to the dialogue. Separating himself from his character, Vonnegut says:

> It's sort of self-congratulatory to be the person
> who walks around pitying other people. I don't do that
> very much. I just know that there are plenty of people
> who are in terrible trouble and can't get out. And I'm
> impatient with those who think that it's easy for
> people to get out of trouble. I think there are some people
> who really need a lot of help. I worry about stupid
> people, dump people. Somebody has to take care of them,
> because they can't hack it. (*WFG* 255)

Bluntly put. While the novel contains a dialogue between Eliot and the senator, then, the third voice is the authorial one implicit in the narration. While it expresses a tougher attitude than does Eliot it is in the main sympathetic toward him, and indeed it validates Eliot's compassion more because it views him with some skepticism than it would be likely to if it were naively his apologist. It is the presence of this third voice, in sum, that saves the novel from the excesses of didacticism or sentiment that might so easily attend its subject matter.

The novel's rationale is effectively written by its own central character. When Eliot Rosewater attends the science fiction writers' convention, he wonders why no good science fiction book has ever been written about money: " 'Just think of the wild ways money is passed around on Earth!' he said." Nor need we look to Tralfamadore for creatures with incredible powers: "Look at the powers of an Earthling millionaire! Look at me!"[2] *God Bless*

You, Mr. Rosewater does look at the wild ways money is passed around, at the powers of a millionaire, and at Eliot Rosewater. It looks at the other side of the coin—or the Rosewater fortune—as well. And it does not simply castigate the "haves" for being rich or for the ways they come by wealth, and plead the case of the "have-nots" or the pathos of their having not. It probes the burdens that can attend wealth, the problems that can accompany giving to the poor, and more than these, it exposes the inversions of values and loss of purpose that can afflict a society that esteems its currency above its people. In short, it shows money as sort of psychological germ-carrier, afflicting both collective and individual man.

Eliot's history of the Rosewater fortune, although obviously not an unbiased record, is one of the several indications of the distortion of social values which comes in the wake of wealth. Eliot theorizes that an error of the Founding Fathers was in putting no limit on the riches of each citizen, out of the misconception that the resources of the continent were infinite, more than enough for everyone. Men like his forefather Noah exploited this omission, grabbing and bribing their ways to wealth. "Thus did a handful of rapacious citizens come to control all that was worth controlling in America. Thus was the savage and stupid and entirely inappropriate and unnecessary and humorless American class system created" (12). In this system, hardworking men who asked for living wages were "classed as bloodsuckers," while riches went to those subtle enough to commit "crimes against which no laws had been passed." And in this system, continues Eliot, "every grotesquely rich American represents property, privileges, and pleasures that have been denied the many" (13). For Noah Rosewater and his ilk, who acquire out of a "paranoid reluctance to be a victim," Eliot contrives two appropriate mottos: *"Grab much too much, or you'll get nothing at all"* and *"Anybody who thought that the United States of America was supposed to be a Utopia was a piggy, lazy, God-damned fool"* (13). Thus the distortion of a potential utopia into a nightmare land of possessiveness, greed, and insecurity. While all of these opinions are ascribed only to Eliot, they deserve reviewing for what they tell us about the protagonist and because they express, by and large, the attitudes adopted by the novel itself.

The early Rosewaters are not the only ones who have come by their money through dubious means and warped ethics. The Buntline fortune began when Castor Buntline set up a broom-making factory employing blind Civil War veterans, cynically recognizing that such men would make compliant workers, that he would be acknowledged as a humanitarian, and that people would buy the brooms out of patriotism. Both early Buntlines and early Rosewaters are unscrupulous in their money making, but are equally fond of Bible quoting and moral preaching. The men who make these great fortunes, goaded by the insecurity that demands more and more, were not simply crooks. Ironically, they could know they were crooks and yet be sanctimonious at the same time. The perversion that comes down to the present generation is that they no longer recognize themselves as crooks to any degree, but are more sanctimonious than ever. Lister Rosewater appears to be one of those Republicans Eliot refers to as being willing to "order the militia to fire into crowds whenever a poor man seemed on the point of suggesting that he and Rosewater were equal in the eyes of the law" (13). He advocates a return to "a true Free Enterprise system" with "sink-or-swim justice," where the swimmers triumph and the others sink quietly away (24–27). The moral line of the Buntlines emphasizes the sanctity of property rather more. It is epitomized in the oath, written by Castor Buntline, which the inmates of the orphanage he has endowed must recite nightly: "I do solemnly swear that I will respect the sacred private property of others, and that I will be content with whatever station in life God Almighty may assign me to. . ." (133).

This is the mentality that defends that "unnecessary and humorless American class system," the characteristics of which emerge repeatedly in the novel. One instance can be seen in the "inner city" and suburban split between Rosewater and Avondale. Rosewater has the high school, the city park, the fire department, and that is about all, since the Saw Company has moved out to a commercial park. Its working class citizenry has become an idle class. Meanwhile, "the few highly paid agronomists, engineers, brewers, accountants, and administrators who did all that needed doing lived in a defensive circle of expensive ranch homes" in Avondale (39). Once these people have observed with contempt the decline of the Rosewater aristocracy, their self-esteem rises: they see themselves not as rising young executives but as the "vigorous members of the true ruling class" (41). As in *Player Piano*, a technological managerial class emerges as the new aristocracy—and it is just as shallow and crass. Meanwhile the "working class" becomes redundant and rejected in another enclave. Thus does a national schizophrenia become manifest in both social and geographical division. Pisquontuit shows the same split personality, being "populated by two hundred very wealthy families and by a thousand ordinary families whose breadwinners served, in one way and another, the rich" (96). Then there are the Rumfoords living in magnificent isolation in their Newport estate. They are required to open their domain to the public once every five years by the will of a forefather who thought it would be to their benefit to catch an occasional glimpse of some of the world's inhabitants. Mrs. Rumfoord indicates the success of the program when she insists that Mushari, whom we are told is prone to see everything as if through a quart of olive oil, had been a sniper in the U.S. infantry. And so the phobias of wealth pile up.

The American class system, the novel argues, in effect institutionalizes money. Like most class systems its function is to protect its aristocracy and keep its masses contentedly, respectfully, and industriously in their places. The American aristocracy may have bought itself refinement in successive generations, but it remains essentially an aristocracy of money. Its orginal power came from money gained by ruthless acquisitiveness, and the laws and ethics it has propagated have been devoted to preserving that power.

The law should ensure the protection of property and the perpetuation of an environment in which egalitarianism is not encouraged. It should curb pressures for such things as higher wages, but not block the tax-evading shenanigans of the rich. The ethic teaches that hard work is a virtue to be accompanied by respect for one's betters (or richers) and contentment with place. To be unwilling or unable to work is sinful. Unless one is rich. But then, of course, the ethic assures that riches never come undeservedly, so the rich deserve to be idle. To be rich means to have one's intelligence and value assured. To be poor implies one is stupid, inferior and valueless. While not very much of all this is new with Vonnegut, his explanations of the social and personal consequences of such a system are penetrating and relevant, particularly in showing the effects upon rich as well as poor. Moreover, Vonnegut does bring new emphasis to the impact of technological displacement upon a nation reared with the work ethic. Above all, his attention to the psychological imbalance that derives such a system, and to the neuroses engendered by it, is fresh and emphatic.

All of these implications of *money* are best demonstrated in the specific. Eliot Rosewater is naturally the one character on whom the moral questions imposed by wealth settle most heavily. His likening of himself to Shakespeare's Hamlet means more than his being the heir in a rotten state. Like Hamlet he faces questions that could drive him mad, like Hamlet his most sane behavior might well appear crazy in a world of inverted values, and like Hamlet he has received a psychological blow that could indeed have unbalanced him. The great shock for Eliot has been that wartime experience in which he mistook volunteer firemen for S. S. troops and killed three innocent men. This prompts his obsession with the propensity of things to combine with oxygen and be consumed, and his passion for volunteer firemen. It also explains at least one of his "crazy" outbursts, and contributes to his later breakdowns and to his drinking. But it also has sharpened his conscience, has given him a peculiar insight into each person's overwhelming responsibility to others, and could have revealed to him, if only subconsciously, the symbol of volunteer fireman as savior which Trout suggests later. Consequently the possibility exists, not just for his detractors but for the detached observer, that Eliot's social conscience and actions are a result of that shock and can be judged unbalanced, just as the probable prior existence of an oedipal complex adds ambiguity to Hamlet's response to the death of his father. That touch of ambiguity greatly enriches the novel. It adds dimension to Eliot's characterization, makes the social criticism exercised through his role less easily propagandistic, and connects the cold subject of money directly with very real human sufferings.

From the start, Eliot's concern with the poor and with the inequitable distribution of wealth is not solely altruistic. One might dispute whether action to relieve the naggings of conscience represents altruism or egocentrism, but in any case conscience works on Eliot, as does a sense of purposelessness. That dissatisfaction creeps through the ironies of the last paragraph of his letter to his heir as he says, "Be generous. Be kind. You can safely ignore the arts and sciences. They never helped anybody. Be a sincere, attentive friend of the poor" (15). Eliot means both that the arts and sciences never helped others—that pouring money into museums and research institutions will give the poor little relief—and that they never really helped the rich donor, either. As he recites on one of those earlier days of running the Foundation:

> Many, many good things have I bought!
> Many, many bad things have I fought!
>
> (17)

The bad things include alcoholism, but he is too drunk himself to read the report on it that he has commissioned. Eliot obviously finds no real purpose, and certainly not enough human contact, in playing the philanthropic mogul.

Those first alcoholic, emotionally distraught junkets that Eliot goes on all point to a search for meaning and purpose. Eliot's seizing upon science fiction writers as the seers of the contemporary world is fraught with comic undercutting, but shows clearly the method in his madness. What he loves about science fiction writers, Eliot says, is that they are the only ones aware of the changes going on around men who care about the future; about what machines, cities, big simple solutions, mistakes, accidents, and catastrophes do to people (18). In the latter part of this, we may see the results of the war trauma working on Eliot, but its application to the general condition of men lacks no logic. In particular, Eliot praises Kilgore Trout for this book *2BRO2B*, a title that casts Hamlet's famous question in new symbols. Trout's novel examines the problems Eliot has alluded to, of life in an automated America where there is no work for people with less than three Ph.D.s, where there are serious overpopulation problems, "Ethical Suicide Parlors" next to every Howard Johnson's, and a general sense of purposelessness. One character voices the question that plagues Eliot and echoes through Vonnegut: "What in hell are people *for?*" (21).

The two questions—"2BRO2B" and "What are people for?"—are connected for Eliot as well as for others. Finding some purpose resolves the question of being. The rub comes in finding the purpose, and that becomes Eliot's search. He writes to his "Dear Ophelia"—Sylvia—from Elsinore, California, that he feels he has an important mission but cannot decide how it should be done (hence his Hamlet complex). Hamlet, he feels, had "one big edge" on him, in having a father's ghost to tell him exactly what to do. But Eliot's instinct for firemen leads him in the right direction. As Trout says near the novel's close, volunteer firemen rush to the rescue of any and all human beings without counting the cost, making them perfect symbols of "enthusiastic unselfishness." What Eliot tries to do in setting up his rescue service in Rosewater obviously parallels a volunteer fire brigade. His two telephones, a red one for fire calls and a black one for humans about to be consumed, emphasizes the parallel. So does the William Blake poem he has painted on the stairs to his office, proclaiming the message so loved by

Gulley Jimson of Joyce Cary's *The Horse's Mouth:* "Go love without the help of any thing on Earth" (51).

"ROSEWATER FOUNDATION. HOW CAN WE HELP YOU?" asks the sign on Eliot's door. The question might almost have been written in response to the name, for Eliot seems as desperately in need of help as most of his clients. But what he does in Rosewater is creditable in deed as well as intention, and makes more sense than his earlier gestures of inviting derelicts off the street to lavish dinners in the Rosewater mansion. His activities are not always the pattern of rationality, and they receive their full share of undercutting. His prescriptions—a glass of wine and an aspirin—and his therapy—organized fly hunts—are often ludicrous, as are his personal appearance and, frequently, his manner. He is even shown to be excessively romantic in his conception of his clients. Senator Rosewater and McAllister may be wrong in their judgment that he "trafficked with criminals," but Eliot "was almost equally mistaken" in taking his following for people like those who "had cleared the forests, drained the swamps, built the bridges, people whose sons formed the backbone of the infantry in time of war—and so on" (56). In fact, we are told, they are both "weaker" and more "dumb" than such people. Those closer to Eliot's description eschew his assistance and try, all too often unsuccessfully, to find work to support themselves. Even the idealism of Eliot's quotation is countered by another from the same poet, scribbled on the hall wall by the senator:

> Love seeketh only Self to please,
> To bind another to Its delight
> Joys in another's loss of ease,
> And builds a Hell in Heaven's despite.
>   (52)

That poem seems hilarious in context—the senator sees his son as delighting in the loss of ease, and certainly views the chaotic office as a Hell built in Heaven's despite—but it also points more seriously to the dangers of egocentrism in Eliot's program.

For all the derision and farce surrounding it, Eliot's rescue service has obvious merits. He may be romantically unrealistic about the heritage of the people he serves, and much of his comforting may be as "hopelessly sentimental" as the music of rainfall that on occasion tellingly accompanies it (60), but he gives "uncritical love" and is not devoid of all practical sense. His remedies, for instance, do not involve the unquestioning distribution of large sums of money, which would surely be the gesture of a man simply trying to assuage feelings of guilt about his own wealth. Giving money generally remains his last resort, and then he will haggle about how much. Nor is he without a sense of humor about what he does, as he shows in the telephone conversation with an anonymous potential suicide. After some verbal exchange, the caller decides Eliot sounds drunk and demands, "Who the hell *are* you?" Eliot replies that if he wants to keep people from killing themselves and he is not a church, he must be either the government or the community chest (76). Joke or not, crazy or not, Eliot gives unstintingly of himself, extends compassion to many who need it and succeeds in making life more bearable for a number of people. In *form* his program may not offer the best solution to the problems of inequities in the distribution of wealth, but it springs from the right principles.

The real measure of Eliot's behavior and sanity is provided in the way other characters' actions are juxtaposed to his. Foremost among these yardstick characters are Norman Mushari, Senator Rosewater, and, to a lesser degree, Stewart Buntline. The obvious basis of contrast between Eliot and Mushari is that the former has wealth, a conscience, and a distaste for acquisitiveness, while the latter has no wealth, no conscience, but great greed. Without question the descriptive odds are stacked against Mushari from the start. He is only five feet three inches tall. Short stature is not necessarily pejorative in Vonnegut, but combine it with his posterior of excessive proportions, his lack of wit, his being tone-deaf, and the fact that his office fellows whistle "Pop Goes the Weasel" as he passes, and we have a clear enough picture. He salivates at the thought of money, and at a moment when she is grieved gives Sylvia "A hideously inappropriate smile of greed and fornication" (54). On top of that his boyhood idols are Senator Joe McCarthy and Roy Cohn. Actually, making Mushari a political conservative seems almost gratuitous. There is little else in his characterization to support his political affinities, except in so far as the novel does align the right-wing of the Republican party with the "God helps those who help themselves to everybody else's" mentality. Mushari's reading *The Conscience of a Conservative* seems rather ironic, in fact, since he has no conscience and is more acquisitive than conservative. There again the connection lies in the play on Goldwater / Rosewater and the satire of the right wing. Mushari's inspiration is a lecture by his favorite law professor, who explains that in every money transaction there comes a moment when the booty has been surrendered by the original owner but not yet received by the new one. This is an astute lawyer's magic moment. "If the man who is to receive the treasure is unused to wealth, has an inferiority complex and shapeless feelings of guilt, as most people do, the lawyer can often take as much as half the bundle, and still receive the recipient's blubbering thanks" (9). To that end, Mushari will try to ensure a divorce between two loving people and will work to prove a man insane. Measured against this young lawyer's calculated schemes, Eliot's earlier outbursts and irrationalities seem both human and moral, and ultimately more "sane." Incidentally, once Mushari has provided that contrast with Eliot, he fades rapidly in the novel, after having been introduced as if he would be a major character. Subsequently his role becomes only a plot convenience, connecting the Pisquontuit Rosewaters with the main narrative and providing the threat of Eliot's sanity hearing.

Senator Lister Rosewater's importance grows as Mushari's fades. For all that his politics are essentially cruel and his values often warped, the senator becomes an almost endearing character. We can well understand why even when suffering his insults Kilgore Trout can enjoy the senior Rosewater for what he is. Even in his "Golden Age of Rome" speech, a classic expression of right-wing paranoia, he somehow emerges more as buffoon than as threat (24–27). His ability to laugh at himself and at the image others have of him, his bluster, and the sheer physical force that emanates from his characterization, all lend him some appeal. We also sense that in his domineering way he genuinely does love Eliot and Sylvia. His social conscience, however, is registered when he speaks of Eliot's activities among his constituents. "In his heart . . ." he says, in a negative echo of Barry Goldwater, "Eliot doesn't love those people out there any more than I do . . . If Eliot's booze were shut off, his compassion for the maggots in the slime on the bottom of the human garbage pail would vanish" (46). For the senator, garbage, slime, or anything other than good clean wholesome living is anathema. To his credit, he does say that he has never thought much about perversion because there never seemed much in it to think about—a reaction we might, like the psychiatrist, find healthier than we expected. But his embarrassment by naked bodies and his aversion to pubic hair seem less healthy. They even afford him a specific definition of pornography: it is anything that calls attention to reproductive organs, discharges, or bodily hair. "The difference between pornography and art is bodily hair!" (72). In short, the senator indulges in a form of superiority complex in which dirt, hair, sex, fat, and inebriation are all seen as aspects of the lower orders of life that he holds in contempt.

The contrast between father and son extends further than one's being dirty, drunk, fat, and intrigued by his own pubic hair and the other's being averse to all these things. (Lister Rosewater has a hygienic mouthwash-cum-cologne sound to it, although the senator is strictly a soap and water man.) It comes down to the fact that Eliot cares for people, accepts their variety, their weakness, their physicality, and is troubled by their suffering, while his father cares little for the mass of human kind and regards most deprivations as deserved. Like the two Blake poems they quote, they represent contrasting aspects of love. Having experienced the consequences of hate and of plain error, Eliot sets himself the awesome task of simply loving without reserve and without help. Lister is also capable of love, but of the individualized, selective and possessive variety. He can love his son or Sylvia, but is appalled by Eliot's general love because it lacks "discrimination." His quotation suggests he sees Eliot's love as the kind which "seeketh only Self to please," as a self-indulgence. Ironically, Blake's phrase aptly describes Lister's love, in that by discriminating between those he judges deserve it and those who do not, he makes his love self-pleasing. Yet there is some support for his charge against Eliot. The psychiatrist suggests that Eliot has "his wires crossed" so that all his sexual energies are directed toward an "inappropriate" object—utopia (73).

At this point we can see how the subjects of love and money intersect. Lister is possessive of money, people, and love, wanting his money to go to those he loves, people who are *his*. Eliot takes the reverse tack, wanting to distribute wealth and love among all people. The capitalistic father sees the free distribution of money and love as indiscriminate, devaluing and contrary to his ethic that both things should be deserved. The egalitarian son feels all people inherently merit their share of both, and regards the hoarding of wealth and the withholding of love from one's fellows as mutually supporting vices. He also recognizes the corrupting influence of money and avoids the mistakes of regarding it as an answer to all problems. The novel vindicates Eliot, but not without reservations. As mentioned earlier, the senator is not made simply unloving, and some of Eliot's performances of love are ludicrous. His distaste for what money does to people leads Eliot into a neurotic wallowing in self-neglect. And Lister's condemnation of the way Eliot has shown love to his father and to the woman "whose only fault had been to love him" hits home. It makes the point that universal compassion can blind people to the responsibilities of personal love as easily as a "nation of two" can be an evasion of wider human concern. Eliot tries to shut out the words, but cannot avoid their truth. Thus begins his last great breakdown.

Stewart Buntline has a lesser but still important role as a figure who contrasts with Eliot. He can be seen as representing what Eliot could have become. In his younger days, he too has been disturbed by the notion that he has so much while others have so little. He goes to McAllister, who guides Buntlines as well as Rosewaters, and says that he has more money than he needs and that he wants to use it to end some of the world's sufferings, buying food, clothing, and housing for the poor. For McAllister this is a familiar line. Numerous young men come to him with the same story. McAllister's argument is simple: a great fortune is a miracle to be learned about and treasured; it is what makes the rich man important in his own as well as others' eyes; without that fortune he would be less happy and free; without it he would be nothing, his descendants would suffer and would regard him as a fool who "piddled a fortune away." Money, McAllister concludes, is "dehydrated Utopia," a miracle that can make life a paradise (119–21). Stewart yields to this, but the paradise he assumes is indeed dehydrated. At forty-odd years of age he is "through with misguided pity," through with sex, through even with his hobby of Civil War history, and spends most of his day sleeping with an untouched Scotch and soda by his side. He becomes so inert that his daughter always checks as she passes to be sure he is not literally dead. Once again, the man who follows the system looks singularly unhealthy in comparison with the "sick" Eliot. On the symbolic scale, Buntline, looking like death and "through with sex," is weighed against Rosewater who at the end plays tennis like a champion and acknowledges fifty-seven "heirs."

Sterility, perversion, or having "wires crossed" so that sexual energies are misdirected—as the psychiatrist says of Eliot—become familiar symptoms in the world of this novel. In Pisquontuit the tone is set by the passing around of *The American Investigator,* with its advertisements for male hair-dressers and swinging couples who want to exchange photographs, executives who want weekday afternoon dates with nonprudes, and prep-school teachers looking for stern Teutonic horse-loving instructresses. Peopling this scene are the suicidal Fred Rosewater, furtively sneaking peeks at sex magazines; his wife, Caroline, who is drunk after lunch daily; Amanita Buntline, a kultchur-vulture lesbian; her daughter Lila, who at thirteen pedals pornography to the children at high profit; and Bunny Weeks, a homosexual who runs a restaurant and gift shop. By mid-afternoon, by the way, all of these people seem to be asleep. The liveliest ones in Pisquontuit are the fisherman Harry Pena and his two sons.

As Harry's last name perhaps too obviously suggests, he stands for virility, fertility, and life. He is surrounded by fish and sea, in case we need more symbols, and tells Fred that the picture of a French girl in a bikini is not a woman but ink on a paper. "If this was a real girl, all I'd have to do for a living would be to stay home and cut out pictures of big fish" (109). Hale, hearty and earthy, Harry Pena becomes a rather romantic and sentimentalized characterization, but he serves a useful function in emphasizing through contrast the aridity and neurosis of the rest of Pisquontuit. His story counterpoints those of Bunny Weeks, Stewart and Amanita, Fred and Caroline, and of Mushari's visit to the Rumfoords. While Harry fishes for "real fish" with his "two real sons" in "a real boat on a salty sea" (111), all else in Pisquontuit is artifice. The homosexual Bunny Weeks gaily paws his female customers, sells seventeen-dollar toilet roll covers and other gimcrackery in his shop or hands out opera glasses so that his restaurant customers can watch the activities of the fishermen. (Caroline watches them and says, "It's so much like life.") Fred Rosewater dreams the afternoon away in his boat, his only consolation the knowledge that when he dies his widow will receive a healthy insurance benefit. Caroline apes Amanita and drinks away her aversion to not living in the style to which she would like to be accustomed. Amanita patronizes Caroline, spends money, patronizes the orphan Selena, spends money, plays Beethoven records at the wrong speed, adores the taste of Bunny Weeks and *Better Homes and Gardens,* and spends money. Stewart sleeps.

The two camps are mutually contemptuous of each other. As the fishermen take the mighty fish, they swear and laugh and feel full of joy. "All three were as satisfied with life as man can ever be. The youngest boy thumbed his nose at the fairy's restaurant, " 'Fuck 'em all, boys. Right?' said Harry" (130). In this restaurant, Bunny judges that the "three romantics out there make as much sense as Marie Antoinette and her milkmaids" (131). Men like that, he says, working with their hands and backs, are not needed any more. They are losing everywhere. Yet with equal contempt, Bunny looks at his fat customers who have all inherited, and at himself who is making money, and says: "And look who's winning. And look who's won" (131). The terrible truth in his comments is that men like Harry are a dying breed, and the number who can find purpose and satisfaction in labor continues to dwindle in an automated America. The irony is that the loser feels happy while the man who is winning and those who have won feel only boredom and resentment. But Harry and his boys are practically unique in this novel, and they too are being hunted down by money since, as Bunny reveals, they are going broke.

The overall portrayal of society in *God Bless You, Mr. Rosewater* is of a sick, sterile wasteland. Hardly a character appears who has not either a psychological or physical ailment. The pathetic Diana Moon Glampers believes that lightning is out to kill her and suffers constantly from psychosomatic kidney pains, while the seemingly prospering fire Chief Charley Warmergran has the "fatal flaw" of not believing that he does have gonorrhea. Until debt catches up with him, at least, Harry Pena appears the one exception, and he derives a sense of purpose from natural outdoor work. There are two conclusions to be drawn from this portrayal of society, and Kilgore Trout—another of Vonnegut's portraits of the artist—makes them both. One is that people need a sense of being for something, of some use or value, and that few of them find this. The second is that in such a world, where so many are afflicted and suffer, "people can use all the uncritical love they can get" (186). There might be a third point to be made—that much of the reason why love has been replaced by self-interest and indifference, and why meaning or purpose has been lost to rich and poor alike, stems from money.

Not surprisingly, Kilgore Trout's commentary on the loss of purpose in a technological world resembles that advanced in *Player Piano*. Machines have supplanted men as producers of goods and services, and are already in the process of doing so as sources of practical ideas in other fields like engineering, economics, and medicine. This leaves an increasing number of people without a function, often without work at all. The American work ethic has taught hatred of people who will not or cannot work, and contempt for oneself in that same situation. Hence the conditions prevailing in Rosewater, where "the Senator's people" who try to work and to keep going themselves despise the welfare recipients and unemployables who gravitate to Eliot, who in turn despise themselves. The lower income echelons feel purposeless either because they have no work or because their work seems meaningless, providing neither satisfaction nor advancement. Senator Rosewater argues that people can still work their way "out of the mire." Trout acknowledges the truth of this, but points out that even so, they or their children are likely to end up "in a Utopia like Pisquontuit, where, I am sure, the soul-rot and the silliness and torpor and insensibility are exactly as horrible as anything epidemic in Rosewater County" (184). As for the rich, we have seen that their inherited wealth leaves them victim to the work ethic, too. Either they work to perpetuate their situation, like Lister, and suffer the moral consequences, or they feel the frustrated purposelessness of Eliot in trying to find a way to make their wealth work to alleviate suffering, or like Stewart they float on their wealth and find no purpose in anything.

As Trout says, "The problem is this: How to love people who have no use?" The answer is to find a way of "treasuring human beings because they are *human beings* . . ." (183). And that, as he says, is not only rare, but difficult in practice. Volunteer firemen provide the model, in that they will aid, rescue, and comfort any man regardless of his worth, esteem, or wealth. Eliot's compulsion to aid and comfort the suffering and to rescue those on the brink of suicide is comparable. The breakdowns of Eliot and Sylvia demonstrate the difficulties of following such a course when it runs counter to the general direction of the society. Sylvia shares Eliot's concerns, and even after her second breakdown demonstrates that she believes in the rightness of what he is doing. Her collapses prove most informative in that they derive almost solely from the stresses of trying to aid the disadvantaged, whereas Eliot's are always complicated by the possibility of their being influenced by his war trauma. Her psychiatrist labels Sylvia's original illness "Samaritrophia," which he describes as "hysterical indifference to the troubles of those less fortunate than oneself" (41). This state comes about when the conscience dominates the rest of the mind, until the other processes rebel, noting that the conscience is never satisfied nor the world ever improved by all the unselfish acts demanded. The other parts of the mind then reject the conscience, following instead Enlightened Self-Interest, whose motto is, "The hell with you, Jack, I've got mine!" (42). The satire in this description, one might think, applies almost universally in our society. But it goes further. The majority of upperclass people in a prosperous, industrialized society, says the doctor, hardly ever hear their consciences at all. Thus he concludes that "Samaritrophia is only a disease, and a violent one, too, when it attacks those exceedingly rare individuals who reach biological maturity still loving and wanting to help their fellow men" (43). Sylvia's reaction follows predictable lines: a complete silencing of conscience and a giving over to self-indulgence. But this too fails, and another breakdown follows, after which Sylvia emerges in a frail condition, obviously believing in the rightness of Eliot's concern but unable to withstand the rigors of the life it demands.

In the touching telephone conversation in which Sylvia agrees to meet Eliot one last time in Indianapolis, it becomes apparent without her making any direct appeal that she desperately needs and wants the love and support of her husband. That Eliot has been too obsessed with his crusade to give her the love she needs has been apparent, and that at heart he knows it is suggested when he breaks down as the senator accuses him of this neglect. As the psychiatrist tells the senator, Eliot's sexual energies have been rechanneled into social reform. This diversion of sexual energy is emphasized in another, comic episode. Reading a pornographic novel by Arthur Garvey Ulm, a writer he had patronized years before, Eliot finds himself with an erection, " 'Oh, for heaven's sake,' he said to his procreative organ, 'how irrelevant can you be?' " And the immediately following paragraph begins with the senator lamenting, "If only there had been a child" (70). It is a telling juxtaposition of lines in a novel where so much emphasis is placed on virility and on real men encountering real life as opposed to perversion, aridity, sterility and artifice. Eliot's erection is as irrelevant as Fred's leching over the bikinied woman who is only paper and ink, but is also irrelevant in the sense that his procreative powers are miscast in the course he has chosen to follow. There appears to be a continuance of the idea expressed in *Cat's Cradle,* that where men see no purpose in existing the urge to reproduce fades or become perverted.

And so Eliot "clicks"—to use the term Noyes Finnerty coins. As Noyes describes it, this happens when a man who has been possessed of some irresistible motivation for years, some secret compulsion always driving him on, suddenly goes flat, empty, dead, that inner force spent forever (164–65). Why does this happen to Eliot? Because he has simply reached the end of his tether? Because his Rosewater project has run its course, with no further possibility of development and no ultimate satisfaction? Because of the charges of his father? Possibly it is because of all these things. Certainly he has become increasingly strained, tired, alcoholic, and even cynical about himself. His father's words do provide the last straw, as if Eliot recognizes that his efforts may after all have been selfish or as though he realizes that even in trying to show love to so many he has neglected and hurt others he loves. His vision of the firestorm as he drives into Indianapolis tends to confirm this surmise. The Trout novel he is reading has just recounted the death of the Milky Way. Eliot looks up to discover that "Rosewater County was gone. He did not miss it" (174). That curious juxtaposition suggests Eliot has more than "samaritrophia," for next comes the Dresden-firestorm-in-Indianapolis, another sort of end of the world. When Dresden was bombed, Eliot recalls, high explosive bombs were dropped before the incendiaries to put the fire brigades out of action. Without them there was no one to counter the final conflagration. Eliot's vision, then, seems to be a manifestation of his perception of a world about to be consumed, about to combine with the oxygen of hate, indifference, greed, self-interest, and purposelessness, with no "firemen" to save it. Perhaps he feels that, in the treatment of Sylvia that Lister charged him with, he has again killed firemen by mistake. Perhaps he feels that he, like the firemen of Dresden, has been bombed underground. Or perhaps he is overcome by the hopelessness of the odds against which he struggles. What precisely goes on in his unconscious we are not told, but the general implications of his breakdown are plain enough. Having the sanity to feel compassion in such a world is enough to drive a person insane. So is trying to act on that feeling, and so is trying to make love work.

Hamlet's struggles to do the right thing perturb his father's spirit and drive the woman he loves mad. Eliot drives his father to distraction, and causes his wife two breakdowns which finally put her in a nunnery where "the rest is silence." Hamlet delays killing Claudius largely on moral scruples, but becomes responsible for the deaths of others and the madness of Ophelia. As Eliot sees things run their course in spite of his efforts, he might be tempted to conclude like Hamlet that "There's a divinity that shapes our ends, / Rough-hew them how we will." Hamlet surrenders to that inevitability and goes to his tragic end. Eliot recovers from his breakdown, confused, uncertain, and looking, as he puts it, like "F. Scott Fitzgerald, with one day to live" (182). But his end is triumphant, if still in a rather crazy way. Eliot has not forced his conscience into an "oubliette," but has learned, or clung to, what Trout affirms as the greatest lesson to be gained from his experiment: "that people can use all the uncritical love they can get" (186). Or as Eliot himself puts it, "God damn it, you've got to be kind" (93). Eliot demonstrates his uncritical love by acknowledging all those spurious offspring as his heirs and by the message he sends them: "And tell them that their father loves them, no matter what they turn out to be. And tell them . . . to be fruitful and multiply" (190).

Once again Vonnegut moves to an ending that meets the requirements of comedy, dark as the comedy may be. The final note is affirmative, with the emphasis appropriately on fertility, love, abundance, and distribution of blessings—more like A Midsummer Night's Dream or The Tempest than Hamlet. Yet it remains something of a throwaway ending, with comic undercutting on the one hand and darkly tragic implications on the other. Eliot's solution—declaring as heirs children who can be proven not to be his—is in effect nutty enough to substantiate the insanity charges it was designed to thwart. It provides a delightful twist to the ending—Eliot beating Mushari on a technicality—but it leaves troubling questions. Is there any way a man can follow his conscience without being judged mad or actually going mad in this society? Is there no more viable solution to the human sufferings, the inequalities, and the neuroses that afflict contemporary America? Is there no more substantial hope than this for the emergence of "uncritical love," for the "treasuring of human beings as human beings" in our society? Vonnegut's answer again comes through Kilgore Trout: "If one man can do it, perhaps others can do it too. . . . Thanks to the example of Eliot Rosewater, millions and millions of people may learn to love and help whomever they see" (187). It sounds more like a prayer than an assurance.

The subtitle of the novel—"Or Pearls before Swine"—introduces the ambiguity that pervades God Bless You, Mr. Rosewater. Obviously it presents two ways of interpreting Eliot's actions: the title reflecting Diana Moon Glampers's response and the subtitle the view of Lister Rosewater. The subtitle is socially satirical, in that the kind of society the novel depicts would see the actions of this latter day Jesus figure as "casting pearls before swine." It might also refer to the fact that in this society the rich get richer, the piggy acquistors being the ones to whom more pearls are cast. And maybe Eliot's well-intentioned actions are as futile as casting pearls before swine. Many such ambiguities operate in the novel—to its benefit. Without them it might easily become too simply moralistic, naive in its social commentary and interpretation of human behavior, and frankly pedantic. As it is, Vonnegut manages to reinvigorate the ancient topic of avarice by giving it topicality, by relating it to recent technological developments and their social implications, by showing it specifically as a part of the American class and value systems, and by emphasizing its role in contemporary society's psychosis.

Notes

1. Kurt Vonnegut, Jr., *Wampeters, Foma and Granfalloons* (New York: Delacorte Press / Seymour Lawrence, 1974); hereafter cited as *WFG*.

2. Kurt Vonnegut, Jr., *God Bless You, Mr. Rosewater* (1965; rpt., New York: Dell, 1970), 21; hereafter cited by page number in the text.

Slaughterhouse-Five

[The Uncertain Messenger: A Reading of *Slaughterhouse-Five*]

Tony Tanner*

. . . Eliot Rosewater's last breakdown is triggered off by his conviction that he can see Indianapolis in the grip of a fire-storm. This illusion is partly a recapitulation of his own war experiences, and partly a projection of a description of the fire-storm in Dresden which he has re-read repeatedly. This is the vision of sudden and unbelievable annihilation which has been somewhere behind all Vonnegut's work, and which was finally brought into the centre of a novel in *Slaughterhouse-Five or The Children's Crusade* (1969). Here for the first time Vonnegut appears in one of his own novels, juxtaposing and merging the fantasies of his own life in a book which seems almost to summarize and conclude the sequence of his previous five novels. Slaughterhouse-Five was the actual address of the place where Vonnegut was working as a prisoner-of-war, and from which he emerged to witness the results of the Dresden air-raid. After seeing that, he tells us, he was sure that the destruction of Dresden would be the subject of his first novel. But he discovered that the spectacle of the Dresden fire-storm was somehow beyond language.

He describes how, over the years, he has tried to put a version together and make a novel, until now, at last, his famous Dresden war novel is finished, "short and jumbled and jangled, Sam, because there is nothing intelligent to say about a massacre," he adds apologetically to his publisher. But of course it is jumbled to very effective purpose. For it is not a novel simply about Dresden. It is a novel about a novelist who has been unable to erase the memory of his wartime experience and the Dresden fire-storm, even while he has been inventing stories and fantasies in his role as a writer since the end of that war. This book too will be a mixture of facts and invention ("All this happened, more or less"—so the book starts), for Vonnegut has created a character called Billy Pilgrim, whose progress entails not only undergoing the wartime experiences which Vonnegut remembers, but also getting involved in the fantasies which Vonnegut has invented. The result, among other things, is a moving meditation on the relationship between history and dreaming cast in an appropriately factual / fictional mode.

*Reprinted by permission from *City of Words* (New York: Harper and Row, 1971), 194–201.

125

Summarizing the line of the story that Vonnegut tells, we can say that Billy Pilgrim is an innocent, sensitive man who encounters so much death and so much evidence of hostility to the human individual while he is in the army that he takes refuge in an intense fantasy life, which involves his being captured and sent to a remote planet (while in fact he is being transported by the Germans as a prisoner-of-war). He also comes "unstuck in time" and present moments during the war may either give way to an intense reexperiencing of moments from the past or unexpected hallucinations of life in the future. Pilgrim ascribes this strange gift of being able to slip around in time to his experience on the planet which has given him an entirely new way of looking at time. We may take Vonnegut's word for it that the wartime scenes are factual, as near as can be attested to by a suffering participant. The source of Pilgrim's dreams and fantasies is more complex. The planet that kidnaps him is Tralfamadore, familiar from Vonnegut's second novel. At the same time it is suggested that the details of his voyage to Tralfamadore may well be based on details from his real experience subjected to fantastical metamorphosis. In his waking life Pilgrim is said to come from Illium (see *Player Piano*); he later encounters the American Nazi propagandist Howard Campbell (see *Mother Night*); in a mental hospital he has long talks with Eliot Rosewater, who introduces Pilgrim to the works of Kilgore Trout, both familiar from Vonnegut's last novel. Pilgrim is not only slipping backwards and forwards in time; he is also astray in Vonnegut's own fictions. Vonnegut himself enters his own novel from time to time (as Hitchcock does his films) and it becomes very difficult to hold the various fictional planes in perspective, as in a picture by Maurits Escher. But the overall impression is that of a man who has brought the most graphic facts of his life to exist in the same medium with his most important fictions to see what each implies about the other. (A relevant comparison may be found in Herman Hesse's *Journey to the East* in which the narrator describes how, on the pilgrimage he took part in, "we creatively brought the past, the future and the fictitious into the present moment." It might seem pointless to bring in this reference from a remote European novel; but as it happens the pilgrimage is also described as "the Children's Crusade" which is the subtitle of Vonnegut's novel. This suggests that Vonnegut may well have read and been influenced by Hesse's book.)[1]

On the one hand the book is obsessed with death. This obsession is noticeable in Vonnegut's earlier works, but *Slaughterhouse-Five* is packed with corpses. It is the force which rigidifies life that holds Vonnegut's attention. He mentions Lot's wife, turned to a pillar of salt; this foreshadows the uncountable rigidified corpses which resulted from the Dresden air-raid. At one point a trainload of American prisoners is described as "flowing" as it unloads like a river of human life. The last man of all on the train, a tramp, is dead. "The hobo could not flow, could not plop. He wasn't liquid any more. He was stone. So it goes." As we have seen, the opposition between the fixed and the flowing is very common in contemporary American fiction. (The property of ice-nine, in *Cat's Cradle*, is to turn everything liquid as hard and fixed as crystal on contact—accidentally dropped into the ocean it starts the end of the world.) At one point Vonnegut recalls a passage in a book by Céline in which he wants to stop everyone moving in a crowded street: *"There make them freeze . . . So that they won't disappear anymore!"* When it comes to freezing people, ice-nine and the Dresden fire-storm are about equally effective. One infers that Vonnegut prefers to see the crowds flowing.

On the other hand, as well as a lot of corpses there are a lot of books in this novel. They range from low fiction (*Valley of the Dolls*), to criticism (*Céline and His Vision*), to documentary studies (*The Bombing of Dresden, The Execution of Private Slovik, Extraordinary Delusions and the Madness of Crowds*), to high-level realistic fiction (*The Red Badge of Courage*), to poetry (Blake is mentioned, Roethke is quoted). One science-fiction book is mentioned, *Maniacs in the Fourth Dimension* by Kilgore Trout. Corpses exist in three dimensions; everything produced by the human imagination (extraordinary delusions, cheap wish-fulfilments or great art) exists in a fourth. Some of the books mentioned, like Crane's *Red Badge of Courage,* are intended to be accurate accounts of the cruel and pathetic maniacs who live in three dimensions; science-fiction goes directly into a fourth. But all the books mentioned form a spectrum which throws light on Vonnegut's own mixed genre (he could be said to be trying to combine Crane and Trout!).

Taken in sum the books have a general significance. They not only serve to extend the setting for Vonnegut's own tale, they are all symptomatic of that human will to communicate which is of central interest to Vonnegut. In this novel he goes out of his way to describe his days as a reporter and the intricate network of pneumatic tubes through which he had to transmit the news. At the time of writing he calls himself a "telephoner," because he likes to call people late at night and try to get through to them. This in turns ties up with the curious way in which Tralfamadorian novels are written. Billy Pilgrim cannot read them, but looking at the script which is arranged in brief clusters of symbols he guesses that they might be like "telegrams." A Tralfamadorian voice tells him he is correct: "each clump of symbols is a brief, urgent message—describing a situation, a scene." These are apparently read all at once, not in sequence. "There isn't any particular relationship between all the messages, except that the author has chosen them carefully, so that, when seen all at once, they produce an image of life that is beautiful and surprising and deep . . . What we love in our books are the depths of many marvellous moments seen at one time." This would seem to be an indirect statement of Vonnegut's own aesthetic, for although, not being from Tralfamadore, one necessarily reads in sequence the many compressed fragments or messages which make up his novels, one nevertheless gets the impression of arrested moments suspended in time. In reading Billy Pilgrim's adventures we too become unstuck in time. As a result we are left with something approaching the impression of seeing all the marvellous and horrific moments, all at the same time. Vonnegut, the telephoner, has condensed and arranged his telegrams to good effect. He starts his account of the adventures of Pilgrim with the single word—"Listen." This is to alert us. We are being messaged.

Billy Pilgrim moves around in time rather as Winston Niles Rumfoord did, and, as was the case with Rumfoord, this gives him an entirely new attitude to the significance and tragedies of those people who still live in an irreversible, linear-temporal sequence. From the Tralfamadorians he learns that all things from the beginning to the end of the universe exist in a sort of eternal present. They can look at time rather as one can scan a wide geographic panorama. Everything always *is*. "There is no why." This being the case everything that happens is exactly what has to happen. To use the Tralfamadorian image, we are all like bugs "trapped in the amber of this moment." The moment always exists; it is structured exactly as it had to be structured. For the Tralfamadorians the strangest thing they have encountered among Earthlings is the meaningless concept of "free will." Clearly this very lofty temporal perspective, like a heightened Oriental view of time, is, from our Occidental point of view, totally deterministic. More than that, it countenances a complete quietism as well. A motto which Billy brings from his life into his fantasy, or vice versa, reads: "God grant me the serenity to accept the things I cannot change, courage to change the things I can, and wisdom always to tell the difference." In itself this is an open-ended programme. But immediately afterwards we read: "Among the things Billy Pilgrim could not change were the past, the present, and the future." Billy becomes completely quiescent, calmly accepting everything that happens as happening exactly as it ought to (including his own death). He abandons the worried ethical, tragical point of view of Western man and adopts a serene conscienceless passivity. If anything, he views the world aesthetically: every moment is a marvellous moment, and at times he beams at scenes in the war. Yet he does have breakdowns and is prone to fits of irrational weeping.

Here I think is the crucial moral issue in the book. Billy Pilgrim is a professional optometrist. He spends his life on earth prescribing corrective lenses for people suffering from defects of vision. It is entirely in keeping with his calling, then, when he has learned to see time in an entirely new Tralfamadorian way, that he should try to correct the whole erroneous Western view of time, and explain to everyone the meaninglessness of individual death. Like most of Vonnegut's main characters he wants to communicate his new vision, and he does indeed manage to infiltrate himself into a radio programme to promulgate his message. He is, of course, regarded as mad. The point for us to ponder is, how are *we* to regard his new vision? According to the Tralfamadorians, ordinary human vision is something so narrow and restricted that to convey to themselves what it must be like they have to imagine a creature with a metal sphere round his head who looks down a long, thin pipe seeing only a tiny speck at the end. He cannot turn his head around and he is strapped to a flatcar on rails which goes in one direction. Billy Pilgrim's attempt to free people from that metal sphere, and teach his own widened and liberated vision may thus seem entirely desirable. But is the cost in conscience and concern for the individual life equally desirable? With his new vision, Billy does not protest about the Vietnam war, nor shudder about the effects of the bombing. The Tralfamadorians of his dreams advise him to "concentrate on the happy moments of his life, and to ignore the unhappy ones—to stare only at pretty things as eternity failed to go by." The Tralfamadorian response to life is "guilt-free." At one point Billy Pilgrim thinks of a marvellous epitaph which, Vonnegut adds, would do for him too. "Everything was beautiful, and nothing hurt." Later in life when a man called Rumfoord is trying to justify the bombing of Dresden to him, Billy quietly reassures him, "It was all right . . . *Everything* is all right, and everybody has to do exactly what he does. I learned that on Tralfamadore." Yet he still weeps quietly to himself from time to time.

Is this a culpable moral indifference? In later life we read that Billy was simply "unenthusiastic" about living, while stoically enduring it, which may be a sign of the accidie which settles on a man with an atrophied conscience. From one point of view, it is important that man should still be capable of feeling guilt, and not fall into the sleep which Germany and Europe slept as eternity failed to go by in the 'thirties. Can one afford to ignore the ugly moments in life by concentrating on the happy ones? On the other hand, can one afford *not* to? Perhaps the fact of the matter is that conscience simply cannot cope with events like the concentration camps and the Dresden air-raid, and the more general demonstration by the war of the utter value-lessness of human life. Even to try to begin to care adequately would lead to an instant and irrevocable collapse of consciousness. Billy Pilgrim, Every-man, needs his fantasies to offset such facts.

At one point when he slips a bit in time he sees a war movie backwards. The planes have a magnetic power which shrinks the fires from the burning city and wraps them up in steel containers which are then lifted into the planes; the men on the ground have long tubes which suck the damaging fragments from wounded planes. It is a magic vision of restored wholeness— "everything and everybody as good as new"—and as such it is the best possible justification for wanting to escape from linear time so that events can be read in any direction, and the tragedy of "before and after" transcended. At the same time we are given some hints about the equivocal nature of Billy's escapism. No one can bear sleeping near Billy during the war because he creates such a disturbance while he is dreaming. "Everybody told Billy to keep the hell away." One man even blames his death on Billy. Later, in the prison hospital, the man watching over him reads *The Red Badge of Courage* while Billy enters a "morphine paradise." In *Cat's Cradle* the narrator admit-ted that there was little difference between a writer and a "drug salesman," and while there is a kind of fiction which tries to awaken men to the horrors of reality (e.g. Crane's book), it is clear to Vonnegut that there are fantasies, written or dreamed, which serve to drug men to reality. When the reality is the Dresden fire-storm, then arguably some drugging is essential.

Billy's Tralfamadorian perspective is not unlike that described in Yeats's "Lapis Lazuli"—"gaiety transfiguring all that dread"—and it has obvious aesthetic appeal and consolation. At the same time, his sense of the futility of trying to change anything, of regarding history as a great lump of intractable amber from which one can only escape into the fourth dimension of dream and fantasy, was the attitude held by Howard Campbell during the rise of Nazi Germany. Vonnegut has, I think, total sympathy with such quietistic impulses. At the same time his whole work suggests that if man doesn't do something about the conditions and quality of human life on earth, no one and nothing else will. Fantasies of complete determinism, of being held helplessly in the amber of some eternally unexplained plot, justify complete passivity and a supine acceptance of the futility of all action. Given the overall impact of Vonnegut's work I think we are bound to feel that there is at least something equivocal about Billy's habit of fantasy, even if his attitude is the most sympathetic one in the book. At one point Vonnegut announces: "There are almost no characters in this story, and almost no dramatic confrontations, because most of the people in it are so sick and so much the listless playthings of enormous forces." It is certainly hard to celebrate the value of the individual self against the background of war, in which the nightmare of being the victim of uncontrollable forces comes compellingly true. In such conditions it is difficult to be much of a constructive "agent," and Billy Pilgrim doubtless has to dream to survive.

At the end of the novel, spring has come to the ruins of Dresden, and when Billy is released from prison the trees are in leaf. He finds himself in a street which is deserted except for one wagon. "The wagon was green and coffin-shaped." That composite image of generation and death summarizes all there is actually to see in the external world, as far as Vonnegut is concerned. The rest is fantasy, cat's cradles, lies. In this masterly novel, Vonnegut has put together both his war novel and reminders of the fantasies which made up his previous novels. The facts which defy explanation are brought into the same frame with fictions beyond verification. The point at which fact and fiction intersect is Vonnegut himself, the experiencing, dreaming man who wrote the book. He is a lying messenger, but he acts on the assumption that the telegrams must continue to be sent. Eliot Rosewater's cry to his psychiatrist, overheard by Billy Pilgrim, applies more particularly to the artist. "I think you guys are going to have to come up with a lot of wonderful *new* lies, or people just aren't going to want to go on living." Of course, they must also tell the truth, whatever that may be. Kafka's couriers could hardly be more confused. What Vonnegut has done, particularly in *Slaughterhouse-Five*, is to define with clarity and economy—and compassion—the nature and composition of that confusion.

Note

1. This suggestion of the relevance of Hesse is reinforced by the fact that Vonnegut published an article entitled "Why They Read Hesse"—"they" referring to the American young—in *Horizon* XII, Spring 1970. At the time of going to press I have not been able to get hold of this article and I am indebted to Mathew Winston of Harvard for informing me of its appearance.

Illusion and Absurdity: The Novels
of Kurt Vonnegut

Charles B. Harris*

. . . . As persistent and significant aspects of American culture, both the illusions fostered by nationalism and the Great-American-Success-Illusion can be viewed as American institutions. Vonnegut believes the responsibility for such institutionalized illusions rests clearly with Americans. Insofar as he treats these kinds of illusions, Vonnegut engages in social protest.

The second kind of illusion Vonnegut examines lies beyond protest. Whereas the first contributes to human despair and should be discarded, the second helps prevent despair and seems essential to human contentment. This is the illusion of a purposeful universe. Those who embrace it believe the world contains plan, meaning and a moral order, and that in the end all things work for the best. The belief in human progress ties in with this illusion. So long as man believes history unfolds as part of a universal drive toward goodness, he can see his own technological and scientific advances as consistent with this drive, as contributing to a universal goal. Strip purpose from the cosmos, however, and man's confidence collapses. Without a context of universal order and direction, progress seems random and arbitrary. The world, no longer explicable in terms of human reason, becomes unfamiliar, and man—in the words of Camus—"suddenly deprived of illusions and of light, . . . feels a stranger." This dilemma, continues Camus, "truly constitutes the feeling of Absurdity."[1]

Vonnegut's belief in a purposeless universe constitutes his main theme. This theme receives its most extensive treatment in *The Sirens of Titan*.[2] More an extended metaphor for an absurd universe than the science fiction novel it is usually taken to be, *The Sirens of Titan* effectively burlesques the entire notion of purpose, but a purpose stranger than any dreamed of in the philosophies of man.

Set some time "between the Second World War and the Third Great Depression" (8), the novel concerns multimillionaire Winston Niles Rumfoord, who "had run his private space ship right into the heart of an uncharted chrono-synclastic infundibulum" (13). Rumfoord and his dog Kazak, who had accompanied him in the space ship, find themselves "scattered far and wide, not just through space, but through time, too" (15). As "wave phenomena," they pulse in "distorted spirals with their origins in the Sun and their terminals in Betelgeuse" (266), materializing on any cosmic body that intercepts their spirals.

Rumfoord's circumstances are governed by the inhabitants of Tralfamadore, a planet 150-thousand light years from earth. In fact, every significant historical event on Earth, both past and present, including a Rumfoord-led invasion of Earth by Martians, has been determined by Tralfamadorians.

*Reprinted by permission from *Contemporary American Novelists of the Absurd* (New Haven, Conn.: College and University Press, 1971), 60–75.

These events form part of a continuous communique from Tralfamadore to Salo, a space-lost Tralfamadorian messenger. Elected to carry a message from "One Rim of the Universe to the Other," Salo experienced space ship trouble enroute and was forced to land on Titan, a tiny planet occupying the same solar system as Earth. After sending a message to Tralfamadore explaining his plight, Salo begins receiving a series of replies. Using a mysterious device called "the Universal Will to Become," the Tralfamadorians influence earthlings to construct these replies to Salo. Stonehenge, for example, means in Tralfamadorian, "Replacement part being rushed with all possible speed" (271). The Great Wall of China means: "Be patient. We haven't forgotten about you" (171). Because the apparatus directing the impulses is often inaccurate, many potential messages go amuck. The decline and fall of great civilizations on earth have been nothing more than communication breakdowns between Tralfamadore and Salo.

The Tralfamadorians use Rumfoord to help get the replacement part to Salo. After various turns of Vonnegut's complicated plot, Salo receives the necessary part and can resume carrying the message that has accounted for all human history. The message is a brief one. "Greetings!" is all it reads. By portraying the whole of human endeavor as nothing more than an exchange of messages between creatures from outer space, Vonnegut effectively debunks beliefs in a purposeful universe, in free will, and in human progress.

These themes recur in Vonnegut's fourth novel, *Cat's Cradle*.[3] Jonah, the novel's protagonist, has decided to write a factual "account of what important Americans had done on the day when the first atomic bomb was dropped on Hiroshima, Japan" (12). He begins gathering information on the late Dr. Felix Hoenikker, "father" of the bomb, whose activities Jonah wishes to include in his book. Jonah does not know that Hoenikker has also invented *ice-nine*, a deadly chemical capable of freezing anything it touches. Jonah's research finally leads him to the island of San Lorenzo, where he converts to Bokononism, a religion that frankly admits its basis in lies. The climax of the novel occurs when, following a bizarre accident, the *ice-nine* contaminated body of "Papa" Monzano, dictator of San Lorenzo, slides into the ocean, immediately turning the whole world to ice.

Like most of Vonnegut's novels, *Cat's Cradle* can be read on one level as a novel of protest, this time against the destructive powers of science. This is especially evident in Vonnegut's portrait of Felix Hoenikker. The epitome of scientific "objectivity," totally uninterested in people, Hoenikker remains oblivious to the effects his discoveries may have on mankind. More a naive child than a father of three, Hoenikker treats science as a game; his discoveries, as happy accidents. When a fellow scientist remarks after Hiroshima that science has now known sin, Hoenikker replies, "What is sin?" (21). Through his burlesque-portrait of Hoenikker, Vonnegut voices his concern that science, removed from a context of humanism, posits a danger to humanity. Despite its danger, however, science continues to be unquestionably accepted, even worshiped, in the novel as "magic that works" (143).

But *Cat's Cradle* goes far beyond protest. Like *The Sirens of Titan*, its main comment is upon the futility of human endeavor, the meaninglessness of human existence. This theme is conveyed primarily through the parables and "calypsos" of *The Books of Bokonon,* the Bible of Bokononism written by Bokonon for his followers. A Negro whose real name is Lionel Boyd Johnson, Bokonon was shipwrecked on San Lorenzo with a marine deserter named Earl McCabe. Dreaming of converting San Lorenzo into a Utopia, Johnson and McCabe supplied the island with a new form of government and a new religion. Johnson designed the religion, becoming a self-styled prophet in the process. His "calypso" on the goal of this new religion expresses both the need for the saving lie of religion and the reality of a meaningless universe.

> I wanted all things
> To seem to make some sense
> So we all could be happy, yes.
> Instead of tense.
> And I made up lies
> So that they all fit nice,
> And I made this sad world
> A par-a-dise. (90)

As is always the case in Vonnegut's novels when a strong man tries to help others, McCabe and Johnson fail "to raise the people from misery and muck" (93). Man, Vonnegut repeatedly emphasizes, can seldom help either himself or others. Julian Castle, founder of the House of Hope and Mercy in the Jungle where the ill of San Lorenzo receive free treatment, also discovers this fact. Like McCabe and Johnson, Castle wishes to help the natives. The futility of his wish becomes especially evident when, during a bubonic plague epidemic, Castle ministers to the stricken for days without sleep, saving so few lives that "a bulldozer actually stalled trying to shove [the bodies] toward a common grave" (111). At the height of the epidemic, Castle wanders into the dark and begins shining a flashlight "over all the dead people stacked outside" (112). Turning to his son, who had followed him, Castle giggles, "Son, . . . someday this will all be yours" (112). In this macabre context, the cliché takes on fresh meaning. Despite Castle's efforts, little change will occur. Life will remain "short and brutish and mean" (119).

Bokonon acknowledges this fact in *The Fourteenth Book of Bokonon* entitled "What Can a Thoughtful Man Hope for Mankind on Earth, Given the Experience of the Past Million Years?" The *Book,* one of the shortest in *The Books of Bokonon,* consists of one word and a period: "Nothing" (164). According to both Vonnegut and Bokonon, history is little more than a sequence of absurd events. Moral progress is illusory. From the localized holocaust of Hiroshima man has "progressed" to the world-wide cataclysm of Hoenikker's *ice-nine*. "History!" writes Bokonon. "Read it and weep!" (168).

Vonnegut's rejection of the idea of human progress reflects the dim view he takes of the human character. This disparaging view of man, along with his belief in a purposeless universe, constitutes Vonnegut's absurdist vision, a vision that overshadows any protest found in his novels. Protest, as indicated in the discussion of *Catch-22*, implies hope for reform. Like most novelists of the absurd, however, Vonnegut entertains little hope for either social or individual reform. Cosmic absurdity informs all things, including man and his institutions. This view of man constitutes a main distinction between Vonnegut's absurdist novels and the novel of radical protest.

Radical protest novels generally view man as the victim of his society. In the protest novels of Dreiser and Steinbeck, for example, a distinction exists between the "decent little people" and the financiers who control conditions. Steinbeck portrays the Joads as decent people who would have remained content cultivating their land had the banks not taken it away from them. Similarly, Dreiser makes it clear that Carrie Meeber's wrongdoings result from the standards of the society in which she finds herself more than from any intrinsic evil in Carrie. As we have seen, Heller's *Catch-22* also portrays potentially decent human beings caught helplessly in the trap of a bureaucracized society. In other words, the social protest novelists could place a certain faith in the masses. The evil these novelists perceive resides in the social system, not in the individual.

For Vonnegut, however, as well as for most contemporary novelists of the absurd, the "little man," while often victimized by a technologically oriented mass society, can seldom attribute his vile, stupid, mean-spirited nature to that society. Whereas the traditional protest novelist believed man would be all right if not for a corrupt social system, Vonnegut views not just man's institutions—but man himself—as absurd.

This theme occurs even in Vonnegut's great anti-utopia novel, *Player Piano*, a novel almost purely of protest. As George Woodcock has indicated, the anti-utopian novel, like the novel of social protest, levels its protest "from the disillusioned left."[4] The difference is that whereas the social protest novel confronts the here and now, the anti-utopia projects a future world. The "fundamental principle" of the latter, to use Mark Hillegas's definition, "is prediction or extrapolation, from existing knowledge and conditions, of things to come."[5] Like the novel of social protest, the anti-utopia "always makes a significant comment on human life: usually it is a vehicle for social criticism and satire."[6] Despite its inclusion in a genre of protest, however, *Player Piano* contains the seeds of Vonnegut's absurdist vision.

Like most anti-Wellsian novels, *Player Piano* takes place in a World State controlled by an elite corps of engineers and managers with the aid of a giant computer, *Epicac XIV*.[7] The mass of men have little to do; most jobs have been taken over by machines. Bored, the masses revolt, but—as in so many Wellsian novels—the revolution fails. Just before their surrender, however, the rebels, whose tactics had involved breaking up the machines in a few cities, begin tinkering with these broken machines, attempting to put them back together again. Vonnegut's irony clearly drives home his point:

even had the revolution succeeded, nothing much would have changed. So much for placing one's faith in the masses.

This pessimistic view of human character recurs in *God Bless You, Mr. Rosewater*. Eliot firmly believes that the people to whom he devotes both time and money are "the same sorts . . . who, in generations past, had cleared the forests, drained the swamps, built the bridges, people whose sons formed the backbone of the infantry in time of war" (69). Vonnegut makes it clear, however, that Eliot is deluded. "The people who leaned on Eliot regularly were a lot weaker than [Eliot believed]—and dumber, too. When it came time for their sons to go into the Armed Forces, for instance, the sons were generally rejected as being mentally, morally, and physically undesirable" (69–70). Similarly, Felix Hoenikker, the Einstein-like inventor of *Cat's Cradle*, acts independently of any institutions, social or otherwise. Indeed, he is called at one point in the novel "a force of nature no mortal could possibly control" (23).

Even the few figures who display strength of character in Vonnegut's novels do little good and receive no reward for their efforts. The attempts of Bokonon and Julian Castle to help the people of San Lorenzo prove futile, and Harry Pena's virility is simply irrelevant. Similarly, Eliot's ministry not only leaves the bootless citizens of Rosewater unchanged, but Eliot is committed to a mental institution for his efforts.

In the face of such all-encompassing absurdity, what is the proper response for man? Vonnegut offers at least three possible answers to this question. Man may practice uncritical love, hoping through kindness and charity to lend some meaning to an otherwise meaningless human condition. Or he can manufacture new illusions to supplant the old—comforting lies that will shelter him from the icy winds of an absurd universe. Finally, he can simply accept the absurdity of his condition, neither affirming nor denying it and never asking the most meaningless of questions, Why?

Several characters in Vonnegut's novels choose love and kindness as the proper response to life. In *Mother Night*, for example, Howard Campbell, Jr., decides to write a book about the love he and his wife shared. "It was going to show how a pair of lovers in a world gone mad could survive by being loyal only to a nation composed of themselves—a nation of two" (37). Eliot Rosewater also associates love and art. He feels the love he extends to "discarded Americans, even though they're useless and unattractive," serves as his "work of art" (47). Like Eliot, Julian Castle gives up a life of affluent ease to establish his Castle of Hope and Mercy in the jungles of San Lorenzo. Finally, in *The Sirens of Titan*, the lesson is that "a purpose of human life, no matter who is controlling it, is to love whoever is around to be loved" (313).

While Vonnegut's sympathy for this position is obvious, his sympathy never gives way to sentimentality. With the possible exception of *Sirens*, nowhere in his novels does charity bring about any meaningful change. Campbell loves his wife, but she is killed in the war. He then falls in love with his wife's sister, who turns out to be a Russian spy who betrays him. Eliot's charitable activities improve nothing, and Castle's efforts as a doctor fail to alter significantly the high death rate of San Lorenzo. On the one hand, Vonnegut agrees with the "one rule" Eliot Rosewater knows: "God damn it, you've got to be kind" (110). On the other hand, he realizes what is stated in *God Bless You, Mr. Rosewater,* that "the outside world has not been even microscopically improved by the unselfish acts" of man (54).

The acceptance of the futility of human endeavor and the purposelessness of the universe lies beyond the capacity of many. These people need illusions to sustain them. As Eliot Rosewater tells a psychiatrist in *Slaughterhouse-Five, or the Children's Crusade,* "I think you guys are going to have to come up with a lot of wonderful *new* lies, or people just aren't going to want to go on living."[8] In that same novel, both Eliot and Billy Pilgrim, the novel's protagonist, have "found life meaningless" and are "trying to re-invent themselves and their universe," turning to science-fiction for ideas.

To offset this general sense of meaninglessness, Bokonon erects his religion upon *foma,* harmless untruths. "Man got to tell himself he understand," he asserts in one of his "calypsos" (124). So Bokonon manufactures purpose. One of his lies, for example, states "that humanity is organized into teams . . . that do God's Will without ever discovering what they are doing. Such a team is called a *karass* by Bokonon" (11). Since, as Bokonon says, one is a fool who thinks he sees what God is doing (13), Bokononists should refrain from attempts to fathom the purposes they serve, remaining content with the knowledge that they serve God's ends. *Foma* such as these, says Bokonon, make it possible for man to be "brave and kind and healthy and happy."

Occasionally, however, Bokonon dispels the illusions he perpetrates, as in the following parable.

> In the beginning God created the earth, and he looked upon it in His cosmic loneliness.
> And God said, "Let Us make living creatures out of mud, so the mud can see what We have done." And God created every living creature that now moveth, and one was man. Mud as man alone could speak. God leaned close as mud as man sat up, looked around, and spoke. Man blinked. "What is the *purpose* of all this?" he asked politely.
> "Everything must have a purpose?" asked God.
> "Certainly," said man.
> "Then I leave it to you to think of one for all this," said God.
> And He went away. (177)

Bokonon's parable exposes the cruel paradox of modern living: "the heartbreaking necessity of lying about reality, and the heartbreaking impossibility of lying about it" (189). Lies, it seems, prove as useless in an absurd universe as charity. The fact of absurdity has become too obvious to conceal.

When both love and lies prove futile as viable responses to the absurd human condition, all that remains—other than suicide—is resignation. True wisdom, Vonnegut implies in *Slaughterhouse-Five*, lies in recognizing the things man cannot change. In the novel Vonnegut also suggests that it would be nice to possess the courage to change the things we can, but the novel offers little indication as to what falls within man's power to reform. "Among the things Billy Pilgrim could not change," for example, "were the past, the present, and the future " (52). The main idea emerging from *Slaughterhouse-Five* seems to be that the proper response to life is one of resigned acceptance.

This resignation undercuts any anti-war sentiment found in the novel. One might as well write an anti-glacier book as an anti-war book, Vonnegut says early in the novel. "And," he continues, "even if wars didn't keep coming like glaciers, there would still be plain old death" (3). In many ways, *Slaughterhouse-Five* is a book about death, an extension of the statement Vonnegut quotes from Celine: "The truth is death" (18). Everytime someone dies in *Slaughterhouse-Five* Vonnegut writes, "So it goes." The phrase occurs over one-hundred times in a one-hundred-eighty-six page novel.

The flippancy of the phrase offers a clue to the effectiveness of *Slaughterhouse-Five*. That effectiveness depends upon the novel's tone, the same kind of tone that colors most of Vonnegut's novels. In these novels, a carefully controlled ironic tension exists between the horrible, often catastrophic, events that make up the content of Vonnegut's novels, on the one hand, and what Richard Schickel calls "the sardonic, unhysteric rationalism of [the narrative] voice" on the other.[9] A second kind of tension also exists in many of his novels. Present in these novels are figures like Julian Castle and Eliot Rosewater, whose concern for humanity contrasts with the absurdity of their surroundings and the hopelessness of the novel's tone. In *Slaughterhouse-Five*, however, no such figure appears. "There are almost no characters in this story." Vonnegut explains, "and almost no dramatic confrontations, because most of the people in it are so sick and so much the listless playthings of enormous forces" (140). So the pervasive hopelessness of the novel's tone remains unmitigated by any character who strives, no matter how futilely, to act in a meaningful manner.

Slaughterhouse-Five is based partially on Vonnegut's own experiences in World War II. Like Vonnegut, Billy Pilgrim is captured by the Germans and taken to Dresden, where he witnesses the destruction of the city by American firebombers. While in Germany, Billy first becomes "unstuck in time." For Billy, "all moments, past, present, and future, always have existed, always will exist" (23). "Spastic in time" with "no control over where he is going next," Billy has "seen his birth and death many times . . . and pays random visits to all the events in between" (20). One of these events involves his kidnapping by Tralfamadorians, who take him via flying saucer to their planet where he lives in a zoo with Montana Wildhack, famous earthling movie star. One of the things the Tralfamadorians teach Billy is that "it is just an illusion we have here on Earth that one moment follows another one, like beads on a string, and that once a moment is gone it is gone forever" (23).

True time is like the Rocky Mountains, permanent, and one can "look at any moment that interests [him]" (23).

In *The Sirens of Titan*, Winston Niles Rumfoord possessed the Tralfamadorian ability to view all of time simultaneously. But, as Salo perceives, "even though Rumfoord was chronosynclastic infundibulated, and might be expected to take a larger view of things," he remained "a surprisingly parochial Earthling at heart" (273). Which is to say, Rumfoord could still become upset, even offended, at the absurdity of things. Billy Pilgrim, on the other hand, learns his lessons well from the Tralfamadorians. Completely resigned to the inevitability of events, Billy finds everthing "pretty much all right" (135). Even the destruction of Dresden, which claimed the lives of 135,000 German citizens, mostly civilians, draws the following response from Billy: "*Everything* is all right, and everybody has to do exactly what he does. I learned that on Tralfamadore" (171).

The first thing Billy learns from the Tralfamadorians is the utter lack of any cosmic purpose. "Why *you?* Why *us* for that matter? Why *anything*" Billy is told upon being kidnapped. "Because the moment simply is. . . . There is no *why*" (60). One searches for meaning in vain. Time, say the Tralfamadorians, "does not lend itself to warnings or explanations. It simply *is*. Take it moment by moment, and you will find that we are all . . . bugs in amber" (74). The world, in other words, is all that the case is, and attempts either to change or to understand it are foredoomed to failure.

The proper response to life, then, becomes resignation. "God grant me the serenity to accept the things I cannot change" becomes the prayer of relevance, one Vonnegut repeats several times throughout the novel. To enhance this serenity, one should "concentrate on the happy moments of . . . life, and . . . ignore the unhappy ones" (168). Billy succeeds in this advice so well that a fitting epitaph for his tombstone, we are told, might read: "Everything was beautiful, and nothing hurt" (105, 106). This, despite a life filled with such violent events as the destruction of Dresden, his own capture by enemy troops, a plane crash in which his skull is fractured, the bizarre death of his wife by carbon monoxide poisoning, and his eventual assassination by a deranged killer!

Such bland acceptance of "things as they are" seems strange in a Vonnegut novel. Initially, one suspects the novel ridicules rather than recommends such passivity. Yet little in the novel supports this contention. In fact, when Vonnegut suggests the epigraph for Billy Pilgrim, he comments upon its appropriateness to his own life (105). A similar sentiment appears in his introduction to *Welcome to the Monkey House*. The "two main themes of my novels," he writes, "were stated by my siblings."[10] Bernard, Vonnegut's older brother, stated the first in a letter home shortly after the birth of his first child. "Here I am," he wrote, "cleaning shit off of practically everything" (xiii). Vonnegut's sister stated the second theme. Dying of cancer, she uttered, "No pain" (xiv). Together, the themes seem contradictory. Can one, aware of how polluted "practically everything" in life has become, remain content with life? Or, to put it another way, why would one able to view painlessly the conditions of life bother to protest those conditions?

The prayer repeated several times in *Slaughterhouse-Five* provides the answer to these questions. "God grant me the serenity," it reads, "to accept the things I cannot change, courage to change the things I can, and wisdom always to tell the difference" (181). Certain things, then, lie within man's control. Included would be those illusions mentioned earlier that make man's life more tedious than necessary, the illusions that contribute to wars and poverty and prejudice. These illusions Vonnegut exposes and ridicules. Most things, however, exceed man's limited control, not to mention his equally limited understanding. True wisdom accepts this fact, acknowledging the lack of universal purpose or meaning or direction. All human activity is blighted by this pervasive absurdity. Since the blight is irremediable, acceptance of it may be the only sane response for man. Indeed, acceptance of absurdity may constitute the only logical extension of the absurdist vision.

The detached tone of Vonnegut's novels is the primary device by which he suggests the hopelessness of the human condition and the resignation he feels is necessary to that hopelessness. As Vonnegut's absurdist vision intensifies with each successive novel, the tone of these novels becomes increasingly "distant." Such "distance" does not suggest "an elaborate novelistic impasse to feeling and judgment," as one critic has maintained.[11] Rather, it indicates Vonnegut's growing resignation to the futility of caring as a viable response in an absurd world. His use of tone constitutes an important part of Vonnegut's absurdist method.

The special use Vonnegut makes of two-dimensional characters also reinforces his absurdist vision. Like Heller, Vonnegut often uses caricature to burlesque certain ideas and philosophies. Intentionally exaggerated figures such as Senator Rosewater, the Reverend Lionel J. D. Jones, Robert Wilson, and Felix Hoenikker are obvious burlesques of the "ideals" they uphold. Yet Vonnegut does not confine his use of two-dimensional characters to satire. In fact, he seldom depicts a "well-rounded" character at all. Almost none of his characters actually develops in the course of the novels.

We know many facts about the life of Eliot Rosewater, for example. We know that he was born in 1918 in Washington, D.C., that he spent much of his boyhood on the Eastern seaboard and in Europe, that he likes to sail and to ski, and that after a brief period at Harvard Law School he enlisted in the infantry, distinguished himself in many battles, and rose to the rank of captain before suffering combat fatigue near the war's end. We also know that while hospitalized in Europe he met and married Sylvia, his nurse, and then returned to Harvard where he earned his law degree and an eventual Ph.D. in international law. We know he was partially responsible for the death of his mother in a boating accident and that while in Europe he accidentally bayoneted two old men and a fourteen-year-old boy whom he mistook for German soldiers. Each of these facts, however, is merely stated. They in no wise contribute to the development of Eliot's character, which remains rather "flat" and two-dimensional; nor do they aid in our understanding of his actions. We never know, for example, why he goes to Rosewater, Indiana. "His Destination is there" (58), we are told—which does not adequately explain Eliot's motivation.[12]

Eliot leaves Rosewater as suddenly and as mysteriously as he arrived. Again, no clear motivation is provided. Dr. Ed Brown, the young psychiatrist who treats Sylvia when she suffers her breakdown, supplies as good an explanation as any. Eliot left Rosewater because he contracted Samaritrophia, defined by Brown as "hysterical indifference to the troubles of those less fortunate than oneself" (54). The disease, which attacks only "those exceedingly rare individuals who reach biological maturity still loving and wanting to help their fellow man" (56), occurs when the conscience is overthrown by the rest of the mind. Brown's prognosis is absurd, of course; but its explanation of Eliot's actions is as valid as a more "scientific" diagnosis would be—which is to say, not valid at all.

The point of Vonnegut's burlesque is that human actions do not always correspond to readily ascertainable motives. The belief that human actions proceed from certain sociological and psychological causes and that these responses can be measured and even predicted, simply constitutes another illusion man has erected to block out the reality of a directionless and chaotic universe. Vonnegut's reluctance to depict well-developed characters and to supply them with conventional motives for their actions serves as a conscious burlesque of the whole concept of realism in the novel. As Robert Scholes has pointed out, novelists of the past century or so have assumed that "a readily ascertainable thing called reality exists and that we all live in it." Thus, reality became "the only thing to write about."[13] This realism extended to characters; consequently, the humorous caricatures common to eighteenth- and nineteenth-century novels gave way to the well-developed, "round" characters of the modern novel—characters who were "psychologically valid." Vonnegut rejects all formulations of reality, whether they be religious, philosophical, scientific, or literary. Psychology is simply another delusive attempt to explain and systematize the inexplicable and chaotic, for man is as absurd as his universe. The well-rounded character whose actions proceed from clearly stated causes, then, represents a falsification. By peopling his novels with oversimplified, two-dimensional figures, Vonnegut mocks the belief that human beings can be understood in all their chaotic complexity, much less captured on the printed page.[14]

From the standpoint of both craft and theme, Kurt Vonnegut, Jr., must be reckoned a serious artist. His novels have progressed from satire to absurdity, from the early protest of *Player Piano* to the almost total resignation of *Slaughterhouse-Five*. Accompanying the gradual intensification of his absurdist vision has been an increased use of innovative techniques that reinforce that vision. Though Vonnegut's angle of vision has become increasingly absurdist, it remains steadfastly comic. Never does he give way to despair or empty cynicism. He has managed to face the absurdity of the human condition squarely without losing his concern for humanity or his sense of humor. Perhaps the comment Vonnegut makes most consistently in his novels is best summed up by Bokonon. "Maturity," Bokonon tells us, "is a bitter disappointment for which no remedy exists, unless laughter can be said to remedy anything" (134). The sincerity of his vision and the skill with which he handles his materials rank Kurt Vonnegut, Jr., among the more significant contemporary American novelists of the absurd.

Notes

1. Albert Camus, *Le Mythe de Sisyphe* (Paris, 1942), p. 18.

2. (New York, 1959). All quotations will be from this edition and will be noted parenthetically in the text.

3. (New York, 1963). All quotations will be from this edition and will be noted parenthetically in the text.

4. "Utopias in Negative," *Sewanee Review*, LXIV (Winter, 1956), 85.

5. Mark R. Hillegas, *The Future as Nightmare: H. G. Wells and the Anti-Utopians* (New York, 1967), p. 9.

6. *Ibid.*, p. 8.

7. Anti-utopian novelists often portray a state much like that envisioned by H. G. Wells. But the result of the Utopians they portray is not human happiness, as Wells envisioned, but human misery and uselessness. Hillegas elaborates this point fully in his excellent study.

8. (New York, 1969), pp. 87–88.

9. "Black Comedy with Purifying Laughter," *Harper's*, CCXXXII (May, 1966), 15.

10. (New York, 1968), p. xiv.

11. Burton Feldman, "Anatomy of Black Humor," in *The American Novel Since World War II*, ed. Marcus Klein (New York, 1969), p. 224.

12. By suggesting "Divine appointment," Vonnegut burlesques the Jonah-theme. This theme also occurs in *Cat's Cradle*, the protagonist of which believes that "Somebody or something has compelled me to be certain places at certain times, without fail" (11). But whereas the biblical Jonah performs a divine mission, saving the city of Ninevah from divinely inspired destruction by converting its inhabitants, Eliot Rosewater reforms no one, and the Jonah of *Cat's Cradle* succeeds only in securing a front-row seat for doomsday.

13. *The Fabulators* (New York: Oxford Univ. Press, 1967), pp. 136–37.

14. Vonnegut also burlesques the conventional novel with his comic use of chapters. In *Cat's Cradle*, a novel of less than two-hundred pages, for example, Vonnegut includes one-hundred-twenty-seven chapters.

Vonnegut's *Slaughterhouse-Five:*
The Requirements of Chaos

Robert Merrill and
Peter A. Scholl*

> I like Utopian talk, speculation about what our planet should be,
> anger about what our planet is.
>
> Kurt Vonnegut[1]

In the recent issue of *Studies in American Fiction,* Lynn Buck presents a
view of Kurt Vonnegut which has become depressingly popular. Her very
title, "Vonnegut's World of Comic Futility," suggests the drift of her discussion. Professor Buck speaks of Vonnegut's "deliberate mechanization of mankind," "the cynicism of the comical world he has created," and his "nihilistic
message."[2] She concludes at one point that "to enter Vonnegut's world, one
must abide by his rules, unencumbered by man-centered notions about the
universe."[3] There is some question, however, as to whether Buck is a reliable guide concerning the nature of these "rules." Her Vonnegut is a man
who cautions against "man-centered notions about the universe," whereas
the real Kurt Vonnegut once told a group of Bennington graduates, "Military
science is probably right about the contemptibility of man in the vastness of
the universe. Still—I deny that contemptibility, and I beg you to deny it."[4]
Her Vonnegut is cynical and nihilistic, whereas the real Kurt Vonnegut
recently said, "My longer-range schemes have to do with providing all Americans with artificial extended families of a thousand members or more. Only
when we have overcome loneliness can we begin to share wealth and work
more fairly. I honestly believe that we will have those families by-and-by,
and I hope they will become international" (*W*, p. xxiv). In short, Buck's
Vonnegut is a fiction. Vonnegut's readers know that he himself believes in
certain kinds of fictions, "harmless untruths" which he calls *foma.* But Buck's
version of Vonnegut is not harmless, for it leads her to distort the meaning of
everything Vonnegut has written.

This reading of Vonnegut is all too representative. Repeatedly, Vonnegut's critics have argued that his novels embody the cynical essence of Black
Humor, a form so despairing as to contrast even with the relatively dark
novels of a writer like Hemingway.[5] The result has been a thorough misunderstanding of Vonnegut's vision in general and the meaning of his novels in
particular. The distortion is most serious with Vonnegut's sixth novel,
Slaughterhouse-Five (1969), for this is his one book that has a real claim to be
taken seriously as a first-rate work of art. For this reason, it is crucial that the
novel be interpreted properly. To do this, the notion that Vonnegut's world
is one of comic futility must be abandoned. It must be seen that Vonnegut's
advice to the Bennington graduates is embodied in his novels as well.

* Reprinted by permission from *Studies in American Fiction* 6 (1978); 65–76.

But I continue to believe that artists—all artists—should be treasured as
alarm systems.

                                              Kurt Vonnegut (*W*, p. 238)

It is safe to assume that novels of social protest are not written by cynics
or nihilists. Surely protest implies the belief that man's faults are remedia-
ble. It is relevant, then, that Vonnegut's novels, early and late, were conceived in the spirit of social protest. Vonnegut has said that his motives as a
writer are "political": "I agree with Stalin and Hitler and Mussolini that the
writer should serve his society. I differ with dictators as to *how* writers
should serve. Mainly, I think they should be—and biologically *have* to be—
agents of change" (*W*, p. 237). This belief informs Vonnegut's first book,
Player Piano (1952), a novel which deserves Leslie Fiedler's elegant com-
plaint that it is excessively committed to "proving (once more?) that machines deball and dehumanize men."[6] It is crucial to *Mother Night* (1962), a
novel which has a rather unquietistic "moral" if the author's 1966 introduction is to be believed: "We are what we pretend to be, so we must be careful
about what we pretend to be."[7] And it is no less central to *God Bless You,
Mr. Rosewater* (1965), a novel in which Vonnegut's attack on capitalistic
practices is unrelenting. These books were all written by the man who once
said that he admired George Orwell "almost more than any other man" (*W*,
p. 94). They were written by the man who likes Utopian talk, speculation
about what Earth should be, anger about what the planet is.

    Therefore it is hard to believe that *Slaughterhouse-Five* is a novel that
recommends "resigned acceptance" as the proper response to life's injustices. Tony Tanner is the only critic who has used the term "quietism" in
discussing *Slaughterhouse-Five*, but most of Vonnegut's critics seem intent
on reading the book as if it *were* the work of a quietist. The problem concerns
Vonnegut's "hero," Billy Pilgrim. *Slaughterhouse-Five* is about Pilgrim's response to the fire-bombing of Dresden. This response includes Billy's supposed space-travel to the planet Tralfamadore, where he makes the rather
startling discovery about time that Winston Niles Rumfoord first made in
Vonnegut's second novel, *The Sirens of Titan* (1959), "that everything that
ever has been always will be, and everything that ever will be always has
been."[8] This proves immensely satisfying to Pilgrim, for it means "that when
a person dies he only *appears* to die. He is still very much alive in the past,
so it is very silly for people to cry at his funeral."[9] Indeed, it is very silly for
people to cry about anything, including Dresden. This is the "wisdom" Billy
achieves in the course of Vonnegut's novel. It is, of course, the wisdom of
quietism. If everything that ever has been always will be, and everything
that ever will be always has been, nothing can be done to change the drift of
human affairs. As the Tralfamadorians tell Billy Pilgrim, the notion of free
will is a quaint Earthling illusion.

    What is more disturbing, Vonnegut's critics seem to think that he is saying the same thing. For Anthony Burgess, "*Slaughterhouse* is a kind of evasion—in a sense like J. M. Barrie's *Peter Pan*—in which we're being told to carry the horror of the Dresden bombing and everything it implies up to a level of fantasy. . . ."[10] For Charles Harris, "The main idea emerging from *Slaughterhouse-Five* seems to be that the proper response to life is one of resigned acceptance."[11] For Alfred Kazin, "Vonnegut deprecates any attempt to see tragedy that day in Dresden. . . . He likes to say with arch fatalism, citing one horror after another, 'So it goes.' "[12] For Tanner, "Vonnegut has . . . total sympathy with such quietistic impulses."[13] And the same notion is found throughout *The Vonnegut Statement,* a book of original essays written and collected by Vonnegut's most loyal academic "fans."[14]

This view of Vonnegut's book tends to contradict what he has said in published interviews and his earlier novels. But of course the work itself must be examined to determine whether or not *Slaughterhouse-Five* is a protest novel. Such a study should reveal Vonnegut's complex strategy for protesting such horrors as Dresden.

> If all time is eternally present
> All time is unredeemable.
> "Burnt Norton"

> When you're dead you're dead.
> Kurt Vonnegut[15]

The key to Vonnegut's strategy is his striking introduction of the Tralfamadorians into what he calls an antiwar novel (p. 3). The fire-bombing of Dresden actually receives less emphasis than Billy Pilgrim's space and time travel, especially his visit with the Tralfamadorians. Vonnegut has played down the immediate impact of the war in order to make "a powerful little statement about the kinds of social attitudes responsible for war and its atrocities," as Harris has remarked of *Mother Night*.[16] By transporting his hero to Tralfamadore, Vonnegut is able to introduce the Tralfamadorian notions about time and death which inevitably call attention to more "human" theories. The status of the Tralfamadorians is therefore the most important issue in any discussion of *Slaughterhouse-Five*.

It is the status of the Tralfamadorians themselves which is in question, not just their ideas. Vonnegut offers many hints that the Tralfamadorians do not exist. Just before he goes on a radio talk show to spread the Tralfamadorian gospel, Billy Pilgrim comes across several books by Kilgore Trout in a Forty-second Street porno shop:

> The titles were all new to him, or he thought they were. Now he opened one. . . . The name of the book was *The Big Board*. He got a few paragraphs into it, and then realized that he *had* read it before—years ago, in the veterans' hospital. It was about an Earthling man and woman who were kidnapped by extra-terrestrials. They were put on display on a planet called Zircon-212 (p. 201).

It seems that the scenario of Billy's life in outer space is something less than original. Pilgrim gets his "idea" for Tralfamadore from Kilgore Trout, just as Dwayne Hoover gets his ideas from Trout in *Breakfast of Champions* (1973). Perhaps this is what Vonnegut had in mind when he said that "*Slaughterhouse* and *Breakfast* used to be one book" (*W*, p. 218). The parallel is instructive, for Hoover is clearly insane. Pilgrim may not literally be insane, but Vonnegut has undermined the reality of his experience on Tralfamadore. Indeed, the conclusion is irresistible that Pilgrim's space and time travel are modes of escape. Surely it is not coincidental that Billy first time-travels just as he is about to lie down and die during the Battle of the Bulge, nor that he begins to speak of his trip to Tralfamadore *after* his airplane crash in 1968. Faced with the sheer horror of life, epitomized by World War II and especially the fire-bombing of Dresden, Billy "escapes" to Tralfamadore.

If the very existence of Tralfamadore is in doubt, one might wonder about the ideas Billy Pilgrim encounters there. Billy takes great comfort in these ideas, but at first glance there would seem to be nothing very heartening in the Tralfamadorian philosophy. After all, the Tralfamadorians think of human beings as "bugs in amber" (p. 86). Like bugs, human beings are trapped in *structured* moments that have always existed and always will exist. For that matter, human beings are not really human: "Tralfamadorians, of course, say that every creature and plant in the universe is a machine" (p. 154). The Tralfamadorians would seem to be as jovial about life as the later Mark Twain.

But the Tralfamadorians have much to offer in the way of consolation. Most crucially, their theory of time denies the reality of death. Further, it allows man to pick and choose among the eternal moments of his existence. If everything that ever has been always will be, one can practice the Tralfamadorian creed and "ignore the awful times, and concentrate on the good ones" (p. 117). If one concentrates hard enough, he can have the same epitaph as Billy Pilgrim: "Everything was beautiful, and nothing hurt" (p. 122). He can be like Billy in other ways, too. He can survive such demoralizing experiences as Dresden. He can return home and complete his education, marry the boss's daughter, make $60,000 a year, father a daughter as capable as Barbara Pilgrim and a son who finally gets "straightened out" by the Green Berets; he can own a fifth of the new Holiday Inn in town and half of three Tastee-Freeze stands; he can be President of the Lions Club and drive Cadillacs with such stickers as "Impeach Earl Warren" and "Reagan for President." He can not only get by, he can thrive.

But all this can be done only by ignoring the wisdom embodied in Billy Pilgrim's prayer: "God grant me the serenity to accept the things I cannot change, courage to change the things I can, and wisdom always to tell the difference" (p. 60). This advice is meaningless for Billy himself, for "among the things Billy Pilgrim could not change were the past, the present, and the future" (p. 60). Billy is one of those people Vonnegut was referring to when he said, "there are people, particularly dumb people, who are in terrible trouble and never get out of it, because they're not intelligent enough. And it strikes me as gruesome and comical that in our culture we have an expectation that a man can always solve his problems" (W, p. 258). Billy is a man who can only solve his problems by saying that they are insoluble.

The irony here is that the Billy Pilgrims of this world *are* better off saying that everything is beautiful and nothing hurts, for they truly cannot change the past, the present, or the future. All they can do is survive. Tralfamadore is a fantasy, a desperate attempt to rationalize chaos, but one must sympathize with Billy's need to create Tralfamadore. After all, the need for supreme fictions is a very human trait. As one of Vonnegut's characters tells a psychiatrist, "I think you guys are going to have to come up with a lot of wonderful *new* lies, or people just aren't going to want to go on living" (p. 101). The need for such "lies" is almost universal in *Slaughterhouse-Five*. Most obviously, it lies behind Roland Weary's pathetic dramatization of himself and two companions as The Three Musketeers (p. 42). It is most poignantly suggested in the religiosity of Billy's mother, who develops "a terrible hankering for a crucifix" (p. 38) even though she never joins a church and in fact has no real faith. Billy's mother finally does buy a crucifix from a Sante Fe gift shop, and Vonnegut's comment is crucial to much else in the book: "Like so many Americans, she was trying to construct a life that made sense from things she found in gift shops" (p. 39). Billy Pilgrim's "lie" is no less human and a good deal more "wonderful."

But finally Billy Pilgrim is not Everyman. One may sympathize with his attempt to make sense of things, but the fact remains that some men have greater resources than others. Indeed, some men are like Kurt Vonnegut. By intruding into his own tale, Vonnegut contrasts his personal position with that of his protagonist. Billy Pilgrim preaches the Tralfamadorian theory of time until he becomes a latter-day Billy Graham (p. 142); Vonnegut looks with anguish at a clock he wants to go faster and remarks, "There was nothing I could do about it. As an Earthling, I had to believe whatever clocks said— and calendars" (p. 20). Billy Pilgrim sends his son to Vietnam and the Green Berets; Vonnegut tells his sons "that they are not under any circumstances to take part in massacres, and that the news of massacres of enemies is not to fill them with satisfaction or glee." Vonnegut even tells his sons "not to work for companies which make massacre machinery, and to express contempt for people who think we need machinery like that" (p. 19). Billy Pilgrim says that God was right when He commanded Lot's wife not to look back upon Sodom and Gomorrah; Vonnegut writes *Slaughterhouse-Five* and so becomes "a pillar of salt" himself (p. 22). As Donald Greiner has said, "while Billy can come to terms with death and Dresden, Vonnegut cannot."[17] Nor can anyone who would be fully human.

This should be clear from a careful reading of Vonnegut's first chapter. Vonnegut's discussion of how he wrote *Slaughterhouse-Five* is not an indulgence, for his difficulties in writing the book are as crucial to its meaning as the story of Billy Pilgrim. As a "trafficker in climaxes and thrills and characterizations and wonderful dialogue and suspense and confrontations" (p. 5), Vonnegut is supposed to create fictions with beginnings, middles, and ends. But how does one create such a structure from the materials of Dresden? One can follow Billy Pilgrim to Tralfamadore and write the Tralfamadorian equivalent of the novel, books which appear to be "brief clumps of symbols separated by stars," where each clump of symbols is "a brief, urgent message" and "there is no beginning, no middle, no end, no suspense, no moral, no causes, no effects" (p. 88). But the burden of Vonnegut's first chapter is that to do so would be to deny one's humanity. Vonnegut can't deny that he is an Earthling who must believe whatever clocks and calendars tell him. Further, he is an intelligent, sensitive Earthling who knows that from a human point of view there *are* causes and effects, not to mention morals. The effects of Dresden are terrible but they can be reckoned. The effects of helping other Earthlings are also real, so Vonnegut can remark that it is "a lovely thing" for Mary O'Hare to be a trained nurse. It is a lovely thing because it is so *human*. Vonnegut also says that he loves Lot's wife for having spurned God's rather Tralfamadorian advice. He himself has become a pillar of salt because, unlike his hero, he cannot reject the burden of being human.

It may seem that Vonnegut has contradicted himself, for Billy's "lie" apparently expresses a profoundly human need at the same time that it denies his humanity. In point of fact, the contradiction is Pilgrim's. Indeed, the pathos of Billy's story is captured in this paradox. Because he is one of those people who are in terrible trouble and not intelligent enough to get out of it, Billy is unable to imagine a saving lie except one that denies personal moral responsibility. Of course, for those who see Vonnegut as a quietist, this is as it should be. These critics see the Tralfamadorian message as an example of *foma,* or "harmless untruths," a concept advocated in an earlier Vonnegut novel, *Cat's Cradle* (1963). Whether this is indeed the case is crucial to any interpretation of the later novel.

It is true that Vonnegut follows such philosophers as Vaihinger in arguing that all human ideas are fictions. As Vonnegut once said, "everything is a lie, because our brains are two-bit computers, and we can't get very high-grade truths out of them." For this reason, man must follow Vaihinger's advice and live by his fictions as if they were "true," as if their validity could somehow be demonstrated.[18] Man must embrace fictions that are "harmless" because their human consequences are benign. In this interview Vonnegut went on to say that while brains are two-bit computers, "we do have the freedom to make up comforting lies." Asked for an example of a comforting lie, Vonnegut replied, " 'Thou shalt not kill.' That's a good lie. Whether God said it or not, it's still a perfectly good lie" (W, p. 240).

So far as *Slaughterhouse-Five* is concerned, the question is whether the theories of Tralfamadore qualify as *foma.* In a very limited sense the answer is yes, for these theories do provide comfort for people like Billy Pilgrim. But what comforts Pilgrim will not do the job for everyone. Finally there is a great difference between the quietistic notions of Tralfamadore and the injunction not to kill. The latter is a truly comforting "lie": it implies that human life is inherently valuable, and it suggests that men are capable of *choosing* whether or not they will destroy their fellow human beings. The consequences of accepting this idea are altogether agreeable. The consequences of believing in Tralfamadore and its theories are something else again. Vonnegut is careful to show that these consequences involve more than enabling Billy Pilgrim to achieve a sustaining serenity. They involve an indifference to moral problems which is the ultimate "cause" of events like Dresden.

Critics of *Slaughterhouse-Five* seem never to notice that it is filled with Tralfamadorians who look very much like human beings. An obvious example would be the German guards who brutalize Billy Pilgrim and his fellow prisoners of war. The connection with Tralfamadorian fatalism is suggested by an interesting parallel. When he is kidnapped by the Tralfamadorians, Billy inquires of his captors, "Why me?" The Tralfamadorians reply, "Why you? Why *us* for that matter? Why *anything?*" (pp. 76–77). Later, one of Billy's fellow prisoners is beaten gratuitously by a German guard. "Why me?" the prisoner asks. "Vy you? Vy anybody?" the guard answers (p. 91). This parallel exposes the inhumane consequences of adopting the Tralfamadorian point of view, for the denial of personal reponsibility easily leads to the brutal excesses of the Nazis. Vonnegut hardly sees the problem as peculiarly Germanic, however. Early in chapter one, he reminisces about his experiences as a police reporter for the Chicago City News Bureau. One day he covered the death of a young veteran who had been squashed in a freak elevator accident. The woman writer who took his report calmly asked him to contact the dead man's wife and pretend to be a police captain. He was to do this in order to get her response. As Vonnegut remarks, "World War II had certainly made everybody very tough" (p. 10). This sort of complacence might be termed quasi-Tralfamadorian. What is missing is an attempt to rationalize the status quo. This comes later from a Marine major at a Lions Club meeting: "He said that Americans had no choice but to keep fighting in Vietnam until they achieved victory or until the Communists realized that they could not force their way of life on weak countries" (p. 59). It seems that America had "no choice" but to remain in Vietnam. But then the Allies had no choice but to destroy Dresden, either, or so Billy is told by Bertram Copeland Rumfoord, a retired brigadier general in the Air Force Reserve and the official Air Force historian. "It *had* to be done," Rumfoord tells Billy. "Pity the men who had to *do* it." Billy assures Rumfoord that he understands: "Everything is all right, and everybody has to do exactly what he does. I learned that on Tralfamadore" (p. 198). As this reply suggests, Rumfoord's statements are in the best spirit of Tralfamadore. The general has obviously read his Pope: Whatever is, is right.

The scene involving Rumfoord and Billy Pilgrim is positioned at the end of *Slaughterhouse-Five* because it is the real climax to Vonnegut's complex protest novel. The object of satiric attack turns out to be a complacent response to the horrors of the age. The horror of Dresden is not just that it *could* happen here, in an enlightened twentieth century. The real horror is that events such as Dresden continue to occur and no one seems appalled. *Slaughterhouse-Five* is filled with allusions to such postwar disasters as Vietnam, the assassinations of Bobby Kennedy and Martin Luther King, Jr., and the riots in American ghettos. Vonnegut stresses the kinship between these events and Dresden, most notably in the scene where Billy Pilgrim drives his Cadillac through a burned-down ghetto which reminds him "of some of the towns he had seen in the war" (p. 59). These are the problems Billy avoids in his life as Lions Club President, Tastee-Freeze entrepreneur, and Reagan supporter. These are the problems the Marine major and Professor Rumfoord would see as "inevitable." But it is one thing to say that human problems are insoluble if one has visited Tralfamadore. It is quite another to support this view from a strictly Earthling perspective. Vonnegut's point is that insofar as men are guided by the likes of Professor Rumfoord, they act as if the Tralfamadorians were real and their deterministic assumptions valid. Yet Rumfoord's assertion that Dresden *had* to be is obviously false. The distinguishing feature of the raid on Dresden is that there was no strategic advantage to it whatsoever. The assertion is not a true example of *foma* because the notion of harmless untruths implies that there are also *harmful* untruths. Man must judge his lies by their consequences, and the consequences are disastrous if people in power believe that Dresden was inevitable. In Vonnegut's view, the consequences are Vietnam, the ghettos, and a social order that seriously considers the election of Ronald Reagan as President of the United States.

What Vonnegut has done in *Slaughterhouse-Five* is "poison" his readers with humanity. The term is his own:

> And it's been the university experience that taught me that there is a very good reason that you catch people before they become generals and presidents and so forth and you poison their minds with . . . humanity, and however you want to poison their minds, it's presumably to encourage them to make a better world.[19]

Vonnegut is not sanguine about the possibilities for this better world, for he believes that the people in power really determine the quality of life in any age. As he once told the graduating class at Bennington, "Another great swindle is that people your age are supposed to save the world. . . . It isn't up to you. You don't have the money and the power. . . . It is up to older people to save the world" (W, p. 167). Alas, the older people seem to respect men like Professor Rumfoord. Yet the effort can and must be made to "poison" the young with more humane values.

Vonnegut's Bennington speech has been grossly misrepresented by those who would characterize him as a quietist. Glenn Meeter, for example, cites the passage just quoted as proof that Vonnegut is a Tralfamadorian at heart.[20] In doing so, Meeter ignores what Vonnegut went on to tell the Bennington graduates: "When it really is time for you to save the world, when you have some power and know your way around, when people can't mock you for looking so young, I suggest that you work for a socialist form of government" (W, pp. 167–68). He ignores Vonnegut's blunt rejection of the Tralfamadorian view of man: "Military science is probably right about the contemptibility of man in the vastness of the universe. Still—I deny that contemptibility, and I beg you to deny it" (W, p. 165).

Slaughterhouse-Five presents much the same argument. The book suggests that if there is any philosophical basis to the actions of men like Professor Rumfoord, it is a callous Social Darwinism. In this spirit Rumfoord tells his doctors "that people who were weak deserved to die." But the doctors disagree, for they are "devoted to the idea that weak people should be helped as much as possible" (p. 193). Vonnegut is devoted to the same idea. He has said again and again that whatever man's limitations he does have the power to change the conditions of human life. Slaughterhouse-Five defends this position so eloquently because it blinks at none of the attendant problems. Vonnegut's self-portrait is again crucial, for the depression he acknowledges in his own history testifies to the terrible effort men must make if they would commit themselves to an all but impossible task. No one knows better than Vonnegut that the vast majority of comforting lies are insufficient. He has recently redefined foma as "harmless untruths, intended to comfort simple souls. An example: 'Prosperity is just around the corner' " (W, p. xv). It will take more than this sort of thing to defeat the "bad" illusions of Marine majors and Air Force historians. But for those who are not such simple souls, the alternative to concerted action is suicide.

Vonnegut's new novel, Breakfast of Champions, is about an unsimple soul named Kurt Vonnegut who does contemplate suicide as a viable option. It is about a man who seriously entertains the Tralfamadorian view of man as machine, who has "come to the conclusion that there was nothing sacred about myself or about any human being, that we were all machines, doomed to collide and collide and collide."[21] It is a novel about a man who is "rescued" from this philosophical cul-de-sac by the assertion of one of his characters that most of man's parts may be "dead machinery," but there is still "an unwavering band of light" in man, his human awareness, which must be seen as sacred (BC, p. 226). Other men must see it this way, too, for as Vonnegut says ". . . there is no order to the world around us. . . . We must adapt ourselves to the requirements of chaos instead" (BC, p. 215). Having so adapted himself, Vonnegut can say, in the subtitle to Breakfast of Champions, "Goodbye Blue Monday!" This assertion is dramatically unimpressive, but it does suggest that the author of Slaughterhouse-Five knows very well that the requirements of chaos demand human vigilance and not "resigned acceptance." Indeed, they demand the insistence on humane practices which is the burden of everything Vonnegut has written.[22]

Notes

1. Joe David Bellamy, ed., *The New Fiction: Interviews with Innovative American Writers* (Urbana: Univ. of Illinois Press, 1974), p. 206.

2. Lynn Buck, "Vonnegut's World of Comic Futility," *SAF*, 3 (1975), 183, 196.

3. Buck, p. 183.

4. Kurt Vonnegut, Jr., *Wampeters, Foma & Granfalloons* (New York: Delacorte Press/ Seymour Lawrence, 1974), p. 165. Future references to this work will be incorporated into the text with the abbreviation *W*.

5. See especially Clinton S. Burhans, Jr., "Hemingway and Vonnegut: Diminishing Vision in a Dying Age," *MFS*, 21 (1975), 173–91.

6. Leslie A. Fiedler, "The Divine Stupidity of Kurt Vonnegut," *Esquire*, 74 (September, 1970), 199.

7. Kurt Vonnegut, Jr., *Mother Night* (New York: Avon Books, 1967), p. v.

8. Kurt Vonnegut, Jr., *The Sirens of Titan* (New York: Dell, 1970), pp. 25–26.

9. Kurt Vonnegut, Jr., *Slaughterhouse-Five* (New York: Dell, 1971), pp. 26–27. Unless otherwise noted, all future page references will be to this edition.

10. "*Playboy* Interview: Anthony Burgess," *Playboy*, 21 (September, 1974), 74.

11. Charles B. Harris, *Contemporary American Novelists of the Absurd* (New Haven: College & University Press, 1971), p. 69.

12. Alfred Kazin, *Bright Book of Life* (Boston: Little, Brown, and Co., 1973), p. 88.

13. Tony Tanner, *City of Words* (New York: Harper & Row, 1971), p. 200.

14. See the following in *The Vonnegut Statement*, eds. Jerome Klinkowitz and John Somer (New York: Delta, 1973): Jerome Klinkowitz, "*Mother Night, Cat's Cradle*, and the Crimes of Our Time," pp. 169, 176; Glenn Meeter, "Vonnegut's Formal and Moral Otherworldliness: *Cat's Cradle* and *Slaughterhouse-Five*," pp. 217–19; John Somer, "Geodesic Vonnegut; or, If Buckminister Fuller Wrote Novels," pp. 230, 237, 242, 251.

15. *Mother Night*, p. vii.

16. Harris, p. 51.

17. Donald J. Greiner, "Vonnegut's *Slaughterhouse-Five* and the Fiction of Atrocity," *Critique*, 14, (1973), 49.

18. See Hans Vaihinger, *The Philosophy of "As If"*, trans. C. K. Ogden (London, 1924). For a discussion of this idea as it is related to literature, see Frank Kermode, *The Sense of an Ending* (New York: Oxford Univ. Press, 1967).

19. Robert Scholes, "A Talk with Kurt Vonnegut," in *The Vonnegut Statement*, p. 107.

20. See Meeter, p. 219.

21. Kurt Vonnegut, Jr., *Breakfast of Champions* (New York: Delacorte Press/Seymour Lawrence, 1973), pp. 224–25. Future references to this work will be incorporated into the text with the abbreviation *BC*.

22. A number of this paper's conclusions are anticipated by Maurice J. O'Sullivan, Jr. in his recent essay, "*Slaughterhouse-Five*: Kurt Vonnegut's Anti-Memoirs," *Essays in Literature*, 3 (1976), 244–50. Published after the present essay was accepted for publication, O'Sullivan's reading of *Slaughterhouse-Five* is much the most persuasive discussion of the book to appear so far, though it does not go far enough in tracing either the logic or the details of Vonnegut's fictional "argument" against quietism.

The Later Works

Vonnegut's *Breakfast of Champions:* The Conversion of Heliogabalus
Robert Merrill*

The reviews of Kurt Vonnegut's *Breakfast of Champions* (1973) are remarkably misleading. Where one reviewer speaks of the book's "gratuitous digressions,"[1] another refers to the "banality, the nearly Kiwanian subtlety of [its] social criticisms."[2] Yet another describes it as "a deliberate curiosity, an earnest attempt to play after getting Dresden out of the way."[3] The reviewers talk much about Vonnegut's "stick figures"[4] and "facile fatalism."[5] Anyone who reads the reviews must conclude that *Breakfast of Champions* is an act of sheer audacity, that Vonnegut has exploited his enormous popularity by throwing between covers nothing but "textural irrelevancies."[6] Yet to speak of *Breakfast of Champions* as "play" suggests an almost absolute misunderstanding of Vonnegut's intentions.

Breakfast of Champions can only be understood as a novel *about* "facile fatalism." Like *Slaughterhouse-Five* (1969), it is a novel in which Kurt Vonnegut is his own protagonist, but the "Vonnegut" of this book is rather less appealing than in the earlier novel—so much so that his facile fatalism and banal social criticisms have tended to alienate his readers altogether. The effect is largely deliberate: *Breakfast of Champions* is "a moving, tortured, and honest book"[7] because in it Vonnegut turns an extremely cold eye on his own artistic practices and philosophical assumptions. In a rather zany way it is a bildungsroman about a fifty-year-old artless artist and facile philosopher. It is also a novel about the regeneration of this sorry figure. Far from being the dispirited effort its reviewers took it to be, *Breakfast of Champions* is an artistic act of faith.

Such assertions must be fleshed out, of course, but one should perhaps also insist on what the novel is *not*. Most crucially, *Breakfast of Champions* is not a traditional novel of character. Vonnegut remarks in *Slaughterhouse-Five*, "There are almost no characters in this story, and almost no dramatic confrontations, because most of the people in it are so sick and so much the listless playthings of enormous forces."[8] The people in *Breakfast of Champi-*

*Reprinted by permission from *Critique* 18 (1977); 99–109. This essay has been slightly revised.

153

ons are "stick figures" for much the same reason, as this novel also examines the apparent sickness and listlessness of contemporary man. The novel's thematic structure requires that Vonnegut's characters seem wooden or mechanical, for they are exemplary figures in a moral fable. As a number of critics have pointed out, all of Vonnegut's novels are such fables.[9] One might wonder whether Vonnegut is capable of writing more traditional fiction in which "rounded" characters are of the essence. Strictly speaking, however, he has never tried to do so.

Still, the novelist of ideas must somehow interest us in the fictional debate that informs his work. In *Slaughterhouse-Five* and *Breakfast of Champions*, Vonnegut dramatizes his own attempt to comprehend the problems of his characters. Vonnegut has said that these two novels were once "one book,"[10] and nothing points up the family resemblance so well as Vonnegut's use of himself as a persona in each novel. His self-portrait is essential to the meaning of each book, though the two personae differ considerably.

The "Kurt Vonnegut" of *Slaughterhouse-Five* is an attractive figure. Above all he is honest. In the first chapter he charts the decline of his youthful idealism. Once he and his wife were World Federalists, but now, as they near fifty, he is not sure what they are. He supposes they are Telephoners (*Five*, 11). *He* is a Telephoner, at any rate, for he admits that he is in the habit of calling up old friends after getting drunk and driving his wife away "with a breath like mustard gas and roses" (*Five*, 4). But if Vonnegut is "an old fart with his memories and his Pall Malls, with his sons full grown" (*Five*, 2), he is an engaging old fart—one who speaks fondly of Guggenheim money ("God love it") and likes to quote dirty limericks (*Five*, 1, 2–3). We are made to feel that Vonnegut's idealism has not really evaporated; rather, it has been challenged by the most fearful of realities: his memories of the firebombing of Dresden. We strongly identify with Vonnegut's predicament, for the first chapter traces his successful attempt to throw off an understandable depression and somehow deal with those terrible memories. Vonnegut may tell his publisher that *Slaughterhouse-Five* is "short and jumbled and jangled . . . because there is nothing intelligent to say about a massacre" (*Five*, 19), but the book still represents one man's attempt to exorcise the numbing sense of helplessness we all must feel in an age of cataclysmic horrors. We love Vonnegut for becoming "a pillar of salt," like Lot's wife (*Five*, 22), for in doing so Vonnegut has looked back. He has asserted, implicitly, that even the worst of modern disasters can be dealt with from a human point of view. Finally, we do not remember Vonnegut's depression so much as his transcendence of this melancholy, reflected in his promise to Mary O'Hare that his war novel will not include a part for Frank Sinatra or John Wayne (*Five*, 15) and in the advice he offers to his sons: "I have told my sons that they are not under any circumstances to take part in massacres, and that the news of massacres of enemies is not to fill them with satisfaction or glee" (*Five*, 19).

The "Kurt Vonnegut" we encounter in *Breakfast of Champions* is a good deal less heroic. He is still self-deprecating, telling us that he feels "lousy" about his book,[11] suggesting that he is "programmed at fifty to perform childishly" (5), but his depression seems rather more serious. Here we get no stirring speeches to his sons; the man we meet here is not so much depressed by inhumane practices as by human nature itself. He suspects that "human beings are robots, are machines" (3); he is tempted to say, when he creates a fictional character, "that he is what he is because of faulty wiring, or because of microscopic amounts of chemicals which he ate or failed to eat on that particular day" (4). Nothing is very amusing about this Kurt Vonnegut; instead of witty limericks he offers us pictures of assholes (5). He does not seem to love anything, not even Guggenheim money.

Of course, both "Kurt Vonneguts" are literary constructs. When Vonnegut tells us his mother committed suicide, we are sure he is telling the truth; but Vonnegut has assimilated such facts into a fictional context, so the question of their "truthfulness" is irrelevant. Vonnegut was probably a slightly happier man while writing *Slaughterhouse-Five*, but his fictional strategy demands that he represent himself as such. Vonnegut's tactic in the earlier novel is to establish a vital contrast between himself and his protagonist, Billy Pilgrim. In writing his novel Vonnegut faces much the same problem as his hero—how does one make sense of such hopelessly irrational events as Dresden? Pilgrim's answer is escapist, involving space travel to Tralfamadore and adoption of the deterministic philosophy he encounters there. Vonnegut suggests the inadequacy of this "solution" by depicting his own inability to rest content in the quietistic assumptions of Tralfamadore. The very meaning of his novel requires Vonnegut to present himself as a sympathetic figure, one who can make speeches to his sons that are anything but quietistic in nature.

The "Kurt Vonnegut" of *Breakfast of Champions* is a different character because this novel treats a different problem. Here Vonnegut does not protest the social attitudes that lead to wars and ultimately to Dresden; instead, he explores the possibility that our attitudes are irrelevant to such events. To do this, he creates a persona who fears that men are machines, utterly without free will. This persona does not say that men *are* machines; rather, he refers to his "suspicion" that this may be true. Moreover, he says that he is "tempted" to see his characters as controlled by chemicals, thus implying an element of doubt. In the course of *Breakfast of Champions* these suspicions are tested and finally exorcised. In a very real sense, then, the novel dramatizes its author's internal debate.

One value of seeing the book in this way is that we can explain its muchlamented "digressions." The novel is filled with social commentary of every conceivable variety, especially a series of rather crude reflections on American hypocrisy. Vonnegut devotes much of his book to insulting the national anthem (8), the idea that Columbus discovered America (10), the nobility of the founding fathers (11–12), the justice of our cause in Vietnam (11–12), and other American myths. These remarks are invariably expressed in the baldest manner possible, as when we are told that "the demolition of West

Virginia had taken place with the approval of the executive, legislative, and judicial branches of the State Government" (123), or when West Point is defined as "a military academy which turned young men into homicidal maniacs for use in war" (157). Given his reputation as a comic novelist, Vonnegut seems oddly humorless here. Even when he provokes a smile, as when he records the size of each character's penis, the humor is soon dissipated in an almost manic repetition. One can understand why a reviewer would speak of the nearly Kiwanian subtlety of the novel's social criticism, for Vonnegut's attack seems to have no subtlety at all—and roughly half the book is given over to it.

Vonnegut's social and philosophical reflections must be seen in the dramatic context suggested above. In his preface Vonnegut[12] explains that he has dedicated his book to an old friend, Phoebe Hurty, who lives in his memory as a child of the Great Depression: "She believed what so many Americans believed then: that the nation would be happy and just and rational when prosperity came" (2). Phoebe Hurty believed in the very myths Vonnegut debunks so gracelessly throughout the novel. As his discussion of Phoebe makes clear, however, Vonnegut attacks these myths from the point of view of a disillusioned "believer": "nobody believes anymore in a new American paradise. I sure miss Phoebe Hurty" (3). To have the faith of a Phoebe Hurty would be wonderful, but we know too much for that. After such knowledge, what forgiveness? Vonnegut turns on the idealistic myths of America with the passion of a betrayed lover. When he tells us that he is "trying to clear my head of all the junk in there" (5), he seems to include all those patriotic ideals that have come to seem the soiled heritage of a past forever lost. Vonnegut wants to believe in this heritage; he says that he "can't live without a culture anymore." But the reality of past and present America is such that he must also say, "I have no culture, no humane harmony in my brains" (6). Vonnegut's social comments reflect his anger and frustration, as if he would cultivate a cynical pose in order to cast out such "junk" once and for all. We see much the same process at work when Vonnegut speaks of his "suspicion" that men are machines. If men are not the noble beings of myth, they must be robots.

This dubious logic also informs the "story" that Vonnegut creates to illustrate his new cynicism. This story involves two characters who embody different aspects of his own personality. Dwayne Hoover represents his Midwestern, middle-class background, while Kilgore Trout is a comic embodiment of his artistic career. Like his creator, Trout has become a devout pessimist in his old age: "But his head no longer sheltered ideas of how things could be and should be on the planet, as opposed to how things really were. There was only one way for the Earth to be, he thought: the way it was" (106). Indeed, Trout thinks that "humanity deserved to die horribly, since it had behaved so cruelly and wastefully on a planet so sweet" (18). It is not clear why humans "deserve" to die horribly if they are mere machines and "there was only one way for the Earth to be"; but Vonnegut contrives to bring Trout to Midland City, Hoover's home town, to confront the folk with these bracing "truths." It seems that Vonnegut wants to rub middle America's nose in the sheer ugliness of life.

Trout's resemblance to Vonnegut is in many ways quite playful. For example, Trout's remarkable anonymity is surely meant to remind us of Vonnegut's early problems in securing hardcover publication, not to mention a significant audience. But *Breakfast of Champions* presents a more serious link between the author and his creation: both are frustrated idealists. We know from the nature of his innumerable publications that Trout once sheltered ideas of how things could be and should be on this planet, as opposed to how things really are. In *God Bless You, Mr. Rosewater* (1965), we learn that "Trout's favorite formula was to describe a perfectly hideous society, not unlike his own, and then, toward the end, to suggest ways in which it could be improved."[13] As summarized in *Breakfast of Champions*, Trout's tales teach such lessons as our tragic failure to communicate (58), the tendency of government to deal with secondary rather than primary causes (74), our disastrous inattention to ecological problems (88–89), our contempt for art (132–33), and our ridiculous obsession with national averages (173). But of course Trout is an unappreciated prophet, almost literally unread, and he has gradually lost faith in the possibilities of reform, finally becoming a rather frightening misanthrope. Early in *Breakfast of Champions* he tells his pet parakeet, "We're all Heliogabalus, Bill" (18), alluding to the Roman emperor best known for entertaining friends by placing a man inside a hollow, life-sized iron bull and lighting dry firewood under the bull (18–19). No wonder each of Trout's three wives has been "shriveled" by his pessimism (113).

The most interesting of Trout's fables, *Plague on Wheels*, radically qualifies his despair. While the moral of the tale is gloomy enough ("There was no immunity to cuckoo ideas on Earth" [27]), the book suggests Trout's unwavering belief in the importance of ideas. As Trout says elsewhere, "Ideas or the lack of them can cause disease!" (15). His very epitaph, taken from his last, unfinished novel, suggests that "we are healthy only to the extent that our ideas are humane" (16). Nothing connects Trout and Vonnegut so securely as this faith in the power of ideas.[14] The Kurt Vonnegut we meet early in *Breakfast of Champions* may be a pessimist, but even he must concede it will take more than chemicals to unhinge his "hero," Dwayne Hoover: "Dwayne, like all novice lunatics, needed some bad ideas, too, so that his craziness could have shape and direction" (14). (Trout, of course, will provide the bad ideas through one of his own books.) As a young man Trout has understood that if bad ideas can destroy us, humane ideas can give us health. He has known that "the purpose of life" is to be "the eyes and ears and conscience of the Creator of the Universe" (68). Implicit here is the notion that we *can* exercise conscience. At the time of the novel Trout has turned away from such ideas, yet in 1981 he will say that we are healthy only to the extent that our ideas are humane. What happens to cure Trout of his misanthropy?

What happens is that both Trout and his creator encounter a *wrang-*

wrang. According to Bokonon, the black prophet of *Cat's Cradle* (1963), a *wrang-wrang* is "a person who steers people away from a line of speculation by reducing that line, with the example of the *wrang-wrang*'s own life, to an absurdity."[15] The narrator of *Cat's Cradle* meets such a figure in Sherman Krebbs, a nihilistic poet. After lending his apartment to Krebbs, the narrator returns to find the apartment "wrecked by a nihilistic debauch" (*CC*, 58). Krebbs has set fire to his couch in five places, killed his cat and avocado tree, and torn the door from his medicine cabinet. He has hung a sign around the cat's neck that reads "Meow." The narrator comments, "Somebody or something did not wish me to be a nihilist. It was Krebbs's mission, whether he knew it or not, to disenchant me with that philosophy" (*CC*, 59). In *Breakfast of Champions* Dwayne Hoover is Trout's and Vonnegut's *wrang-wrang*.

Hoover is a slightly revised version of Billy Pilgrim. Like Pilgrim, he is a successful entrepreneur: besides his Pontiac auto lot, he owns part of the local Holiday Inn, "three Burger Chefs, five coin-operated car washes, and pieces of the Sugar Creek Drive-In Theatre, Radio Station WMCY, the Three Maples Par Three Golf Course, and seventeen hundred shares of common stock in Barrytron Limited, a local electronics firm" (65–66). He lives in "a dream house in Fairchild Heights, which was the most desirable residential area in the city" (17). But Hoover is also like Pilgrim in that he suffers terribly despite his apparent prosperity. While Pilgrim is haunted by memories of World War II, Hoover is burdened with the suicide of his wife, the homosexuality of his son, and a growing sense that his life is meaningless. At one point he even compares himself to Job: "I couldn't help wondering if that was what God put me on Earth for—to find out how much a man could take without breaking" (170). As he first appears in the novel, he is a man in search of "new truths"; he wants to meet artists at the Midland City Festival of the Arts "to discover whether they had truths about life which he had never heard before." He hopes these truths will "enable him to laugh at his troubles, to go on living, and to keep out of the North Wing of the Midland County General Hospital, which was for lunatics" (200). Hoover is in the same position as Billy Pilgrim and Eliot Rosewater in *Slaughterhouse-Five*. In the aftermath of Dresden, Pilgrim and Rosewater find themselves dealing with "similar crises in similar ways. They had both found life meaningless. . . . So they were trying to re-invent themselves" (*Five*, 101). Pilgrim finds his "answer" in the Tralfamadorian theory of time, which offers the reassuring message that "everybody has do to exactly what he does" (*Five*, 198). Dwayne Hoover comes to believe the same thing, but the consequences are something less than reassuring for Trout and Vonnegut.

Hoover discovers his comforting "truth" in *Now It Can Be Told*, a book Trout has carried with him to Midland City. The book is in the form of a long letter from the Creator of the Universe to his experimental creature, a man with free will. In his letter the Creator tells the man, "You are the only creature in the entire Universe who has free will. You are the only one who has to figure out what to do next—and *why*. Everybody else is a robot, a machine" (259). Billy Pilgrim learns something similar on Tralfamadore, though the Tralfamadorians allow for no exceptions: "Tralfamadorians, of course, say that every creature and plant in the Universe is a machine" (*Five,* 154). Pilgrim is pleased by the message, but Dwayne Hoover's response suggests there is another side to this coin. Hoover reasons that if all other men are "unfeeling machines" he can do whatever he wants to them (266). Finally he acts on this belief, beating up everyone around him until he sends eleven people to the hospital, Trout among them. He acts with no sense of shame, for he has been "liberated" from such feelings: "I used to think the electric chair was a shame . . . I used to think war was a shame—and automobile accidents and cancer." But now he does not think *anything* is a shame: "Why should I care what happens to machines?" (270). Why indeed? If men are machines, why should we be horrified by Heliogabalus himself?

Dwayne Hoover's thematic function is to point up the disastrous consequences of adopting a deterministic view of man. Dramatically, his function is to reveal these consequences to Trout and Vonnegut. Following his trip to Midland City, Trout rejects his belief that there is only one way for the Earth to be. He returns to his former task of alerting mankind to its inhumane practices, in the belief that man's capacity to believe anything can be his salvation as well as his cross.[16] As he finally says in 1979 as he accepts the Nobel Prize for Medicine, "now we can build an unselfish society by devoting to unselfishness the frenzy we once devoted to gold and to underpants" (25). Vonnegut's playfulness is not without meaning, for by 1979 Trout has become a true "doctor"—one who would restore us to health through good ideas.

Vonnegut is "rescued" from his own despondency by the negative example of Dwayne Hoover, but also by a speech delivered by one of his other characters, Rabo Karabekian, who has contributed a painting to the Midland City Festival of the Arts called *The Temptation of Saint Anthony.* This huge picture consists of a green field painted in Hawaiian Avocado and a vertical orange stripe. The people of Midland City are outraged that Karabekian has received $50,000 for the picture, but the artist is eloquent in his own defense. He gives his word of honor that the painting shows everything about life that truly matters, with nothing left out: "It is a picture of the awareness of every animal. It is the immaterial core of every animal—the 'I am' to which all messages are sent. . . . It is unwavering and pure, no matter what preposterous adventure may befall us. A sacred picture of Saint Anthony alone is one vertical, unwavering band of light. . . . Our awareness is all that is alive and maybe sacred in any of us. Everything else about us is dead machinery" (226). This speech marks a dramatic reversal in *Breakfast of Champions.* We had been led to anticipate a climax where Trout would teach Hoover everything he did not want to know about the vanity of human wishes. But before this encounter takes place, their creator stumbles upon a "spiritual climax" of his own. Vonnegut tells us that he is "transformed" by Karabekian's speech (223). He had feared that he might kill himself as his mother did (198); he had come to believe that "there was nothing sacred about myself or about any human being, that we were all machines, doomed to collide and collide and collide" (224–25). Karabekian's speech saves him because it suggests how we might "adapt ourselves to the requirements of chaos": by asserting our sacred awareness in the face of chaos itself. As Vonnegut says, "It is hard to adapt to chaos, but it can be done. I am living proof of that: It can be done" (215). By this point Vonnegut's dark "suspicion" about man's nature must be identified with the "bad ideas" Dwayne Hoover learns from Kilgore Trout. At the end of *Breakfast of Champions* Vonnegut rejects both the suspicion and the ideas, just as Trout will do in the last years of his life.

In the novel's final pages the newly rescued Vonnegut bestows a final gift upon his most famous creation. Vonnegut arranges a final meeting where he tells Trout that he is going to follow Jefferson's and Tolstoi's examples and set his literary characters at liberty. From now on, Trout is *free* (301–302). This gesture seems to have been misunderstood, for one critic remarks that Vonnegut "seems to conclude on an even grander destructive note, namely the destruction of his own fictional universe."[17] There is, of course, nothing "destructive" about Vonnegut's final actions. Just before he releases Trout from literary bondage, Vonnegut offers a second gift, an apple. As he tells Trout, "We Americans require symbols which are richly colored and three-dimensional and juicy. Most of all, we hunger for symbols which have not been poisoned by great sins our nation has committed, such as slavery and genocide and criminal neglect" (301). So Vonnegut first offers Trout an apple, a superior symbol, then his freedom. Such an ending is hardly destructive; it might even seem sentimental. To forestall such a reading, Vonnegut has Trout call after him, "*Make me young, make me young, make me young!*" (303). It would seem that freedom is not enough. Indeed, freedom can be frightening. Earlier, Trout offers freedom to his parakeet, but the bird flies back into his cage (35). It is always possible that man will also reject the possibilities inherent in his freedom. What is Vonnegut telling us on every page but that man has been doing just that from the beginning of time? But he also tells us, in the fable he contrives, that only by asserting our freedom can we possibly adapt to the requirements of chaos. We cannot make ourselves young again, but we can make ourselves more humane.

I say that Vonnegut *contrives* this fable because throughout *Breakfast of Champions* he insists on his role as master puppeteer. Here Vonnegut allows no pretense about the status of his fictional creations. Toward the end of the book he even seats himself at the same bar with his characters and proceeds to explain why he has decided to have them act as they do. (This Nabokovian device is, of course, anticipated in *Slaughterhouse-Five*.) This insistence on the artificiality of his dramatic personae emphasizes that there is really only one "character" in *Breakfast of Champions*. That Karabekian's painting is named after Saint Anthony is no accident, for *Breakfast of Champions* is about its author's triumph over a great temptation. Vonnegut's temptation is of the spirit, whereas Saint Anthony's was of the flesh; but we should know by now it is the spirit that both kills and dies. At the end of the novel Vonnegut's spirit refuses to die: "I am better now. Word of honor: I am better now" (199). His hope is that we might all become "better." His message is that to become so we must resist the seductions of fatalism.

Notes

1. Peter S. Prescott, "Nothing Sacred," *Newsweek,* 14 May 1973, 114.

2. Richard Todd, review of *Breakfast of Champions, Atlantic* 231 (May 1973):106.

3. J. D. O'Hara, "Instantly Digestible," *New Republic,* 12 May 1973, 26.

4. O'Hara, 26.

5. Prescott, 114.

6. Peter B. Messent, "*Breakfast of Champions:* The Direction of Kurt Vonnegut's Fiction," *Journal of American Studies* 8 (April 1974):111.

7. Robert W. Uphaus, "Expected Meaning in Vonnegut's Dead-End Fiction," *Novel* 8 (Winter 1975):173.

8. Kurt Vonnegut, Jr., *Slaughterhouse-Five* (New York: Delacorte Press, 1969; rpt., New York: Dell, 1971), 164. Subsequent references to this edition are indicated by the abbreviation *Five.*

9. See, for example, Robert Scholes, *The Fabulators* (New York: Oxford University Press, 1967), 35–55; Raymond M. Olderman, *Beyond the Waste Land* (New Haven: Yale University Press, 1972), 189–219; Karen and Charles Wood, "The Vonnegut Effect: Science Fiction and Beyond," in *The Vonnegut Statement,* ed. Jerome Klinkowitz and John Somer (New York: Delta, 1973), 133–57.

10. Kurt Vonnegut, Jr., *Wampeters, Foma and Granfalloons* (New York: Delacorte Press, 1974), 281.

11. Kurt Vonnegut, Jr., *Breakfast of Champions* (New York: Delacorte Press, 1973), 4. Unless otherwise noted, subsequent references are to this edition.

12. Rather than continue to use quotation marks, I would simply have it understood that the Vonnegut I refer to is the persona who appears in *Breakfast of Champions.*

13. Kurt Vonnegut, Jr., *God Bless You, Mr. Rosewater* (New York: Holt, Rinehart and Winston, 1965; rpt., New York: Dell, 1970), 20.

14. Cf. Vonnegut's personal remarks: "Writers are specialized cells in the social organism. They are evolutionary cells. Mankind is trying to become something else; it's experimenting with new ideas all the time. And writers are a means of introducing new ideas into the society" (*Wampeters, Foma and Granfalloons,* 237).

15. Kurt Vonnegut, Jr., *Cat's Cradle* (New York: Holt, Rinehart and Winston, 1963; rpt., New York: Dell, 1970), 59. Subsequent references to this edition are indicated by the abbreviation *CC.*

16. Cf. Vonnegut's comment in an interview: "But I continue to think that artists—all artists—should be treasured as alarm systems" (*Wampeters, Foma and Granfalloons,* 238).

17. Otto Friedrich, "Ultra-Vonnegut," *Time,* 7 May 1973, 66.

Vonnegut's Comic Persona in
Breakfast of Champions
Charles Berryman*

When an author becomes a character in his own fiction, the traditional result is some form of autobiography. In post-modern fiction the author is more apt to pass through the looking glass into his own creation in order to question the very nature of his art. If the author becomes a naive character, bewildered and lost in his own novel, the result is comedy and satire. No one has presented this aspect of postmodern fiction with more comic delight than Kurt Vonnegut in *Breakfast of Champions*.

Vonnegut was unhappy with his brief venture into drama and television in the early 1970s because in a film "the author always vanishes." Vonnegut's desire to be a character in all his works prompted his return to a narrative form with more scope for self-revelation and parody.[1] *Breakfast of Champions*, largely written by 1971 but not published until 1973, is a novel in which the comic persona of the author holds conversations with himself: " 'This is a very bad book you're writing,' I said to myself . . . 'I know,' I said."[2] No longer content with the limited autobiographical preface common in his earlier books, Vonnegut now introduces himself as a character to observe and participate in the climax of the story. Suddenly the author appears wearing dark glasses in the cocktail lounge of the Holiday Inn where he has assembled the chief characters for their violent interaction.

Vonnegut's appearance in his seventh novel is a natural step in the evolution of his remarkable career. A few years earlier the dark glasses would have been unnecessary—who would have recognized him? In the middle of the 1960s Vonnegut's first four novels and his first collection of stories were all out of print. Despite fifteen years of work as a writer, Vonnegut found himself faced with oblivion. His situation was reminiscent of the career of Herman Melville a century before. If a writer achieves early success with a popular form—Melville with his romances of the South Pacific or Vonnegut with his science fiction—how can he attract a new audience when his craft matures and his metaphysical vision deepens? The skeptical themes and experimental forms of Melville's best novels only found a receptive public decades after his death. Vonnegut was very apprehensive about suffering the same eclipse. The specter of a prolific and misunderstood novelist haunted his imagination in the 1960s. It appeared in his novels as the forlorn and embittered science-fiction writer, Kilgore Trout.

At the nadir of his expectations in 1965 Vonnegut decided upon two strategies that might rescue his career from the fate of his fictional novelist. He decided to separate himself from the label of science fiction and to promote his own image in the public media as often as possible. Consequently he announced in the *New York Times Book Review:* "I have been a

*This essay was written specifically for this volume and is published here for the first time by permission of the author.

sore-head occupant of a file drawer labeled 'science fiction' . . . and I would like out!"[3] He also devoted a considerable time to first-person journalism. Readers of magazines like *Esquire, Life, Playboy,* and *Mademoiselle* were offered Vonnegut's latest opinions on everything from astronauts to mass murderers. Many of his journalistic ventures were designed to impress the public with his image as a social critic and satirist, but the saving grace of this journalism is its mocking tone and occasional self-parody. His piece on the Maharishi Mahesh Yogi, for example, is entitled "Yes, We Have No Nirvanas."

In 1965 Vonnegut also began two years of residence at the University of Iowa Writers Workshop. For the first time he was in daily contact with students and critics who pressed him for explanations about his craft. While such academic debate often paralyzes less experienced writers, it proved to be a significant catalyst for Vonnegut's mature fiction. When his third novel, *Mother Night,* was reissued in 1966, Vonnegut decided to add an autobiographical preface describing his experience during the bombing of Dresden. Two years later he wrote a personal introduction to his collection of stories, *Welcome to the Monkey House,* in which he explored the relationship of life and art. His next novel was *Slaughterhouse-Five* with its opening chapter in the form of an author's confession. Step by step Vonnegut was moving himself onto the stage of his fiction.

Vonnegut seldom explores a possibility for his art without soon beginning to parody its form. The next step for his progressive revelation of self was therefore the self-mocking portrait of the author as character in *Breakfast of Champions.* By the time this novel appeared in 1973 the author was experiencing all the pressures of literary success. His brief residence among the academics, not to mention his advertisements of himself in popular journals, were beginning to pay remarkable dividends. His long-anticipated war novel, *Slaughterhouse-Five,* was welcomed in 1969 by scores of favorable reviews. Vonnegut thus began to enjoy the second audience that Melville never lived to see. The full emergence of Vonnegut as a literary celebrity in the early 1970s provided him with a new public image just ripe for satire in *Breakfast of Champions.* While he was receiving maximum exposure in the various public media, Vonnegut was also devising new ways of representing himself in fiction.

Vonnegut knew that his first novel of the 1970s would attract considerable publicity. Indeed, three book clubs were waiting to offer it as their featured selection. He also assumed that his new novel would be judged against the achievement of *Slaughterhouse-Five.* So much of Vonnegut's own experience had gone into the writing of *Slaughterhouse-Five* that its audience and author alike must have been wondering what he could do next. The novel that comes after a major achievement has always been a special problem for American writers. After the publication of *Moby-Dick* in 1851, Melville's next and seventh novel was the ill-fated *Pierre.* After the success of *Slaughterhouse-Five* in 1969, Vonnegut was afraid that his next book, also his seventh novel, would disappoint his new audience. For a while he delayed publication of *Breakfast of Champions*. Moreover, he built a negative critical response into the book itself. Anticipating an audience now ready to chip away at his new fame and fortune, Vonnegut presents a comic image of the author dissatisfied with his own work and then attacked by a ravenous dog at the end of the book. The writer appears as a character in his own novel, not merely to conduct a dialogue with himself about the relationship of art and life, but also to deflect the charges of his audience. When the dog at the end of the book springs for the jugular vein of the author, our storyteller makes a comic leap over his rented automobile to saftey. Vonnegut's persona thus escapes with his life, but at the same time a local tourist attraction known as *Moby-Dick* is being destroyed by industrial waste.

Vonnegut's appearance in his own novel also allows him to parody his reputation as a hip philosopher. Even his early books attracted a cult following eager to find metaphysical speculation. Vonnegut appealed to this audience by including various fantastic religions such as the Church of God the Utterly Indifferent in *The Sirens of Titan* or Bokononism in *Cat's Cradle*. Despite the comic thrust of his early metaphysical capers, Vonnegut was aware that some readers and critics were solemnly discussing his philosophy. No doubt he found the spectacle amusing. When academic critics began to claim with awe that "Vonnegut is wrestling with nothing less than the cosmological question,"[4] who could blame the novelist for laughing to himself? And he encouraged such discussion by scattering his views on almost every subject throughout the popular journals. During the late 1960s Vonnegut was almost always available for instant wisdom in press interviews, talk shows, commencement addresses, etc. What his audience didn't always perceive, however, was the amount of self-parody inherent in his public image. Vonnegut was performing in the spirit of Mark Twain, pretending to be profound, when all along the joke was on his audience. His metaphysical comedy bred a solemn debate among critics and disciples about his view of a "meaningful existence," and the debate was often held in a nonsense language. "In the post-apocalyptic void," wrote one critic, "all identity is adventitious."[5] The language of critical discussion thus entered the world of chrono-synclastic infundibula without noticing its own comic echo.

Although he may have enjoyed hearing himself praised as "the foremost serious writer in America today,"[6] Vonnegut was experiencing the bittersweet frustration of being praised for the wrong reasons. When would he be recognized as the foremost comic writer? Vonnegut also began to worry about the critics who were seeing through his metaphysical charade without recognizing its comic potential. Leslie Fiedler, for example, was remarking in 1970 that Vonnegut's own spiritual age is late adolescence. The title of Fiedler's article, "The Divine Stupidity of Kurt Vonnegut," and the fact that it appeared in *Esquire*, the home of some of Vonnegut's own writing, were both disconcerting.[7] But a far worse attack was published the next year by

Charles Samuels in the *New Republic*. Samuels declared that Vonnegut "can tell us nothing worth knowing except what his rise itself indicates: ours is an age in which adolescent ridicule can become a mode of upward mobility."[8] Samuels at least did not take Vonnegut's metaphysical performance with great solemnity—"a sententious old salt in ontological drag"[9]—but he still implied that Vonnegut would like his philosophy to be accepted without irony. Nothing could be further from the truth. Vonnegut decided to counter such false impressions by increasing the self-parody in his next novel, *Breakfast of Champions*, and by placing such misunderstandings at the very center of his narrative.

Breakfast of Champions is about a novelist named Kilgore Trout who is invited to attend an art conference in Midland City. There he meets his potential audience, Dwayne Hoover, who rapidly becomes insane after one reading of a Trout novel. The mad rampage of Hoover who injures eleven people and bites off the end of Trout's finger is a mock description of the conduct of Vonnegut's own audience and its penchant for biting the hand that feeds it.

Kilgore Trout, familiar to readers of earlier Vonnegut novels, achieves a new significance in *Breakfast of Champions*. Although he travels to the art conference in order to reveal the face of failure to a naive and uncomprehending audience, he unexpectedly meets his creator and is granted ironic freedom. It is even reported that Trout will soon receive a Nobel Prize. The public will read his science fiction as if it were true, and he will be awarded the Nobel Prize for Medicine. With such bravado Vonnegut is simultaneously mocking the solemn incomprehension of his own audience and exorcising the specter of a failed career. Better the wrong Nobel Prize than none at all!

Trout's fiction is described as "solipsistic whimsy," and the same label has been applied by more than one critic to Vonnegut's novel. The criticism is encouraged by the tone and style of the book, which readers often find exasperating and silly. The tone is deliberately simpleminded. The persona of the author is pretending to tell the story as if he were reporting events on a distant and dying planet. The style includes drawings by the author of such obvious things as a light switch, a cow, and a hamburger. "I've often thought," Vonnegut once declared, "there ought to be a manual to hand to little kids, telling them what kind of planet they're on, why they don't fall off it, how much time they've probably got here . . . I tried to write one once. It was called *Welcome to Earth*. But I got stuck on explaining why we don't fall off the planet."[10] Unfortunately *Breakfast of Champions* often sounds like such a manual, and it is not surprising that so many readers have resented being addressed in such a manner.

The strategy of the novel, however, is less sentimental and patronizing than at first it seems. Vonnegut's satire depends on a perception of the difference between the author and his naive persona. Although the persona does conform with some of the known facts of Vonnegut's life—date of birth, details about parents, and concerns about mental health—the persona is an obtuse, comic self-parody of the novelist.

Vonnegut reveals the identity of the persona very clearly in the novel: "What do I myself think of this particular book? I feel lousy about it, but I always feel lousy about my books. My friend Knox Burger said one time that a certain cumbersome novel 'read as though it had been written by Philboyd Studge.' That's who I think I am when I write what I am seemingly programmed to write" (4). The same voice says a paragraph later, "I am programmed at fifty to perform childishly" (5). The first-person pronoun is prominent, but who is the "I" speaking to us? Vonnegut happens to be fifty at the time, but this preface to the novel is signed by "Philboyd Studge." The comic name belongs to the narrator who serves as a self-parody of Vonnegut, but the name comes from a short story by Saki (Hector Hugh Munro) about the perversity of public taste and the ingratitude suffered by a poor artist. Saki's brief tale, "Filboid Studge, The Story of a Mouse That Helped," tells about an artist who encourages a huge demand for an awful breakfast cereal merely by calling it "Filboid Studge." Vonnegut's *Breakfast of Champions* is not only named after a famous advertising slogan for a breakfast cereal, a registered trademark for Wheaties, it is also narrated by Philboyd Studge, the name created in Saki's story to sell the most unpalatable breakfast cereal of all time. The poor artist in the story advertises the cereal by drawing a picture of hell where a fashionable public is tempted by the cereal just beyond their reach. Filboid Studge is thus the image of what the damned public wants but cannot enjoy, and the artist who gives them the image remains at the end of the story unrewarded. The perversity of public taste and the ingratitude faced by an artist are among the themes presented and mocked in *Breakfast of Champions*.

The style and tone of Vonnegut's novel are consistent with the comic persona called "Philboyd Studge." His are the childish observations about common things. His are the drawings scrawled with a felt-tipped pen. But who wants to read a novel told and illustrated by the namesake of a breakfast cereal? Even if Vonnegut can be successfully separated from Philboyd Studge, the responsibility for creating the self-parody still belongs with the novelist. What advantages, if any, come from having Philboyd Studge serve as the narrator of *Breakfast of Champions*?

If satire depends upon irony, perhaps it is helpful to have a naive storyteller who seems to know less about things than either the author or the audience. This is the familiar strategy of *Gulliver's Travels*, and the adventures of Gulliver are not far removed from the comic accidents of Philboyd Studge. Both serve as first-person narrators telling us about their experiences that neither can fully understand or control. Gulliver's assumed superiority to the King of the Brobdingnagians is just as ironic as the conceit of Philboyd Studge. Gulliver's admiration for the Houyhnhnms is just as ridiculous as the naiveté of Vonnegut's narrator. The misadventures of both storytellers—captured by the Lilliputians or injured at the Holiday Inn—are comic and absurd. The humor comes from our recognition that Lemuel Gulliver and Philboyd Studge, despite their pretensions of superiority, are still quintessential Yahoos. The reputation of Jonathan Swift as the greatest satirist in the English language is commonly accepted even though critics still disagree about how to distinguish Swift and Gulliver and how to interpret Gulliver's final response to the Houyhnhnms. Such critical problems are inherent in satire. Thus it is hardly surprising that contemporary readers have difficulty when it comes to separating Vonnegut from his persona and interpreting the narrator's response. Gulliver's final resentment over the pride of the Yahoos is just as ironic as the last tear shed by Vonnegut's narrator over a fate he cannot understand.

Once the narrator of *Breakfast of Champions* is viewed as a naive storyteller, the many conversations in the novel about the very process of writing are understandable in a new context. When the narrator says to himself, "this is a very bad book you're writing," we should hear the comic despair of Philboyd Studge unable to live up to the standards of the Houyhnhnms. If the dissatisfaction were Vonnegut's, there would be no excuse for publishing the book. But if the feeling belongs to the comic persona, then Vonnegut succeeds in mocking the fears and pretensions of his fictional author.

Vonnegut's narrator assumes a self-indulgent tone at the beginning when he announces: "This book is my fiftieth birthday present to myself" (5). The birthday celebration is viewed as a time to take stock of the many characters in the author's head: "I think I am trying to clear my head of all the junk in there . . . I'm throwing out characters from my other books, too. I'm not going to put on any more puppet shows" (5). Vonnegut is mocking that decisive moment in an author's career when he feels ready to abandon his cast of characters. The best examples in English literature are Shakespeare allowing Prospero to dismiss the "elves of hills, brooks, standing lakes and groves" and W. B. Yeats concluding that his circus animals will no longer be on show.[11]

Prospero's words, which echo Medea in Ovid, are both proud and apologetic. Despite his references to "weak masters" and "rough magic" (lines 41, 50), the poetry reverberates with the proud knowledge of his accomplishments. Prospero has imitated the power of the gods—"to the dread rattling thunder / Have I given fire and rifted Jove's stout oak / With his own bolt" (lines 44–46). Shakespeare is about to retire from the London stage, and it is hardly a time for modesty about his "potent art" (line 50). Vonnegut, however, has no intentions of ending his career, and the farewell gestures of his comic persona are both vain and disingenuous. Vonnegut's narrator has very limited power to create or destroy. He is trapped and victimized in the world of his own characters. Any attempt to assume godlike power leads quickly to a pratfall. The more he tries to clear his head, the faster the junk inside appears to multiply.

His gesture of dismissal—"I'm not going to put on any more puppet shows"—sounds closer to the disappearing circus animals of Yeats, but Vonnegut's narrator is merely exhibiting a false bravado at age fifty, and not the final realization that old themes and characters can no longer be summoned when it is time to "lie down where all the ladders start, / In the foul rag-and-bone shop of the heart" (lines 39–40). Vonnegut's naive persona hides behind his dark glasses at the Holiday Inn and hardly begins to approach his own heart. The comic irony of the narrator is multiplied by the self-indulgent tone of his decision to celebrate his own birthday and the self-deluded gesture of dismissing his own characters.

The full comedy of the author attempting to dismiss his characters occurs near the end of *Breakfast of Champions*. The author in a rented Plymouth Duster is chasing after his most famous creation: " 'Whoa! I'm a friend!' I said . . . 'Mr. Trout,' I said from the unlighted interior of the car, 'you have nothing to fear. I bring you tidings of great joy' " (298). The divine pretensions of the author are immediately mocked when he attempts to turn on the light and merely succeeds in activating the windshield wipers. When it comes to the climactic moment of freeing his character, he invokes the memory of Count Tolstoi freeing his serfs and Thomas Jefferson freeing his slaves, but the great emancipation ironically backfires. When the author says, "Arise, Mr. Trout, you are free, you are *free*" (302), the character suddenly appears to have the face of the author's father, and his last words are: "*Make me young, make me young, make me young!*" (303). The result of bringing the comic author face to face with the image of his own father is to undercut his pride as a creator. He has no more power to set his creation free than he does to make his father young. Indeed, if the character is the father of the author, then the very tables of creation have been turned. Vonnegut, of course, is the father of both the character and the comic author, and the disillusionment of both in the novel completes Vonnegut's self-parody and his satire of the vain delusions of narcissistic authors.

If the chief delusion of an author is the attempt to assume divine creative power, Vonnegut deliberately mocks his comic persona for indulging such pretensions. We should laugh at the vanity of the narrator when he modestly announces: "I was on a par with the Creator of the Universe there in the dark in the cocktail lounge" (205). We might also recall that the same narrator has been complaining about the incompetence, the cruelty, and the indifference of the Creator at frequent intervals throughout the novel. He has often referred to a God who moves in disastrous ways creating tornadoes and tidal waves or destroying a whole galaxy for the mere pleasure of the fireworks. Thus when the narrator introduces himself as being "on a par with the Creator," he is vainly assuming some rather dubious credentials.

The dialogue between the comic author and the bewildered Kilgore Trout is a wonderful example of baffled condescension and suspicious distrust. The author playing God in his rented car has promised "tidings of great joy," but Trout's response to the good news is a noncommittal "Um." Frustrated by the ungrateful response, the author says, "If I were in your spot, I would certainly have lots of questions." Trout's wary reply is "Do you have a gun?" (299). Trout has good reason to be suspicious of anyone approaching him in a car. Earlier in the novel he was "kidnapped by pure evil in a white Oldsmobile" (76) and left unconscious after losing his money. How can Kilgore Trout be certain that the author in the rented Plymouth is not a member of the Pluto gang ready to strike again?

The narrator says that he wants to bless his creation with the gift of harmony: " 'Mr. Trout, I love you,' I said gently. 'I have broken your mind to pieces. I want to make it whole. I want you to feel wholeness and inner harmony such as I have never allowed you to feel before' " (300–1). And what does Trout see in the hand of his benevolent creator? An apple! There is no sign that Vonnegut's comic author in the role of God recognizes what will come from the fruit he so kindly offers. Unknowingly, he is placing his favorite character in the same position that is described in Trout's novel *Now It Can Be Told*. This science-fiction novel is written in the form of a letter from the Creator of the Universe to "the only creature in the entire Universe who has free will" (259). When this message from the Creator was read by Dwayne Hoover, who was just insane enough to believe it, the result was his mad rampage through the Holiday Inn. When the apple of freedom is offered to Kilgore Trout by his naive creator, who believes the apple is "a symbol of wholeness and harmony and nourishment" (301), the poor science fiction writer thinks his creator is merely playing one final joke upon him. The offer of freedom is therefore met with the desperate wish that all the knowledge and experience of the tempting fruit could be withdrawn—"*Make me young, make me young, make me young!*"

Vonnegut, of course, is the creator of the comic author, who in turn plays God and pretends to be the creator of Kilgore Trout, who in turn is the author of *Now It Can Be Told*, which describes the Creator of the Universe making the promise of free will. "My books," Vonnegut has said, "are essentially mosaics made up of a whole bunch of little chips; and each chip is a joke."[12] The humor reflects on all the authors in and out of Vonnegut's book who assume the guise of divine power only to discover the knowledge of evil that comes from their best intentions. The last joke is on author and characters alike—the tidings of great joy become paradise lost.

Notes

1. Kurt Vonnegut, *Between Time and Timbuktu* (New York: Delacorte Press, 1972), xv.

2. Kurt Vonnegut, *Breakfast of Champions* (New York: Delacorte Press, 1973), 198; hereafter cited in the text.

3. Kurt Vonnegut, "Science Fiction," *New York Times Book Review*, 5 September 1965, 2.

4. David H. Goldsmith, *Kurt Vonnegut: Fantasist of Fire and Ice* (Bowling Green, Ohio: Bowling Green State Popular Press, 1972), 10.

5. Richard Giannone, *Vonnegut: A Preface to His Novels* (New York: Kennikat Press, 1977), 61.

6. Jerome Klinkowitz, "Vonnegut in America," in *Vonnegut in America,* ed. Jerome Klinkowitz and Donald L. Lawler (New York: Delacorte Press, 1977), 33.

7. Leslie A. Fiedler, "The Divine Stupidity of Kurt Vonnegut," *Esquire* 74 (September 1970):195–97, 199–200, 202–4.

8. Charles Samuels, "Age of Vonnegut," *New Republic* 12 (June 1971):32.

9. Ibid., 30.

10. Kurt Vonnegut, *Wampeters, Foma and Granfalloons* (New York: Delta, 1975), 276.

11. William Shakespeare, *The Tempest,* ed. Northrop Frye (New York: Penguin Books, 1970), V.i.33, and W. B. Yeats, "The Circus Animals' Desertion," in *The Collected Poems of W. B. Yeats* (New York: Macmillan, 1956), 335–36. Subsequent line numbers will refer to act 5, scene 1 of this edtion of *The Tempest* and to this edition of Yeats's poems.

12. Kurt Vonnegut, "*Playboy* Interview," *Playboy,* July 1973, 58.

Culture and Anarchy: Vonnegut's Later Career
David Cowart*

Any American novelist who came to prominence in the 1960s must feel, a quarter of a century later, like Theseus in the labyrinth. Although the 1960s saw the greatest efflorescence of novelistic talent since the 1920s, they may prove, in retrospect, to have set in motion more experimentation than was good for the larger cause of literature. As Charles Newman shows in *The Post-Modern Aura,* his telling critique of contemporary literary aesthetics, the fruition of the new aesthetics has brought with it a catastrophic diminution of audience and a paralyzing crisis of faith in literature's ability to do more than play with itself.[1] Theories of language and discourse that demonstrate the invalidity of value and reference and meaning tend to undermine the work of contemporary writers who produce realistic, value-centered fiction. At the same time, unfortunately, writers who attempt to base their work on such theories risk a terrible sterility and find themselves apologists for a form of artistic nihilism. But a few writers function amphibiously—they produce postmodern fictions that somehow affirm meaning and value. One such author, Kurt Vonnegut, has made a career of balancing between nihilist despair and humanist affirmation. Recognizing the limits of stylistic self-indulgence, Vonnegut has devoted his artistic energies to defining the cultural malaise and attempting responses to it. Always a moralist, even at his most black-humorous, Vonnegut has come to sound at times like the later D. H. Lawrence, haranguing a sick civilization and devising myths of rebirth.

*This essay was written specifically for this volume and is published here for the first time by permission of the author.

"For two thirds of my life I have been a pessimist," Vonnegut remarks in *Palm Sunday*, the "autobiographical collage" he published in 1981. "I am astonished to find myself an optimist now."[2] Though perennially aware of absurdity as the ground for existence, Vonnegut in his later career emphasizes the hopelessness less and less. He has moved beyond pessimism to introduce more and more positive variations on a theme that has always figured centrally in his work: the need of humanity, especially American humanity, for a sense of community, a sense of living in a cohesive culture. The family, though not the jejune "nuclear" family of the sitcoms, becomes his standard metaphor for this ideal of community. As he remarked to an audience of college journalists in 1980, "Those of you who have been kind enough to read a book of mine, any book of mine, will know of my admiration for large families, whether real or artificial, as the primary supporters of mental health" (*PS*, 66).

Vonnegut, then, identifies the modern malaise with isolation, which he prefers to call by the homelier and starker name of loneliness. As early as *Cat's Cradle* (1963), as critics like Lundquist, Klinkowitz, and Hume have noted, he identifies family, community, and culture as the collective antidote to this loneliness.[3] The author urges these perceptions with increasing emphasis in the later works, those that come after what an early critic, Peter Reed, recognized as the completion of a first cycle of work culminating in *Slaughterhouse-Five*.[4] One sees important signals in the play *Happy Birthday, Wanda June* (1971), written and produced at a time when, as Richard Giannone notes, Vonnegut's own family was dissolving.[5] In the introduction to the published version of the play he speaks of its cast as his "new family,"[6] and in the action proper he examines one family's fragmentation and prospects for a restored wholeness. Fantasy sequences depict heaven as a place of ultimate familial harmony, a place where once-vicious Nazis and innocent little girls live together happily.

In his subsequent work, Vonnegut continues to promote the family and to define it more broadly. In a commencement address collected in *Palm Sunday* he advocates the ideal of community as nothing less than a new religion, the basis of a "*moral code*" (202). He hints at this broader conception of family in the preface to *Breakfast of Champions* (1973), where he declares that one cannot survive without the sense of a shared set of values and myths—all that goes to make up and define that higher family called a culture. In *Slapstick* (1976), in which families swell artificially to thousand-member communities, Vonnegut provides the definitive version of this theme, which he allows to temper an otherwise grim picture of general collapse. In *Jailbird* (1979) he sets out to record the history of the twentieth-century American Left, the history, that is, of those in this country who, in Vonnegut's view, promote the values of a collective standard of social welfare and advocate treating all citizens—not just those who have money or other forms of privilege—as family members. In *Deadeye Dick* (1982) the breakdown of the extended family figures in the shocking metaphor of Midland

City depopulated by the accidental detonation of a neutron bomb, symbolically "the disappearance of so many people I cared about in Indianapolis when I was starting out."[7] In *Galápagos* (1985), finally, he envisions a return to Edenic community as the ironic outcome of a million years of evolution, and one suspects the end of another cycle of Vonnegut's work.

One notes in this connection how often Vonnegut dedicates books to friends and relatives who have died or scattered, robbing him of an extended family of his own. *Breakfast of Champions,* for example, is dedicated to Phoebe Hurty, whom the author had known in Indianapolis during the Great Depression. This woman had provided guidance, comfort, sage counsel, and lessons in irreverence. The perfect aunt, though not actually a blood relation, she had shared her home and family with the youthful Vonnegut. She presides, then, as tutelary spirit over a novel whose central conceit is that human beings have somehow become mechanical and unfeeling—robots incapable of fraternal sentiments and unworthy of inclusion in any human family. Such mechanized people cannot treat themselves or their neighbors with charity. They also cannot treat nature with reverence, and Vonnegut registers some familiar complaints regarding the failure of his fellow citizens to venerate and protect the earth and the life it harbors. Vonnegut expects human beings—if they are to be worthy of the name—to treat all living things with respect and to discriminate, with regard to nonliving things, between the noxious and the benign.

Persons, things, the earth—these are the valenced building blocks of Vonnegut's moral and aesthetic universe, the elements, even, of a kind of ultimate family. In 1971, during the period when *Breakfast of Champions* would have been gestating (the novel grew out of material left over from *Slaughterhouse-Five*),[8] Vonnegut spoke before the National Institute of Arts and Letters and quoted with enthusiasm a description, by anthropologist Robert Redfield of the University of Chicago, of the "folk society," a community in which

> . . . behavior is personal, not impersonal. A "person" may be defined as that social object which I feel to respond to situations as I do, with all the sentiments and interests which I feel to be my own; a person is myself in another form, his qualities and values are inherent within him, and his significance for me is not merely one of utility. A "thing," on the other hand, is a social object which has no claim upon my sympathies, which responds to me, as I conceive it, mechanically; its value for me exists in so far as it serves my end. In the folk society, all human beings admitted to the society are treated as persons; one does not deal impersonally ("thing fashion") with any other participant in the little world of that society.
>
> Moreover . . . in the folk society much besides human beings is treated personally. The pattern of behavior which is first suggested by the inner experience of the individual—his wishes, fears, sensitivities, and interests of all sorts—is projected into all objects with which he comes in contact. Thus nature, too, is treated personally; the elements, the features

of the landscape, the animals, and especially anything in the environment which by its appearance or behavior suggests the attributes of mankind—to all these are attributed qualities of the human person. (*WFG*, 177–78)

The idea of the folk society proves central to Vonnegut's imagining of an alternative to the urban and suburban wastelands and their human automata. But in *Breakfast of Champions* the author is not yet ready to advocate the ideal—at least not as something actually realizable. Instead, he expresses his outrage in an often ill-humored and even strident contumely. Thus the novel opens with something of a philippic against those symbols of the nation—an anthem that is "pure balderdash,"[9] a flag that becomes an idol or graven image, and money that bears the emblems of Masonic tushery—that collectively seem to say: "*In nonsense is strength*" (10). In what follows, the author continues to make plain his disgust at an ecologically benighted society, a society that tolerates—even promotes—pollution, strip mining, and the disproportionate exploitation of energy resources. Unable to eradicate racism, drug addiction, poverty, organized crime, or fascistic tendencies on the part of its police, such a society commits its resources to more and more extravagant weaponry, enshrines materialism and vulgarity while neglecting art, and expunges from its history the record of its founders' rapacity.

Among the neutered products of this industrial leviathan are breakfast cereals that taste like cardboard. Referring to this novel in the *Playboy* interview, Vonnegut provides a hint about the meaning of its title, which echoes a phrase associated for years with a breakfast cereal made by General Mills. "What I say didactically in the introduction to *Breakfast of Champions* is that I can't live without a culture anymore, that I realize I don't have one. What passes for a culture in my head is really a bunch of commercials, and this is intolerable" (*WFG*, 281). Commercials force into one's head advertising slogans like "Breakfast of Champions" and "Goodbye, Blue Monday." Thus Vonnegut's disclaimer regarding the "fine products" (1) of General Mills sounds ironic—especially when he repeats it. The novel's title is intended to include, in the overall indictment of American capitalistic civilization, a direct jab at the consumer society and its holy center—Madison Avenue. The pseudonym with which he signs the preface, "Philboyd Studge," adds to the indictment. Though he identifies by that name a generic author of turgid prose, the self-mockery merely masks a telling allusion, for the name also refers to a breakfast food, the unpalatable Filboid Studge that gives its name to a wicked satire on advertising by H. H. Munro ("Saki").[10]

Yet despite this kind of subtlety, to read *Breakfast of Champions* a decade after its publication is to be somewhat put off by the author's crabbiness, effrontery, self-indulgence, and admissions of mental instability. Indeed, even at the time of its publication, there was a sense that Vonnegut had ceased to be the spokesman for the zeitgeist he had been in the 1960s. The 1960s were no more, and imputations of American fascism and ecological irresponsibility were no longer chic. Critics began to imply that Vonnegut was dated, no longer fresh, artistically spent.

They were premature. However self-indulgent and ideologically unctuous, *Breakfast of Champions* marks a fresh start, and Robert Merrill rightly defends it as "an artistic act of faith."[11] It marks, too, a maturation of the author's political, philosophical, and artistic views. Nor are these in fact so negative as they might seem. Politically, for example, the author conveys a heteroclite patriotism, and the reader may at times recall the spirit in which a Thoreau or for that matter a Thomas Pynchon (notably in *The Crying of Lot 49* and *Gravity's Rainbow*) condemns his country's faults yet communicates an abiding love. As Vonnegut remarks in *Palm Sunday*, "This country has fulfilled more of the requirements of the Communist Manifesto than any avowedly Communist nation ever did" (198). The author's epistemology, too, can be construed as not altogether bleak, for it allows latitude for the emotional and artistic rebirth announced toward the end of the novel.

Breakfast of Champions climaxes with a revelation about consciousness, implicitly defined as integral to the vitality of sentient beings. Without this "awareness," as the sometimes churlish artist Rabo Karabekian observes, human beings are mere machines, the robots over which the narrator has agonized throughout the novel. "Our awareness is all that is alive and maybe sacred in any of us. Everything else about us is dead machinery" (226). Thus the narrator can introduce the scene with Karabekian as "the spiritual climax of this book," the point at which he—the author—is "born again" (223).

The "something sacred" celebrated here, the "unwavering band of light" (231), is another version of that which in *Deadeye Dick* metaphorically defines conscious existence—the peephole that opens at birth and closes at death. In addition to defining life as something richer than mere automatism, this awareness is the hidden constant, the sine qua non, to all physical phenomena, all reality. Thus the narrator observes that the famous formula defining the relation of matter to energy, $E = Mc^2$, ought also to have "an 'A' in there somewhere for *Awareness*—without which the 'E' and the 'M' and the 'c,' which was a mathematical constant, could not exist" (247).

This doctrine hints at an appealing corollary to the classic philosophy of subjective idealism, as propounded by Bishop Berkeley in the eighteenth century. Berkeley argued that external reality cannot be known as an objective phenomenon, since one knows it exclusively through the senses and the mind they serve. Only consciousness is certain—indeed, only the *individual* consciousness. Subjective idealism has affinities, then, with the "solipsistic whimsy" (264) of Kilgore Trout's novel *Now It Can Be Told*, fiction-within-the-fiction whose premise is that only one person in the world—the reader—exercises free will. All others are robots. This novel has a devastating effect on the mentally marginal Dwayne Hoover, but a more stable reader might learn something from it about existential freedom—not to mention postmodernist aesthetics. What does the author of such a book say if he identifies his reader as the only sentient being in a world of robots? He says that people who read redeem themselves—they grow more human, less mechanical. The conceit also provides a paradigmatic illustration of the relationship between a reader and the world of any novel. Robots lacking in free will do in fact populate the universe described by Trout, as they do the one described by Vonnegut. These robots, commonly called "characters," exist to interact with and "test" their free counterpart—the reader of the book in which they appear. Thus Vonnegut invites the reader to practice the postures of free will vis-à-vis this fiction.

Like Trout, or like the deity, Vonnegut is a "Creator of the Universe"; in fact, this novel is ostensibly as chaotic as the universe it reflects:

> Once I understood what was making America such a dangerous, unhappy nation of people who had nothing to do with real life, I resolved to shun storytelling. I would write about life. Every person would be exactly as important as any other. All facts would also be given equal weightiness. Nothing would be left out. Let others bring order to chaos. I would bring chaos to order, instead, which I think I have done.
>
> If all writers would do that, then perhaps citizens not in the literary trades will understand that there is no order in the world around us, that we must adapt ourselves to the requirements of chaos instead.
>
> It is hard to adapt to chaos, but it can be done. I am living proof of that: It can be done. (215)

Although several critics have taken these remarks at face value, they reveal, I think, a calculated irony, for Vonnegut in fact orders this fiction even as he allows it to seem formless, the faithful mirror of an external chaos. At the end, the artifice becomes more and more transparent, with the author, hitherto only a know-it-all narrative voice, actually sitting in a lounge and interacting with his characters—even as he directs their actions. His ultimate gesture is the attempt to confer real existential freedom on one of them, Kilgore Trout. In doing so he echoes the biblical language of revealed supernatural truth: "Mr. Trout . . . you have nothing to fear. I bring you tidings of great joy" (298). "I'm your creator" (299). Eventually he goes so far as to proffer Trout an apple, "symbol of wholeness and harmony and nourishment" (301).

Vonnegut only appears to be revising the traditional symbolism. The apple given to Trout is symbolically the same fruit that brought to Adam and Eve the knowledge of good and evil, made them "as gods," and cost them their innocence. "It is supposed to be good to lose one's innocence," Vonnegut declares in *Palm Sunday:* "I think that is what my novels say" (70). Thus he strips Kilgore Trout of his innocence by providing him with knowledge of his status as fictional character. In conferring freedom on Trout, Vonnegut abandons his character to a bracing existential terror. It is a gesture at once of ultimate bounty and ultimate cruelty—made by a god nearing his fiftieth birthday and wanting to make some spiritual gesture of self-cleansing comparable to that of a Jefferson or a Tolstoy. They freed their slaves, Vonnegut frees his. Like Yeats without his "circus animals," as Stanley Schatt observes,[12] Vonnegut looks forward to producing literary art without his old standby, Kilgore Trout (not that experienced Vonnegut readers actually believe they have seen the last of this literary loser).

What does this amount to? It might seem to amount to "doodly squat." But to dismiss Vonnegut's denouement as mere pretentious twaddle would be to miss its considerable metaphysical power, for it is an acute demonstration of the extent to which we are linguistically bound by our fictions of the world and word. If one tries to free oneself from fictions, if one tries to get beneath language to "reality" or existential bedrock, one finds only the void. As an illustrative gesture, then, the conclusion to *Breakfast of Champions* provides Vonnegut's characteristic admission of ultimate meaninglessness—but with perhaps more real *bite* than all the mannered "poo-tee-weets" punctuating cataclysm. It is the gesture, finally, of a supreme ironist.

In *Breakfast of Champions* Vonnegut manages only a tentative step or two toward the vision of a healthy human community that gradually becomes central to his thinking during this phase of his career. But in his next novel *Slapstick,* the vision begins to take shape, to take on something of the same imaginative power as the celebrated depictions, in the earlier novels, of death, decay, senseless carnage, and apocalypse. Though in his preface he describes *Slapstick* as a book about "desolated cities and spiritual cannibalism and incest and loneliness and lovelessness and death, and so on,"[13] it is also his most straightforward and comprehensive fictional exposition of the oft-desiderated return to human connectedness, the return to "culture" or the "folk society." Again in his preface Vonnegut laments the passing of his own sense of family and community in Indianapolis, Indiana, and notes—as he does elsewhere—the curious fact that people are forever forming themselves into artificial families based on shared problems (Alcoholics Anonymous), shared interests (professional societies), or shared experiences (veterans' organizations). He feels that they come together in this manner in part because of a breakdown in traditional family cohesion, complicated by the attenuation of cultural and communal bonds in modern, industrial society. Unfortunately, such confraternities or families tend to be discriminatory or exclusive—they provide no haven for the poor, the ugly, the disadvantaged.

Repeatedly in *Wampeters, Foma and Granfalloons* Vonnegut touches on his ideal of the family. In the preface he speaks of "providing all Americans with artificial extended families of a thousand members or more" (xxiv), and in a piece on the Biafran war he expresses his admiration for the extended families common in Nigeria. In the *Playboy* interview he imagines creating extended families for Americans by means of government-issued middle names. Though he ascribes the idea to his disreputable alter-ego, Kilgore Trout, the fruit of this speculation turns out to be Vonnegut's next novel, *Slapstick*.

Vonnegut imagines the office of president of the United States occupied by a pediatrician named Wilbur Rockefeller Swain, who ordains the creation of large families based on randomly assigned middle names. One notes that members of the Swain family all have middle names taken from plutocrats: Mellon, Rockefeller, Vanderbilt, and so forth; the intent is presumably to emphasize an automatic membership in the "family" of the rich. In proposing a new set of *middle* names for Americans, Swain repudiates this idea of a rich people's confraternity in favor of something more humane, less discriminatory. He does the same thing in attiring himself in a "clownish" parody of the plutocrat's garb, "a top hat, a claw-hammer coat and striped pants, a pearl-gray vest with matching spats, a soiled white shirt with a choke collar and tie. The belly of my vest was festooned with a gold watch-chain which had belonged to John D. Rockefeller" (47).

Although Swain's scheme does not forestall the collapse of American civilization, it makes the death agonies more bearable and even provides a sensible basis for life in the ruins.[14] It is another paradigm of Vonnegut's characteristic stance, his intriguing mix of pessimism and utopian vision: things are going to hell regardless, but there are things humanity might do to minimize the pain and the chaos. This advocacy of striving to ameliorate a desperate situation may be behind the candlestick motif in the novel. Dr. Swain becomes the King of Candlesticks because he is thought to value them especially when he comes to New York. He owns a thousand of them, and his recollection of being surrounded with burning candles on his last birthday concludes his narrative: "Standing among all those tiny, wavering lights, I felt as though I were God, up to my knees in the Milky Way" (228). Vonnegut reveals the negative side of this image in the preface to *Wampeters, Foma and Granfalloons,* where he argues the appalling emptiness of the cosmos: "All the twinkles and glints in the night sky might as well be sparks from a cowboy's campfire, for all the life or wisdom they contain" (xxiii). But one finds also a positive side, a proverbial one: Dr. Swain is a person who, rather than cursing the darkness of his times, lights a candle. The candles all around him at the end are equal in number to the relatives that he—like all his people—enjoys as a result of his extended family scheme.

Vonnegut's meditation on loneliness and its antidotes begins with an idyllic fantasy of twin "monsters," Wilbur and his sister Eliza, who grow up together as fated siblings in an enchanted castle surrounded by apple trees. These primal twins, like Adam and Eve, must undergo an archetypal encounter with knowledge and give up their paradisal home. It is paradise in large measure because time—except for regular birthday observances—is largely banished, and because of the perfect sense of community that obtains there. Significantly, the familial ideal is essentially artificial, since the consanguineous relations—the mother and father—are not part of the circle. But the siblings enjoy a "family"—themselves and their servants—that is virtually perfect.

As twins, moreover, they enjoy special mythic stature, for as Vonnegut would know from reading Sir James George Frazer's *The Golden Bough* (he holds a master's degree in cultural anthropology from the University of

Chicago, after all), twins have been taboo—in both the positive and negative senses—in many cultures and in many times.[15] "Yet whether their bond be love or hate or death," declares a character in John Barth's *The Sot-Weed Factor*, anatomizing the phenomenon of twins, "almost always their union is brilliance, totality, apocalypse—a thing to yearn and tremble for!"[16] The incestuous yearnings of Wilbur and Eliza—which on two occasions cause them to be parted disastrously—would be sanctioned in a primitive culture. Among the ancient Egyptians, Incas, and Persians, for example, incest between a royal brother and sister was not only tolerated but enjoined. The impunity with which, say, pharoanic siblings broke the taboo (no divine wrath ensued) was taken for a sign of their own quasi-divine status. Small wonder, then, that Eliza takes up residence in Machu Picchu, ancient capital of the Incas, or that in the primitivized future into which Wilbur eventually survives he finds himself assisting, like an ancient Egyptian, at the erection of a funerary pyramid.

As doomed as the mythic Teutonic siblings Siegmund and Sieglinde, parents of the great Siegfried, Wilbur and Eliza produce no heroic offspring. They do, however, contribute signally to the solution of famous problems—from squaring the circle to child-rearing, not to mention gravity, loneliness, and the shortcomings of Darwin's theory of evolution. One of the book's central ironies is that the ideal of family—brain child of Wilbur and Eliza—comes to humanity more or less simultaneously with the destruction of the paragon of family that the twins and their childhood circle constitute. The sundering of Wilbur and Eliza, along with the dissolution of their circle, announces a mythic fall into division that echoes Blake (the dissolution of Albion) and has its roots in the myth—most famously developed in Aristophanes and Plato—of a primal oneness that degenerates into twoness and thereby brings gender itself into existence. The myth is especially powerful now because the fall into division is precisely the fate of modern civilization—Vonnegut's great subject and frequent theme.

It is typical of Vonnegut, at least at this point in his career, that he should temper his vision of familial utopia by setting it against an imagined collapse of American civilization. Much the same doubleness of vision obtains in the author's next fictional effort, for *Jailbird* turns on a similar vision of something of immense cultural value subverted by invidious, built-in social and cultural mechanisms. *Jailbird* culminates in revelations about Mary Kathleen O'Looney, a bag lady who happens to own a corporation—RAMJAC—of mythic proportions. RAMJAC, incredibly, is the opposite of every corporate cliché: instead of being consecrated to profits at any cost, it functions as the arm of Mary O'Looney's charity—or, more precisely, as the model of an enlightened economics advocated by its ardently leftist owner. It is another extended family. Unfortunately, in this novel the extended family cannot survive in its original character after the passing of the matriarch. It proves subject to economic, cultural, and social laws that subvert enlightened efforts to consolidate fraternal relations within the family of human beings.

Jailbird is also Vonnegut's reflection on twentieth-century American political and economic history, especially in regard to the aspirations of the Left. A recurrent motif in the novel is "the Harvard man"—usually invoked at the expense of this entity. Harvard has always had a reputation for its liberalism (as opposed to that bastion of conservative sentiment, Yale), and yet it furnishes a remarkable number of tarnished angels to the halls of corrupt power. Though the novel ostensibly focuses on Watergate, the infamous scandal is something of a red herring, for Vonnegut is not analyzing the criminal failings of the Nixon administration so much as the fate of leftist millenarianism from the labor agitation early in the century to the still-controversial Sacco and Vanzetti case to the McCarthy hearings and on to the embattled Left of the Nixon era (curiously, the liberal Kennedy-Johnson era receives no attention at all). The theme of the novel is perhaps expressed best by the judge who summons Starbuck and gives him a dressing-down for his folly in giving the reactionary Right ammunition to use against "pity and brains." Starbuck, says the judge, has "set humanitarianism back a full century."[17] To set back humanitarianism is to set back prospects for returning society to familial standards of decency—to postpone the millennial "folk society."

In its place we have the Darwinian Right, led by Richard Nixon. Starbuck, like his namesake in *Moby-Dick,* is one of the more morally earnest members of a monomaniac's administration; while Richard Nixon pursues the white whale of a viable Vietnam policy, his advisor on youth affairs supposedly helps him to deal with youth-centered protest of the war effort and other policies. Though readers expecting a roman à clef will not find Starbuck among those actually prosecuted and imprisoned for their part in Watergate, he does resemble at least one historical figure. Like Whitaker Chambers, the renegade Communist who fingered Alger Hiss as a fellow party member, Starbuck destroys the career of Leland Clewes, an old friend whose previous political sympathies he reveals in the McCarthy hearings.

Whether or not one accepts the similarity between Starbuck and Chambers as intentional, a comparison with another work in which the renegade Communist figures—Lionel Trilling's *The Middle of the Journey*—should prove worthwhile. Trilling's novel, a liberal's rigorous critique of liberalism, concerns the inability of the liberal visionary to accept the constraints of reality. The novel shows this ideological tenacity first in Arthur and Nancy Croom, who are made extremely uncomfortable by talk of their friend John Laskell's brush with death. The Crooms, Communist "fellow travellers," are appalled at the stark reality of death, so utterly unamenable to visionary ideology. By the same token, they cannot accept the shocking revelations of a formerly committed Communist named Maxim Gifford (the Whitaker Chambers character), who has rejected communism for Christianity. They reject out of hand Gifford's attempts to convince them of the reality of Stalinist terror—which he himself has promoted. Laskell is the book's enlightened liberal, chastened by experience to renounce certain of the more egregious pipe dreams of the Left. In defining a position between communism and Christianity, he charts a course between equally absurd absolutist ideologies. Humanity, too, says Trilling, must steer between ideologies too extreme to be defended. Humanity is neither the evil carrier of Original Sin, dependent on supernatural means for redemption, nor the angelic inheritor of the utopia of tomorrow. Like the individual human being, humanity collectively must conceive of itself as part beast, part angel—and order its society and its political destiny accordingly.

Vonnegut, by contrast, offers a far less neat package. Much less analytical than Trilling, he remains far closer, emotionally, to both the Christian and the political visionary (he describes himself as an atheist with a profound respect for the Sermon on the Mount). Nevertheless, unlike Arthur and Nancy Croom, he always admits the existential facts and their corollaries: nature is sublimely indifferent to human ideas of justice or purpose, wisdom may "be as impossible in this particular universe as a perpetual-motion machine" (180), and "the economy is a thoughtless weather system—and nothing more" (231). The linking of the economic and existential realities— the subordinating, that is, of the one to the other—hints at a truth that everything else in the novel resists: that all the enlightened commitment in the world will not bring social justice, will not forestall our collective degeneration as we squander available sources of energy and persecute those among us who insist quixotically on the continuing validity of the Sermon on the Mount as a set of moral guidelines.

Early in the novel Starbuck thinks of his wife Ruth, a concentration camp survivor who "believed . . . that all human beings were evil by nature, whether tormentors or victims, or idle standers-by. They could only create meaningless tragedies, she said, since they weren't nearly intelligent enough to accomplish all the good they meant to do. We were a disease, she said, which had evolved on one tiny cinder in the universe, but could spread and spread" (23). Late in the novel Starbuck reflects bitterly on the absurdity of human aspirations in the face of an indifferent universe. "We are here for no purpose, unless we can invent one. Of that I am sure." No matter what he had done with his life, he thinks, "the human condition in an exploding universe would not have been altered one iota" (236).

Yet such bitter recognitions have begun to figure less and less prominently in Vonnegut's work, and they tend either to come from characters from whom the author maintains some moral distance or to be qualified by an ultimately more positive slant. Though honest enough to let Starbuck articulate the cruel truths about politics, economics, and the cosmic void, Vonnegut resists final pessimism. Like Starbuck in his better moments, Vonnegut remains committed to the ideals enunciated in the Sermon on the Mount. Starbuck invokes that most hopeful of New Testament texts early on, along with a composite myth (the Cuyahoga massacre) of labor exploited, oppressed, and resistant. Thus, too, he invokes Sacco and Vanzetti throughout, from the epigraph (xxxix) to the closing passages. He elevates these anarchist martyrs and their fellow-traveller, an actual criminal named Celestino Madeiros, to Christ-figures of the Left: "As on Golgotha, three lower-class men were executed at the same time by a state. This time, though, not just one of the three was innocent. This time two of the three were innocent" (172). Author and persona coalesce, finally, in celebrating the sacrifice of those who died at the hands of benighted and rapacious authority. Vonnegut defines anarchists here as "persons who believe with all their hearts that governments are enemies of their own people" (175); elsewhere he calls himself an anarchist (PS, 122).

Though *Jailbird* ends with the RAMJAC family subverted, the novel's liberal passion delivers it from negativism. Not so with Vonnegut's next work, *Deadeye Dick*. If, as I am suggesting, Vonnegut's later career follows a trajectory toward realization of an ultimately sanguine vision, perhaps one should expect that, before the full maturation of that vision in *Galápagos*, the author would produce something as cheerless—and as undistinguished—as its predecessor. Darkness commonly intensifies before dawn.

The narrator of *Deadeye Dick*, Rudy Waltz, chronicles the attenuation of his family, his circle, and his community. Rudy begins life with a pair of supremely ineffectual parents who do little to provide him with a sense of protection from the world's complexity and danger. Strike one for the ideal of family. Encouraged by his father to handle guns, he accidentally shoots a pregnant woman and suffers extensive hatred and abuse from his community. Strike two. Eventually that community perishes in a neutron bomb's problematic detonation. Strike three. In the end, like Candide or Rasselas, Rudy cultivates his garden in Haiti, his "family" shrunk to a brother, a sister-in-law, his lawyer, and the headwaiter of a hotel he now owns. As Vonnegut explains in his preface, he identifies with this character's shrinking circle.

A shrinking circle suggests an iris, and this connection may in fact dictate the novel's most prominent metaphor, the "peephole" of consciousness. Vonnegut has invoked something like the peephole motif before—in *Breakfast of Champions,* where a minor character named Eddie Key, who has memorized his family history back through the generations, imagines himself "a vehicle, . . . his eyes . . . windshields through which his progenitors could look, if they wished to" (278). But the peephole of *Deadeye Dick* defines consciousness far more narrowly. It opens at birth and allows the living creature only a brief and limited view before it closes. The same conceit figures in Beckett's celebrated line: "They give birth astride of a grave, the light gleams an instant, then it's night once more."[18] Nabokov also expresses the idea movingly: "The cradle rocks above an abyss, and common sense tells us that our existence is but a brief crack of light between two eternities of darkness."[19] But where a Beckett or a Nabokov renders the insight poetically, Vonnegut contrives to render it with laconic austerity. The peephole, that inadequate iris, suggests a blinkered, provisional quality to consciousness; it hints, even, at an element of wan prurience. Without the peephole, one remains a "wisp of undifferentiated nothingness," something not so different from the "wisp of an implication" Vonnegut speaks of in the double-talk cosmogony he sets forth in the preface to *Wampeters, Foma and Granfalloons* (xxiii, xxvi).

The peephole image has its complement in the ironic sobriquet that gives the novel its title and in the bull's-eye motif that decorates each chapter head. The novel's narrator, the "neuter" Rudy Waltz, seems incapable of capitalizing on consciousness; his is a "dead eye" recording a world at the mercy of blind chance complicated by human folly and cupidity. Like the optometrist Billy Pilgrim in *Slaughterhouse-Five* or the Pontiac dealer Dwayne Hoover in *Breakfast of Champions* (Dwayne appears as a minor character in this novel as well), Rudy makes his living in a proverbially neutered and unglamorous profession. He becomes a pharmacist, too chastened by his father's artistic failure to develop his literary talent. Yet however neuter, he is not without humanity, and Vonnegut hints in his preface at the affinities between himself and his "viewpoint character." Rudy is the familiar Vonnegut persona, a kind of nebbish or schlimazzle (or child, as he has it in *Palm Sunday* [58]) whose general incapacity for passion nevertheless allows some latitude for moral nuance, for a certain wry and enervated disgust at nuclear waste, suburban vacuity, police brutality, fascism, racism, drug abuse, confiscatory litigation, the misvaluation of art, and weaponry from handguns to the neutron bomb.

These horrors create an environmental chaos that Rudy can do virtually nothing to alleviate. One of Vonnegut's teachers at the University of Chicago explained to him that "the artist says, 'I can do very little about the chaos around me, but at least I can reduce to perfect order this square of canvas, this piece of paper, this chunk of stone' " (*PS*, 321). This observation reveals the poignance of Rudy's devotion to cookery. The recipes that punctuate the book, "musical interludes for the salivary glands" (ix), hint at a realm of order and control that Rudy only occasionally glimpses. The recipes yield consistent results, taming life's confusion on a small scale. They are minor art, a way to gustatory Shangri-la for Rudy, "always trying to nourish back to health those he had injured so horribly" (130).

Vonnegut ends this book with the bitter remark that "we are still in the Dark Ages" (240), but in his next novel, *Galápagos*, he takes his readers into a Darwinian Renaissance a million years hence. In *Galápagos* the author argues that the freakishly large human brain, an evolutionary mistake, causes an immense variety of afflictions, threatening the future of the human race as well as other species and the planet itself. The loathesome "big brain" generates an appalling amount of irresponsible intellection, notably the anguished perception—so common in Vonnegut's work—of life as a "meaningless nightmare."[20] Both the novel's narrator, ghost of Leon Trout, and a prominent character, the captain of the *Bahia de Darwin*, agonize over the ultimate cosmic emptiness: "The Captain looked up at the stars, and his big brain told him that his planet was an insignificant speck of dust in the cosmos, and that he was a germ on that speck, and that nothing could matter less than what became of him. That was what those big brains used to do with their excess capacity: blather on like that" (197).

In the million years covered in this tale, humanity sheds the oversized brain as well as those mischievous, tool-making and weapon-wielding hands and becomes a race of seal-like "fisherfolk"—pacific, Angst-free, and ecologically in harmony with other species and the environment. These features of the story, along with its Japanese characters and its premise of evolution reversed to take humanity back to the sea, make *Galápagos* resemble prominent Japanese novelist Kobo Abé's *Inter Ice Age 4*. In the Abé novel the threat to humanity comes from the melting of the polar ice caps, which submerges the world under water; the research of a doomed computer genius, Professor Katsumi, allows scientists to modify human embryos to live in water, thus enabling humanity to survive as an "aquan" species. Vonnegut, too, imagines the species returning to its thalassic cradle, and he, too, introduces a doomed computer genius, Zenji Hiroguchi, into the action. But where Abé imagines human ingenuity as the agent of evolutionary development, Vonnegut insists that only a largely accidental evolutionary development—the diminution of big brains—will deliver humanity from oblivion.

In imagining such a happy evolutionary outcome Vonnegut realizes his long-standing desire to see modern urban humanity reborn in a folk society. He accounts for this devoutly-to-be-wished consummation in terms of Darwin's law of natural selection. But where Darwin allowed for accident (accidental mutations, for example), Vonnegut imagines a comic proliferation of chance developments. Thus the survival of humanity depends on the inclusion on the fateful voyage of the Kanka-bono girls, the desertion of the competent First Mate, and the bombing of Hiroshima, which results in the felicitous mutation of Akiko. Captain von Kleist's fortuitous freedom from Huntingdon's Chorea also figures—as does his stupidity, which proves a valuable contribution to the genetic makeup of a small-brained and hence ecologically viable future humanity.

Though thoroughly "Darwinian" in this tale, Vonnegut also—as readers of *Wampeters, Foma and Granfalloons* might expect—waxes thoroughly subversive of Darwin. He subverts chiefly the doctrine of "survival of the fittest," commonly invoked to oblige acceptance of a biological bias in favor not only of hardiness, wiliness, and adaptability but also of ruthlessness and unhindered predation. As in his other novels, Vonnegut suggests that mindless (or rather mentally twisted) human predation is merely Darwinian mechanism gone malign, promoting ecological catastrophe rather than orderly evolution. And of course he recurs repeatedly to the magnitude of the evolutionary mistake of the big brains, merely the latest and most appalling evolutionary misstep in a series that includes the Irish elk and the dodo: "The brain is much too big to be practical" (81), Leon Trout declares. "Even at this late date, I am still full of rage at a natural order which would have permitted the evolution of something as distracting and irrelevant and disruptive as those great big brains of a million years ago" (174).

Mythically and allusively, *Galápagos* proves one of the richest of Vonnegut's later novels. The name of the *Bahia de Darwin*'s master, for example, seems to invite a connection with the German playwright Heinrich von Kleist (1777–1811), a man who, like Vonnegut's captain, combined considerable comic gifts with military inadequacy and a general incapacity for practical living. The story of Captain von Kleist's command, moreover, echoes the stories of Adam and Eve, Noah's Ark, *The Tempest, Das Narrenschiff, The Nigger of the Narcissus,* and, as noted above, Kobo Abé's *Inter Ice Age 4*. Subsuming them all is the work of Charles Darwin, creator of the powerful modern myth of evolution—and with it much of the character of modern consciousness.

Because Vonnegut takes a keen interest in the extremes of innocence and knowledge, he often alludes to the myth of Adam and Eve, the apple, and the Garden of Eden. One encounters some reference to the myth, for example, in *Jailbird,* and, in the attention to the ancient problem of free will (not to mention the author's gift to Kilgore Trout), in *Breakfast of Champions*. In *Deadeye Dick* the apple offered to Celia by Otto Waltz is associated with both the apple of discord in Greek myth and the apple of primal transgression in Genesis. The narrator of *Slapstick,* Wilbur Daffodil-11 Swain, harks back to a strangely privileged childhood with his twin sister on a remote estate full of apple trees. He and his sister are expelled from this Eden when they admit to knowledge and loss of innocence. In *Galápagos* the myth is especially prominent, since the story concerns humanity coming full circle to something like Edenic innocence once again. Thus Captain von Kleist and the Kanka-bono harem he unwittingly impregnates are explicitly related to Adam and a collective Eve. Mary Hepburn is also Eve-like, not only on Santa Rosalia but also in the midwestern nature preserve where she meets her Adamic future husband. The apple in *Galápagos,* symbol of ambiguous human knowledge, is the supercomputer Mandarax. When von Kleist loses patience with Mandarax, he rids himself and his community of the tiresome machine, and the narrator observes: "As the new Adam, it might be said, his final act was to cast the Apple of Knowledge into the deep blue sea" (62).

Many of Vonnegut's other allusions here direct the reader to a variety of archetypal sea stories, especially those that invite one to interpret a sailing vessel as a microcosm, its passengers and crew representative of frail humanity at the mercy of a great existential sea. These stories have as their common ancestor the story of Noah's Ark, in which the human and animal macrocosm quite literally shrinks to the scale of the microcosm. In the ark a representative remnant of the earth's living creatures survives apocalyptic destruction; according to patristic exegesis, the ark prefigures the Church, which will deliver another privileged remnant from the more profound apocalypse to come at the end of time. In a setting of ultimate catastrophe, therefore, Vonnegut freights his ill-manned vessel with nothing less than human destiny. "The *Bahia de Darwin* wasn't just any ship. As far as humanity was concerned, she was the new Noah's ark" (215).

Vonnegut's story of a brave new world on a strange island at times resembles Shakespeare's *The Tempest* as well. Its tendency, like that of Shakespeare's play, is ultimately comedic, as evil dissipates and virtue triumphs. Its characters, similarly, compose a fairly extensive moral spectrum. Though the closest it can come to a Caliban is the marine iguana, which merely *looks* fearsome, it is replete with a bevy of Mirandas (the Kanka-bono girls), a disembodied spirit increasingly impatient for his release (the ghost of Leon Trout), and an inept Prospero[22] (Captain von Kleist) who happily fails to impose his will on "Mother Nature Personified" (95), as Mary Hepburn's students once called her. For Prospero's staff we have Mandarax, renounced and buried certain fanthoms at a climactic moment. The island is spared a vicious Antonio or Sebastian, for the wretched James Wait dies before landfall.

The confidence man's name, of course, links the story to Conrad's *Nigger of the Narcissus*, whose title character, that principle of evil vacuity against which the microcosmic community must struggle to define itself, is also named James Wait. Vonnegut evidently wants to correct Conrad's casual and unreflective racism; thus he makes this latter-day James Wait a white man and notes the moral superiority of the partly negro Kanka-bonos. But Vonnegut's Wait, like Conrad's, provides the tension of evil through much of the story; his exclusion from the landfall—and with it the symbolic hint of humanity's exemption, at long last, from its own home-grown evil—comes as a delightful twist to the variations on the role of chance in the Darwinian scheme of things. As Albert Guerard says of Conrad's enigmatic character, James Wait is *"something the ship and the men must be rid of before they can complete their voyage."*[23] In Conrad, the death and burial of Wait are followed by the rising of a redemptive wind, and Vonnegut echoes this powerful conceit in naming the first male child born on Santa Rosalia Kamikaze, which means "sacred wind" (272).

Of course Kamikaze has other connotations as well. One ought, perhaps, to think of spermatozoa, those "determined, resourceful, microscopic tadpoles" (157) that fling themselves ova-wards like the suicidal Japanese pilots who attacked Allied warships late in World War II. Indeed, one recognizes the *Bahia de Darwin* itself as a solitary spermatozoan, fighting its way blindly toward the waiting ovum of Santa Rosalia. This symbolism accounts for the otherwise gratuitous eroticism of the Peruvian pilots' attack on Guayaquil: their orgasmic bombs propel the *Bahia de Darwin* across a sea whose salinity, Vonnegut notes, matches that of amniotic fluid (58). This metaphorically exhilarating reminder of the tenacity of life's reproductive mechanism, however, figures in a larger, ironic context. To see the ultimate irony of this particular strain of symbolism, the reader should keep in mind why everything rides on the viability of the Santa Rosalia colony: apocalypse comes to the rest of the world not with a bang but a whimper, as the old human race perishes in an epidemic of universal sterility (162, 233).

As in *Slapstick*, Vonnegut places his imagined communal advance in a setting of general collapse for human civilization as it has previously existed.

But for the first time the meliorist vision proves ultimately triumphant, subsuming as it does evolution itself. Thus in *Galápagos* Vonnegut contrives his most sanguine fantasy—of evolution triumphant, of Eden restored, of all humanity as an extended family, a folk society. The routine recitations of despair recur in this novel, but now they carry less authorial endorsement than ever. Instead of a Ruth Starbuck, the concentration-camp survivor who defined humanity as a disease, Vonnegut invokes Anne Frank, another victim of the Nazi death camps, and invites his readers to accept at face value the famous words from her diary: "In spite of everything, I still believe people are really good at heart."

Vonnegut's strength in his work since *Slaughterhouse-Five* is the acuteness with which he diagnoses the problem central to modern life, the breakdown of community and the dissolution of culture. If one must critique his vision of the folk society—at the heart of so much that Vonnegut has written—one must admit that its specifics, notably the idea of large, artificial families, hardly provide realistic antidotes either to current despair or to imminent apocalypse, whether it come as fiery cataclysm or a slow wasting away. Nevertheless, the attempt to promote such a meliorist fiction reveals once again the humane sanity that has always distinguished Vonnegut and his work. It also reveals a principled resistance to the nihilistic seductions of postmodernism, which more and more contemporary novelists have instinctively or consciously recognized as a moral and aesthetic dead end. Postmodernist artists and critics have so "deconstructed" Sidney's famous dictum "the poet nothing affirmeth" as to make a powerful and distressing case for the final impossibility of *all* meaning—literary or otherwise.

But because he demonstrates an awareness of linguistic determinism (in *Breakfast of Champions*, for example) and dabbles in black humor and self-reflexivity, Vonnegut might best be thought of as a bridge between modernism, which sees the fragmentation of culture and advocates classical standards and values as antidote, and postmodernism, which returns artists to a condition of polymorphous perversity, in which they can spin out intertextual self-parodies that reveal only the inevitability of fictions and the nothingness they mask. Vonnegut plays the game, but he also quietly hangs on to ideas of meaning and value. A moralist, he dares the postmodernist maze but unreels a thread connecting him with standards of humanism that may yet deliver him—and his readers—from the minotaur.

Notes

1. Charles Newman, *The Post-Modern Aura: The Act of Fiction in an Age of Inflation* (Evanston, Ill.: Northwestern University Press, 1985).

2. Kurt Vonnegut, *Palm Sunday: An Autobiographical Collage* (New York: Delacorte, 1981), 209; hereinafter cited in the text as *PS*.

3. James Lundquist, *Kurt Vonnegut* (New York: Ungar, 1977), 13–14; Jerome Klinkowitz,

Kurt Vonnegut (New York: Methuen, 1982), 21–22, 28; Kathryn Hume, "The Heraclitean Cosmos of Kurt Vonnegut," *Papers on Language and Literature* 18 (Spring 1982):218–19.

4. Peter J. Reed, *Kurt Vonnegut, Jr.* (New York: Warner Paperback Library, 1972), 218.

5. Richard Giannone, *Vonnegut: A Preface to His Novels* (Port Washington, N.Y.: Kennikat, 1977), 98.

6. Kurt Vonnegut, Jr., *Happy Birthday, Wanda June* (New York: Delacorte, 1971), xvi.

7. Kurt Vonnegut, *Deadeye Dick* (New York: Delacorte, 1982), xii; hereafter cited parenthetically in the text.

8. As the author remarked in the *Playboy* interview. See *Wampeters, Foma and Granfalloons* (New York: Delacorte, 1974), 281; this collection of occasional pieces is hereafter cited in the text as *WFG*.

9. Kurt Vonnegut, Jr., *Breakfast of Champions, or Goodbye Blue Monday!* (New York: Delacorte, 1973), 8; hereafter cited parenthetically in the text.

10. For "Filboid Studge, the Story of a Mouse That Helped," see *The Short Stories of Saki* (New York: Viking, 1930). For more on this allusion, see Charles Berryman, "Vonnegut's Comic Persona in *Breakfast of Champions*" in the present collection.

11. Robert Merrill, "Vonnegut's *Breakfast of Champions:* The Conversion of Heliogabalus," *Critique* 18 (1977):99.

12. Stanley Schatt, *Kurt Vonnegut, Jr.* (Boston: Twayne, 1976), 98.

13. Kurt Vonnegut, *Slapstick, or Lonesome No More!* (New York: Delacorte, 1976), 18–19; hereafter cited parenthetically in the text.

14. Peter J. Reed argues the numerous qualifications and ironic underminings of the family scheme but concludes that "while Vonnegut laughs at the craziness likely to come with such a scheme, and recognizes limits to its effectiveness, he seems serious about some of the benefits it might achieve. Above all, he remains deadly serious about the psychological and social ills which the extended families are intended to alleviate. He uses a 'modest proposal' to expose the nature of the malady which needs cure." "The Later Vonnegut," in *Vonnegut in America*, ed. Jerome Klinkowitz and Donald L. Lawler (New York: Delacorte, 1977), 178–79.

15. Charles Berryman, in "After the Fall: Kurt Vonnegut," *Critique* 26 (1985):98, makes the acute observation that "the twins in this novel are a typical gothic device for dramatizing a mind on the verge of schizophrenia." He goes on to compare them to Roderick and Madeline Usher. It is interesting to note, in this context, Robert Merrill's suggestion that in Dwayne Hoover and Kilgore Trout, in *Breakfast of Champions*, Vonnegut presents "characters who embody different aspects of his own personality" (103). See also Reed, "The Later Vonnegut," 158ff, and Kathryn Hume, "Vonnegut's Self-Projections: Symbolic Characters and Symbolic Fiction," *Journal of Narrative Technique* 12 (Fall 1982):177–90.

16. John Barth, *The Sot-Weed Factor*, 2nd ed. (Garden City, N.Y.: Doubleday, 1967), 497.

17. Kurt Vonnegut, *Jailbird* (New York: Delacorte, 1979), 76; hereafter cited parenthetically in the text.

18. Samuel Beckett, *Waiting for Godot* (New York: Grove, 1954), 57.

19. Vladimir Nabokov, *Speak, Memory* (New York: Putnam's, 1966), 19.

20. Kurt Vonnegut, *Galápagos* (New York: Delacorte, 1985), 127; hereafter cited parenthetically in the text.

21. Vonnegut makes clear at a couple of points in this volume (186, 238) that he deplores the tendency toward "social Darwinism" still prevalent among certain elements of capitalist society.

22. For a discussion of the Prospero figure in Vonnegut's novels from *The Sirens of Titan* to *Slapstick*, see John Updike, "All's Well in Skyscraper National Park," *New Yorker*, 25 October 1976, 186–87.

23. Albert J. Guerard, *Conrad the Novelist* (Cambridge, Mass.: Harvard University Press, 1958), 109.

Vonnegut and Evolution: *Galápagos*   Charles Berryman*

Imagine a Vonnegut novel that pays comic tribute to Darwin's *On the Origin of Species by Means of Natural Selection*. The setting would be the natural home of marine iguanas and larcenous frigate birds. The cast of characters might include vampire finches and flightless cormorants. The theme, of course, would be evolution, and the tone would be a casual blend of humor and sharp observation. *Galápagos* (1985) is Vonnegut's eleventh novel, and it is a wry account of the fate of the human species told from a million years in the future.

How far will a writer go to acquire material for his next book? Vonnegut and his wife took a cruise to the Galápagos Islands. "Of course, I was fascinated by the island's natural life," Vonnegut reports. "I spent as much time there as Charles Darwin did—two weeks. We had advantages that Darwin didn't have. Our guides all had graduate degrees in biology. We had motorboats to move us around the islands more easily than rowboats could when Darwin visited the Galápagos in the 1830s. And most important, we knew Darwin's theory of evolution, and Darwin didn't when he was there. His *Origin of Species* came out 20 years after his journal of the voyage on H. M. S. Beagle."[1] Vonnegut published *Galápagos* within four years of his visit to the most famous natural laboratory for the study of evolution.

Despite his claims of objectivity—"I've tried to make the book as responsible as possible scientifically"—Vonnegut's novel is a sad and comic farce about the human condition. *Galápagos* is a mixture of early Charles Darwin and vintage Kurt Vonnegut. Scientific observation is taken over by a familiar blend of social commentary and science fiction. The evolution of humanity is predicted for the next million years. The species will be limited to the Galápagos Islands, and evolve into creatures with flippers and beaks. "If my predictions in the book are wrong," Vonnegut laughs, "I will return all the money."

The evolution of Vonnegut's own craft as a novelist may not be a subject of debate for the next million years, but the question of progress or decline should be reviewed in light of *Galápagos*. Vonnegut's recent novels have all been compared unfavorably with *Slaughterhouse-Five*, but some critics have welcomed *Galápagos* as a decided improvement over *Slapstick, Jailbird,* and *Deadeye Dick*. The praise, however, has been far from unanimous. While one reviewer may applaud the novel's "whimsical charm," the next

*This essay was written specifically for this volume and is published here for the first time by permission of the author.

will condemn its argument as a "sophomoric cliche."[2] The pros and cons in Vonnegut criticism have become all too familiar, but in reviews of *Galápagos* the differing positions have reached a new stage of self-parody. Which critical voice is more embarrassing: the claim that Vonnegut's observations "are the sort that high-school juniors will find profound" or the suggestion that "we may find ourselves reeling with delight at the density of the linguistic brilliance [Vonnegut] is treating us to"?[3]

Inflating the rhetoric in the debate over the faults and merits of Vonnegut's style may be a common feature in the reviews of *Galápagos*, but nothing can be resolved as long as the argument fails to connect the critical methods with the central theme of evolution. The setting, the characters, and the narrative strategy are all closely related to the theme. Indeed, the interdependence of all elements to the central vision of the novel is what makes *Galápagos* more coherent and satisfying than its immediate predecessors.

The novel has two settings that are connected by the hapless voyage of the *Bahia de Darwin*, the cruise ship used by Vonnegut as a contemporary Noah's Ark. The voyage from the mainland of South America to the most remote of the Galápagos Islands is the symbolic turning point in evolution from the present to the start of a bizarre future. The setting for book 1 is the city of Guayaquil on the coast of Ecuador. Here the characters assemble who expect to take the "Nature Cruise of the Century" to the Galápagos Islands. Many celebrated men and women have signed up for the well-advertised cruise—Jacqueline Kennedy Onassis, Mick Jagger, Henry Kissinger, among them—but financial panic and spreading violence in the Third World prevent all but a few of the intended passengers from ever reaching South America. The setting of book 1 allows Vonnegut to survey the faults in human society that ought to be left behind by a new chapter in evolution. The title of book 1, so filled with signs of greed, deceit, and violence, is simply "The Thing Was." Vonnegut's familiar complaints about the human condition are set in a context of evolution where the novel's characters are examples of a species in danger of destroying itself. It may be rather fortunate that book 1 takes up more than three quarters of the novel, because Vonnegut is typically better at describing the problem than he is at imagining the cure.

The characters who do assemble for the Nature Cruise of the Century include a science teacher who has recently lost her husband, a con man who preys upon unsuspecting widows, a business tycoon with his blind daughter, and a Japanese computer genius with his pregnant wife. The characters are all described as having reached the stage of evolution when human brains are too large for their own good. "Can it be doubted," asks the narrator, "that three-kilogram brains were once nearly fatal defects in the evolution of the human race?"[4] The characters are plagued by several forms of deceit and violence that may be traced to their oversize brains. The mind of the con man spins out false stories to trap his next victim; the businessman is plotting to take over the failing economy of Ecuador; and the computer genius feels as if his head is ready to explode. Small wonder that "the oversize human brain" is cited again by the narrator as "the only real villain in my story" (270).

The men are prevented by madness, violence, and death from ever reaching the island that Vonnegut chooses to be the cradle for the future of the human race. The business entrepreneur and the computer scientist are shot unexpectedly by a deranged soldier. Only the con man is taken aboard the cruise ship, but he dies the next day of a heart attack, and his bones are later mixed with the remains of exotic birds and animals. While the men are scheming to get ahead in a world that will soon disappear, the women are haunted by visions of suicide. The science teacher nearly suffocates herself in a plastic garment bag, and the blind girl does eventually walk hand in hand with the Japanese woman to meet death in the ocean.

Violence and death are hardly new ingredients in Vonnegut's fiction, but in *Galápagos* they are given motive and coherence by the central theme of evolution. His earlier novels are haunted by scenes of destruction that often remain inexplicable. Vonnegut confesses in the opening chapter of *Slaughterhouse-Five* that the bombing of Dresden is beyond the conventions of fiction to fully present or explain. The book is "so short and jumbled and jangled," declares the persona of the author, "because there is nothing intelligent to say about a massacre."[5] At least this confession is appealing for its frankness and humility. Not so with the smug and evasive statement that comes from Bertram Rumfoord near the end of the novel. When the official historian of the war defends the bombing of Dresden by saying "It *had* to be done," he echoes the false wisdom of Tralfamadore—"There is no *why*." Such bland irresponsibility was not acceptable to Vonnegut, who had studied anthropology and wanted to understand the roots of evil in the human condition. Vonnegut should not be confused with Billy Pilgrim who neither questions the wisdom of Tralfamadore nor the weak excuses of Bertram Rumfoord. Nevertheless, the full horror of the Dresden experience in *Slaughterhouse-Five* tends to overwhelm any possible explanation. Vonnegut does implicate the pride and delusions of the human condition, but he spares any larger force operating throughout the natural world. Thus nature itself is presented as innocent, and the novel ends with the springtime sound of birds. Thanks to Darwin, however, and his theory of evolution, all natural creatures in *Galápagos* will be competing for survival, and the birds in the novel will be flightless cormorants and bloodsucking finches.

The novels between *Slaughterhouse-Five* and *Galápagos* are filled with random violence and death. Various female characters in *Breakfast of Champions, Slapstick, Jailbird,* and *Deadeye Dick* are eliminated by suicide, car accidents, gun shots, and radiation poisoning. The tide of industrial waste threatening Midland City in *Breakfast of Champions* is a comic exaggeration of real environmental concerns, and the story of a massacre reported in *Jailbird* has some precedent in history, but the death and violence described in *Slapstick* are merely whimsical and weightless. When the narrator's sister in *Slapstick* is killed by an avalanche on Mars, the notion of unexpected destruction has reached an absurd limit. The accounts of changing gravity and a mysterious plague only confirm the fundamental absurdity. Without any believable reference point in history or science, *Slapstick* has generally been dismissed as the least consequential of Vonnegut's recent novels. The social and historical connections, however, that Vonnegut attempts to forge in *Breakfast of Champions* and *Jailbird* are not much more convincing; they hardly achieve the coherence and unity given to *Galápagos* by the story of evolution.

Without a larger perspective for violence and death, the novels before *Galápagos* are loosely structured around the psychological state of a single character. Thus the principal focus of *Slaughterhouse-Five* is the schizophrenic, traumatized consciousness of Billy Pilgrim whose life has been a series of encounters with death. His shock treatments range from an early swimming lesson that almost drowns him to a late plane crash that he alone survives. The most traumatic event, of course, is the bombing of Dresden. The psychological damage to Billy Pilgrim in turn dictates the schizophrenic narration of the book. The same principle of psychological unity is carried forward with less success in the next four novels until it is more or less exhausted in *Deadeye Dick*. The victims in *Breakfast of Champions, Slapstick,* and *Jailbird* are less interesting psychological cases than Billy Pilgrim. It is hard to care about Dwayne Hoover, whose madness erupts at a Holiday Inn, or about Wilbur Swain, whose sister is killed on Mars. The narrator of *Deadeye Dick,* who suffers from the guilt and shame of accidentally killing a pregnant woman, is presented as such an extreme psychological case—"so sexless and shy that he might as well be made out of canned tuna fish"—that further psychological study may have seemed pointless to Vonnegut as well as to his critics. In any event, he shifted the focus of his next novel to the larger perspective of evolution.

Instead of identifying the characters in *Galápagos* as psychological victims, Vonnegut describes them as natural experiments. The con man, for example, is presented as "Nature's experiment with purposeless greed," and the Japanese woman is described as "Nature's experiment with depression" (82). The words "greed" and "depression," of course, still suggest moral and psychological qualities, but they are subordinated to "Nature." Instead of unifying the novel by the style and substance of a tormented mind, Vonnegut achieves the coherence of *Galápagos* by subjecting all characters and events to the impersonal force of evolution.

In light of Darwin's law of natural selection the instances of violence and death in *Galápagos* assume a meaning and order not often found in the earlier novels. The devastation of New York by random gravity in *Slapstick* was a whimsical application of science fiction. The depopulation of Midland City by a neutron bomb in *Deadeye Dick* was a poor attempt at political satire. Vonnegut's imagination has been haunted by visions of destruction, but after portraying the bombing of Dresden in *Slaughterhouse-Five* he has had difficulty finding an objective correlative for such visions in his fiction. Retelling the story of the Cuyahoga Massacre in *Jailbird*, or reporting an avalanche on Mars in *Slapstick*, only reveals a tenuous and unbelievable connection to history or science fiction. The law of natural selection, however, allows Vonnegut to describe events as if their history were part of a million years of scientific change. To be sure, Vonnegut is exaggerating both history and science to create a comic fable about the future, but the wild visions are at least supported by the central perspective of evolution. Thus he may report the end of life as we know it with just a few bold strokes of explanation: the financial collapse of Third World countries, the spread of a virus that prevents human reproduction, and the start of a world war. The reviewer who chides Vonnegut for this "Rube Goldberg apocalypse" misses the point.[6] It is not necessary for Vonnegut to dwell on the mechanics of change. The medical, financial, and military crises have some obvious connections with current events, some recognition value, but the narrator is looking at the present stage of evolution from a million years in the future. If the human race in *Galápagos* is on the verge of extinction, the particular mistakes and follies of the moment are less important than the narrow escape to a new and different future. Thus all difficulties are attributed to oversize brains, and survival will demand a new direction for evolution.

The focus on basic change for the species also explains why events are so often described in sexual and reproductive terms. The description of war, for example, includes the "mating" of a rocket missile and a radar dish. Vonnegut's narrator makes the point too obvious: "The launching of the missile, in fact, was virtually identical with the role of male animals in the reproductive process" (189). Anthropological clichés about sexual identity and warfare no doubt inform this observation, but all that matters in the context of Darwinian survival is reproduction or extinction. Vonnegut ironically suggests that warfare conducted in the guise of sexual aggression may aim for survival and reach extinction. He quotes Hamlet's famous words—"'Tis a consummation / Devoutly to be wish'd"—knowing full well that such consummation means death.

Vonnegut's decision in *Galápagos* to present characters in the context of evolution may be a response to critics who have often complained that his flat and undeveloped characters are "stick figures."[7] Various reasons have been offered for the lack of development in other novels. The characters in *Breakfast of Champions*, for example, were defended by James Lundquist who argued, "Vonnegut's reluctance to depict well-developed characters and to supply them with conventional motives . . . serves as a conscious burlesque of the whole concept of realism in the novel."[8] Vonnegut does experiment with the conventions of fiction, and the spirit of mockery is often conspicuous in his work, but the weak characters in novels from *Breakfast of Champions* to *Deadeye Dick* are hardly redeemed by this excuse. Readers and critics are still apt to dismiss characters who lack motivation and energy. How can the author make his readers care about the burlesque of realism? Perhaps the best defense of undeveloped characters comes from Vonnegut himself in *Slaughterhouse-Five:* "There are almost no characters in this story, and almost no dramatic confrontations, because most of the people in it are so sick and so much the listless playthings of enormous forces" (164). The success of *Slaughterhouse-Five* has much to do with the fate of characters at the mercy of "enormous forces." Whatever his limitations as a listless plaything, we never lose sympathy with Billy Pilgrim because the destruction of Dresden looms over the novel as a fact of history. Without a force or event of comparable power in the next few novels, however, the characters who are free of history often seem more appropriate for comic books. Vonnegut only finds the convincing sense of "enormous forces" again when he subordinates his characters to the long process of natural selection.

The characters who are least fit to survive do not even begin the "Nature Cruise of the Century." The business tycoon and the computer genius are the first to be eliminated. Vonnegut has never shown much fondness for such types, but their extinction in *Galápagos* indicates the law of natural selection at work. The businessman with his raging ego and blind daughter has marred the essential work of reproduction. The inventor of new computers has attempted to substitute machines for human intelligence. Nature has its revenge, however, when the computer is finally eaten by a great white shark. The machine with its codified information and inappropriate quotations is a reminder of the useless wisdom that comes from an oversize brain. The men who define themselves in terms of business and computers may be the most intelligent in the novel, but given the logic of the book that is the very cause of their early demise.

The next most intelligent character is James Wait, the con man who has married seventeen different widows in order to take over their property and break their hearts. It is natural for Wait to be the next to die, and appropriate that the cause should be a heart attack. James Wait's very existence is one of nature's experiments; he is the product of incest between father and daughter. Nor is it surprising that his only offspring is the homosexual piano player in *Breakfast of Champions*, the character who thinks of himself as the despised son of Dwayne and Celia Hoover. The belated news of Celia's adultery with the young James Wait may help to explain her suicide and perhaps her husband's rampage at the Holiday Inn. (Vonnegut never tires of making new connections among his novels.) The early death of James Wait may be regretted because his talent for duplicity makes him an interesting character, but as a genetic experiment it is clear why he does not survive.

If all three men who signed up for the cruise are dead before it reaches the Galápagos Islands, who will be the father of the next stage in human evolution? The ship's captain will contribute the seeds of future life, but he doesn't know at the time that his sperm will be used to inseminate six primitive girls of the Kanka-bono tribe. He in fact doesn't want offspring because he fears transmitting defective genes likely to cause madness and disease. The captain is a successful comic figure who seldom knows where he is or what he is doing. His sheer incompetence proves to be the decisive factor in securing a future for the human species. After wildly steering the ship away from its target, he runs it aground on the island where evolution turns in a new direction. If all human beings in the future are descendants of this reluctant Adam, it is not hard to see why the new thrust of evolution is in the direction of smaller brains. At least the captain didn't have the gene for Huntington's Chorea that he so feared, and he does live longer on the island than any of the original survivors. Senility brings few changes. He is finally attacked by vampire finches and eaten by a hammerhead shark described as a "flawless part in the clockwork of the universe . . . perfected by the Law of Natural Selection many, many millions of years ago" (289).

The character responsible for the artificial insemination is the widowed science teacher. She is the only figure in the novel who knows and understands the evidence for Darwin's theories. She has taught evolution to high school students for many years, and repeatedly shown them a film about the Galápagos Islands. It is appropriate for her to be the one who allows evolution to continue; her students haven't nicknamed her "Mother Nature Personified" for nothing. Vonnegut's method of characterization may be too obvious and arbitrary, but in a novel about evolution the most important character is bound to be "Mother Nature." At least the science teacher is given several human touches. She doubts at times the subject that she teaches; she almost commits suicide before the "Nature Cruise of the Century" is scheduled to leave; and she is finally consumed by a great white shark as she vainly attempts to retrieve the computer with its useless information.

The ambivalent presentation of this character suggests a question at the very heart of the novel. In so far as she is "Mother Nature Personified," the science teacher represents the force of life that evolves in keeping with natural selection. Thus she passes on the captain's sperm to the fertile characters on the island. But insofar as she is revealed to be a teacher who occasionally doubts her subject, a woman who cannot have children of her own, and a stubborn individual who retains her intellectual curiosity against all odds, she cannot merely be accepted as some impersonal force of nature. The question at the heart of the novel is whether human intelligence may have a role in evolution, and if so, whether it is a positive or negative one. The narrator knows how much intelligence has been wasted on the rockets and weapons of destruction, and he repeatedly blames the near extinction of the species on "those great big brains of a million years ago" (174). It is the quick thinking of the science teacher, however, that saves her fellow creatures from extinction, and she is praised by the narrator as "the most important experimenter in the history of the human race" (46).

The science teacher also tries hard to preserve the remains of human culture and knowledge represented in the small computer. It is a sad moment when she loses at the end to raw nature in the form of a great white shark. Nor is it a cause for celebration when the human species she has saved gradually evolves into a new form of amphibious life. The law of natural selection may work its mechanical and impersonal destiny, but after a million years the colony on the island is no longer human in any meaningful sense. If this is Vonnegut's conclusion, what reader could find it satisfactory? (Unless the novel is meant to be read by marine iguanas and blue-footed boobies as some Vonnegut critics have implied.) When the science teacher is killed by a shark, it may seem that her intelligence and her understanding of evolution have all been for naught. When the species then evolves into creatures with more use for flippers than brains, the narrow escape from extinction may hardly seem worthwhile. Perhaps the science teacher should have left the seeds of life in her barren womb. Vonnegut, however, does not give the last word to the voice of some natural law. Indeed, the whole novel is told by a particular narrator who is both human and supernatural, and the irony of his point of view finally informs the story of evolution.

The narrator of *Galápagos* is none other than the headless ghost of Kilgore Trout's son, Leon Trotsky Trout, who waits a million years before joining his father by entering "the blue tunnel to the Afterlife." Vonnegut's boldest experiments in fiction have always been with narrative strategy. Kilgore Trout is a familiar alter-ego, a very prolific and unappreciated author of science fiction, and his stories have been retold in several novels to multiply the narrative point of view. The idea for Tralfamadore, for example, comes from a Kilgore Trout book that Billy Pilgrim had read in *Slaughterhouse-Five*. Another of Trout's stories, "Now It Can Be Told," provokes the madness of a main character in *Breakfast of Champions*. Vonnegut has been intrigued by what happens when an unstable personality is exposed to the dangers and delusions of science fiction. If merely reading one or two books by Kilgore Trout is enough to provoke signs of madness, imagine the effect of being raised as Kilgore Trout's son! What are the chances that Leon Trotsky Trout could have anything like a normal life? Nor is it encouraging that his mother was a red-headed, left-handed woman who walked out on the family when Leon was a child. Small wonder that Leon feels abandoned by his parents and later betrayed by his government. He walks away from the mistake of Vietnam like his mother attempting to leave behind a bad marriage. He then escapes to the protection of neutral Sweden only to lose his head in a bizarre shipbuilding accident. Leon Trout surely belongs on the list of Vonnegut figures who are forlorn and abject playthings of fate. Given the oddity of his genetic inheritance and the horrors of his experience, he can be expected to narrate a story about evolution from his own unusual perspective.

Vonnegut hides the background for this bias, however, by introducing Leon Trout with stray bits of information that are scattered throughout the novel. The narrator's identity is not announced until the reader is well into the book, and the details reported in the previous paragraph only come together near the end. At first the narrative strategy is bewildering. When the identity of the narrator is still undisclosed, the reader assumes that the point of view belongs to a persona of the author and not one of his characters. The reader who makes the same assumption with the preface to *Breakfast of*

Champions is surprised to discover that it is signed by "Philboyd Studge." Vonnegut likes to play games with narrative perspective—witness the sly intrusion of a first-person narrator into the text of *Slaughterhouse-Five*. Given the fact that all Vonnegut narrators tend to communicate in the same casual style, it is often hard to believe in the distinctions. If it is true that Trout's voice sounds so much like Vonnegut's, then why bother to distinguish them? It is typical, however, for the meaning of a Vonnegut novel to depend on just this kind of distinction. If readers do not separate Vonnegut and Billy Pilgrim, despite all they have in common, the novel's point of view will be confused with Pilgrim's fantasies. The importance of sorting out differences between narrator and author is even greater in *Galápagos*. If the biased perspective of Leon Trout is not kept in mind, the antihuman point of view will be taken as Vonnegut's. If the irony of a headless ghost is ignored, the story of evolution will be reduced to its face value. Such is the mistake of a reviewer who says that "Vonnegut's solution for human problems is to revert back to unthinking animals."[9]

After the initial confusion, the effect of the narrator's delayed introduction is to make each new piece of information about him seem more valuable. The reader is asked to begin to assemble the pieces and to guess at the full picture. When it is revealed that the narrator's father has spent his life vainly writing science fiction, what reader of Vonnegut's novels doesn't start to think about Kilgore Trout? Such thoughts, however, are not confirmed until many pages later. Thus the reader is teased with possible answers, and the narrative strategy is heightened with anticipation and suspense.

The effects of evolution have been a concern for three generations of the Trout family. Kilgore Trout was born in Bermuda where his father worked for the Royal Ornithological Society protecting "the only nesting place in the world for Bermuda Erns." When all efforts failed to save the giant birds from extinction, it was young Kilgore Trout who was given "the melancholy task of measuring wingspreads of the corpses." This early lesson in evolution is cited in *Breakfast of Champions* as the cause of Kilgore Trout's depression, which in turn has a negative effect upon his own family—eventually driving away his wife and only son. Leon Trout has more than sufficient cause to resent the effects of evolution.

The details of the narrator's sad life and early death that are scattered in *Galápagos* add up to an ironic pattern of repeated failure. Each time he attempts to improve his situation, he only succeeds in making it worse. When he tries to escape his unhappy childhood by joining the military, he discovers the horrors of Vietnam. When he seeks refuge and work in a peaceful country, he is killed and decapitated. Despite his intelligence and sensitivity, Leon Trotsky Trout is a born loser. Perhaps his middle name is meant to indicate the failure of utopian hopes and the final hazard of exile and escape. Even as a headless ghost the narrator of *Galápagos* continues to be a forlorn and unlucky figure. Despite repeated invitations from his dead father, Leon Trout misses the blue tunnel to the afterlife for a million years.

The narrator's life from childhood forward has apparently given him ample reason to doubt the value of human intelligence, but his experience in Vietnam is cited as the most disillusioning. "When I was alive," says Leon Trout, "I often received advice from my own big brain which, in terms of my own survival, or the survival of the human race, for that matter, can be charitably described as questionable. Example: It had me join the United States Marines and go fight in Vietnam" (29). This bitter report ends with a typical expression of the narrator's sarcasm: "Thanks a lot, big brain." His exposure to war gives the narrator an education familiar to several Vonnegut characters. His worst recollection of war includes shooting an old woman who had just killed his best friend with a hand grenade. Trout is haunted by this memory of violence in much the same way that Eliot Rosewater can never forget killing a young civilian in Germany. The shooting of the old woman is followed by the massacre of the whole village. The future narrator is thus supplied with a vision of destruction that is both common in Vonnegut's fiction and crucial to the theme of evolution in *Galápagos*.

An immediate consequence of the massacre in Vietnam is that Leon Trout is hospitalized for "nervous exhaustion." His condition is reminiscent of Billy Pilgrim's after the trauma of Dresden. The shock treatments administered to Pilgrim in the veterans' hospital are sad attempts to cure his suffering with more of the same. The hapless narrator of *Galápagos* does not fare any better. He contracts syphilis while supposedly recovering from his nervous debility. Billy Pilgrim was seduced by the false comfort of science fiction when his roommate at the veterans' hospital introduced him to the books of Kilgore Trout. The doctor consulted by Leon Trout for syphilis turns out to be the only other fan of his father's novels. This is also the doctor who advises the narrator to seek political asylum in Sweden. Small wonder that it proves to be no more a viable escape than Billy Pilgrim's fantasy of Tralfamadore.

Leon Trout finds a job in Sweden as a welder in the shipbuilding industry. When he is assigned to work on the *Bahia de Darwin*, the very ship destined to serve as a second Noah's Ark for the Nature Cruise of the Century, he is "painlessly decapitated one day by a falling sheet of steel." Thus he becomes the headless ghost who haunts the *Bahia de Darwin* and its survivors throughout the novel. What advantages are there in having a ghost serve as narrator for a story of survival and evolution? Vonnegut's bold experiment combines the virtues of first-person and omniscient narrative. The voice of Leon Trout is associated with the history and point of view of a particular character, but the character is now a ghost who can manage his own invisibility, live inside the heads of other figures, and tell his story from the perspective of a million years. Vonnegut advertised *Slaughterhouse-Five* as "a novel somewhat in the telegraphic schizophrenic manner of tales of the planet Tralfamadore," but the character who believed he had been to another planet wasn't the narrator of the novel, and Pilgrim's travel in time was only a symptom of his troubled mind. The ghostly narrator of *Galápagos*, however, does have the ability to move back and forth in time because he enjoys the hindsight of so many centuries, and he does transcend his mortal self when he becomes the invisible eyes and ears of the narrative. Vonnegut has struggled for a long time to combine first-person and omniscient points of view. (What better way for a writer to play God?) He has at last found the perfect vehicle in *Galápagos*.

The most important scene for understanding the significance of the narrator may be late in the novel when he has a conversation with his dead father. Kilgore Trout chides his son for lingering on earth as a headless spirit, and encourages him to move at once into the afterlife. The father's attitude is hardly surprising, his faith in the value of human life having been lost in his youth, but the cynical advice from Kilgore Trout gives his son a chance to explain why he wants to remain on earth a while longer: "I had chosen to be a ghost because the job carried with it, as a fringe benefit, license to read minds, to learn the truth of people's pasts, to see through walls, to be many places all at once, to learn in depth how this or that situation had come to be structured as it was, and to have access to all human knowledge" (253). This may sound like eloquent testimony for the motive and profession of a writer, but the narrator's father who was a writer merely replies in scorn: "The more you learn about people, the more disgusted you'll become." The son, however, resists the father's deep-rooted cynicism. He doesn't want to join his father in the afterlife because he decided years ago that his father was a failure. Instead, he would like to meet the spirit of his mother whose favorite words from Anne Frank are used as the novel's epigraph: "In spite of everything, I still believe people are really good at heart."

Leon Trotsky Trout, of course, is a true combination of his father and mother. He has become a writer to "have access to all human knowledge"; he has told a story of evolution that often resembles the bizarre science fiction of his father; and he has retained his mother's belief in human goodness. Vonnegut's success with *Galápagos* owes much to this winsome and paradoxical mixture of curiosity, wry cynicism, and tragic hopefulness. It may seem a long way from Darwin to Anne Frank, and at times Vonnegut's reach surely exceeds his grasp, but the narrator of *Galápagos* tells the story of evolution from a human point of view that is wise beyond its years, high spirited, and doomed.

When crossing the ocean in a terrible storm the narrator's ghost is seen at the mast of the ship holding gallantly to his severed head. What a perfect image for Vonnegut's place in contemporary literature! *Galápagos* is Vonnegut's best novel since *Slaughterhouse-Five*.

Notes

1. Herbert Mitgang, "Advantages Darwin Lacked," *New York Times Book Review*, 6 October 1985, 7.

2. Michiko Kakutani, "Books of The Times," *New York Times,* 25 September 1985, 21, and Gregory Benford, *"Galápagos," Los Angeles Times,* 29 September 1985, 11.

3. Robert Towers, "Three-Part Inventions," *New York Review of Books,* 19 December 1985, 25, and Loree Rackstraw, "Blue Tunnels to Survival," *North American Review* 270 (Winter 1985):78.

4. Kurt Vonnegut, *Galápagos* (New York: Dell, 1986), 8; hereafter cited in the text.

5. Kurt Vonnegut, *Slaughterhouse-Five* (New York: Dell, 1971), 19; hereafter cited in the text.

6. Benford, *"Galápagos,"* 1.

7. J. D. O'Hara, "Instantly Digestible," *New Republic,* 12 May 1973, 26.

8. James Lundquist, *Kurt Vonnegut* (New York: Ungar, 1977), 74.

9. Benford, *"Galápagos,"* 1, 11.

General Studies

Kurt Vonnegut and the Myths and
Symbols of Meaning
Kathryn Hume*

Many reviewers treat Vonnegut's pessimism as a kind of intellectual body odor—an unnecessary offence against good taste. Because they find the bleak outlook pervasive yet unconvincing, they resent its inescapability and decry Vonnegut's indulgence in lamentation when he could make constructive suggestions instead. Christopher Lehmann-Haupt registers his protest with a flippant rapier thrust: "Well, of course one didn't believe him; he [Vonnegut] was just walking his despair around the block."[1] In a notorious *Newsweek* review of *Breakfast of Champions*, Peter S. Prescott bludgeons Vonnegut with such terms as "cretinous philosophizing" and "pretentious, hypocritical manure," in part for what he considers Vonnegut's "smug pessimism" and "facile fatalism."[2] As if the pessimism were somehow irrelevant to the presentation of values, another reviewer complains that "the reader will search in vain for a vision of the proper order of things."[3]

Vonnegut's writings are pessimistic, but not to the degree so often assumed. Especially since his Dresden book, he has struggled to identify values in human nature and society that he can affirm despite the events of our century. Overall, there is a tension in his work between the pessimism born of experience and the optimism stemming from background and values. This tension confuses readers, and the clash of values it reflects has made authentication of his artistic vision difficult for Vonnegut. In book after book, he has had to grapple with an intractable problem: how can a novel convey a sense of affirmation without relying on traditional symbols or becoming preachy? Vonnegut has experimented with standard devices for imparting positive meaning and has found them wanting. The myths and symbols of "a proper order of things" are empty because his personal experiences have destroyed their significance for him. But how can he communicate his sense of life's meaning if not through the conventional symbols and myths? These are questions whose import reaches beyond the works of Vonnegut, but his

*From *Texas Studies in Literature and Language* 24, no. 4 (Winter 1982); pp. 429–447. Reprinted by permission of the author and the University of Texas Press.

novels exemplify with exceptional clarity the results of a clash between an artist's experience and his culture's symbols.

To understand Vonnegut's dilemma, we need to consider how a work normally projects a sense of meaning. Literature can convey at least four possible kinds of meaning in addition to an explicit didactic message. We find one kind of meaning in the plot structure, or mythos, in which the author has embodied his sentiments. A romance, or hero monomyth-based story, encourages the reader to value individual aspiration and action. A comedy affirms belief in the renewability of society. Similarly, tragedy and satire reinforce certain basic interpretations of experience. The values implicit in these mythoi are absorbed by the reader as part of the narrative's meaning, and they contribute to the work's vision of order. We find a second kind of meaning in a work's symbols and symbolic situations. Let an author call attention to a cruciform shape, even in an albatross, and that author can draw on the cross's encrusted layers of formal significance. Likewise, a scene suggesting death and rebirth, or a monster fight—both symbolic situations— gives the reader a sense of affirmation. A third kind of meaning is psychoanalytic. According to critics like Norman Holland, this sort of meaning grows out of the author's infantile traumas and manifests itself in the author's choice of words and situations. For example, readers will feel tension and relief as they react unconsciously to disguised anxieties over oral engulfment. Their heightened emotional response to what they are reading seems evidence to them of the story's rightness or truth, and hence of a kind of emotional meaning. The fourth sort of meaning is perhaps the simplest. A story may uphold a code of behavior without preaching it, and the coherence and strength of that code will come across as a form of meaning. In the *Odyssey*, for instance, self-control and generosity toward guests are basic virtues. These are not part of the story's mythos but rather its ethos, and insofar as the virtues operate powerfully within the tale, readers will tend to absorb them as a form of meaning.

The myths and symbols of his culture stir an author's imagination in its developing stages and later shape his sense of literature. However, the ability to work successfully with these inherited signs is affected by personal experiences as well as by talent and practice. Kurt Vonnegut's works offer a fascinating study in the way that experience can adversely affect an artist's ability to use the conventional materials of his culture. Vonnegut started his career by trying to use his culture's traditional devices for imparting a positive sense of meaning. Only gradually has he realized that he is up against some fundamental limits inherent in the symbols and up against another set of limits within himself. The traditional forms, especially the hero monomyth with its archetypal situations, clash too directly with Vonnegut's experiences for him to use them effectively. In his recent books, he works out new symbolic fantasies and situations that let him project different kinds of order in his stories.

I would like to use Vonnegut's artistic development as the basis for a study of this problem of incompatibility between personal experience and cultural heritage. My aims are twofold. I want to explore the literary ramifications of an artist's need to integrate personal values with inherited value structures if he is to communicate a sense of purpose and order. And I wish to show specifically in Vonnegut's case how one artist has begun to create new tools for expression because the traditional ones failed him. His early books show Vonnegut struggling with the symbolic situations that constitute any storyteller's stock-in-trade—the hero monomyth. In his more recent novels, he has turned to different kinds of myth and to symbolic distortion in an attempt to express values he can believe in.

VONNEGUT'S STRUGGLE WITH
TRADITIONAL MYTHS AND SYMBOLS

Vonnegut's early novels exhibit an obvious and troublesome self-contradiction. Again and again, Vonnegut's overt pessimism is undercut by his use of the hero monomyth, which affirms the value of the individual and the desirability of that individual's finding a suitable role in society. Many of his stories follow a monomythic quest pattern, but usually the pattern is uncomfortably distorted. Vonnegut's experiences do not let him use it without strain.

The monomyth is the basic optimistic mythos for structuring meaning in our literature. It gives the standard plot to legends, folktales, romances, and most popular forms of literature, including science fiction.[4] Northrop Frye identifies its ultimate concern as the loss and regaining of identity and calls this romance pattern "the framework of all literature."[5] The pattern has three parts. During the first, the initial equilibrium, the hero is at one with his society. During the second, he undergoes a quest or test while separated from the props and supports which society can give. Finally, the hero achieves a new equilibrium in which he reaches adulthood, becomes an individual, reintegrates with society, and starts trying to help others instead of serving only himself. Joseph Campbell gives us labels for this monomyth's most common symbolic situations. He derives the terms from their occurrence in myth, and they sound alien and oversimple when applied to contemporary literature. When reading contemporary novels, we rarely find a literal meeting with a goddess or atonement with a father, apotheosis or ultimate boon. But these and other Campbell terms can usefully point to the underlying symbolic functions of episodes in recent novels as well as traditional myths. I shall try to use the terms descriptively when they fit Vonnegut's stories, for they provide a list of checkpoints at which one can compare the personal experiences of the author with the underlying meanings in his fiction.

Consider, for instance, the situations which arise when the hero confronts a hostile woman, a common component of both monomythic adventure and realistic novel. Woman can be the ultimate enemy, associated with the Other and with death; and in this powerful form, she manifests herself as goddess, witch, vamp, and siren. In these guises she threatens the hero with annihilation, or at least with psychological maiming. According to psychoanalytic theory, such goddess figures take some of their coloring from the creator's own mother. When this archetypal figure appears in a fictional plot, we know that what she offers the hero may destroy him, particularly if he is at an early stage of his development.[6] Sir Gawain deals with her in two forms, as Morgan le Fay and as seductive hostess. Odysseus battles her importunities in Circe and the Sirens. In a conventionally handled monomyth story, victory gives the hero a psychological boost and helps confirm him in his heroic identity.[7]

In Vonnegut's novels this archetype of female power is heavily influenced by the author's mother, who committed suicide. In his early works, the eternal feminine is an absence, a gap through which a chill wind blows. The mothers of Paul Proteus, Malachi Constant, and Howard Campbell are distant or missing. Eliot Rosewater feels responsible for killing his mother, for she drowned in a sailing accident in which he was involved. Billy Pilgrim always pretends to be asleep when his mother visits him in the nursing home and thus punishes her with his absence. Vonnegut faces his resentments directly in *Breakfast of Champions*. In this book Celia Hoover, who shares some of his mother's peculiar habits, commits suicide in an especially punishing fashion: she swallows Drano. Vonnegut admits that his mother's example has been a nagging temptation to suicide whenever life seemed unpleasant, but declares in this book that he has defeated that temptation. Nevertheless, the declaration of victory is low-keyed and lacks the jubilation that should accompany full success. Because of its timing, his mother's suicide appears to have been a gesture directed at her son. His mother thus made herself an almost archetypal figure, a siren luring him to death, a maenad seeking to dismember her Orphic son. What should have been victory under more favorable circumstances proves Pyrrhic. The emptiness of mere survival is painfully described in *Cat's Cradle,* in which the earth is locked in frozen death and is consequently referred to as "a very bad mother."[8] No actively helpful mother figures have yet appeared in Vonnegut's fiction. Traditionally the confrontation with this dangerous feminine power would reinforce optimism by bringing the hero to victory, but this archetypal situation does not fit Vonnegut's experience. Mothers, for him, will probably never embody the eternal feminine in any very positive way.

Of course the feminine need not be negative. The damsel rescued from the dragon inspires and rewards the hero. In Neumann's terms such damsels represent the anima in its transformative function. In a sense they represent his unconscious creative abilities which must be raised to consciousness. Such an anima figure is the muse who inspires, the goddess who helps, the young woman who understands.

Again, this very common literary figure has been contaminated for Vonnegut by a close member of his family. What happened to her affects his ability to employ this symbol. In the prologue to *Slapstick*, Vonnegut says that his sister Alice "was the person I had always written for. She was the secret of whatever artistic unity I had ever achieved. She was the secret of my technique" (p. 15). She died of cancer in 1958 when she was only forty-one. He goes on to note that Nature was nice enough "to allow me to feel her presence for a number of years after she died—to let me go on writing for her" (p. 15). Vonnegut acknowledges that Wilbur and Eliza Swain, the grotesque twins of *Slapstick*, are projections of himself and Alice. They interact like the two hemispheres of a single brain—brilliant when together, stupid and incomplete when apart. In this story the power of this anima figure is so overwhelming—possibly in part because of its incestuous nature—that it wrecks the relationship. However, in *Jailbird*, this anima power is distributed among three women—Sarah, Mary Kathleen, and Ruth—with the result that Starbuck is not overcome by contact with any of them. True, they complicate his life, but they enrich it and him in many ways, as anima figures normally do.

Clearly these various images of the feminine are powerful in Vonnegut's work. Their power is primarily threatening because of the author's personal experiences. Memories of members of his family personalize and distort the archetypes. Once Vonnegut has managed to free himself from the shadow of his mother's death, he finds it possible to create more positive female characters and his fictions take new directions. We should note, however, that these new characters are less successful than traditional anima figures. Even when the three powerful women in *Jailbird* work to transform Starbuck, they prove unable to save him from his own second-rateness.

In the monomyth the hero often meets some form of monster. "The central form of quest-romance is the dragon-killing theme."[9] Slaying the monster, be it a beast, a computer, or a human, is not a task for which Vonnegut has any stomach. A monster must be evil: killing benign giants or large herbivores wins a hero no fame or joy, as Orwell found when shooting an elephant. To believe in monsters, an author must enjoy seeing the world as black and white, with good and evil polarized. This particular oversimplification is wholly foreign to Vonnegut's thinking. Even in his Luddite fable, *Player Piano*, he upholds the value of some mechanization. In his college writing and in *Mother Night*, he shows himself unable to accept the comforting myth of Germany as undiluted evil and America as moral perfection. A German name and some relatives who still spoke German remind him all too forcefully of might-have-beens: "If I'd been born in Germany, I suppose I would have *been* a Nazi, bopping Jews and gypsies and Poles around" (*Mother Night*, p. vii). Campbell of *Mother Night* finds at least as much monstrosity in the American, O'Hare, as he ever did in his high-ranking Nazi acquaintances. Nazi war criminals, in Vonnegut's fiction, are mostly rather ordinary-seeming people. So is his Watergate conspirator. So is the man who dropped the bomb on Nagasaki (a minor character in *Breakfast of Champions* and *Happy Birthday, Wanda June*). To find monster fights symbolically satisfying, an author must content himself with seeing only the evil aspects of the adversary. Vonnegut is unwilling to secure his own ease of mind so crudely, in part because of his German-American heritage.

Another common climax to the monomythic hero's trials is atonement with the father. The father may be divine, political, genetic, social, psychological, or just the "wise old man" of Jung's archetype. In one form or another, this reconciliation is a common organizing principle in fiction. "The hero's search for a father"—the theme Maxwell Perkins suggested to Thomas Wolfe—produces such variations as the atonement in C. S. Lewis's *Out of the Silent Planet*, the coming together of Stephen and Bloom in *Ulysses*, the resolution of Oedipal hatreds and the commencement of love in Zelazny's *Chronicles of Amber*, and the ironic reconciliation of Smith to Big Brother in *1984*.

Far from declaring peace with their fathers and father figures, Vonnegut's characters nourish implicit or explicit resentment. Psychological readings of his fiction disclose a very angry and unhappy strain of Oedipal tension. Paul Proteus, Malachi Constant, Howard Campbell, the Hoenikker children, Eliot Rosewater, Billy Pilgrim, Dwayne Hoover, Wilbur Swain, and Walter Starbuck—all are estranged from their fathers. Lynn Buck points out that "just as Vonnegut's earthly fathers are cold and indifferent toward their sons, unpredictable and frequently destructive, his God is a disinterested Creator, remaining aloof from His earth creatures except to punish them occasionally when they step out of line. The chilling parallel between celestial and terrestrial fathers is too strong to ignore."[10] In another psychoanalytic reading, Josephine Hendin notes that hopelessness in *Cat's Cradle* is a "parental gift": "Vonnegut's fictional children always inherit killing coldness."[11] In the prologue to *Jailbird*, Vonnegut describes trying to write a short story about his father. "I hoped in the story to become a really good friend of his." It did not work out. Although the story took place in heaven, Vonnegut found himself embarrassed and irritated by his father and kept having to shout, "For the love of God, Father, won't you please grow up!" (pp. xiii–xv). Vonnegut concludes: "It insisted on being a very unfriendly story, so I quit writing it."

Vonnegut has reached no fictional atonement with either the distant father or the withdrawn deity, but that failure may be good. Of all the tensions underlying his work, this Oedipal stress seems to be one of the most basic. The fathers in his books embody most of what is wrong with his fictive worlds. The anger behind his attacks comes from personal experience, as does the force motivating Paul Proteus in *Player Piano*. Were Vonnegut to come to terms with this archetypal force in his inner pantheon, he might well cease to write, for much of what he says grows out of this tension. Atonement, for Vonnegut, would mean acceptance of the world as it is and might therefore prove a creative and moral dead end.

Another common symbol for the monomythic hero's success is the boon that he brings back, a gift from the special world that may take the form of treasure, but which ultimately signifies knowledge of some sort: knowledge which helps the hero escape the confines of his own ego, or knowledge of some message that may save his society. Vonnegut would clearly like to find such a message.[12] Malachi ("faithful messenger") Constant lives in the hope of finding "a single message that was sufficiently dignified and important to merit his carrying it humbly between two points" (*Sirens of Titan*, p. 17). In *Breakfast of Champions*, Vonnegut emphasizes Kilgore Trout's apothegms by awarding him the Nobel Prize for messages such as "We are healthy only to the extent that our ideas are humane." The ultimate boon is the cure needed by the monomythic hero's society, but the problems that engage Vonnegut are so deeply rooted in human nature that he can find no one-line solutions to them. Messages prove inadequate. In *Jailbird* he tries to put forward the Sermon on the Mount as such an ultimate message, but even though we may stop to readmire its sentiments, we see all too vividly how ineffective that message has been, historically speaking.

Epiphany, illumination, and even apotheosis are crowning adventures that may befall a monomythic hero of exceptionally spiritual capacity. Vonnegut explores the potential of these symbolic situations, with predictable results. In *Slapstick*, Wilbur achieves a kind of epiphany on the last day of his life: "Standing among all those tiny, wavering lights [a thousand candles], I felt as though I were God, up to my knees in the Milky Way" (p. 228). As an atheist (however often he may mention God as a convenient fiction), Vonnegut can find no higher power than man; so Wilbur enjoys a flash of feeling himself the creator of the universe, but makes no contact with any power higher than himself. In *Breakfast of Champions*, Vonnegut plays with the idea of himself as creator of his fictive universe, but he finds no comfort in the notion because if he is the creator he is responsible for the anguish of his characters. The experience is depressing rather than enlightening, and apotheosis, like other symbolic situations, fails to convey the conventional optimistic sense of meaning.

Only once does the epiphanic breakthrough work for Vonnegut with something like its traditional power. In *Breakfast of Champions*, he concludes that individual consciousness is a pure, unwavering band of light, and claims that the awareness it represents is "all that is alive and maybe sacred in any of us. Everything else about us is dead machinery" (p. 221). This mystic revelation strikes him so powerfully that he declares himself "born again." This success with a conventional symbol is unique.

Confrontation with the goddess, transformation through the aid of the anima, atonement with the father, apotheosis and epiphany, and winning the ultimate boon—all these trials are major functional units of the monomyth. From them come the majority of traditional stories and a great many episodes in contemporary novelistic narratives as well. At each of these possibilities Vonnegut is blocked by personal experience. This blocking persists even if we view the hero's road of trials in its broader functions.

Campbell identifies the series of trials as a "descent into the underworld," or adventure "in the belly of the whale." The trials await the hero in a special world—underworld, belly, land of spirits or of the dead—which is cut off from the ordinary realms of human action. Once the hero enters, he cannot retreat. He must complete his quest in order to reemerge. In initiation ceremonies, this land of spirits is endured after the ritual celebrating death-as-a-child and before the ritual symbolizing rebirth-as-an-adult. Emerging from it should bring the initiate or hero a strengthened ego and a new identity.

Vonnegut uses some situations reminiscent of the monomythic descent into the underworld, but experience again distorts this archetypal situation. In Dresden, POW Vonnegut was marched to a deep subterranean meat locker, and there he survived the fire bombing. So too, Billy Pilgrim descends deep into the earth and survives the holocaust. But the world does not survive. When both prisoners come forth, they might as well be on the moon, or in the land of the dead, for all that remains are 135,000 corpses. In *Cat's Cradle* the narrator descends into a dungeon fitted out as a bomb shelter, and there he weathers the monstrous tornadoes that follow upon the freezing of all the earth's water into Ice-9. When he emerges, the world is dead, and corpses dot the landscape, frozen monuments to man's stupidity. In *Jailbird*, Starbuck descends to the vasty halls of a train station below Grand Central, where he witnesses the death of a crazy but passionately optimistic bag lady. While he does not find the rest of the world destroyed when he remounts the stairs, he does feel that Mary Kathleen's death signifies the death of all youthful innocence in the world.

For Vonnegut, the belly of the whale becomes a tomb. The underworld is not just a temporary testing ground, but a labyrinth which imprisons the living dead; though still in the flesh, they will wander its corridors through the rest of their miserable lives. Vonnegut feels no confidence that the soul will ascend renewed, once it has descended in this standard symbolic ordeal.

Part of the psychic texture of the descent into the underworld is the related image of death and rebirth. If the land of the dead provides the landscape for the ordeal, death and rebirth begin and end the sequence. That symbolism does not work well for Vonnegut. In the initiation ordeals he describes, innocence is not laid aside, to be replaced in the natural course of things by knowledge and maturity; innocence is murdered, and only a void remains. Billy Pilgrim is dumb innocence personified; the war so blows Billy's emotional fuses that he emerges a passive wreck. In *Slapstick* one of the central images is a pyramid erected over the grave of a male fetus, an obvious monument to dead innocence.

The death and rebirth ritual often makes use of fire or water or pain as the purifying medium, but if ever fire had positive and purifying connotations for Vonnegut, Dresden destroyed them. Fire is his cosmic and personal nightmare. To a Dresden survivor, no fiery furnace, no gold being tried, no vision in the flames, makes emotional sense as positive symbol. The epiphany with candles in *Slapstick* is the closest Vonnegut comes to being reconciled to fire. Even this truce does not last, for in *Jailbird*, Starbuck daydreams of becoming a skid-row drunk and of being doused with gasoline and set alight by toughs.

Water, the opposite of fire, fares little better in Vonnegut's work. Jess Ritter argues that "water images abound, water representing fertility and life (Ice-9, frozen water, *death-in-life*); pools and fountains (both flowing, and dry and barren) recur; Eliot Rose*water* and Kilgore *Trout* represent life-giving water forces; rivers (and canals) with 'carp the size of atomic submarines' figure in *The Sirens of Titan, God Bless You, Mr. Rosewater,* and *Slaughterhouse-Five*."[13] Pertinently quoting Vonnegut as saying, "In the water, I am beautiful," Peter B. Messent points out that in *Breakfast of Champions* Dwayne Hoover can only find complete relaxation on a water bed; that Sugar Creek (in both *Breakfast of Champions* and *Happy Birthday, Wanda June*) epitomizes humanity's careless pollution of once-beautiful water.[14] Vonnegut's use of water seems less positive in implication than Messent suggests. Sugar Creek—to judge from its name—was once lovely, but all we are shown is its stinking corpse. Similarly water destroys the world when it turns to Ice-9. Moreover, Alice Miller, Olympic swimming champion, is not idealized; she is a child with chlorine-ruined eyes, whose father turned her into an outboard motor. As an atheist, Vonnegut finds no sacred baptismal imagery in water. He often mentions as the quintessential scientific dilemma his brother Bernard's experience. Bernard developed techniques for seeding clouds to cause rain. He had been proud of his contribution to mankind until he learned that the technique was being used in Vietnam to flood crops and starve the North Vietnamese. Although water carries none of the onus of fire in Vonnegut's vocabulary, it remains stubbornly nonmystical and is symbolic only in minor and fleeting ways.

After descent, and after death and rebirth, the hero monomyth usually goes on to the hero's homecoming—the last symbolic situation I wish to discuss. This return to the normal world rounds out the hero's adventures and ushers him back into society. Except where writers deliberately foil our expectations, a homecoming ultimately celebrates welcome, acceptance, and confirmation of identity. But Vonnegut's experience destroyed this archetype too. "Shortly after transferring to the Carnegie Institute of Technology, Vonnegut enlisted in the army and became an infantry combat scout. He obtained leave to visit his parents on Mother's Day, 1944; but the night before his arrival his mother took a fatal overdose of sleeping pills."[15] Even a more euphemistic account of the event brings out elements which would have caused anguish and guilt: "Mrs. Vonnegut was distressed by her son's participation in a war she abhorred, and her health began to fail. She died in May 1944, when her son was home on leave."[16] With personal experience again having made a mockery of the archetype, we should not be surprised that homecomings bring little joy to Vonnegut characters. In *Mother Night* the return to America is to friendless emptiness; in *Slaughterhouse-Five* it is to a nursing home. In *Jailbird* the release from jail makes painfully obvious the lack of home. The whole of *Happy Birthday, Wanda June* takes Odysseus' homecoming and undercuts most of Homer's assumptions about what should seem valuable or enduring. The hero feels little love for home and hearth. His wife has outgrown him intellectually. He cannot even commit suicide successfully. The happiest homecoming in Vonnegut's canon is that of Malachi Constant, who returns to earth and promptly freezes to death, made happy in the process by a dream about afterlife that has been implanted by posthypnotic suggestion.

Thus, point for point, Vonnegut's experiences contradict the basic symbolic situations of the hero monomyth, our culture's primary literary structure for conveying an optimistic sense of life's meaning. From the stories, from the obvious attempts to find values he can affirm, we can see Vonnegut's desire to project positive messages, but clearly his primary option for expressing this outlook is not adequate to his personal needs. Little wonder that critics find no "right order of things" if they seek an inhering sense of value in the symbolic terms that would traditionally be used to put it across.

MYTHIC EXOSTRUCTURES

The symbols which focus and reinforce meaning within the hero monomyth are not the only possibilities open to Vonnegut. If an internal mythos does not spontaneously shape a story, the author can work from the outside. He can use a preexisting story or myth to structure his material. Joyce's *Ulysses* is the classic example. Other recent authors, struggling with a sense of the exhaustion of literature, have sought such external or "exo-" structures to give form to their matter. Heinlein, in *Time Enough for Love*, uses Otto Rank's interpretation of the Don Juan legend to give an overall outline to his hero's life and amours. John Barth uses the Greek legends of Perseus and Bellerophon and the Arabian story of Scheherazade to create modern metafiction. Vonnegut has experimented with such mythic exostructures with varying results. His most overt example is *Happy Birthday, Wanda June*, in which he rewrites the *Odyssey*. *Breakfast of Champions*, written at the same stage in his career, also seems to echo the *Odyssey*. In *Jailbird*, Vonnegut tries out Christian myth and American labor history as a way of embedding meaning in the text.

The *Odyssey* seems to have been polymorphous in its meanings for Vonnegut. Sometimes he sees positive power in its values, sometimes only negative. In *Breakfast of Champions*, it lies behind and beyond the text, an example of a world totally opposite to the one he describes. The *Odyssey* tells of life in a traditional world, where "vertical" values link past and future, father and son, the gods above and the land of the dead below. Athene contrives an unnecessary skirmish in which Laertes, Odysseus, and Telemachus fight shoulder to shoulder in order to reaffirm their relationship in a continuum. Even though Odysseus is so exalted a hero that he is a consort desired by a goddess, he accepts the definition of himself as Lord of Ithaca and member of a human family. He is offered immortality and eternal sensual pleasure, but rejects them and accepts instead the human limitations of sickness, age, and death. He knows his wife is no goddess, and Ithaca only a rocky islet, but these traditional values give him his sense of identity.

Breakfast of Champions shows the contemporary world where all values run "horizontally" rather than "vertically." There is no God, except as metaphor, and no afterlife. Characters have no sense of past or future; they are trapped in an eternal present. All relationships between parents and children are warped, brutal, anguished, and destructive. Kilgore Trout, like Odysseus, is on a long journey. He travels toward an arts festival and arrives after having been robbed at one stage of his adventures and given free transport at another stage. His brushes with pornography stores and blue movie houses correspond to Odysseus' adventures with Circe and the Sirens. He sees trucks labeled Pyramid and Ajax. He hears a truck driver recount the plot of one of his books, an experience almost as disturbing for him as was Odysseus' hearing the bard, Demodocus, tell of the wily hero's Trojan exploits. Trout too survives a general "slaughter" at the end of the story. Whereas Odysseus can refuse immortality in order to accept life, and with life accept death, Trout has no such inner values to support him. He cries out, "*Make me young, make me young, make me young!*" (p. 295). When Odysseus reveals himself to Laertes, he identifies himself by laying claim to certain fruit trees, and clearly the fruits symbolize wholeness and the good things of life. Vonnegut offers Trout an apple, telling him it is a symbol of wholeness; but this is disingenuous, for an apple brought about the fallen world and the punishment of death, at least in the popular mythology of our culture. Trout's odyssey ends not in affirmation, but in futile rebellion against the blight which man was born for. In *Breakfast of Champions*, the exostructure of the *Odyssey* points up the failure of contemporary values.

In *Happy Birthday, Wanda June*, an exostructure is far more evident. Harold Ryan, big game hunter and mercenary soldier, has been missing for seven years when he returns without warning to his wife, Penelope. Like Odysseus, he is furious over her suitors (a vacuum salesman and a doctor), and he proves ugly and vengeful. We are accustomed to think of Odysseus as a hero and sometimes forget that he relished the excuse to castrate and torture one of the suitors. Harold's values revolt us, and once we acknowledge our disgust, we realize we must reassess Homer's values too. In Odysseus' world a hero can boast of the great warriors he has killed; when Harold does the same, we gag. Homer's Penelope could win respect only by worshiping her husband's memory and by holding herself apart from any personal life. She gives up twenty years of her life, and that is considered proper. The modern Penelope has gone back to school, gotten an M.A. in English, and has developed a set of personal beliefs and ethics. Whereas Odysseus' wife could only obey or disobey the immutable laws, Vonnegut's character has a number of valid choices. Vonnegut the anthropologist and Vonnegut the humanitarian see very different values in Homer's story of a hero's homecoming. On the one hand, the vertical values and extended family give members of society a sense of belonging. On the other, the ethos accompanying them is not always attractive or humane. For both of his probes into the values of the *Odyssey,* Vonnegut takes plot and basic situation from Homer, and then develops his comment on values as an ironic counterpoint to the story. He manages thus to exploit the inadequacy of the traditional symbols rather than fight to make them work for him in conventional ways.

In *Jailbird,* Vonnegut tries a Christian exostructure, not for the main plot line, but for a secondary plot in which he works out the basic values for life. Having accepted the sacredness of human awareness as he does in *Breakfast of Champions,* Vonnegut feels driven to ask what an individual can do to alleviate the pain inherent in the human condition. Sacco and Vanzetti and other martyrs to the American labor movement offer paradigms for right action, and to make their action significant, Vonnegut invests it with Christian overtones.

He begins the story with an account of the Cuyahoga massacre. Vonnegut puzzles over the enigma of how armed men could bring themselves to fire on unarmed men, women, and children. This slaughter of innocents takes place on Christmas morning. The capitalist owners who crush the workers are the same enemy confronting Sacco and Vanzetti. Vonnegut calls the execution of these two "a modern Passion." "As on Golgotha, three lower-class men were executed at the same time by a state. This time, though, not just one of the three was innocent. This time two of the three were innocent" (p. 172). The Pontius Pilates "would be in favor rather than against the death penalty this time. And they would never wash their hands. They were in fact so proud of what they were about to do that they asked a committee composed of three of the wisest, most respected, most fair-minded and impartial men within the boundaries of the state to say to the world whether or not justice was about to be done" (p. 179). Sacco and Vanzetti worked to help their fellow men through the labor movement. Trying to improve the lives of others comprises Vonnegut's definition of right action. Their dedication to the welfare of other people calls forth reference to the Sermon on the Mount. The Sermon, indeed, crops up whenever ordinary characters try to commit themselves to meaningful and significant action. Vonnegut lets Christian ethics, if not Christian theology, suggest the way in which men can find meaning through devoting their energies to helping others.

Vonnegut plays with Christian myth in other novels, but never before so explicitly as here. Kilgore Trout is a messianic figure, and his plots are parables. Bokonon, too, is a messiah. The radium-poisoned clock-face painters are martyrs, though not specifically religious. Sacco and Vanzetti, with Christ's life imposed on theirs, are Vonnegut's main essay at a religious mythic exostructure. This technique allows him to push beyond his pessimism and make a positive statement, which I see as an artistic advance for him, given his experience with the optimistic monomyth symbols. *Jailbird* is more optimistic than any of his earlier books. Falling back on a public value system has helped him escape, at least in part, the destructive effect that his personal experience has had upon his use of standard literary archetypes. Some tension and unease result from his use of a Christian ethical system whose underlying theology he denies, but overall, Vonnegut has here one solution to his problem of projecting a "right order of things."

CONCLUSIONS

I started this article by pointing to Vonnegut's pessimism as an artistic problem. Critics have felt this pessimism to be inauthentic because it clashed with his monomythic symbolism and his obvious attraction to the bourgeois verities. Critics have also complained that Vonnegut's pessimism is aimless and demanded a more positive approach to the world's problems. Vonnegut's own bourgeois values have certainly predisposed him to attempt affirmative statements, but conventional symbols for such expressions have failed him. Until *Breakfast of Champions*, we see a constant inner tension between the symbolic situations he presents and the grotesque turns his experiences compel him to give those situations. With *Breakfast of Champions*, his one effective epiphany, Vonnegut freed himself from some of the darker shadows of his past. After all his literary questing for a message, for a positive value, he found one. He then had to decide where to head with that insight.

Since 1977 he has been exploring new forms of action and mythic exostructures to see if they can be of any use to contemporary humanity. In a curious way, Vonnegut has recapitulated some of the most basic literary patterns. As Borges says in his short story, "The Gospel according to Mark," "generations of men, throughout recorded time, have always told and retold two stories—that of a lost ship which searches the Mediterranean seas for a dearly loved island, and that of a god who is crucified on Golgotha."[17] In abstract terms Vonnegut has experimented with the quest for meaning on the individual, human level of the monomyth and the *Odyssey* and then has gone on to the transpersonal, sacred level of sacrifice and tragedy. Vonnegut has explored the monomyth with all that it stands for—quest, heroism, homecoming, romance, lasting love, happy ending—and found it wanting as a means of representing his sense of reality. His exploration of the more tragic realm of sacrifice and martyrdom in *Jailbird*, seen in the subplots involving labor history and Christian myth, promises to be more productive for him. People who choose to work for others, he finds, can at least buy something meaningful with their lives and sacrifices, even if it is only a sense of their own meaning. Vonnegut presents significant action so relatively positively in *Jailbird* that he appears to be finding it a foundation capable of sustaining his natural optimism. Helping others rather than trying to make sense of one's own life is, at least for now, his central idea. And of course, helping others sometimes makes one feel that one's own life has meaning.

Vonnegut is not relying on this one idea or on mythic exostructures as his only means of expressing a sense of meaning. He is developing another technique as well. Although it first appeared in *Sirens of Titan* and is arguably present in any Tralfamadorian scenes he has written, it vanished, not to return until *Slapstick* and *Jailbird*. This method amounts to new symbols, generated by a vein of fantasy that distorts the physical world. In *Slapstick* he uses grotesque bodily form, varying forces of gravity, and miniaturization of humans. In *Jailbird* we find the immeasurable immensity of the RAMJAC fortune; the infernal subdepths of a train station beneath Grand Central; the soaring heights of the Chrysler Building, where harps are sold in a warbler-filled anteroom to heaven. These distortions are treated as if they exist on the same fictional plane as his realistic scenes and characters. Like the distortions and transpositions of a Picasso painting, these changes in normal shapes let the artist both express his sense of the unreliable nature of the cosmos and stress those parts of it which seem in need of special comment. For Vonnegut these include the inequalities of wealth, beauty, and health; the usefulness of light gravity (i.e., humor), and the shattering extremes of sunny heights and dark depths to which life exposes us.[18] This vein of fantasy lets him communicate feeling—if not ideas—expressively and lets him reinforce the sense of meaning he is projecting by means of his mythic exostructures and his ideas.

In a recent essay, John Barth predicts that postmodernist fiction will be easier to read and less in need of a tenured priesthood devoted to expounding its mysteries.[19] Vonnegut's writing shows some of the simplicity that Barth is looking for, and predictably such writing upsets the priests, whose livelihood rests on explication. They prefer to call it simple-minded. But Vonnegut's values cannot be identified solely with the one-liners that point his morals and adorn his tales. His sense of meaning functions at several levels: in generic form, in symbols and symbolic situations, and in his use of exostructures and fantastic distortions. Nor is Vonnegut, as some reviewers have charged, just a lazy spouter of antisocial values which he sweetens up for general consumption. As an artist, he has struggled to work out a value system for our age. He is no Pollyanna, but neither is he totally pessimistic or cynical. His last three novels take affirmative stances and work to support these in the face of humanity's inhumanity. Had Vonnegut been comfortable with the monomythic symbols, he might have become the science fiction writer for whom many critics still mistake him. In this regard his limitations and experiences may actually have worked to his advantage, since that sort of speculative fiction does not appear to be his forte.

The odd mixture of optimism and pessimism in Vonnegut's works has caused reviewers considerable discomfort. His pessimism, though often explicit, is not as unrelieved as Beckett's, for example, and so cannot be admired for its obsessive purity. But Vonnegut's symbolic situations yield no satisfying outcomes, and this inability to gratify the expectations of optimism has proved equally discomfiting to critics. However, Beckettian singleness of vision is not an automatic literary virtue; so Vonnegut's departure from it need not be held against him. Vonnegut tries instead to do justice to the complex coexistence of our criminal as well as our generous impulses. Many of his observations are depressing, but many are also funny. He has worked throughout his career to hammer out positive values which are defensible despite the Medusa-face our era has worn. His recent works show modest progress in this difficult quest, no mean achievement for someone who once felt he had been turned to a pillar of salt by witnessing the destruction of a city of the plain.

Notes

1. Christopher Lehmann-Haupt, review of *Slapstick, New York Times,* September 24, 1976, p. C19.

2. Peter S. Prescott, "Nothing Sacred," *Newsweek,* May 14, 1973, pp. 114–15.

3. About *Jailbird,* from an unsigned notice in *National Review,* 31 (August 17, 1979), p. 1045.

4. For studies of this pattern in its various manifestations, see Erich Neumann, *The Origins and History of Consciousness* (orig. German, 1949; trans. R. F. C. Hull, Bollingen Series 42, Princeton: Princeton University Press, 1970); Mircea Eliade, *Rites and Symbols of Initiation,* trans. Willard T. Trask (New York: Harper & Row, 1958); Joseph Campbell, *The Hero with a Thousand Faces* (1949; 2d ed., Bollingen Series 17, Princeton: Princeton University Press, 1968); Vladimir Propp, *Morphology of the Folktale,* trans. Laurence Scott (orig. Russian, 1928; 2d ed. of trans., Austin: University of Texas Press, 1968); and my "Romance: A Perdurable Pattern," *College English,* 36 (1974), 129–46. Vonnegut himself discusses some variations on the pattern in *Palm Sunday* (New York: Delacorte, 1981), pp. 312–15.

5. Northrop Frye, *The Educated Imagination* (Bloomington: Indiana University Press, 1971), p. 55. See also his discussion of the romance mythos in *Anatomy of Criticism* (1957; paperback ed. Princeton: Princeton University Press, 1971), pp. 186–206.

6. For a detailed analysis of this archetype, see Erich Neumann, *The Great Mother: An Analysis of the Archetype* (orig. German, 1955; trans. Ralph Manheim, Bollingen Series 47, paperback ed. Princeton: Princeton University Press, 1972).

7. Derek Brewer (*Symbolic Stories* [Cambridge: D. S. Brewer, 1980]) suggests that this maternal power is perceived as more threatening than the paternal in European folktales and romances.

8. Quotations from all the texts are from the Dell/Delta paperback editions, except for references to *Happy Birthday, Wanda June* and *Jailbird,* which are cited from the Delacorte Press editions of 1970 and 1979 respectively. The quotation from *Cat's Cradle* is from p. 180.

9. Frye, *Anatomy,* p. 189.

10. Lynn Buck, "Vonnegut's World of Comic Futility," *Studies in American Fiction,* 3 (1975), 181–98, quotation from p. 190.

11. Josephine Hendin, *Vulnerable People: A View of American Fiction since 1945* (New York: Oxford University Press, 1978), pp. 34, 35.

12. For an analysis of Vonnegut's search for a message, see Tony Tanner, "The Uncertain Messenger," in *City of Words: American Fiction 1950–1970* (New York: Harper & Row, 1971). Several Vonnegut heroes link their picture of themselves to that of Jonah, messenger of God to the people of Nineveh. See Stanley Schatt, "*The Whale and the Cross:* Vonnegut's Jonah and Christ Figures," *Southwest Review,* 56 (Winter 1971), 29–42; and also his book, *Kurt Vonnegut, Jr.* (Boston: Twayne, 1976).

13. Jess Ritter, "Teaching Kurt Vonnegut on the Firing Line," in *The Vonnegut Statement,* ed. Jerome Klinkowitz and John Somer (New York: Dell, 1973), pp. 31–42, esp. pp. 38–39.

14. Peter B. Messent, *"Breakfast of Champions:* The Direction of Kurt Vonnegut's Fiction," *Journal of American Studies,* 8 (1974), 101–14, esp. p. 105.

15. Schatt, *Kurt Vonnegut, Jr.,* p. 15. See also "An Account of the Ancestry of Kurt Vonnegut, Jr. by an Ancient Friend of his Family," *Summary,* 1 (1971), 76–118, esp. p. 115: "Kurt, Jr. got leave from his regiment to come home and spend Mother's Day in May, 1944 with his family. During the night before, Edith died in her sleep in her fifty-sixth year on May 14, 1944. Her death was attributed to an inadvertent overdose of sleeping tablets taken possibly by mistake."

16. Jerome Klinkowitz, "Vonnegut in America," in *Vonnegut in America,* ed. Jerome Klinkowitz and Donald L. Lawler (New York: Dell, 1977), p. 12.

17. Jorge Luis Borges, *Doctor Brodie's Report,* trans. Norman Thomas di Giovanni (New York: E. P. Dutton, 1972), p. 19.

18. For critical analyses of Vonnegut's sense of the universe and of man's place in it, see Stanley Schatt, "The World of Kurt Vonnegut, Jr.," *Critique,* 12 (1971), 54–69; Jerome Klinkowitz, "Kurt Vonnegut, Jr., and the Crimes of His Time," *Critique,* 12 (1971), 38–53; Max F. Schulz, "The Unconfirmed Thesis: Kurt Vonnegut, Black Humor, and Contemporary Art," *Critique,* 12 (1971), 5–28; and my "Vonnegut's Self-Projections: Symbolic Characters and Symbolic Fictions," forthcoming in *Journal of Narrative Technique;* and my "The Heraclitean Cosmos of Kurt Vonnegut," *Papers on Language and Literature,* 18 (1982), 208–24.

19. John Barth, "The Literature of Replenishment: Postmodernist Fiction," *Atlantic,* 245 (Jan. 1980), 65–71, esp. p. 70.

The Heraclitean Cosmos of Kurt Vonnegut

Kathryn Hume*

Vonnegut's fictional cosmos is one of flux and transformation. We catch glimpses of metaphors as tenor dissolves into vehicle. Events, words, people, and ideas—apparently unconnected—turn out to be complexly interrelated. Characters reappear in two or more of his books, often so totally transformed that one would not recognize them as the same people if they did not have the same name. The force of gravity, the freezing point of water, the necessity of breathing: such fixities of human life come unstuck. What we are accustomed to count on as stable, and enduring, shifts shape and evanesces in Vonnegut's cosmos.

The recycled characters are mentioned in any assessment of Vonnegut's works, for this technique is peculiar to his fiction. Reviewers and critics occasionally mention other fluctuating elements too. Curiously, their response to all these transmutations is often hostile and uncomprehending. Charles Samuels is typical: "Vonnegut is celebrated for his power of invention, but he is uninventive to the point of repetition. Not only do names of

*From *Papers on Language & Literature* 18, no. 2 (Spring 1982): 208–24. © 1982 by the Board of Trustees, Southern Illinois University. Reprinted by permission.

places and characters continuously reappear; so also do devices within a single novel. . . . In Vonnegut [the repetitions] express not a way of seeing but a way of frugally husbanding the little one has been able to imagine."[1] Who could possibly create the series of Kilgore Trouts, so varied in personal history and outlook, out of a failure of imagination? Choosing different names from a telephone book would have been easier than conceiving of the cracked messiah and the gentle jailbird as one being. Had Vonnegut made a habit of alluding to *Verfremdungseffekt* or *ostraneniye*, "estrangement" or "defamiliarization," his reception might have been more to Vonnegut's tastes, for few literati would admit that they have let themselves be too alienated by simple dislocations to see the real issues. Whether such critical misunderstanding discredits Vonnegut's artistry is debatable, but I think not, for reviewers too often treat a single book rather than all his works. One must examine the mutations through which Vonnegut's kaleidoscopic cosmos passes, for they shape his most striking literary techniques, they help explain his plots and his favorite anthropological issues, and they provide the terms for him to express some of his basic philosophical beliefs. No one who misunderstands the nature of Vonnegut's cosmos can expect to make much sense of his canon, for all his works form parts of a single tapestry. Some panels stand out for their use of one or another color or style, but the background—this fluctuating and coruscating cosmos—underlies all the plot patterns and situational metaphors and gives his works a coherence that otherwise remains elusive.

1

Verfremdungseffekt and *ostraneniye* are both terms for discussing one of art's possible functions. An artist must startle his audience out of its stock responses and must force it to work through the artifices to underlying truths. Brecht wants the audience to forego its illusion of the invisible fourth wall, the illusion of its own non-presence, and the illusion that the actor is the character. Forcing the audience to recognize the artificiality of the theatrical experience should make them wonder what justifies the antics of costumed pretenders prancing and prating before silent spectators. Within a play or a work of fiction, an author can force contradictions on the audience by disrupting conventional plot patterns or by raising expectations and refusing to gratify them. Such violence within the author / audience relationship should make the audience react without the normal damping and numbing effect of automatism. Victor Shklovsky laments that habitualization, the automatic and even unconscious handling of routine, devours our lives. Those who live at a low level of consciousness make their lives worthless. "Art exists that one may recover the sensation of life; it exists to make one feel things, to make the stone *stony*."[2] *Verfremdungseffekt* and *ostraneniye* do not require a self-asserting author. Techniques of estrangement are important to jokes, to metafiction, to epic and romance, and to traditional realistic novels. An author can efface himself and avoid flashy gimmicks that call attention to his artifice, yet make readers respond to the stoniness of the stone simply by describing it with engaging and vivid realism.

Vonnegut uses his sense of the world as flux to create many touches of defamiliarization. One of his defamiliarizing techniques amounts to digging the literal out of what have become dead metaphors. Suddenly, the dead words take on meaning. For example, Kilgore Trout notices a truck belonging to the Pyramid Trucking Company and wonders why someone would name such a company after "buildings which haven't moved an eighth of an inch since Christ was born."[3] Or Vonnegut draws a beaver (the rodent) and then a picture of a crotch like those seen in magazines bearing the label "Wide-open beavers inside!" He continues, "It was the duty of the police and the courts to keep representations of such ordinary apertures from being examined and discussed by persons not engaged in the practice of medicine. It was somehow decided that wide-open beavers, which were ten thousand times as common as real beavers, should be the most massively defended secret under law" (BC, 24).

Another strategy to estrange his readers from unthinking acceptance is his description of metamorphoses. He calls attention to transformations that we prefer to repress. Thus, in *Breakfast of Champions*, he refers to a fried chicken franchise; he then describes a chicken and draws one—a cheerful, stupid-looking but animated bird. Then he shows how it is transformed into buckets of crispy, impersonal, inanimate pieces of eating matter: "The idea was to kill it and pull out all its feathers, and cut off its head and feet and scoop out its internal organs—and then chop it into pieces and fry the pieces, and put the pieces in a waxed paper bucket with a lid on it, so it looked like this" (BC, 158). A picture of the bucket follows. He similarly transforms a cow into hamburger and the "blood" of maple trees into maple sugar. He sports with some of the transformations, glorying in their incongruity. Alcohol he defines as "a substance produced by a tiny creature called yeast. Yeast organisms ate sugar and excreted alcohol. They killed themselves by destroying their own environment with yeast shit" (BC, 208). He also shivers at the ugliness of some transformations: "Celia had committed suicide, for instance, by eating Drāno—a mixture of sodium hydroxide and aluminum flakes, which was meant to clear drains. Celia became a small volcano, since she was composed of the same sorts of substances which commonly clogged drains" (BC, 65). All such simple defamiliarizations remind us of the chemical and material truth underlying and delimiting our consciousness. They also allow Vonnegut to express his condemnation of man as a greedy consumer.

Another kind of cosmic flux that startles the audience is Vonnegut's interrelating of disparates. We think of Stonehenge, the Great Wall of China, and the Kremlin as separate entities but common evidence of man's engineering prowess. Each has its own cultural function and history. However, in *Sirens of Titan* Vonnegut makes them all messages of comfort to a stranded Tralfamadorian. Indeed, every part of human history turns out to have been caused by these aliens in order to produce and transport the replacement part for the Tralfamadorian's space ship. Disparates are also linked, and illusions broken, when Billy Pilgrim goes to the latrine and witnesses an American POW purging, and the narrative voice remarks, "That was I. That was me. That was the author of this book" (*SHF*, 109). In *Jailbird* two of Starbuck's women, though socially miles apart, coincidentally share a tragedy: Sarah Wyatt's family owned a clock factory where women of the neighborhood painted dial faces with radium. Mary Kathleen O'Looney was the daughter of one of the radium-poisoned dial painters. Vonnegut revels in these crazy linkages. When Kilgore Trout's jacket acquires a smear of dogshit on one shoulder, Vonnegut remarks that "by an unbelievable coincidence, that shit came from the wretched greyhound belonging to a girl I knew" (*BC*, 198). Vonnegut exalts such astonishing interrelatedness into a major tenet of the Bokononist faith.

Apparently, Vonnegut alienates some of his readers by recycling characters, leaving his audience unhappy that personality, identity, and even biographical fact are unreliable. Bernard B. (or V.) O'Hare appears in three books, each time as a totally different person, yet he is always an American in uniform. The O'Hare of *Slapstick* is the honor-bright boy (though now quite old), naïve, eager, and easily dazzled by conventional symbols. The O'Hare of *Slaughterhouse-Five* is Vonnegut's old war buddy and a Dresden survivor—a stolid man, later a Pennsylvania District Attorney, a man who likes facts and provides them for Vonnegut's use. He is noted, however, for having few memories of the war. As his wife, Mary, insists, " 'You were just babies in the war—like the ones upstairs' " (*SHF*, 13). Innocent during the war and forgetful after—and therefore perhaps capable of perpetuating wars? Bernard O'Hare of *Mother Night* is the righteous American, sure that he has God's approval and sure that his enemy is the devil incarnate. Arrogant and violent, abusive and drunk, a failure as a civilian, he is a man looking for a myth to give his life substance. Nothing since the war, when he could kill Germans and feel justified, has given him a sense of meaning. All three O'Hares embody part of the American war experience and attitudes toward service in the army. All three men are naïve and unthinking in their basic acceptance of the American position—they merely vary in the maturity with which they can relate to life and other people.

The inconsistency of O'Hare's middle initial is typical of Vonnegut's minor changes when recycling characters. Dr. Schlichter von Koenigswald (*CC*) and Major Siegfried von Konigswale (*HBWJ*) are both Nazi war criminals, men with horrendous pasts, who nonetheless manage to appear ordinary. Stony Stevenson is the hearty and humane army commander in *Sirens of Titan* who gets strangled for trying to figure out who runs his world. Stony reappears as a wispy wanderer, a starchild, in *Between Time and Timbuktu*. Both, however, try to find out what governs their made worlds. Diana Moon Glampers, in *God Bless You, Mr. Rosewater,* is the quintessence of the poor in spirit. She is a hypochondriac with a crushing inferiority complex. She babbles endlessly on the phone to Eliot Rosewater, bidding for attention and sympathy. She is "a sixty-eight-year-old virgin who, by almost anybody's standards, was too dumb to live. . . . No one had ever loved her. There was no reason why anyone should. She was ugly, stupid, and boring" (*GBYMR*, 56). In the short story "Harrison Bergeron," and in the scene based on that story in *Between Time and Timbuktu*, Diana Moon Glampers is a hardbitten, middle-class harridan who adjusts handicaps in a society of forced equality, where no one ever need feel inferior to anyone else. She sentences beautiful people to wear hideous masks; the physically talented wear weights and harnesses; the intelligent wear earphones that blast them with jagged explosions of sound, thus making concentration and thought impossible. Behind her name is a problem—the ease with which people feel miserably inferior to others—and Vonnegut considers this problem from two angles by embodying it in his two Diana Moon Glamperses. To someone reading only one book, Diana Moon Glampers, or Stony Stevenson, or Bernard O'Hare is only one person. To someone enjoying more of Vonnegut's canon, they represent complex attempts to make sense of the elements in human nature which puzzle Vonnegut.

Kilgore Trout is Vonnegut's chief avatar of human transformation. He appears more often than any other character and has far more substantial roles. Furthermore, the numerous summaries of his plots give him special weight and influence. In *God Bless You, Mr. Rosewater* Trout is a bearded novelist who looks like Christ and makes ends meet by redeeming stamps at a redemption center. His role in *Slaughterhouse-Five* is to ride herd on newspaper boys. Not until *Breakfast of Champions* is he given a past. His pessimism has shrivelled three marriages. His son has defected to the Viet Cong. He installs storm windows for a living. In the course of going to the Midland City Arts Festival he has adventures with muggers, porn stores, blue movies, and truck drivers. He gets his finger bitten off, his feet plasticized. He also meets his creator. Yet this contradictory and complex man, and all his previous incarnations, might never have existed when Vonnegut comes to create a Kilgore Trout for *Jailbird*. In that book Kilgore Trout is the pseudonym for Bob Fender, a Korean War soldier who is serving a life sentence for having harbored a North Korean girl who turned out to be a spy. He has never been married. A veterinarian by training, he is now in charge of the prison's clothing depot. In his spare time he writes science fiction under the names of Kilgore Trout and Frank X. Barlow. Trout's role as writer and the zany nature of his plots confirm his identity as a kind of alter ego for Vonnegut, but one may still wonder why Trout should have been so contradictorily presented.

The answer lies in Trout's complex relationship to Vonnegut.[4] Trout is a means for Vonnegut to deal with problems that affect him as artist, and those problems shift throughout his life. In early novels Trout wrestles with obscurity; he is a messiah with no followers. *Breakfast of Champions* shows Trout in midcareer, getting extreme (if unbalanced) reactions from such figures as

Eliot Rosewater, Dwayne Hoover, and Milo Maritimo. He is promised a Nobel Prize in medicine for such insights as: "we are healthy only to the extent that our ideas are humane" (BC, 16). His world makes no sense, and he is harshly buffeted by its vagaries, but he survives the senseless ups-and-downs of life. For Vonnegut, as for Trout, *Slaughterhouse-Five* and *Breakfast of Champions* represent a turning point. Vonnegut comes to terms with large segments of his past, especially Dresden, his mother's suicide, long obscurity, and wild and sometimes insane recognition. Trout does not appear in the next book, *Slapstick*, but he returns in *Jailbird* to face new problems. The continued contempt and hostility shown by reviewers provokes a paranoid reaction in Vonnegut.[5] In *Slapstick* Vonnegut projects himself as a neanderthaloid grotesque, whose intelligence is not recognized by the adults around him. They only see the idiot exterior. In *Jailbird* Starbuck is a victim / scapegoat who goes to jail. Trout too is in jail, and his actions sound essentially innocent, so this self-image also embodies Vonnegut's sense of persecution and misunderstanding. In both these books, Vonnegut introduces women characters in a new manner. They seriously complicate the lives of the protagonists—Izumi, after all, gets Trout jailed for life—but they also enrich the protagonists' lives and symbolically represent creativity, affirmation, action, and meaningfulness. Trout is different in this latest book because Vonnegut is different. The reader tends to forget that Trout is a metaphor, so his changes are not realistic and novelistic, but symbolic.

Trout's plots offer Vonnegut yet another form of transmutational *Verfremdungseffekt;* they constitute a kind of allegorical defamiliarization. Trout tells of helpful aliens who try to communicate warnings using their only methods of talking—tapdancing and farting. Earthlings, unable to get the message, attack them. He tells of a planet run by animate automobiles who destroy the planet and ultimately themselves. He tells of two yeast organisms wondering what life is all about as they smother in their own excrement, never dreaming that they are making champagne. Alien dirty movies consist of a family eating itself into a stupor at a feast and then throwing out large amounts of waste food. These allegories are not subtle; they force the reader to work through the artifice to truth and to see the world change before his eyes. The reader's casual acceptance of feasts, for example, is shaken by seeing them as obscene.

Vonnegut uses other forms of defamiliarization such as skewed statement of the obvious: a gun is "a tool whose only purpose was to make holes in human beings" (BC, 49). One of his favorite estranging techniques is the creation of distortions and exaggerations of physical form—size, height, shape, and the like. These are important as visible manipulations of the material world, and they contribute to the kaleidoscopic effect of Vonnegut's cosmos. Examples appear in most of his works, from the inconceivable massiveness of the crazily won fortune bequeathed to Malachi Constant in *Sirens of Titan* to the subterranean depths of train stations beneath train stations in *Jailbird*. The notorious penis statistics in *Breakfast of Champions* contain a variant on this form of exaggeration. After reducing to its inherent silliness the standard male anxiety about size by bombarding us with sizes, Vonnegut puts man in perspective by announcing the size of a blue whale's penis. More important, he describes "the most decorated veteran in Midland City" as having "a penis eight hundred miles long and two hundred and ten miles in diameter, but practically all of it was in the fourth dimension" (BC, 202). Given the many novelistic and psychiatric connections between American involvement in Vietnam and other twentieth-century wars, and American male sexual problems, Vonnegut's description is an effective, estranging joke designed to make us see that connection. An argument which takes Norman Mailer two novels (The Naked and the Dead and Why Are We in Vietnam?) Vonnegut delightfully compresses into a single sentence.

The clusters of exaggerations and distortions are especially prevalent in Slapstick. First come the twins—monsters two meters high with six toes and fingers on each extremity, and multiple nipples. Then there is the variation in the forces of gravity, such that on some days people nearly float while on others they scarcely crawl. The Chinese, in an attempt to cut food consumption, manage to miniaturize themselves to sixty centimeters high. To some extent, these distortions are a bit like mannerist or cubist paintings. The disturbing shapes of early Picasso pictures call attention to the subject behind the artifice. With Vonnegut, these distortions often add symbolic meaning: when Wilbur talks about his activities on days of light gravity he establishes a connection between light gravity and non-seriousness. As a Vonnegut self-projection, Wilbur thus makes numerous comments that apply to Vonnegut's own writing.

The elasticity of Vonnegut's universe is just one more way of focusing attention on underlying ideas.[6] His cosmos, consisting of endless transformations, provides him with many of his literary techniques for guiding the reader's attention. Yet critics have had trouble with these effects—the distortions, the recycled characters, the interrelated disparates, and the metamorphoses whose middle stage we tend to repress. S. K. Oberbeck complains of "guru gooiness" in Breakfast of Champions, especially in respect to maple sugar coming from the "blood" of maple trees. Philip Stevick dislikes the naïve statements of the obvious, which make the book seem trivial to him. Roger Sale complains that Slapstick enshrines and embodies semi-literacy as slick and acceptable, in part because he dislikes the passages involving transformations, the simple statements, and the repetitions of phrases. Jack Richardson finds Vonnegut's flat statements and easy-to-read truisms rather juvenile.[7] Since many of Vonnegut's flat statements and truisms are part of his game of transformations, these reactions are triggered by his alienating cosmos.

Vonnegut is an expressionistic writer in more than one sense. He uses distortions and symbols to give objective form to inner experience. Critics have had trouble with his symbols because Vonnegut's canon is interlocked; the symbols and meanings of one book make far more sense if studied in relation to all the books rather than just within the one. Each Bernard

O'Hare alone is a pasteboard figure, a simplified model of one facet of the problem of what happens to Americans when they don uniform. But all the O'Hares together make an important comment on Americans who adapt to the army. Likewise, the two Diana Moon Glamperses, if both are known to the reader, form a more complex and suggestive commentary on inferiority complexes than can either one alone. Vonnegut's truisms about guns, body bags, women being big mammals with large brains, alcohol, and the like allow him to look at life as process, in order to decide what, if anything, redeems it—especially what may redeem American consumerism, war-behavior, and a life of relative misery. He asks his questions with childish directness. But if the emperor parades in the nude and we ignore this, should we turn angrily on the naïf who wonders why in a penetrating voice? Vonnegut's naïveté and over-simplifications are real, but so are the issues he insists on raising.

2

When Vonnegut's characters are confronted with the shifting currents of his universe, they are naturally insecure. They want meaning, or at least a recognizable pattern. They want stability or escape. They struggle with loneliness; they recoil from massacres; they cringe at evil. Like all people in all societies, they both inherit and make bulwarks against the flux. Vonnegut describes these attempts and comments upon them. Vonnegut studied anthropology at the University of Chicago; this may have sensitized him to the ways in which man creates such security blankets. He specifically makes an anthropological analysis in *Breakfast of Champions* when he contrasts American black and African extended families with the feeble family structures of the whites of Midland City. Although he is less explicit in his other novels, he works with characteristically anthropological themes and problems. Noting his anthropological interests helps the reader to understand Vonnegut's main themes and to make sense of such ideas as the change of personal name.

Throughout his writings Vonnegut pays attention to the ways in which traditional value structures and institutions have helped people face uncertainties. One of his longest-standing interests is the way people use names. Members of the computerized society of *Player Piano* could wangle minor privileges if their fathers were famous. Name will give Eliot Rosewater's fifty-seven "children" rights to his family fortune. Some of Vonnegut's characters relish their famous names, depending heavily on them for meaning; others change their names to take on a different identity. Rural Elihu Swain changes his middle name to Roosevelt; in part because of this lie, his descendants come to move in social circles that include Roosevelts, Duponts, and Rockefellers. Walter Starbuck enters life as Stankiewicz but takes on Nantucket respectability by adopting this New England name.

Vonnegut analytically examines the effect of names in *Slapstick* when he has Wilbur Swain try out a scheme for creating artificially extended families.

The computer assigns middle names—Daffodil, Pachysandra, Eagle—and a number, thus giving everyone a nationwide family. All Chipmunks belong to an extended family; all Chipmunk-5's belong to a smaller, inner family. The groups are inclusive rather than exclusive; all members are accepted for life, no matter what their mistakes or crimes. Wilbur tries to banish loneliness by creating these families, and he appears to be at least partially successful. People seem to get enough psychic support from their name-groups to survive the disintegration of the nation that takes place when fuel runs out. These family structures also help prevent impersonal massacres. Wilbur witnesses a battle and reports that though some of the participants were killed, many threw down their weapons and embraced "relatives" in the opposing army. Wilbur concludes that the battle was no massacre—an important statement since it ultimately comes from the pen of a Dresden survivor and from the creator of the Cuyahoga massacre. Vonnegut shows some cynicism and dismay at the traditional use of family name, especially if the name gives the bearer money and privilege, but in his latest books he turns to name for possible benefits. In family name, he finds a traditional structure of meaning which, if suitably modified, may yet help people face the swirling changes of life.

Traditional society also uses social hierarchies to structure experience and meaning. In the earlier novels, Vonnegut attacks several caste systems and ways of according honor: IQ, the army, political in-groups, inherited money, and traditional hero status. In *Slapstick*, however, one finds kings and dukes, seraglios and slaves. Given Vonnegut's hostility to slavery, as expressed in *Breakfast of Champions*, this apparent acceptance of it is strange. But in *Slapstick* he shows that society needs value structures and will create them however it can. He may deplore destructiveness when that is part of the value structure, and he certainly deplores the eagerness with which men want others to take care of them and think for them, but he knows, anthropologically, that they will gratefully submit to imperfect and even destructive systems rather than live without order.

Vonnegut also examines romantic love and the family as means of making life seem meaningful. He finds both woefully lacking. Passionate "kingdoms of two" appear in *Mother Night* and *Slapstick*. In the former, the relationship allows Howard Campbell to hide from responsibility for his actions; in the latter—which happens to be an incestuous symbiosis between twins who function like the two hemispheres of a single brain—the relationship proves to be so powerful that the twins choose to separate. The women in Starbuck's life have some positive effect, but his various loves can hardly be said to improve or change him in major ways. Relationships across the generation gap are no more successful. Whereas traditional societies exalt the ties of blood, as Athene does the shoulder-to-shoulder stand of Laertes, Odysseus, and Telemachus, contemporary, rootless American society encourages no such continuity, and neither does Vonnegut.[8] Without exception, his fictional parents and parent figures are at best distant from their children, and often their relationship is bitterly hostile and the children are warped by their upbringing. The nuclear family, with its romantic basis, wins no praise from Vonnegut as anthropologist, but when he writes *Jailbird* he is ready to accept whatever support, no matter how feeble, a family can give. In his recent books, he seems to feel that relationships which are less exclusive and demanding, which rest on courtesy and decency rather than on love, are more durable. Extended families, being less exclusive than nuclear families, seem more flexible and promising to him as bulwarks against the flux of the cosmos.

Religion, traditionally the most obvious way of coping with the apparent meaninglessness of the flux, is also explored anthropologically. In *Cat's Cradle* two characters invent a religion to give the miserable natives of a Caribbean island some satisfaction in their poverty-stricken lives. Bokononism both parodies and yet embodies many qualities of Christianity, creating tensions and awareness by engaging everyone in the great battle between light and dark. Bokononists enjoy all the spiritual advantages of persecution with few of its penalties. Their faith encourages them to believe themselves part of a karass—a group bonded by its carrying out a mission for God. Members of a person's karass are rarely known, and a list of them would seem random, yet a mysterious order in such seeming disorder is the basic tenet of their faith. Bokonon knows that man cannot understand whatever order may exist, but he also knows that man desperately needs to feel that order is there: "Man got to tell himself he understand" (*CC*, 124). Bokononism offers attitudes and sayings that help man cope with the indifference of the universe. Significantly, Bokononism preaches love to all, not the exclusive love of marriage. It also helps its followers to face the ultimate transformation—death. While Bokononist rites comfort the dying, this religion, like all the rest, fails to prevent the destruction of the earth. It cannot help its followers shed a selfish greed for happiness that causes the apocalypse. Religion, like families and love, ultimately fails as a source for stability and order. Ironically, Vonnegut shows religion as most effective in helping man and the world on their way to oblivion.

In *Jailbird* Vonnegut explores another bulwark for establishing values amidst the chaos. For once, he appears to have found one that is at least partly successful. The new bulwark is significant action, especially action that helps others. Of the earlier heroes, only Paul Proteus managed any actions that would qualify as significant. Up to *Slaughterhouse-Five* (1969) and *Breakfast of Champions* (1973), Vonnegut seems most concerned with finding a narrative stance for describing Dresden and with determining what, if anything, he can affirm as a value for our violent, unattractive species. In *Breakfast of Champions* he finds he cannot dismiss pain and misery with mechanical and chemical hypotheses; he affirms consciousness as sacred, and with that affirmation forces himself to continue to face the problem of evil. In *Slapstick* and *Jailbird* he starts exploring what man can do to alleviate evil. *Slapstick* tackles loneliness, and, more generally, the problems of alienation that beset contemporary society. *Jailbird* looks at what may be done to ameliorate the inequities of society.

He finds three principal kinds of action that seem significant (beyond those actions which stem from personal love). The first is embodied in Christ as a mythic paradigm of right action; the second appears in figures of the labor movement, the real Sacco and Vanzetti, and Powers Hapgood, and the fictional Kenneth Whistler; the third appears in ordinary people who generously give comfort rather than pain when confronted with an unprepossessing specimen of humanity. The last-named are called "saints." There are religious overtones in his portrayal of all these exemplars. Of Powers Hapgood he says, "I have always been enchanted by brave veterans like Powers Hapgood, and some others, who were still eager for information of what was really going on, who were still full of ideas of how victory might yet be snatched from the jaws of defeat. 'If I am going to go on living,' I have thought, 'I had better follow them' " (*Jailbird*, xiii). Powers Hapgood's way of justifying his labor activities and his support for Sacco and Vanzetti was to cite the Sermon on the Mount.

Vonnegut is not a writer who promises rosy rewards to those who work for others. Paul Proteus will presumably be executed for his attempt to help the masses. Mary Kathleen O'Looney and Eliot Rosewater go crazy in their frustrated attempts to help the poor. Powers Hapgood could not save Sacco and Vanzetti. At best, some characters manage to ameliorate small miseries and, with vast effort, effect small improvements in the living and working conditions of others. Vonnegut offers no heaven on earth, but he has brought himself to argue that there is some hope. Actions that help others make life seem significant.

When critics respond to some element of Vonnegut's anthropological concerns, they tend to find him impractical, over-simple, sentimental, and subjective. If a writer proposes something like Wilbur's naming scheme, they feel, the writer should do so seriously and didactically; he should work out the implications with the utmost rigor, and provide a blueprint for implementations. But Vonnegut is not a didactic writer. He is reactive, not active. He works with emotions and metaphors, not with logical arguments and instructive blueprints. He is subjective. Studying one's society anthropologically is difficult, for subjectivity and social conditioning create blind spots. Vonnegut's refusal to lay out dogmatic answers is a way, implicitly, of inviting us to analyze our own defenses against chaos. His answers are liberal and simple, but so, for example, are the prescriptions of the New Testament. His low-keyed and loosely structured presentation lets us make our own comparisons and judgments. That we re-evaluate our own perceptions is more important than that we accept his.

3

The protean nature of Vonnegut's fictive cosmos is not merely a literary characteristic. It represents a major component of Vonnegut's philosophical outlook, a fact on which few critics have commented.[9] Vonnegut's relationship to the universe is indeed metaphorically akin to that between Menelaus and Proteus. Menelaus, hoping to learn what he must do to reach home, struggles with the infinitely changing and transforming Old Man of the Sea. The classical hero conquers Proteus and wrests from the god what he wants. Vonnegut is not able to exert brute force against his universe. It still twists and writhes in his grasp, as it has ever since he wrote his first book, whose hero was named Proteus. Vonnegut's perspective on the phenomenal world can be compared to the comments of other artists and philosophers who have also perceived the universe as myriad processes of transformation and flux. Ovid, Shakespeare (in *Hamlet*), Heraclitus, and Gerard Manley Hopkins, oddly assorted though they may seem, shed light on the implications of Vonnegut's outlook.

Ovid's metamorphoses, with their doctrine of change, come to mind as philosophically similar in some ways. Ovid too enjoys yoking disparates and showing zany interrelatedness: Myrrha becomes a tree; her son, after enjoying the love of a goddess, becomes a flower. The blood from Medusa's horrible head brings forth the loveliness of Pegasus. Perseus is born because Danae did not use an umbrella. Ovid's world is one of fascinating interchangeability. But ultimately this flux is not reassuring. Having revelled in the peccadilloes of Jupiter, Ovid does not sound sincere when he solemnly invokes the sky god at the end of *Metamorphoses*. Having presented so many transformations lightly, Ovid does not comfort us with the deification of Julius Caesar. Underlying Ovid's flashy and entertaining universe is a kind of emptiness, and his ending does not fully disguise his *horror vacui*. Similarly, Vonnegut's metamorphic Glamperses and Trouts, his cows transformed into hamburger, his yeast dying to make champagne—all his networks of linkages and random interrelationship—serve more as reminders of the emptiness they try to fill than as reassurances that the void has indeed been given form by their tenuous connections.

That transformation and flux can represent the ultimate horror to some men is succinctly stated in *Hamlet* (5.2.211–18):

> Alexander died, Alexander was buried, Alexander
> returneth to dust; the dust is earth; of earth we make loam;
> and why of that loam whereto he was converted might
> they not stop a beer barrel?
> Imperious Caesar, dead and turned to clay,
> Might stop a hole to keep the wind away.
> O, that that earth which kept the world in awe
> Should patch a wall t'expel the winter's flaw![10]

Hamlet avers that noble deeds do not consecrate mortal remains. The dust of the ruler of the world fares no differently from the dust of a beggar. Nothing can be counted on. All the mortal certainties in Hamlet's personal world have recently become unfixed and fallible; now he sees this unreliability mirrored by and possibly ensured by the transmutable material universe.

Vonnegut too faces mortal certainties coming unfixed and gives them free reign in plots that feature changing gravity, pills that replace breathing, and new forms of water. Everything in his universe tells him to despair, but Vonnegut is not temperamentally inclined to accept that answer. Despite the evidence, he keeps casting around for some intelligent response that will allow him to continue to hope.

Another philosophical analogue, and one with surprising congruities, is Heraclitus' world of cosmic flux, in which divine fire is the ultimate element. Everything changes and flows, feeding the divine fire, being changed by it. Strife and war are important terms for the nature of change in the Heraclitean world. For Heraclitus, this concept of divine fire as the ultimate basis for reality is a positive idea. Fire means motion, purity, rebirth. Fire also permeates Vonnegut's picture of the cosmos, but Dresden fire, not ethereal. Rebirth through fire is not an image that makes emotional sense to him. For Vonnegut fire is the ultimate nightmare. It is apocalyptic. However, for Vonnegut the universe itself is not inherently malevolent. The mutability of all he sees is not in and of itself cause for despair. And like Gerard Manley Hopkins, he finds a way of redeeming the world of flux, poetically speaking. In "Nature is a Heraclitean Fire and of the comfort of the Resurrection" Hopkins marvels at the transformations and changes in his stippled and whirlwind-swiveled world. Time beats level everything, whether cloud puffballs or nature's clearest-selved spark, man. But a final transformation banishes the horror and gives meaning to all the transmutations:

> I am all at once what Christ is, since he was what I am, and
> This Jack, joke, poor potsherd, patch, matchwood, immortal diamond,
> Is immortal diamond. [11]

Vonnegut makes no such passionate affirmation, but he too finds something at the heart of things which appears to be stable, unchanged by the gliding shapes of life. In *Breakfast of Champions* Rabo Karabekian says of his minimalist picture (a vertical orange tape on a green background):

> the picture your city owns shows everything about life which truly matters, with nothing left out. It is a picture of the awareness of every animal. It is the immaterial core of every animal—the "I am" to which all messages are sent. It is all that is alive in any of us—in a mouse, in a deer, in a cocktail waitress. It is unwavering and pure, not matter what preposterous adventure may befall us. . . . Our awareness is all that is alive and maybe sacred in any of us. Everything else about us is dead machinery. [*BC*, 221]

Vonnegut may not be able to find an ultimate Heraclitean benefit in fire, but fire's visible element, purified and intensified, with its wavering and fluctuations gone, is light. Light is not so destructive. Light has associations with spiritual enlightenment, with rising above the self. In the shifting worlds of his books up to *Breakfast of Champions* Vonnegut struggles to make sense of meaninglessness and evil. In *Breakfast of Champions* he affirms the identity of individual consciousness with this band of light. This metamorphosis of fire to light is central to Vonnegut's development as a writer. Having found something stable in the world, he turns in his later works to the problem of what can be done to ameliorate man's lot.

Flux is permanent. Our world will die if someone halts the flow, as happens in *Cat's Cradle*. Interrelatedness is total; no man is an island. People are protean, and so are places and things. Knowledge is relative. Because things flow and change, Vonnegut is rarely willing to polarize and separate people into camps of the good and the bad. In his world one cannot count on anything staying the same, and often one cannot prevent gold from turning to lead. But the horror of instability and flux no longer haunts him. Vonnegut no longer needs to feel like a pillar of salt looking back on the destruction of the cities of the plain. Vonnegut has explored this flux as madness, as the product of evil, as the result of man's consuming greed, and as the result of natural forces. He has looked anthropologically at man's defenses against the instability, and he has explored man's ways of keeping the tides of change at bay. More important, Vonnegut has found his own way of anchoring his perceptions amidst the flow. What he can accept as fixed may be very limited, but he has found some stabilities—human consciousness, helpfulness, decency—and from these he is beginning to build further fictions.

Understanding Vonnegut's assumptions about the world is important for making sense of his writings. Too often reviewers have noticed small details like the multiple Kilgore Trouts and have rejected them, unaware that these details relate to a complex network of images and philosophical values. By comparison, most art critics would find it a bit odd if someone were to review one scene in the Bayeux Tapestry and castigate it for its mode of representing action. The way of showing action is stylized. Those trained in the art of other periods may not like it. But taking a single scene does not do justice to the effect and achievement of the whole. Likewise, Vonnegut is a writer who needs to be seen in full.

Notes

1. "Age of Vonnegut," *New Republic*, 12 June 1971, p. 31. This is a retrospective review of all the fiction up to and including *Slaughterhouse-Five*.

2. "Art as Technique," in *Russian Formalist Criticism: Four Essays*, ed. and trans. Lee T. Lemon and Marion J. Reis, Regents Critics Series (Lincoln, 1965), p. 12. Brecht's many comments on *Verfremdung* as a theatrical device are scattered through the essays gathered in *Brecht on Theatre: The Development of an Aesthetic*, ed. trans. John Willett (New York, 1964).

3. *Breakfast of Champions* (New York, 1973), p. 109; cited hereafter in my text as *BC*. All references to Vonnegut's works, cited in my text, are from the following editions: *Player Piano* (1952; rpt. New York, 1974); *The Sirens of Titan* (1959; rpt. New York, 1970); *Mother Night* (1962; New York, 1974); *Cat's Cradle* (*CC*) (1963; rpt. New York, 1970); *God Bless You, Mr. Rosewater* (*GBYMR*) (1965; rpt. New York, 1970); *Slaughterhouse-Five* (*SHF*) (1969; rpt. New

York, 1970); *Happy Birthday, Wanda June (HBWJ)* (New York, 1971); *Between Time and Timbuktu* (New York, 1972); *Slapstick* (New York, 1976); *Jailbird* (New York, 1979); and "Harrison Bergeron," in *Welcome to the Monkey House* (New York, 1970).

4. For a more thorough analysis of Trout as a projection of Vonnegut, see my forthcoming article, "Vonnegut's Self-Projections: Symbolic Characters and Symbolic Fiction."

5. The paranoid nature of these images is analyzed in more detail in "Vonnegut's Self-Projections: Symbolic Characters and Symbolic Fiction."

6. Critics who have linked Vonnegut's universe to his artistic stances include Stanley Schatt, "The World of Kurt Vonnegut, Jr.," *Critique* 12, no. 3 (1971): 54–69, and his book, *Kurt Vonnegut, Jr.* (Boston, 1976); Jerome Klinkowitz, "Kurt Vonnegut, Jr., and the Crimes of His Time," *Critique* 12, no. 3 (1971): 38–53; and Max F. Schulz, "The Unconfirmed Thesis: Kurt Vonnegut, Black Humor, and Contemporary Art," *Critique* 12, no. 3 (1971): 5–28.

7. See, respectively, *Book World*, 13 May 1973, pp. 2–3; *Partisan Review* 41 (1974): 302–4; *New York Times Book Review*, 3 October 1976, pp. 3, 20, 22; *New York Review of Books*, 2 July 1970, pp. 7–8. For criticism of the stylistic repetitions, which is based on genuine aesthetic considerations rather than on misunderstandings, see Peter B. Messent, *"Breakfast of Champions:* The Direction of Kurt Vonnegut's Fiction," *Journal of American Studies* 8 (1974): 101–14.

8. The unhappy relationships between parents and children in Vonnegut's fiction have been analyzed—interestingly and differently—by Lynn Buck, "Vonnegut's World of Comic Futility," *Studies in American Fiction* 3 (1975): 181–98; and by Josephine Hendin, *Vulnerable People: A View of American Fiction since 1945* (New York, 1978), chap. 2.

9. The critics mentioned above in note 6 are those who have noticed, however fleetingly, the connection between Vonnegut's cosmos and his outlook. Max Schulz sees Vonnegut's world as "fragmented into multiple realities," and interprets this as an argument in support of Vonnegut's status as a black humorist. Stanley Schatt mentions Vonnegut's involvement in a pluralistic universe, especially in connection with such characters as Howard Campbell, who cannot tell what is real from what is play-acting. Jerome Klinkowitz relates the unverifiability of Vonnegut's universe to Vonnegut's concern with schizophrenia, a disease characteristic of our times.

10. Ed. Edward Hubler (New York, 1963), p. 165.

11. *The Poems of Gerard Manley Hopkins*, 4th ed., ed. W. H. Gardner and N. H. Mackenzie (London, 1967), pp. 105–6, 106 for the quotation.

INDEX